Wilmer, Richard Hooker, Thomes William Henry

Running the blockade

U. S. Secret Service adventures

Wilmer, Richard Hooker, Thomes William Henry

Running the blockade
U. S. Secret Service adventures

ISBN/EAN: 9783337377472

Printed in Europe, USA, Canada, Australia, Japan

Cover: Foto ©ninafisch / pixelio.de

More available books at **www.hansebooks.com**

Running the Blockade;

OR,

U. S. SECRET SERVICE ADVENTURES.

BY

W. H. THOMES,

AUTHOR OF "THE GOLD HUNTERS' ADVENTURES IN AUSTRALIA,"
"THE BUSHRANGERS," "THE DEAD ALIVE, OR THE GOLD
HUNTERS IN EUROPE," "A SLAVER'S ADVENTURES,"
"A WHALEMAN'S ADVENTURES," "LIFE IN
THE EAST INDIES," ETC.

ILLUSTRATED.

BOSTON:
LEE AND SHEPARD, PUBLISHERS.
NEW YORK:
LEE, SHEPARD AND DILLINGHAM.
1875.

TO MY FRIEND

AVERY SMITH, ESQ.,
OF NEWARK, NEW JERSEY,

FOR HIS UNCEASING DEVOTION TO THE UNION, DURING
ALL ITS TRIALS AND TRIBULATIONS, AND HIS
SINCERE AND UNSELFISH ADMIRATION FOR
THE REGULAR AND VOLUNTEER
SAILORS OF THE UNITED
STATES NAVY,

This Book is Respectfully Dedicated

BY THE AUTHOR.

CONTENTS.

CHAPTER I.

An Introduction. — The House of Blank, Hawser, & Co. — An Inducement. — An Apparition. — A Lost Heart. 9

CHAPTER II.

An Unexpected Meeting. — The President serves me a Good Turn. — An Encounter. — The Result. — In New York. — An Important Interview. — For Nassau. — Strange Companions. 41

CHAPTER III.

A Mysterious Passenger. — A Blunt Kentuckian. — A Quarrel and Reconciliation on the Passage. — Our Arrival at Nassau 75

CHAPTER IV.

An Encounter. — The Streets of Nassau at Night. — The American Consul. — A Row. — A Foul Blow. — On a Blockade-runner. — An Impressment. — A Friend in Need. — The Suspicious Steamer. — A Signal. — Harry Bluff and his Station in Life . . 112

CHAPTER V.

The Chance. — A Signal. — A Response. — A Surprised Master. — An Apparition. — More Trouble for the Pet. — Three more Steamers in Sight. — Pooduck's Blood is up. — A Meeting. — A

Tight Spot. — A Prize to the Stingeree. — A Bluff Captain. — A Surprise. — Harry and Old Ben in New Parts. 143

CHAPTER VI.

Mrs. Gowen and the Captain. — A Special Plea. — A Release. — Harry Bluff and I join Forces. — A Row at Nassau. — "Up, Stingerees, and at 'Em." — A Reconciliation. — I am welcomed by Colonel Rhett. — A little Questioning. — A Change of Scene. 172

CHAPTER VII.

A Sudden Attack. — A Rescue. — On Board the Spitfire. — A Capture. — John Bull makes a Discovery. — A Chase. — A Recognition, and what came of it. 204

CHAPTER VIII.

At Sea. — A Strange Steamer. — Colonel Rhett turns up again. — His Story. — A Stern Chase. — A Run for Charleston. — Running the Blockade. — The Signals. — A Hail. — A Close Shave. — A Ruse. — Making Signals. — A Cross Admiral. — Colonel Rhett again in Trouble. — Insulting an Admiral. — Colonel Rhett explains. — An Invitation, and what came of it 241

CHAPTER IX.

A Prisoner. — A Negro League. — A Fellow-sufferer. — Bowmount in a Trap. — He finds a Chisel. — At Work to get out. — The Kentuckian escapes. — Some Old Friends appear. — A Moment of Peril. — Timely Arrival of the Kentuckian. — The Tables turned. 277

CHAPTER X.

A Plea for Mercy. — A Flogging for Hanging. — On the Belle. — A Carouse. — Harry undertakes an Expedition. — The Charleston Iron-clads. — I see some Old Friends, and am surprised at meeting them. — Harry and his Uncle. — Valuable Papers, and what I did with them. — Sam is Penitent. 323

CHAPTER XI.

A Visit to the City Prison. — Officer's Opinion of the War. — Colonel Rhett and John the Mulatto. — Their Release. — Escape of Harry and Companion. — Sailing of the Belle. — A Dark Night, and an Anxious one. — Running the Blockade. — A moment of Peril. — A Sharp Pursuit. — More Treachery. — Arrival at Bermuda. — Despatch-bag and its Contents. — Old Acquaintances. . 358

CHAPTER XII.

A Complete Surprise. — A Union Spy. — An Interview with Captain Switchell. — Mrs. Gowen and her Husband. — A Painful Scene. — The Kentuckian in a New Character. — A Terrible Revelation. — The Kentuckian's Story. — Magnolia's History. — A Share of the Profits. — Sale of the Belle. — Meeting of Old Friends in New York. — Off for Washington. — Promotion to the Rank of Commander. — Smith is Astonished. — A little Love-making. — An Interruption. — A Stern Parent. — Terms. — An Agreement. — A Wedding. 413

RUNNING THE BLOCKADE.

CHAPTER I.

AN INTRODUCTION. — THE HOUSE OF BLANK, HAWSER AND CO. — AN INDUCEMENT. — AN APPARITION. — A LOST HEART.

A WOUND, no trifling one, has laid me on the shelf for some months. My hull is shattered with rough weather, hard work, and constant excitement and peril. Yet I am a young man, not over twenty-eight, and at one time possessed a constitution as tough as a nor'wester, and the strength of a steam-tug. Rest may restore me, medicine may heal my wounds, kind treatment may banish the fancies that at times take possession of my mind as I think of the past; but no earthly power can ever make me forget all that I have endured and suffered for the Union's sake.

And now, while I am racked with pain, unable to muster at quarters, with no immediate chance of once more snuffing salt water, I can while away my time by writing an account of my adventures, more for the purpose of showing how secret-service duties were carried on, and what means our government resorted to for the purpose of entrapping the rebels, breaking up blockade-running, and gaining information of Southern movements, than for personal aggrandizement, or pecuniary benefit.

One word as to my previous history, for I want to commence my yarn with a fair wind and a smooth sea, so that my readers may understand me and my motives. I always like to have a plain talk with my men when I sail from port, so why should I not call all hands aft on this voyage, and tell them all about my personal affairs?

I arrived home, in the year 1862, in command of an East India ship, owned in Boston by Blank, Hawser & Co., for whom I had sailed ten years, as boy, man, mate, and master. The firm was an old one, rich and influential, with stores and warehouses located on Lewis's Wharf, with nice, carpeted offices, old, gray-headed clerks, ponderous books, formidable safes, and colored charts of all parts of the world, which hung on the walls, and were often consulted by the house when a ship was to be despatched on a long and uncertain voyage.

I had a warm reception from the firm. Perhaps it was owing to the fact that I had brought home a valuable ship and cargo, that I had escaped the perils of the sea, had outsailed a privateer, which chased us for twelve hours, and only gave it up when night, a gale of wind, rain and fog hid us from the sharp eyes on board of the steamer. These things may have influenced the house in giving me a reception warmer than that which had been given to any master in their employ since the time when old Crosstree arrived from San Domingo with his brig loaded with plate, pictures, books, and gold and silver coin, all of which had been put on board by the residents just before a massacre of the whites by the blacks. The owners never called for their property. No wonder. They were sent to that unknown world where man is not supposed to care for wealth, or the vanities of the earth. The negroes made sure work of it, so much so that Blank, Hawser and Co. were enabled to estimate the profits of the year at something prodigious; while old Crosstree retired from the sea altogether, with money enough to enable him to spend a portion of his time wandering around State Street, with nothing to do, except to chew tobacco and read the morning papers in the insurance offices. It was always remarked that the captain never boasted of the manner in which he acquired an independence. In fact, he never once alluded to San Domingo, or acknowledged that he had traded at the island, during his long and eventful life.

But I have to deal with the house of Blank, Hawser & Co., so I will leave the ancient mariner, and resume the thread of my own yarn. In other words, I will make sail and keep on my course, although we may not come to anchor for some months.

As I said before, the house gave me what was called a warm reception when I landed, and reported myself and ship. Mr. Blank, a precise old gentleman, with a red nose and white hair, a keen black eye and sharp face, black clothes and spotless linen, a lover of good dinners, a gallant old beau, gave me two of his white fingers, and said that he was glad to welcome me home, and trusted that I was well, and that the ship I commanded, the Laughing Mermaid, sailed very well and was in good condition, and that the cargo had escaped damage.

And then Hawser, the jolly man of the firm, a gentleman with a large stomach, a fat face, a loud laugh, slapped me on the back, and swore that I had arrived just in the nick of time, and that the government wouldn't catch them on the new tariff. Not a bit of it. Two days made a difference of some fifty thousand dollars. And would I take a drink?

I did not refuse the drink, because Hawser would have felt offended at my refusal, and because he always kept good liquors in his private room, and was rather liberal with them; while Blank, that tall, stately man, would have felt insulted had he been asked to touch glasses with one of his masters.

While the ship was unloading, I was a frequent visitor at the counting-room, confidently expecting that I should again have the vessel, and wondering where I would be sent, when one morning Mr. Blank sent for me to enter his private room, and talk on business.

"Now for it," I thought. "He is about to offer me the ship and increase my wages. Another trip to San Francisco, and then Calcutta and a market, I suppose."

Such were my reflections; but they were not quite correct, as the conversation proved.

"Ah, good morning, sir," and Mr. Blank looked up as I entered the room. He held out two fingers, and allowed me to hold them about as long as a man would care to hold two hot iron balls. "Take a seat, sir."

I dropped the fingers, and took a seat.

"Captain Constant," the head of the firm said, and as he spoke he trimmed his nails with a penknife, "we have been much pleased with the manner in which you have conducted yourself since you have been in our employ, over ten years, I believe?"

I bowed. He was complimenting me in a manner such as I never expected to hear from his lips. He certainly will increase my wages I thought.

"Yes, sir, through all the changes which you have passed, while in our employ, from seaman to mate, and from mate to master, you have satisfied us that you intend to do your duty under all circumstances."

Once more I bowed. "At least twenty-five dollars per month to be added to my wages, or else he will offer me a percentage," I thought.

"Therefore, we conclude it best, under the present disturbed state of the country, to offer you—"

"Certainly, sir, I accept with much pleasure. I want

no better ship than the Laughing Mermaid. She is fast, a good sea-boat, and I know just how to sail her."

"How!" cried the head of the firm, and opened his black eyes to their widest extent.

"The Laughing Mermaid," I faltered, fearing that I had been too precipitate.

"O, yes; didn't I tell you that we intended to lay her up for a season?"

"No, sir, you did not intimate such a thing."

"Then I'm sure that I committed a great oversight, for —"

Just at that moment one of the clerks opened the door, as though to speak a word to Mr. Blank, but before he could utter a syllable was pushed gently aside by a young girl, a vision of loveliness, who entered the room, and danced towards Mr. Blank.

"O, papa," the little beauty said, "they told me that you were engaged."

"That is more than you will be unless you leave off some of your mad pranks," replied Mr. Blank, with a merry twinkle of his eye, while a look of affection mantled his face, stealing through the crusty, port-like blossom of his countenance, like a coat of paint to the bare bends of a ship.

"Engaged," — and here the young lady tossed her head, and made an attempt to smile in a scornful manner; "I can be engaged at any moment, but I don't want to be the slave of any man. I like my freedom too well. No tangled engagements for me."

"I believe it;" and the father laughed in a gratified manner.

"Besides, I like my home too well, and those who make my home happy, to care to leave it;" and the beautiful girl bent her head to her father's shoulder, and allowed her rich peach-like cheek to rest for a moment against his face.

I sat where I could not help noting the scene. The parties seemed to have forgotten that I was present, so absorbed were they in each other. I could see that the father loved his child most dearly. That he was proud of her beauty, her pert, saucy ways and winning manners; and I did not blame him for the affection he displayed, for the young lady seemed most worthy of it, and I felt a pang in the region of my heart as I sat and looked at her, and thought that some day a fine, dashing young fellow would come along, throw her his handkerchief, and carry her off in triumph a wife, but one not loved half as much as such a beautiful little piece of angelic creation should be loved.

I had often heard of the only child of Mr. Blank, but never had expressed the least curiosity regarding her. When the clerks in the counting-room had raved, and declared that she was as lovely as Venus, I had manifested the most supreme indifference on the subject, and laughed at the love-stricken lubbers, as I termed them. But now, as I sat and stared at that well-formed head, covered with masses of dark brown hair, looking soft and wavy; a face that was Grecian in its character, the rich blood showing beneath the transparent skin; the sweet hazel eyes, veiled with long dark lashes, like pickets thrown out in front of a powerful army; a form that was plump and well-proportioned as a first-class clipper ship. Well, I no longer wondered that the clerks were madly in love with the lady.

"Come, darling, sit down for a moment," said the fond father, patting the young lady's soft hair, "or else tell me what you want, if you are in a hurry."

"You know what I want, well enough now."

She laughed and clapped her gloved hands as though she had uttered a good joke.

"Where is the last I gave you?"

"Gone, papa."

"How?"

"A muslin, a bonnet, a silk dress of lovely shade, and charity; you shall see it."

"What, the charity?"

"No, the silk dress, you provoking papa. I shall wear it to church next Sunday."

"And the bonnet, puss?"

"Will also add to my attractions. I intend you shall be proud of your daughter."

The father smiled and pinched her cheek. It was evident enough that he was proud of her, without her gay rigging and trappings, and I was satisfied that Miss Hatty Blank, the full name of my little beauty, loved her father with a devotion that was rather unusual in these days of selfishness.

All of a sudden Miss Hatty turned her hazel eyes on me, for I had coughed in a slight manner to show that some one was present. They rested on my face for the space of a second or two, a haughty, well-bred stare, not impolite, but inquisitive, as much as to say, —

"Pray, who are you, sir, with your black eyes, sunburnt face, and curly hair?"

Truth compels me to state that I so far forgot myself as to return her stare with such intense admiration that Miss Hatty was compelled to lower her eyes and turn her head, while a blush passed over her face that was like the glow on the water in a tropical climate at sunset.

Mr. Blank — happy man to be the father of so much loveliness — did not note the exchange of glances between his daughter and myself. He was too much occupied in looking over a letter to regard us; but his daughter, after one more effort to catch a glimpse of my face, and finding that I was still looking at her, laid her hand on her father's arm, and said, —

"Papa, you are not paying the least attention to me, or this — this — "

She stole a third look at me, and then finished her speech —

"Gentleman."

I had won the victory. I had extracted the word from her in defiance of her will. She had acknowledged my gentility in spite of her wish not to do so.

"I beg your pardon, my dear child; but I was not aware that you were of so much importance."

"But perhaps this gentleman has business with you that requires haste."

This time there was no hesitancy when the word gentleman was used.

"He has business with me, but is not in haste," was the father's reply.

There was no offer at an introduction. The rich merchant did not think that the master of one of his ships was a suitable person to favor with an introduction to his only child. Perhaps he feared that I might claim the honor of her acquaintance on the strength of it. I felt my heart swell within me at the thought; but I restrained all outward sign of emotion, for I had learned that severe trial at an early day. Self-discipline was one of my virtues. I could always wait with some degree of patience for events.

Just at this moment the office door opened, and a favorite clerk entered with some papers in his hand. He was a man nearly forty years of age, with iron-gray hair, a smooth face, clean shaved, thin lips, eyes that never met your own; always meditating, never surprised; civil to all, yet exchanging words with but few. Such were the traits of Kiner King, who had been in the house for thirty years, rising from the position of office boy, errand boy, entry clerk, to that of a favorite clerk, at a salary of two thousand dollars per annum.

Kiner stopped when he was near Mr. Blank's desk, and

looked as though undecided whether to move on or retreat.

"Excuse me, sir," he said, addressing the merchant. "I was not aware that you had company in your room. Shall I retire?"

Even as the man spoke, he had time to make a most profound and respectful bow to Miss Hatty, as though she must not judge him harshly for what he had done. But Miss Hatty appeared to be obdurate, for she tossed her pretty head, and looked as if she was not in a gracious mood with the favorite clerk.

"O, speak on, Kiner," answered the merchant. "I am not particularly engaged at this moment. What is it you want?"

"A few papers to sign, sir. Shall I leave them on your desk?"

"Yes. I will look over them in a short time."

The smooth-faced clerk laid the papers on the desk, and then turned to leave the room, but for one moment he stopped near Miss Blank, and while rubbing his hands, as if to promote warmth, said, —

"I hope that Miss Blank is enjoying good health at the present time."

"Yes."

The answer was pert and curt, and such the young lady intended it, for she left her chair, turned her back on Kiner, and walked to the window.

The favorite clerk did not manifest the least sign of displeasure; but he glanced at me, as if to note the effect of her conduct, and then his dull, leaden eyes were lowered, and he left the room, stealing through the doorway like a snake that was in search of a field-mouse.

I noted all, and considered. "There is some mystery here," I thought.

As Kiner closed the door, Miss Hatty left her position

at the window. She appeared to recover her spirits the instant the favorite clerk was out of sight.

"Now, papa, give me the money I asked you for, please."

He laughed, went to the safe, took out some bills, and handed them to her.

"Will that be enough, pet?"

"I will make it go just as far as possible, papa; but you don't know how many things I have to buy."

Her father laughed. The young lady stowed the money in her purse, gave me a glance of her eyes, and then danced from the private room to her carriage at the door; but when she left the apartment she carried my heart with her, more securely imprisoned than the greenbacks which she had secured in her purse.

As the door closed upon the retreating form of Miss Hatty Blank, I felt that she had taken all the sunshine and light of the room with her; but from these reflections Mr. Blank aroused me.

"Now, Constant, we can proceed to business, having got rid of that troublesome magpie. As I said before, we have resolved to let the ship lay up for a season, on account of the rebel privateers. We don't feel like transferring her flag, and if we did, we should have to employ an Englishman to command her. You would not care to take a mate's berth once more?"

I shook my head.

"No, I suppose not, and I don't mean to offer it to you; but I have something else to give you that I think will be acceptable."

I looked at him, wondering what was coming.

"The day after your arrival home, I wrote to Mr. Welles, the Secretary of the Navy, mentioning some of your good qualities, and recommending that you should be appointed a volunteer lieutenant in the navy, and despatched on secret service, or else sent down to do blockade duty. Let me see, are you acquainted with the harbors on the Southern coast?"

"Yes, I have sailed from Wilmington, Savannah, Charleston, Mobile, and New Orleans, and have a thorough knowledge of the places named."

"Then you are just the man that government wants. But stay, I'll read the secretary's letter, and let you hear what he says."

Mr. Blank read a document, and I found that Mr. Welles was anxious to see me before he gave me the appointment, and that he expected I would visit Washington without delay, and confer with him on matters which were for the benefit of the country.

At any rate, Mr. Welles promised that I should be taken care of, and receive an appointment according to my merits.

"I have taken this trouble," said Mr. Blank, "in your behalf, on account of the long time that you have been in our employ, and the sincere esteem which I have for you. Our country needs just such men as you are, — bold, active, and enterprising."

I had not listened to one half of this address, for my thoughts were far away, in a certain carriage that was moving along through Washington Street, freighted with a load more precious than a homeward bound East Indiaman. I imagined the lady looking to the right and left, bowing to this one, smiling to that, happy and free of trouble, as all young girls should be. When I looked up and saw that Mr. Blank expected an answer, and that he had waited some seconds for one, while I was up in the clouds, or becalmed among the curls of his daughter's hair. I blushed a little, when I was restored to my senses, for allowing such weakness to overcome me.

"Well," asked Mr. Blank, after waiting, and finding

that I was not disposed to answer him, "what do you think of serving your country for a season? I tell you candidly, that you can't do better. If you want time to consider the matter over, why, take a few days, and then let me know. Of course, after the war has ceased, we shall welcome you back to our employ with much pleasure, provided you want to come. In case you decide to accept Mr. Welles's offer, take his note with you to Washington. It is a letter of introduction, and will secure you some little favor at the hands of the officials."

He nodded his head, and took up a letter from his desk, as though he desired to close the interview. I arose, but as I did so, I happened to look down, and saw lying on the floor a card. I picked it up, and was about to hand it to Mr. Blank, when I noticed that it was a photograph of his daughter, which she had accidentally dropped while in the room.

Instead of handing it to the merchant, I put it in my pocket, and rejoiced to see that Mr. Blank was too much occupied with his letter to notice the act. As no more words were needed on my part, I bowed, and retired from the room.

In the next apartment I encountered the favorite clerk, Kiner King, with his fish-like eyes and smooth face, his cold hands and calm looks.

"Well," he asked, "shall we welcome you as one of Uncle Sam's men?"

"Perhaps."

"Are you in earnest?"

"Yes."

I think the man's face expressed a little astonishment, but his looks were always so well guarded that I could not tell whether he was surprised or not. Just as I was going out of the office, the favorite clerk called out to me, —

"By 'the way, captain, did you ever see Miss Blank before?"

"Never had that honor," I remarked, in a gallant tone, for I thought Kiner meant to say something complimentary.

"O, never did, eh? That's all."

Down went the fellow's head on his book, and he appeared to have forgotten me.

"Look here, Kiner, what in the devil do you mean by such talk? Speak out in ship-shape fashion, and don't be beating all round the bay."

The man looked up, closed his book in a soft, cat-like manner, and then approached me, and whispered, —

"She's a dangerous person to be acquainted with, captain. I noticed that you seemed to be a little struck with her beauty. Think no more of it, and if you should again get sight of her, make sail and claw off as fast as possible. That is all, captain."

I could not help laughing a scornful, defiant laugh at such advice.

"Why, you lubber," I said, in a tone that was half sarcastic and half joking, "do you think that I would run from a pretty face and a petticoat?"

He made no reply, and I walked out of the office, wondering what the deuce was the matter with Kiner.

"He must have intended to play a game on me," I thought. "He noticed, probably, that I was a little struck with Miss Blank's face and form, and thought he would have a joke. Sharp fellow, that Kiner."

And then I dismissed Kiner from my mind; but Miss Hatty was not put off so easy. I passed the day doing nothing with my hands, yet my brain was busy at work over the proposition which Mr. Blank had made, and the daughter which Mr. Blank owned. Of the two, as became a high-toned sailor, I thought most of the lady; and while I was thus engaged, who should slap me on the shoulder but Crosstree, who had formerly sailed for the firm of Blank, Hawser & Co., and made his money through the San Domingo massacre. The old fellow was somewhat bent with age, his hair was white, and his teeth false, but his eyes were as sharp as ever they were, and his wits as keen as when he calculated how much his share of the plunder would amount to after arriving in Boston.

"Well," growled Crosstree, "what in the devil's name are you looking so sober for? What's the matter?"

"Matter enough. The house intends to lay up the Laughing Mermaid."

"Well, there's other chances for a smart young fellow." Old Crosstree had sunk his voice to a hoarse whisper as he uttered the sentence. I did not comprehend the man's meaning, so only stared at him.

"Do you take?" whispered Crosstree, and punched me in the ribs.

"No."

"Don't you know a thing or two?"

"Hang me if I do! Come, pay out cable, so that I can ride free."

"Do you like money?" whispered the old salt.

"Yes; I wish I was worth half a million dollars."

"You can nearly reach that figure if you are bold and lucky!" cried Crosstree, and the old fellow rubbed his hands.

"Then I'm the man for the money," said I, in a jesting tone. "I want a pile of greenbacks, and I don't mind running some risk to obtain it. Come, out with your scheme, and let's overhaul it."

"Don't speak so loud," the old sea-dog whispered, clutching my arm to impose more caution. "We must move carefully in the matter, and take soundings, 'cos we are surrounded by spies. They are all on the watch to spile a nice little speculation."

I began to have some misgivings that the scheme which

Crosstree desired to impose upon me was not exactly the one that would bear the evidence of a man's loyalty. But I desired to hear more before I decided on the steps I would take in the premises.

"Come this way!" the old captain cried in an eager tone. "So, that's well. Now no one can hear us. Listen. Do you know the firm of Brass, Iron & Co.?"

"Yes."

"Do you know how they made all their money?"

"No; I never gave the subject a thought."

"Well, I have;" and here old Crosstree chuckled, and added, —

"I'm bound to make my pile in the same manner. You can join me if you like."

"Name the business."

Crosstree put his mouth close to my ear and whispered, —

"Blockade running."

"What, help the enemies of the North?" I demanded.

"No, we help ourselves — to cotton. You see, it's worth a dollar a pound here in Boston, and we can buy it at the South for about eight cents, in the way of trade. Just see the margin for profit. Five hundred bales would set us on our pins, and put us among the nobs of State Street."

"And what would you give in exchange?" I asked.

Crosstree did not look me in the face as he answered, —

"Well, shoes go well down there, and so does medicines, and clothes — dark gray fetches a big price — and they say that powder, revolving rifles, and swords are snapped at by all sorts of fellows. Never fear but what we can pick up a load of stuff."

With an effort I suppressed my indignation, so that I could learn more of the old rascal's plans.

"You see, we can ship what we want to Bermuda,

Havana, or Nassau, and then buy a steamer and slip into one of the Southern ports on a dark night, and out in the same manner, with cotton and turpentine. If we are lucky, our fortune is made."

"And if we are not?" I asked.

"Well, then, we must grin and bear it, and try again. But there ain't much to fear or risk to run. The fellers on the blockading fleet are asleep half the time, and we can slip in and out without waking 'em up."

"Captain Crosstree," I asked, "would you really turn against the North, and help the South in the manner proposed?"

"I must make some money," he grumbled, with an averted face. "I must live."

"Then, in the name of Heaven, if you must live, try and live in such a manner that your friends won't have occasion to blush for you after you are dead. I'll be —— if I won't live and die poor before I resort to blockade running and aiding the South."

Crosstree did not look up. His hands played nervously with his watch seal, and he appeared most heartily ashamed of himself. He had made a full confession to me, thinking that I would join him; but when he found that I would not, he did not exactly know what to do.

"Come, Crosstree," I said, after enjoying his embarrassment for a few moments, "you are not so bad or so mercenary as you appear. You have been testing my loyalty, I know, to see if I am suitable to enter Uncle Sam's service. Come, own up that such is the case."

"Yes, yes — he, he! — you're right. A devilish good joke. I played it well — didn't I?"

"Yes, you did; but be careful that you don't put such jokes into practical operation. If, as you say, there are spies about, take care that they don't report one of your little funny affairs. If they should, you might find yourself in Fort Warren."

Crosstree's false teeth chattered as he listened.

"But as it was only a joke, you know, you won't say a word about it, will you?" pleaded Crosstree, with a most anxious look.

"No; I'll keep your secret; but let me advise you to turn your attention to other matters, if you wish to die in your bed."

"But there's so much money to be made in running the blockade," whined Crosstree. "Brass, Iron & Co. have made a whack, and they're just as much thought of as other people. The banks all trust 'em, and all the nobs bow to 'em. It's hard if other people can't do as they do."

"If they are traitors, it is no reason why we should be; and the few words that we have exchanged convinces me of one thing."

"Yes, what is it?"

"That it is my duty to enter the navy, and help the country. I shall no longer hesitate."

"Well, you won't split on me. Say that you won't peach, and I'll give up (here he hesitated for a moment) all thoughts of running the blockade."

Of course I consented to keep quiet, and then I left the old fellow; but a few hours afterwards, while passing through State Street, I saw Crosstree and Kiner in close communication, and I had no doubt they were planning some outside job that would put money in their purses.

Before the next morning I had concluded that I would enter the naval service, and serve my country to the best of my ability, provided I could obtain a position that was suited to my capacity. When I announced to Mr. Blank that such was my intention, he looked as pleased as a man can look who cares but little about the subject under discussion. He gave me a letter to Mr. Secretary Welles, shook hands with me, and then bowed as though the interview were closed.

I would have given something to have asked after his daughter, and known that she was well; but I would have given much more if I could have caught sight of her sweet face, and once more witnessed some of her pert airs. But this was one of the impossible things, and with a sigh I left the building.

Three days afterwards I started for Washington, where I arrived without accident. It was my first visit to the city. I found it full of drunken officers, loafers, contractors, blacklegs, blackguards, thieves, bold-faced women, Congressmen willing to sell themselves and country, whiskey speculators, and, lastly, office-seekers, who were drunk two thirds of the time, when they could get trusted or treated, and were clamorous and complaining when sober.

I went to bed early, and the next forenoon started to find the Navy Department and Mr. Welles.

I was a little uncertain about the direction I should take; so I wandered on, through the dirty streets, over the dirty, uneven, tobacco-covered sidewalks, meeting smart negro girls and lazy negro men, — the former with an air that seemed to establish their worth in their owners' estimation, and the latter creeping along as though fearful some one would ask them to do a job of work.

Washington was full of life at that time, although it was a period of great national depression. The people were trembling with fear of further disaster, yet, at the same time, were hopeful as to the final result. No one, to have seen faces, careless and gay, that I saw that morning, would have supposed our country was the scene of a terrible civil war, and that men were falling like leaves in autumn, giving lives and limbs for the sake of the Union.

After I had wandered along Pennsylvania Avenue for a mile or more, I asked a cabman where the Navy Department was located.

The knight of the ribbons looked at me for a moment, with a species of contemptuous pity, emptied his mouth of an enormous quantity of saliva, and then asked, with an insolent leer, —

"D'ye want a carriage to go thar?"

"No."

"Then go to ——, whar ye b'long."

With these refined words, the man put a fresh piece of tobacco in his mouth, and devoted himself to staring at negro wenches.

At first, I thought that I would thrash the man within an inch of his life, but prudence whispered to me that it was better to pass on, and not touch pitch and become defiled.

As I wandered along the avenue, I nearly stumbled over a tall, dark-complexioned man, whose clothes were none too neat, apparently made without regard to symmetry or shape, with many a wrinkle in the back of his coat, and pants that were baggy at the knees, a vest that was buttoned awry, the bottom turned up, as though in open remonstrance at being required to enclose the form of so uncouth a looking person as the one who stood before me. Yet, in spite of the huge, bony hands, the rough face, with a sparsely settled beard on some portions of it, as though the whiskers were uncertain on what part of the countenance they should find rest and protection, I did not fail to notice that there was a certain air of dignity in the appearance of the tall man, which told me that he must be above the ordinary run of Washington visitors; so I at once pronounced him a representative from one of the Western States, out for an early walk.

"Well, stranger, you do not keep as nice a lookout as you might," the tall man said, in a good-humored manner, as we both stopped and looked at each other after the collision.

"I might use the same argument," I answered. "It's as much your duty to keep your eyes open, as for me, mine."

"Yes, I reckon such is the case; but, my young friend, they pull the wool over mine in the most awful manner sometimes."

"But wouldn't it be advisable to wash your eyes, and clear them, before venturing into the street?"

"Ah, my young friend, there you mistake Washington. It would be better if I did not see any one while in the streets of the city. I must see a great deal or nothing — and that reminds me of a story."

"O, hang your stories!" I exclaimed, a little roughly; "tell me where the Navy Department is anchored, and I will thank you."

"So you want to find the sword of Gideon — do you?" asked the tall man, without manifesting the least excitement. "In search of an office?"

"That's my business."

"You are a stranger here, ain't you?"

"Yes, and I'm glad of it; for half the people I meet are either drunk or crazy; and some are impertinent."

"That's as true as preaching," laughed the tall, thin man, who did not appear to think that I was in the least personal. "There's more impudence in Washington than you'd encounter on a Mississippi flat-boat, in the halcyon days of flat-boatmen."

"I have no doubt of it, sir; but you have not answered my question. Where is the Navy Department?"

"I am going there, and will take pleasure in showing you where Gideon reposes. Come, right about face. There is more of a sailor about you than a soldier. I can tell that much by the manner in which you turn."

"You are right. I have spent many years on the ocean. I like it. It is a home to me."

"Then you should enter the navy. Just such men as you are wanted. Bold and active young fellows rise rapidly, and make their fortunes capturing blockade runners. Come, have confidence in me. Acknowledge that you seek the Secretary of the Navy for the purpose of obtaining a commission."

"You are mistaken, sir," I answered coldly; "I have made no application for a commission; but I was informed that one awaited me, so I came to Washington to see what it would amount to."

The tall, ungainly man listened to me in silence as we walked along; but at last he began to ask questions relating to my past life, and soon discovered that I had commanded a ship, that I was ambitious, and that I was loyal and patriotic as a man could be who believed in the old flag, the Union, and the blessings which the country granted to all.

The information which I gave the tall, ungainly man seemed to afford him the greatest satisfaction. He rubbed his large, bony hands, and smiled in a manner that seemed to strike a darkey whom we met as something wonderful, for the negro stopped and took off his hat, and as he bowed, said, —

"Glad to see dat grin on yer face, massa, 'cos it looks as though we had licked 'em d—d rebels. Ha, ha! guess we hab done it. Massa has news dat de rest of us no get."

The tall man raised his hand — a sort of military salute in acknowledgment of the bow — but took no notice of the negro's words.

We passed on; the conversation continued.

"You think that it is my duty to accept a commission?" I asked, after a moment's silence, for I began tó be convinced that my companion was something not often found in Washington — an honest man. Therefore I was inclined to put more confidence in him than I otherwise should have done.

"Not only your duty, but the duty of every able-bodied man in the free States to do all that lies in his power to crush the enemies of the government."

I looked at the man's lank but vigorous form, and a question entered my mind.

"If you have such patriotic thoughts, why don't you enter the army or navy?" I demanded, in a blunt tone.

"Well," answered the tall man, "I would if it were not for some few ties that bind me in Washington. I am fearful that I could not get away."

"And yet you were just telling me that all ties should be broken for the sake of the country."

The tall man laughed, and rubbed his hands.

"You've caught me," he said, "and I don't blame you for hitting me a dig; and now that I think of it, I'm reminded of a little story. A number of years ago, there lived in Illinois an old codger, named —"

Just at this instant we passed a hospital where there were sick and wounded soldiers, and two sentinels were standing in front of the door. The soldiers no sooner caught sight of the tall, dark man, than they seemed imbued with new life, for from a lolling position, half leaning on their guns, they came to an upright, and even presented arms; although why they should do so, when no one but themselves were near in uniform, was a matter of surprise to me.

But all seemed to be taken as a matter of course by the dark man. Up went his large, long hand as an acknowledgment of the salute, and for a moment he stopped, and asked, —

"Well, my boys, do you get enough to eat?"

"Yes, sir," both answered, with one accord.

"Then you are satisfied?"

"Yes, sir; with all but the coffee — that's bad. Nothing but peas and beans, and sour at that."

"Ah! Have you complained to your captain?"

"Yes, sir."

"And what does he say?"

"Twice he was too drunk to say anything, and the other time he threatened to put us in the guard-house if we made more complaints."

The face of the tall man grew dark and stern, as he said, —

"The number of your regiment, and captain's name."

Both were given, and noted down in a small memorandum-book, and then we passed on.

The tall man saw my look of surprise, and said in explanation, —

"The fact of it is, the soldiers round here look upon me as a father, and so they don't hesitate to tell some tales out of school. I shall have these complaints investigated, and if they are true, that captain will lose his place, and the quartermaster of the regiment will be overhauled and looked up; and that reminds me of a little story. When I was practising law in Illinois, a man came to me one day, and said that his neighbor had stirred him up, and he wanted redress. Well, after a long cross-examination, I found that my client had been in the habit of stealing wood from his neighbor's wood-pile, and had taken a log that contained a canister of powder, placed there for the purpose of blowing up the man who stole it. The scheme was successful, for my client was thrown out of one window, his wife out of another, and a grandmother and two children were lodged in a garret, while the stove went up the chimney, and did not again come down as a stove. My client wanted redress for the damage which he and his family had received; for he went on the principle that there was too much of a stir for so small a stick of wood."

I said that I couldn't see the point of the joke.

"Ah!" said the tall man, "that is unfortunate. I am afraid that I must tell you another story — one with an application more plain. But here we are at the Navy Department, and I must postpone the matter till another opportunity. Step light, for we don't want to wake them up if they have not turned out."

I knew what the tall man alluded to. At that time the loyal press was calling upon Mr. Welles, the Secretary of the Navy Department, to resign, and give place to some one who was wide awake, and capable of infusing a little life into the office, so that the privateers could be swept from the ocean, and some of the blockade runners captured or destroyed. I had paid but little attention to the charges brought against Mr. Welles, simply because I knew that our newspapers were fond of grumbling, and if they could not praise, they were pretty sure to condemn.

As the tall man made the remark about stepping lightly, I noticed that he laughed, but in such a manner that I was certain he did not believe the caution necessary. He appeared like a person who would enjoy a joke even if it was at the expense of a friend; although I could see nothing in his face that indicated ill-nature or vindictiveness. He looked like a man who would not feel offended if an acquaintance should get the best of him in telling a story: so I put him down in my own mind as the chaplain of a western regiment, a favorite with his companions, and a man more noted for his desire to see justice done to the soldiers than for his piety.

But, as we entered the Navy Department, I saw that many of those whom we met were quite profound in their manifestations of respect, bending low as they passed us, and apparently anxious for a kind look, if not a word. All the clerks seemed to suddenly find something to occupy their attention; and one fat-faced fellow, who was paring an apple, while seated at his desk, dropped apple and knife the instant he caught sight of the tall man and myself, as though detected in a most flagrant breach of decorum, and then bent over his book, pen in hand, as if spurred to renewed exertions by the sight of that plain, homely face.

"He's a government detective," I thought, when I noticed the signs of fear, and just as I arrived at this conclusion, some one threw open a door leading to the Secretary's private room, and in went the tall man, without being announced, although I could see that a dozen or twenty people were waiting for an opportunity to speak to Mr. Welles.

For a moment I held back, but the tall man looked over his shoulder, and said, with a smile, —

"Come in;" and in I went, and found myself in the presence of Mr. Welles and his assistant, Mr. Fox, both of whom seemed a little surprised at the visit.

I won't say that I did not feel a little abashed when I was thus unceremoniously introduced into the presence of these two gentlemen, who appeared to be consulting together on some matter that was of great importance. On a table were spread maps and papers, rulers and dividers, models of monitors, iron-clads, and double-enders; while in one corner were flags taken from the enemy, relics of captured vessels, and other articles presented to the department by enthusiastic naval officers.

As I entered the apartment, I thought that I was injuring my prospects by the abrupt manner in which I had dropped alongside of Mr. Welles; but a glance at the tall man's face, so full of assurance and confidence, rather helped to restore me, and I was enabled to watch the manner in which the two gentlemen who were examining the maps received my companion.

To my surprise they did not manifest the least displeasure. They left their employment, came towards the tall man, shook hands with him, glanced at me as though wondering who I was, bowed, and then placed chairs for both of us.

"Well, Welles," asked my companion, in a free-and-easy tone, as he slapped the veteran of the Navy Department on the back previous to sitting down, "have you captured the Alabama yet?"

"Not yet, sir; but I have despatched no less than ten vessels in search of her. It is impossible for the pirate to elude us much longer."

"O, gammon!" interrupted the tall man, crossing his legs, and then uncrossing them for the purpose of putting his feet on a vacant chair. "You have repeated that story so long that I really think you believe it. I tell you, Welles, you must wake up and put your finger on that pest. The people complain."

"One moment, sir, and I think you will acquit me of all blame in the premises," replied Mr. Welles. "Look, sir, and see what the department has done. On several occasions it has saved an army, it has reduced forts, it has fought battles, and never yet has it been defeated, or spared the blood of those who man our ships. I wish to institute no invidious comparisons between the army and the navy, for I can afford to let history and the world judge of such things; but I tell you, sir, that when thinking men write of the present rebellion, and the efforts made to put it down, the heroes of the navy will illumine many pages, and their bravery and services will not be eclipsed by the army."

"Hang it, Welles, I know all that! God bless the navy, and the brave men who man it, and the heroes who have given their lives and their blood for the flag and the Union! You have done all that man can do, but if you would only make a stir in the world, and sink those confounded privateers. And that reminds me of a story."

"I beg your pardon, sir, but you have not mentioned this gentleman's name," Mr. Welles said, and pointed to me.

I had listened in silence to the conversation that had ensued, and it struck me that it was not intended for heads like mine. I was astonished at the turn affairs had taken; but even while I listened, I could not help wondering how the tall, dark man should dare to intrude his advice and satire upon one of the most important departments of the country.

Of course, when Mr. Welles alluded to me, all eyes were turned in my direction, and this seemed to recall the tall man to the fact that he had brought me in the room when he entered.

"O, this gentleman," replied the tall man, with a careless laugh, "is one I picked up on the avenue this morning. He was inquiring his way to the Navy Department, so I undertook to pilot him here."

"Good Heaven!" ejaculated Mr. Welles, with a vigorous tug at his beard.

"My God! how imprudent!" remarked Captain Fox, in an almost inaudible tone, as though he felt more than he dared to utter.

My lank companion laughed, as if he rather enjoyed the surprise of the two gentlemen, while the reader can imagine that my situation was far from being agreeable; so I arose, and prepared to retire as rapidly as possible; but, before I retreated, I said, —

"This intrusion is none of my seeking. The gentleman invited me to enter the apartment, and I did so, but with great reluctance."

Mr. Welles and Captain Fox stared at me as though they could hardly believe that I was speaking the truth.

"He don't know me from Adam," said the tall man, with a smile that was intended to be reassuring. "You see that he don't. Come, don't frown, Welles; I've brought you a recruit, and one that will do honor to the navy. Sit down, Constant, and we'll settle this matter before we leave."

Messrs. Welles and Fox did not look quite satisfied, but still they seemed a little reassured, as though they could not help themselves, and had better put the best possible face on the matter.

"Yes," continued the tall man, caressing one of his long legs, and beaming on all three of us as though he really enjoyed what was going on, "I found this young man on the avenue, looking for the Navy Department, so I took him in tow, and brought him here. He wants a commission, Welles, and must have one. Give him a lieutenant's berth, and then set him to work on that mission we were speaking of."

"But he has not been examined as to qualifications. We know nothing of his seamanship or intelligence," pleaded Mr. Welles.

"O, fudge! I can tell what a man 'is made of the instant I talk with him. Come, don't play offish with this man, when you have commissioned a dozen who didn't know one of your double-enders from a flat-boat."

"But he has no references," pleaded Mr. Welles.

"Yes, he has. Show the Secretary the letter from the firm you sailed for."

In obedience to this command — for it sounded like one — I handed Mr. Welles the letter that Blank, Hawser & Co. had given me. The Secretary read it carefully, and then handed it to Mr. Fox.

"The letter is a sufficient recommendation," Mr. Welles said. "I have had quite a correspondence with Messrs. Blank & Co. on the subject. Mr. Constant is here at my request."

"O, he is. Well, why didn't you say so in the first

place, and not make me plead so long? I told you I could pick out a loyal man as soon as I put my eyes on him."

"But, Mr. President, you make some mistakes," laughed Captain Fox.

"Mr. President!" I thought, "what does the man mean?" and all at once it struck me that I had been the companion of President Lincoln, the Commander-in-chief of the Army and Navy of the United States.

"Mr. President," I said, rising, "I had not the slightest idea that you were what you are. Had I been aware of your rank, I should have been more guarded in my speech. I pray you to excuse me."

"I have nothing to excuse, my young friend. I like to hear a man talk just as he thinks, because then I know that his words come from his heart. To hear the truth, a man must mix with the world, and be prepared to take the world's opinion. How would you like that, Welles?"

"I am content to be judged by the world after the bitterness of the contest has passed away," replied the Secretary. "History will do us all justice, I have no doubt."

"Yes, I have no doubt that it will; still, it seems rather hard that one can't be justified while living. But we'll drop that subject now, and attend to business. What do you mean to do with the young man? He is just what you want."

"I will have a lieutenant's commission made out for him."

"Now for that service," said the President, when I had signified that I accepted the appointment of volunteer lieutenant in the navy of the United States.

The President looked at the Secretary, and the latter looked at the former, and then commenced operations on his long, white beard.

"You know what we were talking about, Welles. Put the question to him. He won't squawk, I reckon;" and once more the President nursed his long legs.

"Hem! well, the fact of it is, Lieutenant Constant, we want you to undertake a secret-service expedition. No one must know, but the persons in this room, that you are on duty, or what your business is. Even the firm of Blank & Co. must be kept in ignorance of your plans, for it would be dangerous to yourself to divulge them, and would render our schemes useless."

Mr. Welles paused, and looked at the President. The latter looked at Mr. Welles, and nodded his head, as much as to say that the right tacks were aboard, and the sailing quite plain.

"The scheme that we propose to you," continued Mr. Welles, in a low, confidential tone, "is one of danger, but still highly honorable, and, if successful, will be lucrative in the extreme. The capture of one cotton-loaded ship through your means would place you above want — in fact, make you independent."

"Rich as Illinois mud," the President said in a half whisper.

"And this secret service is not so honorable as some others," I remarked in a quiet tone.

All three gentlemen exclaimed against such an imputation. There was no way I could serve my country so effectually as by secret service: patriotism called me to the work, and as a man I could not decline the position that was offered me.

"But you have not yet explained to me what is needed," I said, after a pause.

"Give it to him in full, Welles," cried the President. "Make a clean breast of it. He isn't the man to back water after he is once floating down the river. I know him by his looks."

Thus urged, Mr. Welles proceeded to unfold his plans; and I will briefly relate them for the benefit of those who have but a slight idea of the workings of the secret-service force. . He said that the government had been mortified at the escape and success of blockade runners, which left Nassau, Bermuda, and Havana. at certain stages of the moon, for Charleston, Mobile, Wilmington, and certain parts of Florida. He wanted me to disguise myself as a common seaman, to ship on board one of the blockade runners, to find out the signals, and to do all that man could do, without exciting suspicion, to enable the United States cruisers to make a capture of the steamer that I was on.

If I was captured, I was to communicate with the captain of the United States vessel, but in a private manner, so that no one would suspect me; and then I was to be set at liberty, or allowed to escape from the vessel, so that I could return to my post as soon as possible.

"That is," I said, after a moment's reflection, "you want me to act a spy's part."

"No, not exactly that," returned Mr. Welles. "I shouldn't say a spy. You wouldn't say a spy — would you, Mr. President?"

"No, I should think not," returned the President, balancing his tall form on two legs of a chair. "Of course not. The spy service is different — entirely different."

"Upon my word, I can't see the difference," I answered.

"Tell him the rest, Welles," the President remarked.

"All the captains of our cruisers will have orders to look out for you and your signal, and if, through your instrumentality, a blockade runner is taken, you will share in the prize money the same as a first lieutenant. If you are as successful as I think you will be, you will rank as a rich man before many months."

"And marry the girl of your heart," echoed the President. "No man can do more for his country than you can, if you have a mind to."

"But it seems to me that you have laid out a large amount of work for one man," I said. "I can't be in Bermuda and Nassau at the same time. A dozen men might find employment in looking after blockade runners. In fact, I should think that a hundred might be stationed at different ports."

"Ahem!" coughed Mr. Welles, and recommenced combing his beard.

"Ahem!" coughed Captain Fox.

"Ahem!" coughed the President. "Well, we won't say but that we have a few agents at some of the English ports; but how many, you won't care to know. If you consent to undertake the service, I will furnish you with a signal by which you will be enabled to recognize all those who are engaged in the same work as yourself, so that you can co-operate, if necessary. It is just the work for a man of ambition and nerve, who desires to make money and fame at the same time."

I could easily imagine all that I would have to undergo, dressing and acting the part of a common sailor, or shipping as a petty officer, receiving hard knocks, and giving them with a will when it was necessary. I would much rather have preferred some other position; but as my country seemed to require that I should take the part that Mr. Welles assigned me, I reluctantly consented.

"That's right!" cried the President, with animation. "Give me your hand, young man. I hope I shall one day have the pleasure of commissioning you as admiral."

He slapped me on the back in his hearty, bluff manner, and then shook hands with me with renewed energy.

"Come to me to-morrow morning, and you shall have full instructions regarding your new business," Mr. Welles remarked, as he rose to intimate to me that the interview was closed. "I shall want you to leave for Nassau in the course of a week. An English steamer starts from New York on the 10th, I think. You must ship on board of her as a seaman, and receive your discharge at Nassau. But we will talk this matter over to-morrow. I need not remind you that you must keep your own counsel in this. Be as secret as the grave."

"If I would avoid filling one," I remarked.

"Not so bad as that, I hope," the President said, and then he whispered for a moment or two with Mr. Welles and Captain Fox, and left the apartment the same moment that I did.

"Come," said the President, passing his arm through mine, as he left the building. "I'm going to the White House. Will you go with me?"

CHAPTER II.

AN UNEXPECTED MEETING. — THE PRESIDENT SERVES ME A GOOD TURN. — AN ENCOUNTER. — THE RESULT. — IN NEW YORK. — AN IMPORTANT INTERVIEW. — FOR NASSAU. — STRANGE COMPANIONS.

I won't say that I did not feel a little elated at the familiar manner of the President; for it was something to boast of to have him put his arm through mine and walk along Pennsylvania Avenue, talking in a natural and unaffected manner of the future and the past, of the failures and the triumphs, the hope and despair of the nation, as we advanced or retreated from the work that was before us.

And thus we chatted until we were near the White

House, when I noticed a party of ladies and gentlemen coming towards us. They appeared to have just left the President's mansion; and I supposed that they had called to pay their respects to Mr. Lincoln, and, not finding him at home, were about drifting back to their hotel.

There were four ladies and two gentlemen; and a lively party it was — laughing, chatting, and admiring or condemning, as they looked to the right and left, and saw things which pleased or displeased their fancy.

Not until we were close to them did the conversation of the ladies subside into inaudible murmurs.

"It is the President," I heard a young lady whisper to a gentleman on whose arm she was leaning.

I looked at her and the gentleman with a strange thrill in the region of my heart. I could not forget the sweet face that I saw before me. It was Miss Hatty Blank and her father, in company with several Boston friends.

I think I stared so hard at Miss Blank, that she dropped her hazel eyes, and blushed as if she were not accustomed to admiration.

"I say, Constant," whispered the President, "there's a confounded good-looking girl. Do you know her?"

The President would have passed on without further notice of the party, if I had not detained him; for Mr. Blank had recognized me, and bowed in a much more familiar manner than was his custom, for was I not walking with the highest in the land — a man who commanded, and was obeyed? And being in such company entitled me to some respect at the hands of Mr. Blank.

I introduced the party to Mr. Lincoln, and the President shook hands with all of them in the most affable manner. To Hatty he said a word or two relative to her beauty, and complimented Boston on producing such charms.

"So you have been to the White House to see me, have you?" asked the President. "If you will return, I'll endeavor to entertain you for a short time; and for the ladies I'll provide a treat in the shape of handsome bouquets fresh cut from the hot-house. Come, Miss Blank, take the arm of my young friend here, while I walk on with your father. Don't shake your head, and say that you are not acquainted with him; for this is Lieutenant Constant, of the United States navy. Good name for a lover — eh, Miss Blank? But of course you never thought of such a thing as a beau. Well, well, never blush about it. Here, Constant, look after her a bit, while I talk with Blank about Massachusetts politics."

I must have been somewhat embarrassed at the position in which we were placed, for I know that I blushed like a schoolboy, and looked at Miss Hatty as though asking her to take pity on me; which appeal must have touched her heart, for she laughed, and whispered, —

"Isn't the President funny? But he isn't handsome. Do you think he is?"

In the mean time I had exchanged a few words with her father, and been introduced to the rest of the party — all from Boston, and all married except Miss Blank. Mr. Blank was so much elated at the condescending manner of the President, that he was quite willing to forget his daughter, and permit her to walk with whom she pleased; while the rest of the party kept close to the President's heels, for the purpose of listening to one of those celebrated stories for which Mr. Lincoln was noted. So Miss Hatty and I walked along in the rear, quite unnoticed; she looking very demure, and I rather flushed and trembling, not exhibiting that composure and firmness which a lieutenant in the navy should always show when in the presence of an enemy or a piece of dimity.

I have read in books how some fellows would have conducted themselves if they had been situated as I was. They would have thought nothing of vowing love to the girl; making her promise to give her hand, and then eloping with her, and marrying her, all within an hour's time, and in spite of the vigilance of friends. I wondered if such dashing lovers would have dared to utter a word to Miss Hatty, and how they would have succeeded. All this I thought of as we walked along; but still I did not find that strength which novel-heroes always have.

Presently Miss Hatty looked up and shot a glance at me with her dark hazel eyes, and with the glance a bright smile, as though she were thinking what a goose I was.

"We have met before, have we not?" the young lady asked.

"Yes; I saw you once at your father's office. It was nearly two weeks since. I have not forgotten the day or the hour."

"Indeed! how strange!" and then she flashed a glance at me, as if to judge how sincere I was in my expressions.

"Not so strange, Miss Blank, when you recollect that sailors are rather susceptible, and love to look at a handsome face as well as sail a clipper ship."

"How singular! I suppose that in foreign ports you see many beautiful women, with dark eyes and hair, as graceful as ballet dancers, and as indolent as first-class beauties have a right to be?"

"I have seen handsomer women in my own country than I ever saw in foreign ports," I replied, with a low bow and so ardent a look that the young lady could not misunderstand my meaning, so she blushed and changed the conversation.

I feared that I had offended her, but her face did not show that she was very angry, so I amused her with my adventures in Washington, my first meeting with the President, the mistakes I had made in talking with him, and other matters that interested her, for she laughed quite heartily, so much so that the President turned and asked,—

"Constant, what is it you are telling the lady? Some good story, I'll warrant. You are making yourself quite agreeable for a naval officer. Recollect, I'll have no love affair, for the nation wants you at this time."

I felt my face burn, and, to add to my confusion, Mr. Blank and the ladies of the party all turned and looked at me, some with surprise, and others with a haughty stare of contempt that was almost maddening, for it showed me that the estimation in which I was held was not of the highest order, in spite of the appointment which I had just received, and the affability of the President.

Had I been a regular officer in the United States navy, one who had been educated at the expense of the nation, I should have been considered the equal of any man or woman present; but as I was only a volunteer officer, who entered the navy for the purpose of receiving hard blows and aiding the country, it was not meet that I should be treated like some of the gentlemen who affected to think but lightly of volunteer officers.

I did not talk much after the President fired his shot. Miss Hatty noted the change and was also silent, and not even the President's jokes could rally us.

We entered the White House, and were escorted to the East Room, looked at the pictures, and then were conducted to an ante-room, where Mr. Lincoln made us drink a glass of wine, told us some stories, and dismissed us in a pleasant manner, with an invitation to call again.

"Constant," Old Abe said, as he shook hands with me at the door, "let me see you before you leave Washington. I have some good advice to give you. I want you to take care of yourself, and come back deserving the thanks of your country. Don't forget that. Always bear it in mind in all your undertakings."

"I will," I answered.

"And one thing, Constant," the President continued,

still retaining his hold of my hand, " I noticed one thing while you were walking with that young lady. You needn't blush, because she is a pretty girl, and I don't blame you for falling in love with her — most men would. I remember when I first commenced practising law in Illinois, I saw a young girl that I took an awful shine to, but she wouldn't have me because my prospects were so uncertain. Now your prospects are uncertain; but there is no reason why you should not rise to a position in life that is equal to mine. The father don't suspect that you are hankering after his daughter, so I didn't let on, but I just put in a few words in your favor that made an impression. He has other ideas for his child, but don't you give up the ship just yet. There is time enough. If I can make you a captain before the war closes, I'll do it. But do your duty, and promotion will come. Now run and gallant the girl to her hotel, for I see that she is looking around for you. Say nothing to Blank, for he is a proud man, vain of his wealth, position in the world, and all such nonsense; but still keep up hope; and, speaking of hope, reminds me of a little story. When — "

Luckily for me, Mrs. Lincoln appeared at this moment, and so I made my escape; but instead of attaching myself to Miss Blank, after I had overtaken the party, I walked with her father, who immediately commenced pumping me on certain points, one of the most important being the station to which I was ordered for duty.

I had half a mind to let Mr. Blank know the secret service which I had undertaken; but I remembered Mr. Welles's warning, not to hint to any one the duty I had promised to assume, so I wisely held my tongue; and months afterwards I had cause to be thankful that I did not confide in Mr. Blank, or expose the secrets of the Navy Department.

"So, Constant, you don't know to what part of the world you may be ordered?" asked Mr. Blank.

"No, sir; I don't think that the department has yet made up its mind what to do with me."

"Well, I suppose that you will soon learn. Do you remain long in Washington?"

"No, sir; I think not."

"Well, I would not if I were you. This is an expensive place; and one meets so much bad company here, the morals of the best of men are soon corrupted. Nothing would bring me here but business. Hatty, my dear, that is General McClellan whom you see on horseback. He is our young Napoleon."

Of course all the ladies cried out in one breath that he was splendid, handsome as Adonis, and other remarks equally complimentary; and while all were looking at the man, as he galloped along the avenue at the head of his staff, I managed to take my leave almost unperceived; for I thought that I was no longer wanted in that select circle, whose pride was built upon money, whose hopes were based upon money, and whose thoughts were upon money.

As I walked towards the hotel, thinking of the various scenes which I had witnessed since I had left it, I chanced to look up, and saw that Miss Blank was just in advance of me, and that she was alone, having left her father and party for a moment to do a little shopping.

This was a most imprudent act on the part of Miss Hatty, and if she had been acquainted with the morals of Washington, she would never have ventured on such a course; or, if her father had stopped to consider that the Washington of to-day is not the Washington of twenty years back, he would have accompanied her on her little excursion among the dry goods stores of the capital of the United States. But it was fated that he should not; and so I had an opportunity to once more run alongside, and speak to her.

It happened in this manner: I noticed the dainty form

of the young lady, as she tripped on before me, so I quickened my steps for the purpose of keeping close to her, admiring her, and wishing that she would turn her head so that I might make my presence known. But she did not look back, although she glanced from side to side, as though in search of a certain kind of store, and could not find what she wanted.

Those eyes of hers, and the glances combined, were the means of producing trouble; for an officer, a young fellow who looked as though he had been doing guard duty all night and part of the morning over a spirited fortification of bottles, imagined that those eyes and glances were for his especial benefit, and that the owner of them was rather struck with his form and face, the latter puffed out and inflated as though the veins were filled with a mixture of liquor and gas, and the former all stomach, and very little shoulders.

This interesting youth noted Miss Hatty's eyes and face, and he was just vain enough to think that he had created a sensation in the region of her heart. He saw she was unattended, and supposed that she wanted company, like many of the young women of Washington society, where at times it is hard to discriminate between the good and the bad.

The officer's brain was stupefied with liquor, or he would have noticed the difference between the pure and the impure. I am glad that he was drunk, or too much under the influence of liquor to make nice distinctions, and the reason for such feeling will soon be apparent.

The military man touched his cap as he passed Hatty. She did not notice the act, or even look at the fellow, for her thoughts were on other matters; but he supposed that she made a sign, so he turned and hastened after her.

"My pretty little posy-osey," the drunken fool said, as he came alongside of the lady.

She looked at him with a haughty stare of astonishment. She did not comprehend the man.

"Does my little ducky want company?" asked the officer, and he put out one of his arms as though he intended to throw it around her.

She avoided the embrace, yet was not frightened, for she was a girl of courage and decision in spite of her little vanities.

"Don't you fight so blamed shy!" the man cried. "I know you, and want to talk with you. You'd better confide in me. I have influence with the provost marshal."

Once more he approached her, and stretched out his arm. She avoided him, and began to look a little anxious, as though she had encountered something really serious.

The officer shook his head, and attempted to scratch it with his dirty fingers. As no new ideas entered his brain by such means, he stopped working amongst his hair, uttered an oath or two by way of gaining fresh audacity, and then ran towards the young lady.

"I'll have a kiss," he said, "if it costs me all my postal currency!"

He threw his arms around her waist, and made a dash for her lips; but Miss Hatty dodged her head and uttered an indignant remonstrance, at the same time she called for help.

She did not have to call more than twice before I was alongside, and ready to grapple with her foe; and I never felt more gratified at the prospect of a row than I did at that moment, when Miss Hatty was to receive the benefit of my strength and devotion.

I laid one hand on the officer's collar, and the other in the region of his coat tail, and then with a sudden jerk I sent the fellow flying into the gutter, where he struck with such force that the blood spirted from his nose, but he had too much liquor aboard to be deprived of his senses.

He scrambled to his feet in a moment or two, and then came towards me, revolver in hand.

I don't know how it happened: but, when I had sent the drunken fellow to the gutter, I put out my arm and placed it around the waist of Miss Hatty; for it seemed to me she was so much agitated that she must faint. But I afterwards found that she was not one of the fainting kind. Although somewhat frightened, she did not think it necessary to lose her senses; but, for all that, she did not entirely repudiate the support of my arm when I placed my body as a shield between herself and the savage drunken officer.

As the ruffian stood up, covering me with his pistol, the blood streaming down his nose, his hair in disorder, his face bloated and flushed with passion, he did not look very inviting, and it struck me that the present was an excellent opportunity to utter a prayer or two, for the purpose of keeping an anchor to the windward in case of serious accidents; but just at that moment I could not think of a suitable one, and, if I had, Miss Hatty would have interrupted it, for she made a faint struggle when she saw that I stood as a shield between her and danger, and exclaimed, —

"O, no! You must not. You are too kind and too generous. Let me be exposed, not you."

But I could not heed her remonstrance. I thought at the moment that I would give my life for her own, so I stood firm, at the same time keeping my eyes on the officer, expecting him to fire every moment.

"You have insulted a gentleman!" the drunkard bellowed. "You shall pay for it. I'll shoot you."

"You had better not," I returned as calmly as I could. "Think better of it, and give up the idea. Even in Washington assassination is not common, so you may be punished."

AN ENCOUNTER AT WASHINGTON. — Page 50.

"Never. You have insulted me. Death to you and the young —— on your arm."

As he spoke, he took aim and fired: but, luckily for Miss Hatty and myself, most of the officers who loafed around Washington instead of being at the front in those days, were more familiar with the contents of black bottles than those of revolvers; so, as a matter of course, the ball whistled within a foot of my head, and lodged in the side of a house.

When the drunkard discharged his revolver he was not more than two fathoms from me, so the moment the shot was fired I made up my mind what to do. I knew if I turned and ran a second shot would follow, and perhaps wing me, while if I advanced I might escape.

I resolved on the latter course as the boldest, and the one calculated to produce the most effect on Miss Hatty; for I did not want her to think that I was a coward, or capable of deserting her at the first appearance of danger.

I removed my arm from the lady's waist, and then, with a sudden rush, was within reach of the man before he had time to cock the pistol and take a second shot.

"I'll kill you!" the ruffian said, and put his thumb on the cock of the revolver; but, before he had time to do more, I planted my fist beneath his nose, and over he went like a dead man.

He did not move after he fell, but lay as though stunned by the blow and fall; but for fear that he should revive, and once more make trouble, I took his revolver, discharged the loaded barrels, then threw the weapon in the mud, and once more joined Miss Hatty, who remained on the sidewalk, seemingly quite interested in all I did.

"Now, Miss Blank," I said, in as calm a tone as I could assume, "if you will suffer me to conduct you to your hotel, I should be proud of the honor."

She looked at me with a wondering pair of eyes and a pale face.

"Are you sure that you are not hurt?" she asked.

"I am quite certain on that point. The fellow missed me. He will not be likely to use his pistol for some time to come."

"I am so glad that you are not injured, for do you know that it was quite noble in you to come to my assistance in such a brave manner? I don't believe that many of the young gentlemen of my acquaintance would have acted as you have."

"Will you walk along with me?" I asked, for a crowd of loafers began to collect around the officer, and the usual amount of bickering and pocket-picking commenced, while several dark darkies were already seated on the curbstones addressing the fallen hero in tones of comic commiseration, and I heard one of them say, —

"What for you down thar for, wid yer nose all bunged up? Say, massa ossifer, can't you talk?"

And then the companions of the negro yelled with laughter, for they had found something that was lower even than their own social scale.

Hatty laid her hand on my arm, and I led her away, fearing more disturbance, several military officers having arrived on the spot, and were evidently inclined to avenge the wrongs of the insensible man.

We did not hasten our steps, for I scorned to run away, and I think that Miss Blank was equally as proud as myself on that point.

"I am thankful that I was so near as to render you some assistance," I said, when we were beyond the crowd's observation.

"Goodness knows, I am ever so glad!" replied Miss Blank. "I don't know what I should have done had you not come to my aid. The man was drunk, and I don't like to have a drunken man near me. Will you let me thank you for what you have done? But I will thank you, whether you want me to or not. It was a real brave act on your part, and but few of my gentlemen acquaintances would have done the same. Come, don't blush. You didn't blush the first time I saw you."

"Do you recollect the first time I ever saw you?" I asked, and stole a look at her handsome, glowing face.

"Of course I do; and I thought you a very impertinent man."

"For what reason?"

"Because you stared at me in such a rude manner."

"But it takes two persons, Miss Blank, to effect a stare such as you complain of."

"O, does it? Well, do you mean to say that I looked at you in a rude manner?" and Miss Hatty tossed her head, and attempted to frown.

"Miss Blank is never rude. Indeed she could not be."

"Thank you for the compliment, sir. I did not think that sailors, with their honest heartiness and bluffness, could flatter, but I find that I am mistaken. I am sorry to think that I have been laboring under such a misapprehension."

I laughed at her wilful, playful ways, and grew more confident as I began to realize my position and present happiness; for it was happiness to be in her company, to hear her voice, and feel the pressure of her little hand on the sleeve of my coat.

"But tell me one thing," I said. "Do you forgive me for offending you the first time we met?"

"You did not offend me. I noticed that you stared at me as though you thought I was an awfully wild girl, and I am afraid you think so now."

"I do not know what I think," I replied; and it seemed as though I must pour out the burden of my heart, tell her that I loved her, and would die for her if it would afford her the least satisfaction; but, by an effort, I managed to prevent making a fool of myself, and that is something to be wondered at, for a pretty girl can turn the head of the most obdurate of men.

"Do not think harshly of me, at all events," she said. "I have my sober moments as well as other people. Now, to prove it, I have a great mind to tell you something."

"I should be delighted to hear it. Do favor me."

"Well, I will. Just before I was insulted, I was thinking of you."

"Indeed! I am most happy to hear it. Pray, tell me of your thoughts."

"I will; but you won't laugh?"

"No."

"Well, I was thinking that it was very singular we should meet in Washington; and I wondered if we should often see each other. Now don't laugh."

I did not feel in the least like smiling after such a confession.

"And I, too, have a secret to confide to you. Would you like to hear it?" I asked.

"Yes, indeed I should."

"Perhaps you will be offended with me for being so frank."

"No, I hope not. But I can't tell till I hear what it is."

"You say that you feel grateful to me?"

"Yes, very grateful."

I stole a quick look at her face, and saw that her bright eyes were dimmed with tears. She was thinking of the insults of the drunken officer.

"If such is your feeling, then I have no doubt but that you will pardon me. I will confess my crime in a few words. The day I saw you at your father's office you dropped a photograph of yourself."

She looked up with a knowing smile. She began to comprehend my meaning.

"That photograph," I continued, "I picked up and placed in my pocket, intending to keep it. Here it is. What shall I do with it?"

She just glanced at it, but did not offer to take it.

"It is a horrid likeness," she said. "Somehow the artist did not get a good light, and I had on the most unbecoming dress that I ever wore. I have always felt ashamed of the picture."

"And you will allow me to retain possession of it?"

"Why, yes, I suppose so. That is, if you want it. I would rather you had a better one. I don't see how I happened to drop it; but I suppose that it fell from my card case. I am sure I don't see what you want of such a fright."

I placed the photograph in my breast pocket, and as I did so, I noticed a look of satisfaction on the face of Miss Hatty. She was flattered by the reverence with which I treated her picture.

We walked on a short distance in silence, and then Miss Hatty suddenly looked up, and withdrew her hand from my arm.

"O!" she cried, "here is papa. He has come to look for me."

Mr. Blank had waited at his hotel some time for the return of his daughter, but as she had not arrived as early as he expected he had started out to find her, feeling a little uneasy at her absence."

"O, papa!" Miss Hatty cried, starting forward, and clasping his arm, "such an adventure! I am sure I am almost frightened out of my wits, and should have died if it had not been for Captain Constant. He saved me, papa! indeed he did."

"How? What is the meaning of all this?" asked Mr.

Blank, who began to tremble, fearing that something serious had happened.

Miss Hatty, like all young ladies under similar circumstances, commenced shedding tears, and those only added to her father's perplexity.

He looked at his daughter, and then at me.

"Who has dared?" he asked, and then stopped.

"Explain this matter, sir," he said, as though I was the culprit, and had presumed to offend the only daughter of the rich Boston merchant.

"O, he is not the one," sobbed the young lady. "He would have given his life for mine; he is all that is brave, noble, and generous."

"Brave, noble, generous? What in thunder does this mean?"

By this time the usual Washington crowd commenced gathering around us, and one pickpocket, more bold than the rest, made a dash for Mr. Blank's watch; but the timekeeper was secured by a secret guard, so the attempt failed, and the fellow retired, and allowed some other expert to make a trial.

Just then a carriage passed us. I hailed the driver, and engaged him to take us to the hotel where Mr. Blank was stopping.

When the coachman slammed to the door, and drove along the avenue, Mr. Blank said, —

"Now, pet, dry your tears, and tell me all that has transpired. Let me know what has happened from your own lips. Who has dared to insult a daughter of mine?"

I interrupted him, and said that I would give him a full account of all that had happened, but the offer was not accepted.

"No, sir; let my daughter tell me all that she recollects of the matter. Come, darling, don't be frightened. I am here to protect you."

Thus encouraged, Miss Hatty related all that had passed, — how the officer had insulted her by putting his arms around her waist, and offering to kiss her; and how I had come to her rescue, and saved her, although I had endangered my life in so doing.

Her father listened in patience to all that she told him, and when she had concluded, he kissed her, and congratulated her on her narrow escape; but not one word did he think of addressing to me until his daughter reminded him that I deserved her thanks, and the thanks of all her relatives.

"O, yes! I nearly forgot that, Captain Constant. Allow me to thank you for what you have done. It is just what I should have expected of you. Hatty, my dear, have you thanked the captain?"

"O, yes, papa! some time since. I did not wait to be told."

"Ah! quite proper and right. But you don't understand these things like men. We have a more unceremonious method of doing business than you women. Ah, here we are at the hotel. Will you go in with us, captain?"

He asked the question in so indifferent a tone that I was indignant.

"If he can't treat me with some show of politeness," I thought, "I will spare him the annoyance of my company. At least he might be grateful and courteous at the same time."

But it was not in the man's nature to be courteous to a person of my station in life. What I had done he regarded as perfectly proper, and he would have blamed any of his employees who had declined the same kind of service. In fact, if a man lost his life while serving Mr. Blank, it was not regarded as a serious matter, but a just tribute to the virtues of Mr. Blank's position that had been built up with gold, and hedged in with exclusiveness.

"Won't you come in with us?" asked Hatty, who noted the manner in which I had received the invitation from her father.

We were standing on the sidewalk in front of the hotel at which Mr. Blank was stopping.

Her father had turned his back, and was about to enter the hotel without another word; but when he heard his daughter's invitation, he stopped, turned half round, and awaited the result of the request. He did not join her in making it; he thought that he had performed his duty in speaking as he had.

"I have business that will prevent me from accepting your kind invitation."

"Won't you come in for a moment?"

I shook my head. With a woman's quick perception, she saw what was the matter, and was anxious to make amends for her father's rudeness. I appreciated her motives, but at the same time would not violate the resolution which I had formed not to force myself into the society of Mr. Blank.

As Miss Hatty spoke, Mr. Blank manifested symptoms of impatience.

"Come, child, come!" he said. "Don't loiter on the sidewalk."

"I shall see you again before you leave Washington?" Miss Hatty asked.

"I think not. My business is pressing."

She looked grieved for a moment, and an impatient command from her father cut short all discussion. She held out her hand.

"Good by until I see you again. I shall never, never forget the service you have rendered me. Be assured of that."

For one moment I held her hand. Then she withdrew it, and turned away; but there was a look in her eyes that was eloquent of feeling and gratitude.

She put her hand on her father's arm, and together they entered the hotel, Mr. Blank looking neither to the right nor left.

I caught one last glimpse of the lady's face, and then, with a sigh, moved in the direction of my hotel.

The day and night passed, and, punctual to the minute, I presented myself before Mr. Welles and Captain Fox at the Navy Department.

The Secretary of the Navy was very deep in thought, and his fingers were lost in the tangled locks of his beard when I entered the apartment which was used as his private office; while Captain Fox was examining the model of a double-ender, pondering over it as though he was endeavoring to convince himself that a steamer, built after the pattern before him, could move as fast through the water while going one way as another.

Both gentlemen looked up as I entered the room, and both of them left their occupations to attend to my business.

"You are punctual," said the Secretary. "This looks well for the future."

I bowed, and accepted the chair that the Secretary pointed to.

"Captain Fox, is Mr. Constant's commission made out?" Mr. Welles asked.

Captain Fox said that such things were never forgotten at the department, and as proof of his words selected a parchment from the midst of a hundred others, and handed it to Mr. Welles.

"You accept the commission of lieutenant, do you?" asked the Secretary of the Navy, after a glance over the document.

"Yes, sir."

"Then take it. Now I shall order you to perform the duty that I spoke to you about yesterday. You recollect it?"

"Yes, sir."

"And have you thought of the matter? Have you weighed the whole affair in your mind?"

"Yes, sir; I have considered all the dangers and the hardships."

"They shall be paid for out of the secret-service fund; and in addition to the regular salary of a lieutenant. This is something that I should not offer to every one; but I have taken a fancy to you, and think that —"

"He's just the man for the place," interrupted Captain Fox, who saw that his chief was hesitating for a word.

"Precisely: just so. The man for the place. That's it. There are but few in whom we would put so much trust; the business is so peculiar."

"Requiring so much tact and self-possession," hinted the captain.

"All that you can summon," continued the Secretary. "But now for the final instructions. Captain Fox, you have given some attention to the subject. Explain all that is necessary to Lieutenant Constant — the secret signals, and all;" and then Mr. Welles turned me over to his subordinate, and plunged into a mass of correspondence.

It is not necessary that I should enlighten the world relative to my instructions, the signals which I were to make if I had an opportunity, the signals which I were to recognize when I encountered one of our gunboats, the commanders of our national ships, the American consuls at all ports where blockade runners congregated, and nearly all persons who were engaged in the same business as myself; and it was intimated that I should meet several of them on land, on shipboard, and in the queerest of places.

"Understand me distinctly," said Captain Fox. "The commanders of our national ships alone have the key to the signals which I have imparted to you. No other person on board knows anything about them. Our captains are instructed, that if their ships are in danger of capture, the signal-books must be destroyed at all hazards, even at the sacrifice of life; so you see that your secret is secure. The consuls keep their secret instructions locked up in their safes; and as they are burglar-proof, there is no fear of their being stolen. Now let me see if you can go through with all the minute instructions which I have imparted to you. It is necessary that you should commit all to memory, for we don't dare trust papers to men who are compelled to play such hazardous parts."

I have a most retentive memory, and can learn quick. I caught the spirit of his meaning at once, and was enabled to repeat all the signals; the grip of hands, the position of the head, even the wearing of the hat, cap, or clothes, was significant of something connected with secret service; and all were so well arranged, so entirely unsuspicious, that no one could have detected, unless initiated, that men were working in common for some great purpose.

For nearly two hours did I go over the lessons with Captain Fox; and at the end of that time he said I was text-perfect, and congratulated me on my retentive memory, which he thought promised great results.

"And now, one word," he said, as he arose to intimate that our interview was about to close; "you are to embark on the most dangerous business that the department can send you to look after. A word, a glance, or even a suspicion, will be enough to end your days with a rope around your neck, or a toss overboard some dark night. Now I think we understand each other."

"I am positive that we do."

"Well, such being the case, you must get away as soon as possible. An English steamer leaves New York for Nassau in the course of a few days. On board that steamer you must embark, either as a sailor, working your way before the mast, or as a rabid secessionist, anxious to aid the South, and despising the North. But you must not overdo the thing; and above all, remember that the Southern gentleman always detests one who agrees with him in all things. You have a peculiar part to play, but I think that I can trust to you to enact the *rôle* I have marked out. Of course you are acquainted with parties at the South, so that if necessary you can mention their names?"

"Yes."

"And are familiar with some town, so that you can hail from the place in case it is necessary?"

"Yes."

"Then you are all right. After you reach New York, you can decide whether you go to Nassau as a sailor or sympathizer. If the latter, call on the collector of the port, and he will furnish you with money for your passage. Now take leave of Mr. Welles, and then you can go."

Mr. Welles was reading a letter and combing out his beard when we ventured to disturb him. He extended his hand, gave me an anxious glance, and asked, —

"Does Lieutenant Constant know all?"

"Yes; I have given him full directions," answered Captain Fox.

"And he agrees to all the proposals?"

"Yes, sir; without the least reservation."

"Then he will be successful. Mark my words, Captain Fox: Lieutenant Constant will give a good account of himself. Farewell, sir;" and Mr. Welles resumed his paper and beard at the same time.

I left the Navy Department, and then thought of my promise to the President, and concluded that I would call on him, and bid him farewell.

No sooner was the thought formed than I determined to

execute it. I walked slowly along Pennsylvania Avenue, thinking of Miss Blank, and wishing I could obtain another glimpse of her sweet face without seeking her at the hotel, and wondering if she had given me a thought since we parted the day before, when who should I encounter but the drunken fellow who had insulted Miss Hatty. He was in company with a brother officer; and as they were near me, and talking in rather a loud tone of voice, I could hear all that passed between them.

"I tell you what it is," said the fellow who bore the marks of punishment, "if I could find him, I'd skin him."

"And yet you say you insulted the girl?"

"Yes; but I thought she was a —"

"Never mind what you thought. You were free and easy with her, and the chap struck you. Now you had better let the matter drop, because, if you don't, it may turn out that the girl is the wife or daughter of one of our Congressmen, and then you can judge where you would be. I tell you, they'd strip the bars off your shoulders in no time."

Just at this instant I was close alongside of the speaker, and looked him full in the face. He knew me in an instant, for he was not so drunk the day before but that he could recollect.

"By Heaven, there is the man!" cried the military genius, clutching the arm of his judicious adviser.

"Well, all that I can say is, that he has a smart look," replied the latter; "so let him alone."

But this advice was unheeded. My antagonist broke away from the restraint imposed upon him, and came towards me.

"Sir," he asked, "did you, or did you not, strike me yesterday?"

"Yes, for insulting a lady; and, if you should repeat such conduct while I was near, I should repeat the dose that was administered."

"You have insulted me, and I will have satisfaction. Who are you? Give me your card."

"What kind of satisfaction do you require?"

"An exchange of shots."

"Well, you owe me one. Recollect that you fired at me yesterday; so stand off six paces, that I can have a fair chance. I know that I can hit you."

"Would you murder me?" demanded the fellow.

"No; but you attempted to murder me. I mean to wing you so that you will no longer disgrace the army. I will shatter a leg or arm, whichever you prefer."

"I want a fair exchange of shots: that is all I desire," remarked the officer. "Will you grant me my request?"

"Why, you want all the advantage. You have had one shot, and now you want another — two to my one. Don't you see the injustice of such a request? Come, be reasonable, and let us settle this matter in a fair way. I'll fire at you; and then, if I don't maim you, you can have another turn, on an equal footing."

"I won't fight in that manner."

"I hope that you are talking of fighting the enemies of your country," said a calm, cheerful voice at my elbow.

I turned, and saw that President Lincoln had approached us unperceived. How much of the conversation he had heard I was unable to determine, for I could tell nothing by his face.

The two army officers took off their caps, and bowed most profoundly, while the President laid his hand on my shoulder, and asked, —

"What is the meaning of this, Constant?"

"O, these gentlemen and myself were having a little fun owing to something that happened yesterday."

"Yes; I have heard of the affair. Blank told me about it last night. I saw him at Seward's; I knew that I had not misjudged you. I can generally tell what a man is by the look of his face. You are as ready to fight for a lady as your country."

"I did what honor commanded me to do," I remarked.

"And honor in that instance was a good prompter; but it is not at the present time. Come with me. I want to speak with you."

As I turned to follow him, he addressed my late adversary,—

"Go to your regiment, and report yourself under arrest for creating a disturbance in the street, and for drunkenness. I will see that you have justice."

The military officer marched off with a halting step, while his companion took an opposite course, and seemed to feel thankful that he had escaped some kind of punishment.

"Constant," said the President, as we walked along, "you did a good thing yesterday when you protected that girl. She will recollect you for it. I know that she will, by the way her eyes sparkled last night when she told me how you managed. Good-looking, isn't she? Will make some man happy."

I sighed when I thought that such might be the case.

"I don't know that you have told your love," continued the President, with a laugh, "or whether you have let it lie concealed in your damask cheek. But my opinion is, go in, and win glory and lots of prize money. Those things will tell, if they are backed by devotion and good looks."

"Yes; but how can I win glory by acting the part that I must act?"

"By serving your country. It is not the station, nor the duties, but the zeal that proves a man's patriotism. Do your duty where fate or chance may cast you, and you will find that your own conscience will approve; and that is glory enough for most any man."

"But not enough to win the heart of a handsome, romantic girl," I remarked in a sad tone.

"I tell you what," cried the President, "if a man makes love to a girl, and that love is rather acceptable than otherwise, she won't look for glaring deeds. Now, I once courted a girl in Illinois, when I studied for the bar, and she told me that I could never make a show in the world, because I wasn't a rising man. I was not so tall then as I am now. In fact, I thought I was running to seed; but I sprouted after a while, and here I am as high as any of them."

Of course I thanked the President for his kind advice, and then pleaded an engagement, and was let off with good wishes for my success, and a hearty shake of the hand. That was the last I saw of President Lincoln for some months.

In due time I arrived in New York, and made inquiries respecting the sailing of a steamer for Nassau. I soon found that I had several days to spare, so concluded to run on to Boston, and settle up some little affairs I had left undisposed of; and this done, I returned to New York, and commenced working in earnest.

Remembering what Captain Fox had told me about consulting with the collector of the port of New York, and obtaining some hints respecting my future conduct, I determined to call and see him; so about eleven o'clock I started for the custom-house.

It was a long time before I could obtain an audience, and I did not succeed until I had written my name on a slip of paper, and then just beneath the signature drew a few flourishes, which no one would have noticed, and yet they were very significant to the initiated. It was a stroke of secret-service diplomacy that Captain Fox had taught me to use when an important interview was to be obtained with some member of the government who did not wish to be annoyed with bores.

No sooner did the collector receive my name as it was written, than a change took place in his disposition. He gave such imperative orders that I should be admitted immediately, that all the clerks in hearing thought I was to have an office in the custom-house.

The usher bade me follow him, and then I was introduced into the presence of the great man.

He was seated at his desk, and near him were some dozen or twenty people — some writing, and some talking.

The collector looked at me with a keen glance, and made an almost imperceptible sign. In an instant I had answered it, and then gave the sign that followed recognition. It was returned. The collector rose, and extended his hand. I gave him the grip that he was expecting.

"You want to see me on particular business?" he asked.

"Yes; I should like a moment's conversation with you."

He led the way to a private room, and then closed and locked the door.

"Now, sir," he answered, "I am ready to hear all that you have to offer. I find that you are on secret service."

I then informed him of my errand, and for a moment the collector pondered. At last he took from a safe a thick book, looked over its pages, read for a moment, and then said, —

"You must leave in the English steamer that sails to-morrow. If you engage a passage, you will be looked upon with suspicion; for no less than a dozen sympathizers start for Nassau in the vessel. Do you think that you can hold your own in boasting of the resources of the South?"

"I can try."

"Yes; but you must be careful, and keep within bounds. If you ship as a common seaman, there will be but little chance of your learning secret movements. Yes; my advice is, that you engage passage, give out that you belong to some Southern town where there are but few inhabitants, or else to some city where there are many. You can judge which is best."

"I shall be prepared for that point," I answered. "I have already determined what to do."

We shook hands and parted, but my pockets were heavy with the weight of gold I carried away.

During the day I engaged passage on the Dragon, and was told to be on board at nine o'clock, sharp, for delays were not submitted to.

The next morning at eight I was landed on the steamer's deck, — an independent Southern gentleman, who had seen something of sea life, and wanted to see more.

On the quarter-deck I found a dozen or two serious-looking people — most of them dark and bilious, all nervous, all suspicious of each other. Those who came on board were glared at, and all who were glared at returned the glances with interest.

I underwent the general scrutiny with perfect composure; and so well did I perform my part, that a lady, who was seated near a tall, white-headed man, who seemed to be in feeble health, — for he moved with great difficulty, and only with the aid of a cane, — remarked loud enough for me to hear, —

"I know he ain't a Yankee."

"Now," I thought, "is the chance to make a 'ten-strike.' I shall never have a better opportunity."

In an instant I had turned towards the lady and her white-headed, feeble companion, and, raising my hat, said, —

"No; I thank God no Yankee blood runs in my veins!"

The old gentleman with the cane made a desperate attempt to gain his feet, while the lady sought to check him.

"I will, child! I will!" he said. "Don't attempt to restrain me. I must shake hands with a gentleman who boasts that he has no Yankee blood in his veins."

"But consider the consequences, papa. Do be calm and quiet, at least until we are at sea. When we are once upon the blue water, you can open your mouth, and give vent to the indignation that stirs your heart. But now, within sight of Fort Lafayette, it is dangerous."

"I have seen too many dangers, and faced too many, during the past two years, to tremble at the sight of a fort. A colonel in the confed—"

His daughter uttered a little shriek, threw her arms around the old gentleman's neck, and placed a little hand on his lips.

"O, papa! would you ruin all with your Southern impetuosity?"

I managed to smile, as I said, —

"Colonel, it is for me to ask the favor of shaking hands with you. It is an honor that I desire. Keep your seat, sir, for I notice that you are feeble."

The colonel had attempted to rise when I extended my hand, but I prevented him.

At any rate, we shook hands in the presence of the passengers — a scene that was regarded with much interest by them; but not a word was uttered by those who were looking on.

The colonel seemed pleased with my politeness and attention. He motioned to a seat by his side, and made me sit down; while his daughter, a dark brunette, with splendid eyes, full of fire and mischief, flashed a smile on me that was intended to thank me for my attention to her parent's whims. She was a beautiful woman — a type of Southern loveliness; just such a girl as would turn the heads of mankind.

"Allow me to introduce myself," said the colonel, as I

took a seat by his side, while a grim smile passed over his face. "My name is Alfa Rhett, Colonel of the Second Virginia Cavalry. We did good service at the battle of Bull Run. Some of my black-horse cavalry struck terror to the hearts of the Yankees on that day. Gods! how we cut them up! To the right and left, on all sides, we charged on them. I won my eagles on that glorious day."

"You old scoundrel!" I thought, "I should like to pitch you overboard. You deserve hanging and drowning at the same time."

"This is my daughter," the colonel said, pointing to the young lady who sat by his side; "Miss Magnolia Rhett, sir; and although I have no desire to boast, yet I will say that we belong to the first families of Virginia. The name of Rhett is old, sir. There are several branches of the family in Virginia and South Carolina. I belong to the Gordonsville branch."

"I suppose, colonel," I said, "that you would like, after your confidence, to learn a little of my history?"

"If you please, sir."

The young lady smiled encouragingly, and seemed prepared to give her very best attention.

"I cannot boast of belonging to the first families of the South," I said; "but all of my relatives are respectable, I believe, and most of them own a few niggers. I'm a South Carolinian, and belong in Charleston."

"Give me your hand once more!" cried the impetuous colonel. "I honor the people of South Carolina. They were the first to see the danger in which we were falling, and they were the first to dissolve the Union. Glorious old South Carolina! how I honor you!"

"South Carolina be d—d!" some one said. "She's all bluster and fuss, like a barking dog."

I turned and saw a pock-marked man, with a shaggy coat and rough wide-awake hat, standing near us. He had overheard our conversation, and was now ready to take part in it.

The traducer of South Carolina noticed our looks of surprise and indignation, but still did not seem in the least disconcerted. He returned our stare with interest, as he said, —

"If it hadn't bin for the whinin', and kickin', and grumblin', and groanin', of that same South Carolina, the Union would have bin all right at this blessed minit; and all the brave fellers what has fallen, and is now under the turf, would now be alive, drinkin' their reg'lar drink of whiskey, and smokin' their reg'lar smokes, like the rest of us."

"Keep cool, my young friend," said the colonel, when he saw that I was inclined to answer the pock-marked man, and defend the State that I had just claimed for my nativity. "Let me answer him. Magnolia, you remain quiet."

It was well that he spoke to the young lady, for she manifested a Southern girl's desire to make a quarrel out of the matter. Her lips were curled with the most perfect contempt for the opinion and matter-of-fact words of the pock-marked individual.

"O! let the gal talk," said the stranger. "I likes to hear a handsome gal talk. They can't make me mad, if they tries ever so hard. Young ladies like this one has fired the Southern heart all along, and done lots of mischief. Shucks! it would have been better if they had held their tongues, or else went in for the good old Union."

"Stranger," said the colonel, "you are not a Southern man."

"Yes, I be. I'm a Kentucky man — from Louisville. Isaac Bowmount is my name."

"Ah! Kentucky has not done much for our cause,"

murmured the colonel's daughter; and I thought that her eyes flashed fire at the thought.

"She's done a shucks sight more'n she ought to do," growled Mr. Bowmount, whose truthfulness and frankness I began to like, although I knew that it would not do to acknowledge it.

"Stranger," the colonel remarked, "you have never struck a blow for our independence. If you had, you'd hate the Yankees as bad as I do."

"That don't foller," said the Kentuckian. "I reckon I has seen some fightin'; I was at the battle of Bull Run, I was at Donelson, and half a dozen other places, where I commanded a regiment of as stout men as Old Kentuck could muster; but, for all that, I can't say that I like fightin' the Yanks."

"Fighting!" repeated Miss Rhett, with scorn in her voice and eyes: "they never yet stood firm enough to fight."

"It strikes me that you is wrong, miss," returned the Kentuckian. "They held us a tough one at Bull Run, and they gave us shucks at Forts Henry and Donelson. By the Lord Harry! but some of us didn't lose time when the Yanks advanced on our works. We left in a hurry, we did, or them what could get away. Bah! don't tell me that the Yanks won't fight: 'cos I knows better."

The venerable colonel allowed his lips to curl with indignation, as he remarked, —

"Had you owned slaves, you would have remained in the country, and fought until our independence was secured."

"Shucks! didn't I own 'em? I had fifty of 'em when the war commenced, and now I haven't one; and I don't want no more sich property."

"Did they run away from you?" asked the colonel.

"Some of 'em did, and the rest I sold. Shucks! if I had kept 'em, they'd all gone."

"And yet you feel no hatred towards the Yanks?" asked Miss Rhett, in a tone of reproach.

"No: the Yanks ain't to blame. They don't love slavery, and no more does I. The niggers don't love it, so they cuts and runs when they gets a chance. I don't blame 'em: I'd do the same. It would have been money in my pocket if there hadn't been a slave in Kentuck for the last ten years. What do you think of that, South Carolina?"

Mr. Bowmount turned to me as he asked the question.

"South Carolina will fight for her institutions," I replied, in a petulant tone.

"And so will old Virginia!" cried the colonel and his daughter.

"Bah!" retorted the Kentuckian, in a tone of contempt. "I'm a Southern man. I was born South; I had the small-pox South; I made all my money South; but I tell you, that we'd better have kept friends with the Yanks. Them is my sentiments; and I don't care who knows 'em."

The passengers had gradually edged their way towards us, so that they could hear what passed.

The Kentuckian glanced around, and examined the company by which he was surrounded. He noted each face slowly and carefully, as though he wished to be certain before he spoke.

"Gentlemen," he said at length, "I 'spose you is all Southern men?"

No one answered.

"Come, don't be afeared to speak. No one will harm ye. The Yanks will only be too happy to get us out of the country to interfere with us now. Come, which of yer hates the Yanks?"

We all made a simultaneous movement that did not escape the sharp eyes of the Kentuckian. A grim smile passed over his homely, rough face.

"Ah! you all hate the Yanks, do you?"

Another significant gesture on our part.

"Well, gentlemen," said the Kentuckian, "as you all hate the Yankees, why don't you remain in the Confederacy, and help fight her battles?"

This was a stunning question to most of the party; so some of them turned away and looked in another direction, while others stammered an excuse that they could serve the Confederacy in a much more efficient manner than by shouldering a musket.

"O! can you?" retorted the square-shouldered Kentuckian in a contemptuous tone; and then he asked, "Yet you believe in the South?"

"Yes," was the unanimous response.

"Well, now, I've bin in seven battles, I have, and I never seed one of your faces where the fire was hot and the lead flew around like shucks. I've looked you all over, and I don't remember you; so it seems to me that your patriotism don't amount to much. Eh, colonel?"

The colonel brought his cane to the deck with an emphatic whack, as though to confirm the assertion, while his dark-eyed daughter manifested her contempt for the deserters around her, and then her eyes fell on me, with an imploring glance, as though she would have me acknowledge some little deed of daring.

"By George, I will!" I thought. "I'll invent something to suit her."

"I can't boast of military deeds," I said, as soon as I had made up my mind what to say, "but I've seen a little service on the water; and, when Fort Sumter was battered, I was in command of a steamer, and did good work. Since then I have been employed on the Mississippi, seen much service, have been under fire a number of times, and am now bound to Nassau to wait for something to turn up. My name is Barnwell."

Miss Rhett gave me a radiant glance, but just then all conversation was interrupted.

"All aboard!" shouted the captain of the steamer, and with the words the plank was drawn in, and we backed from the dock into the river, and were under way for Nassau.

CHAPTER III.

A MYSTERIOUS PASSENGER. — A BLUNT KENTUCKIAN. — A QUARREL AND RECONCILIATION ON THE PASSAGE. — OUR ARRIVAL AT NASSAU.

No sooner was the head of our vessel pointed towards Sandy Hook, steaming along at the rate of ten knots an hour, the Cross of St. George flying overhead, English officers on the quarter-deck strutting and fuming, and casting contemptuous glances at our gunboats, at the forts, and at everything that was sheltered by the American flag, than the passengers began to recover their spirits, which they had appeared to lose while lying at the docks. Some were even bold enough to walk the deck, and whistle "My Maryland;" and others turned down the collars of their coats, as if no longer ashamed to show their faces.

All these signs the colonel and his handsome daughter noticed; and I observed that once in a while they communicated together as though comparing opinions respecting the company that promenaded before them.

We were about five miles from Castle Garden, when I noticed a Whitehall boat, containing a man in the stern sheets and one at the oars, shoot out from the land, and pull so as to head us off or cross our bows. The person in the stern of the boat waved a white handkerchief, as though to attract our attention; and instantly the eyes of the passengers were centred on the craft, and numerous speculations were made regarding the wishes of the occupants.

The captain of the steamer levelled his glass at the boat, and made a long and careful examination of both men. Then he handed the glass to a passenger who had kept his face hidden by the collar of his coat, and who looked suspiciously at every one on board, as though fearing treachery at the hands of all who were near him.

This latter individual — a dark, hard-featured individual, with restless eyes and nervous movements — had no sooner placed the glass to his eye than he said, speaking to the captain. —

"It is he."

At these mysterious words, the captain of the steamer stepped to the house over the engineer's quarters, and touched a bell. In an instant the steam was shut off, and the wheels stopped, while the vessel slowly made its way through the water; and thus, drifting with the tide, the boat shot alongside, and up the ladder sprang the person who had sat in the stern sheets, and who had waved his handkerchief to attract attention.

"Push off, Bob," the man said as soon as he touched the deck. "You had better wait till the tide turns, and then drift back to the city. Don't attempt to land on the Jersey shore, for some one might attempt to pick you up. Detectives are more plentiful over there than fiddlers in a certain hot place in the other world. Good by till I see you again. Tell the folks that I'm all right."

The boatman nodded, and pushed off, pulling slowly towards the city; while the person who had boarded us in so unceremonious a fashion commenced removing a wig from his head and a pair of grizzly whiskers from his face, revealing the countenance of a good-looking young man, full of determination, dash, and generosity.

"By St. George and the dragon!" he said, as he threw aside the things he had taken off, "I have cheated the Yankees once more, thank fortune!"

The colonel and his daughter, as though delighted with the information, manifested some anxiety to see the man who had outwitted the Yankees. They leaned forward, and I am convinced that nothing but the lameness of the colonel prevented him from starting up, and rushing forward to shake hands with the young fellow.

"Soulé," said the man who had looked through the captain's spyglass, walking towards the young fellow who had shed so much false hair, "I am glad to see you. I feared that we should miss you."

They shook hands with much earnestness, and the man who was called Soulé laughed as he replied, —

"I have been on the watch for you since sunrise. I knew when you started to a minute; for half a dozen boatmen telegraphed the fact by the aid of their oars. I knew that I should hit you; but I feared that some of the sneaking Yankee detectives would investigate a little before I left. Half a dozen of the curs were near me all night; but I shouted strong for the Union, and threw them off the scent."

"You are always lucky; and your boldness makes you so, I believe. But did you succeed?"

"Yes: better far than I could have hoped for. But more of this at another time. Who have we on board?"

The young fellow glanced over the passengers in a condescending manner, until his eyes lighted on the handsome face of Miss Rhett. Here he allowed them to remain for a moment or two, or until she had met his half-admiring, half-impertinent gaze with one of defiance, disdain, or maidenly modesty, I didn't know which. At any rate, she appeared to have made an impression, and one that was rather favorable; for young Soulé whispered to his bilious friend that she was a "devilish handsome girl, and that he must be introduced to her."

Miss Rhett heard the compliment, and cast a triumphant glance towards her father; but the old gentleman frowned at her for indulging in such petty triumphs and vanities; and that look was enough to restore her to all the dignity of the first families of Virginia. She lowered her eyes, and whispered to me, that men were so very rude nowadays that there was no enduring them.

Mr. Soulé and the bilious-looking passenger together entered the cabin; and then the rest of the people who were on the quarter-deck paired off, and talked in low tones of their private affairs, while Colonel Rhett and daughter, and Mr. Bowmount and myself, discussed the prospects of the Southern Confederacy until the pilot left the vessel. When that individual went over the side of the steamer, he was pleased to say that all she wanted was a secession flag to make her a bully confederate craft; and with something like a curse, at least it sounded like one, he dropped into his little dingey, and pulled for his pilot boat.

"Come, Barnwell," said Bowmount; "you and me won't quarrel 'cos we b'long to different States. South Carolina is a mean State, and won't compare with Old Kentuck; but I don't intend to boast; so take a cigar, and let's go forward and have a smoke. Don't refuse; 'cos I'm rather a good fellow after all, and have taken a likin' to you."

"If I could only join you, I should be pleased," cried Colonel Rhett. "But active service in the field has lamed and stiffened me; so I will remain with my daughter, in the hopes of soon being able to shake hands with that young Soulé. I know that he has been doing something to bother the Yankees, and I must find out what it is, so that I can rejoice with him."

Bowmount and I walked towards the smoke-stack, where we could enjoy our cigars without fear of being disturbed. After we had taken a puff or two, the Kentuckian remarked, in his energetic manner, —

"Shucks! what mean men Old Virginny does raise now! don't she? They all belongs to the fust families. Cuss me, if I ever seed one that belonged to the second class; did you?"

He didn't wait for me to reply, but chewed away at the end of his cigar, as though he was masticating some of the pretensions of the Virginia people.

"They is all mighty fine for talk, and sich like," muttered the Kentuckian; "but darned if they can hold a candle to our folks for real pluck."

"South Carolina," I said, in a tone that I thought might resemble one of the fire-eaters of the Palmetto State, "is a State that will turn her back to —"

"O, shucks!" interrupted the blunt Kentuckian; "South Carolina had her belly full of fight in the old Revolution. She was all full of sound and fury, like a bladder with peas in it. No offence to you, old feller, 'cos I really like yer, yer seem so different from them ere fire-eatin' chaps what talk fight, but don't fight."

I made some little pretension to being indignant, as a true blustering son of South Carolina naturally would under the circumstances. I actually turned away, and said that I would hear no such insulting talk, and that, when we arrived at Nassau, he should hear from me; but the Kentuckian didn't seem to care for my anger, for he continued to smoke his cigar, chewing the end like a cud, until I turned to leave him, when he laid one of his heavy, rather dirty hands on my arm, and said, —

"Don't be a fool, Barnwell. You know you has more sense than most of the low cusses of your State; so let's talk, and make use of each other."

He offered his hand, and after some little hesitation, I accepted it.

"That's hearty. Now to business. What do you mean to do after you lands at Nassau?"

"That will depend on circumstances," was my cautious answer.

"Just so. I 'spose you wants to make a few dollars, if you can do it in a neat manner."

"The temptation would be strong," I replied. "But I don't know as the confederate naval department would let me do what I wish to."

"O, blast the naval department! It's only a name. Where's its ships? where's its sailors? O, shucks! don't talk, or I shall laugh at you, even if you has served on an iron-clad, and helped drive some fifty or sixty half-smothered men out of Fort Sumter. Come, you'll allow that was mean, won't you?"

"No, sir; I won't. The hated flag —"

"O, shucks! don't talk sich gammon to me. That will do for the poor whites of the South; them dirty cusses what don't know how to read, write, or talk in a civilized manner. But it won't do for me. The flag was well enough afore we struck it down, and we is all going with it; more fools we. But, shucks! it's no use to talk; so let's drop the subject, and see if we can't put our heads together and make a few dimes while the fools is fightin'."

"Yes; go on. How can we do it?"

"Well, there's only one way. We might go into the blockade-running."

"I've thought of that," I said, in a meaning tone.

"Then so much the better; 'cos now is the time to think of it in earnest. Money is there. Shucks! don't I know it?"

At this instant I happened to look up, and saw Miss Rhett standing on the other side of the funnel, with her back towards us; but how she had gained such a position without being noticed, was more than I could tell. There she stood; but I could not even guess how long she had been there, or why she had left her father's side, to take up such an uncomfortable position as the one she had taken near the hot smoke-stack, and near to the strong-smelling machinery, a snuff of which is enough to make a woman sick, even if she is strong in the region of the stomach. Had she overheard our conversation? That was a question that I could not answer; for her back was towards us, and I was not aware how loud we had conversed.

I made a sign to the Kentuckian, and pointed to the girl.

"Shucks!" he said, in an indifferent tone, "what do I care for her? She may hear all my plans if she wants to. She can't do us any harm, 'cos where we is goin' is as much a confederate port as Charleston. I know it. She's a Southern gal, and knows what's good for the old first families of Virginia; don't you, Miss Rhett?"

It was a little singular that she could not hear the Kentuckian, although he spoke in rather loud tones; and we were compelled to pass round the smoke-stack to attract her attention.

We found she was humming, in a low tone, "My Maryland," with her eyes fixed upon the land that now began to grow dim and fog-like; and were forced even to touch her arm to recall her wandering senses. But when she saw us standing near, she started, and covered her face with her hands, as though she did not desire that we should notice her emotion.

We waited until she looked up, although Bowmount said, —

"Shucks, miss! what's the use of cryin' when you is leavin' a land of sich everlastin' tyranny? Recollect, you can't see none but hateful shores here, and them, you say, ain't worth a tear."

"I know," the young lady responded, dashing away the marks of tears; "but then it is my native land, after all."

"But it ain't Old Virginny, is it?" demanded the Kentuckian.

"No," with a deep sigh, and fresh evidence of tears.

"A State what used to produce more office-seekers to the acre than any other State in the Union. O, shucks! what patriots them fellers would be when they flocked in the hotels of Washington. There wasn't one of 'em but was willin' to lay down his blessed life for the good of his country, and a fat office; and then they was so disinterested! They was allers willin' to fight all men from other States what wanted a office; and I really believe that Old Virginny, in her best days, could have furnished the men for all the offices in the Union."

"You really must not abuse my State in the manner that you do," Miss Rhett murmured. "I will not listen to it. It hurts my feelings, and it hurts the feelings of pa; and now that he is so used up with hardships, he can't endure much joking."

"Then we won't rub him hard," responded the Kentuckian. "We'll praise Bull Run and Virginny, and we'll bring him round."

Miss Rhett said that the Kentuckian was a wicked man, and that he was full of his fun.

"But we want to ax your opinion on a p'int that is interesting," the Kentuckian said. "Now, my friend and me has been talkin' over some matters of business, and he was afraid that you would overhear him. I said I didn't care if you did, and that I would ax your opinion on the p'int. Now, it's this. We can make money by runnin' the blockade. Wouldn't you do it?"

For one or two seconds the girl's eyes wandered over

our faces, as though to read their expression; and I thought she seemed a little startled by the suddenness of the question.

"Why do you ask me?" she demanded, with a flushed cheek, and eyes that sought the deck, as I thought, in maiden simplicity and timidity.

"Because I wanted to show this South Carolina chap that I ain't afeared to tell everybody on board the ship that I mean to make money by runnin' the blockade. Now, wouldn't you do it?"

"But suppose you should get caught? Then you would lose all; and the Yankees would rejoice, confound them."

"Yes; the loss would be heavy, but the profits big if successful," responded the Kentuckian.

"Then I'd run the risk, and cheat the Yankees," exclaimed the girl, with a laugh, clapping her hands as though it was a good joke.

"We are all justifiable in cheating them. I have done so many times, and I hope to many times more."

We turned, and saw that Colonel Rhett had approached during the discussion, leaning on the arm of young Soulé, the man who had come on board but an hour or two before.

"Miss Rhett," said the colonel, with a wave of the hand in the Virginia style of politeness, "this is Vincent Soulé, of New Orleans. He hates the Yankees, and has done them some injury, and hopes to do more."

"Unless they should sue for peace, and ask our pardon for past offences. In that case, we will agree to forgive them, and only kick them when they come in our way."

"He's a true Southerner," cried the colonel, rubbing his hands, and emphasizing his remarks with a rap of his cane. "None but a high-toned Southern gentlemen would utter such words."

"High-toned fiddlesticks!" snorted the Kentuckian. "You all talk as though the Yanks was a parcel of niggers, and would hold still while you slapped their chops and kicked 'em. Shucks! none but cussed fools would talk that way. Now, you just let me have my say," — for young Soulé was about to interrupt him with an angry exclamation, — "and then you may talk as much as you please. Now, I've fit the Yankees, and I've drunk with 'em, and I've seen 'em under all circumstances; and I tell you that they is just as brave as we is, and can fight and kick just as well. You hit one of 'em, and he'll hit you back. You kick one of 'em, and he'll kick too, and just as hard as you kick. They ain't all the time pickin' up quarrels, like some of our folks; but they won't stand much nonsense, now I tell you; so the man what says he would go through the world booting Yanks, don't know what he's talkin' about."

Young Soulé commenced to grow indignant; for he did not expect such words from a Kentuckian.

"Sir," cried the young fellow, in a swelling tone, "you have insulted a son of Louisiana, and you must answer for it."

"O, shucks! go away with your boyish nonsense. I'm a Kentuckian, and speaks my mind just as I find it. There ain't no bounce about me, if there is about you. I've allers fit the Yankees in a fair, stand-up manner; but I never fit 'em by spyin' about their cities."

The young fellow seemed to be almost beside himself with rage, and once I saw him place his hand in his breast as though feeling for the handle of a knife; but at this instant the dark, bilious man, Mr. Newman Fudge, of Tennessee, a confederate agent, laid his hand on Soulé's shoulder, and spoke to him.

"No quarrelling," the agent said. "The South has none too many such men as you two. Come; stop this misunderstanding, or I will report you both."

"Report and be d—d!" replied the blunt Kentuckian. "If a man makes a fool of himself, I shall tell him so; and if he don't like it, he must do the next best thing. All men what respects himself will have some respect for his enemies; and although I has fit the Yanks, yet I don't think they is what some of our folks call 'em. In fact, I rather likes 'em, 'cos they is smart."

"Then you should have staid with 'em," retorted Miss Rhett, with a curl of her thin lips, and a flash of her black eyes.

"Thank you, Miss Rhett; but I think I can make more money by running the blockade. Besides, I don't believe the Yanks would let me rest in their cities, as I'm fresh from the battle-fields where I has fit their brothers and relations. You needn't scorn me, miss, 'cos I'm a man, and can't take any notice of it from you; but I can look around and see if you has any relatives, and take satisfaction out of them."

This hint seemed to have some effect on the young lady, for she recollected that she was endangering her father; and I think that the colonel noted the fact also, for he took his child's arm, and hobbled aft, as though to get out of the way of trouble.

"Come, Bowmount," said the confederate agent, "you and Soulé must shake hands. If I did not know you both, I would not interfere. But Bowmount has fought well, and served out his time at the head of his regiment. Soulé has had battles, but they have not been in the field; he has performed just as good service, however, as though he had been under fire for the last two years. Come; forget, and shake hands."

"O, yes!" said the Kentuckian, "I will." And the two men shook hands; but as Bowmount handed me a cigar, and walked with me forwards, he whispered, —

"That Soulé is a confounded confederate spy, and has a

whole carpet-bag of information about the Yanks, which he is going to send to Richmond by a blockade-runner. I know it."

These words set me thinking; and I determined to obtain possession of that carpet-bag before the voyage ended.

The night before we dropped anchor at Nassau, I observed that Miss Rhett was particularly confidential with Mr. Soulé. She flirted with him, laughed, and listened to his stories, flashed her eyes at him, sat by his side, and would not let him leave her even for a moment.

And the colonel, the venerable gray-headed colonel, who belonged to one of the first families of Virginia, smiled at the happiness of his daughter, and seemed pleased to think she was enjoying herself.

I think that it was about ten o'clock at night when the colonel, whose infirmities seemed to decrease quite rapidly, left the party of men with whom he was conversing, and approached his daughter and Soulé.

"I am going below a few moments," he said. "I have a little writing to do. Will you come with me, or remain?"

"O! don't take her away," cried Soulé. "The night is so pleasant that no harm can come to her while remaining on deck."

It did seem that a significant glance passed between the father and daughter, but I might have been mistaken. It was probably a look of parental anxiety.

"Well, take good care of her, Mr. Soulé," said the fond parent. "I will join you in a short time."

Colonel Rhett, with more lameness than he had manifested for some time, entered the cabin, and, I supposed, retired to his state-room, for I saw the light from his lamp shine through the dead-light that was let into the deck.

I walked towards the smoke-stack, and thought over something that had been on my mind for several days. It was a question how I should secure the carpet-bag that Soulé had brought on board, and which Bowmount had hinted contained valuable secrets, collected for the rebels under circumstances of considerable peril to the compiler.

I had not seen the carpet-bag since Soulé had brought it on board. Where he concealed it, I did not know; but I thought that the government would esteem it a duty on my part to make a strike for the bag, and destroy its contents, or else preserve some of the papers for future reference.

I glanced along the quarter-deck, and thought that now was my chance if ever. Soulé was engaged with Miss Rhett, the rest of the passengers were either laughing or whispering, or else relating the stories of their wrongs at the hands of the Federals, who were painted as monsters of cruelty, vulgarity, and ignorance. These were the men who considered themselves better than Northern mudsills; while they indulged in language and debauchery such as none but the most degraded would countenance. They would drink whiskey and chew tobacco from the time they arose until they went to bed, and seemed to think that such conduct exhibited a noble spirit of Southern independence. I need not say that it disgusted me; yet I had to avoid showing it, and sometimes drink when it was nauseating to do so. It did not seem to me that my fellow-passengers could represent true Southern gentlemen, and I afterwards discovered that they did not.

Bowmount was lying on a settee amidships, smoking a cigar, and dreaming of the profits which he would make in running the blockade, while the cabin servants were all yarning it forward, confident that their services would not be needed for some time to come.

"Now or never," I thought; and, after a hasty glance all over the deck, entered the cabin.

All was quiet. The cabin lamp that hung over the dinner-table burned low and dim, for it had been turned down when the servants finished their work. No one was to be seen. None of the state-rooms were occupied, and the only one that was lighted was Colonel Rhett's.

For a moment I stopped and looked around so to be certain that I was not observed; then I crossed the cabin without noise, and laid my hand on the knob of Soulé's state-room door.

I pushed hard and firmly, but the door was locked, as I half expected it would be; so I quietly returned to a sofa at the head of the dining-table, and laid down to think of the matter.

Just as I had stretched out, the door of Colonel Rhett's state-room opened, and the colonel's venerable head appeared, and then the colonel's sharp eyes were cast about in all directions with such rapidity that it seemed as though he must take in everything at a glance; but he did not, for I was partly concealed by the table, and the light did not reveal where I was lying.

I was about to speak; but the colonel's movements and looks were so suspicious, that I remained quiet, and watched him.

For a moment the colonel stood still, and listened. Then he stole to the door of the cabin, making no sound of footsteps, from which I gathered that he was in his stocking-feet.

"What in the deuce is he after?" I asked myself.

Then the colonel showed what he was after; for he glided to the door of Soulé's state-room; and, while he was crossing the cabin, I noticed that the limping, slow-moving invalid had given place to an active-motioned man, without a limp, or the least sign of age.

"This becomes interesting," I thought. "I will keep quiet till I see what is up."

As soon as the colonel reached the door, he did not waste time in trying if it was locked. He appeared to be aware that it was, and I supposed that he had tested it when first entering the cabin. At any rate, he appeared to take a piece of wire from his pocket, inserted it in the keyhole, worked it about for a moment or two, and then I heard the bolt of the lock slip, and the door was thrown open.

Once more the colonel stopped and listened. No one was coming.

His keen eyes glistened as he waited: but, finding that the coast was clear, he entered the state-room, leaving the door open.

"He is on the same errand as myself," I thought. "But he must not get the start of me."

I pulled off my boots, and placed myself near the door, waiting till he once more entered the cabin.

I do not know how long I had to wait. It might have been five minutes, and it might have been ten. Time passes quickly under such circumstances. I only know that I could hear the colonel fumbling in the berth, and under it, for the carpet-bag, and that at last he found it; and then the noise of a sharp knife, as it cut the bag, was heard, a rustling of papers, and I knew that the colonel had possession of the documents which I so much desired.

When assured of this fact, I returned to the sofa, and once more laid down out of sight; but with my eyes open, and senses on the watch.

In a moment or two the colonel stole out of the room, glanced around the cabin to see if any one was watching his motions, then locked the state-room door, and was gliding towards his own quarters, when I arose from my reclining position.

"Ahem," I said.

The colonel started as though he had been struck by

the knife of an assassin. He quickly turned to see who was watching his motions, and his eyes looked fiendish when they rested on me.

"Ah, colonel!" I said, still looking at him in a calm, steady manner; "I thought you were in bed. I did not expect to find you wandering about like a distressed spirit."

"No," stammered the scion of one of the first families of Virginia; "I haven't retired just yet. In fact, I don't feel sleepy."

"O! you don't? Then that is the reason you wandered into Mr. Soulé's state-room by the aid of a skeleton key."

He looked as though about to commence blustering; but, as I did not quail beneath his dark, vicious eyes, thought better of it.

"What do you mean?"

"Just what I have said. I was lying on this sofa, and saw all your movements; and now I have but to raise an alarm, and you stand before the passengers as a thief and a burglar — a fit subject for a pair of irons, and a berth in the run of the ship."

The colonel looked particularly vicious as he took a step towards me, with his right hand raised as though to strike; but, finding that I did not retreat or move, he said, —

"You are a brave fellow. Come; let us be friends."

He extended his hand; but I assumed a perfect South-Carolina look as I drew back.

"No, sir. I do not shake hands with thieves and burglars."

"By Heaven!" he cried, "you shall repent this. If I live to set foot on shore, I'll have satisfaction."

"Dog!" I said, with an effort at virtuous indignation that was quite creditable, "do you dare to threaten me? I have a great mind to give you up, miserable impostor that you are."

This appeared to touch him, for he assumed a humble look as he asked, —

"What can I do to make you my friend?"

"Your friend! Don't insult me. I have no such friends as you are. My friends are all gentlemen, and would scorn to steal into a state-room."

He rather winced at this, and I intended that it should cut deep; for only by such a course could I accomplish the end I had in view.

"What terms can I make with you?" asked he, "so that you will pledge me your word not to mention what you know and have seen?"

"Give me the papers that you hold in your hand."

He hesitated for a moment, and was about to remonstrate.

At this instant we heard some one entering the cabin; so I motioned the colonel to a seat, and told him not to move until I ordered him to.

It was not my purpose to let any one know that Colonel Rhett had entered Mr. Soulé's state-room, and stolen valuable papers — so valuable, in fact, that I wanted them for my own use, thereby confusing the rebel government a little, and confounding some of its emissaries. I had a game of bluff to play, and held a good hand to back up my bets; but, to win, it was necessary that I should have no one looking over my shoulder, or interfering with the cards.

All these things passed through my mind the instant I heard a person entering the cabin. It would not answer for us to be seen near Soulé's door, so I pointed to the sofa, and whispered the colonel to take a seat.

To my surprise as well as pleasure, the colonel obeyed me with the utmost alacrity, and without a word.

We had but just taken our seats when the lank, bilious rebel agent entered the cabin. I hastily began a conversation with the colonel on the first subject that entered my mind, and we appeared as though very deeply interested in it.

"Holloa!" said the agent; "what do you remain here for when the night is so pleasant on deck?"

"Because we have been so much interested in conversation that we had forgotten how pleasant it is up there," I answered; and the colonel, taking the hint, rambled on respecting some of the battles he had been engaged in, and the large number of Yankees he had slaughtered during certain charges of his cavalry at Bull Run and Ball's Bluff.

"Well," said the rebel commissioner, after he had listened for a moment, "I'll leave you to talk, while I light a cigar, and go on deck. I've heard of those battles before."

I think he had heard the colonel relate the exploits which he had performed in those battles until he was a little tired of the subject. Man is such an envious mortal, that he does not like to listen to personal exploits unless the narrator is as modest as he is brave. The colonel was not a modest man, by any means; but, according to his own accounts, he was as brave as any officer in the confederate service.

The bilious-looking agent lighted his cigar, and went on deck; and glad enough I was to get rid of him, for I was desirous of paying my respects to the colonel. As soon, therefore, as the agent had left the cabin, I turned to him, and said, —

"You see that I have spared you; I have thus far refrained from exposing you; but pity for your daughter has prevented me. Now, will you do what is right?"

"I am sure my daughter has a great regard for you," replied he with a quick look at my face, as though to judge what effect such an announcement would have.

"I am glad to hear it," I replied, with some show of

pleasure — just enough to make him think that I was flattered.

"Yes; she noticed you the first day that you came on board, when I shook hands with you for denouncing the Yankees."

During all the time that we were on the sofa, I had closely watched the movements of the colonel, although he had not been aware of the fact. The corner of one eye had been on him; and I had seen some of his motions, sly and cautious as they were.

I remained quiet until satisfied that he had gone too far to recede, when I said, —

"Colonel, we will resume our conversation, if you please. You have entered a passenger's state-room, and stolen papers. I shall expose you within ten minutes unless you return them to the carpet-bag."

"You apply a harsh term to a little joke of mine."

"You will find it no joke, I assure you. Will you decide what you do? Come; time is getting short."

"You are a funny man," said the colonel, with a horrible attempt at a smile. "I suppose that I must comply with your request. I will go at once."

As he moved towards the state-room, a bright thought entered my head, and I commanded him to stop.

"If you return the papers to the bag," I said, "and then leave the latter in the state-room, Soulé will know that some one has meddled with his private affairs."

"That is so," the colonel answered. "What had I best do?"

"Put the papers in the bag, and drop it out of the cabin window. All evidence of fraud will then be destroyed."

"By George! that is an idea," cried the colonel, his face expressing great signs of relief. "No one will ever suspect us if we resort to such a dodge."

"No one will suspect *you*, I suppose you mean," I said, with the air of a fire-eater. "Recollect, sir, I have not dishonored the Palmetto State by stealing private papers."

This made him wince a little, and I thought I heard him utter a damn on the fate of the State which I represented.

"Yes, of course," he said. "It's all right: I meant that I alone was to blame. I will never do so again, if you will not expose me this time."

"Well, well; drop the bag overboard; and for your daughter's sake, I will pledge my word not to utter a syllable regarding this matter. Be quiet about it."

He made a desperate effort to take my hand; but I refused him with such a haughty glance of disdain, that he appeared to wilt under it; and, without another word, went into the state-room.

No sooner had he disappeared than I returned to the sofa, inserted my hand under the cushion, and pulled out a package of papers which I had seen the colonel place there when he thought I was not noting his movements.

Thrusting the papers in my bosom, and thinking how surprised the colonel would be when he found them gone, I returned to the state-room door just as the Virginian was coming out with the carpet-bag.

"I have it," he said.

"So I see," I replied. "Now overboard with it."

He did not wait for a second bidding; but, stepping to the open cabin window, threw it out, and, as it struck the water, gave a chuckle that seemed strange to me.

"Were the papers in it?" I asked, in a whisper.

"Yes;" with a face that looked quite composed and truthful.

"Not one left?"

"Not one."

"Upon your word and honor?"

"Upon my word and honor."

"What a precious liar you are!" I thought. "I wonder if all the first families of Virginia are as bad."

"Now, we will keep this thing a secret?" whispered the colonel. "That is understood, I believe."

"Yes. But tell me one thing. Why did you rob Soulé?"

"Of course you want to know the truth?" he began.

"Certainly."

"Well, sir, I belong to one of the first families of Virginia —"

"So I have heard you say before," I interrupted. "Do all take articles that don't belong to them?"

The colonel winced again; but in a moment he was composed, and replied, —

"I have all a parent's feelings, sir; and, when I saw Soulé was so marked in his attention to my daughter, I determined to learn more about him than he was willing to admit. For that reason I entered his state-room; on account of my affection for my child, I took the papers, intending to return them after I had learned something in regard to his prospects."

I bowed with mock gravity.

"How do I know," he continued, "but that he is a base Yankee spy, or a traitor to our Southern Confederacy?"

"To be sure," I replied. "Those who talk the loudest are not always the most zealous patriots."

I thought that the Virginia colonel seemed a little cut at this remark; for he added, in a hasty tone, —

"I hope that you don't suspect me of not being a true friend of the South. I've given my blood for the cause, and would give my life rather than see it dishonored."

"Those are proper sentiments, sir," I replied, "and I respect you for them. But we've no time to talk further on this subject. We must return on deck in order to avoid suspicion. Keep your secret, and I will retain it with you. I am doing wrong; but, for your daughter's sake, I'd do much more."

"Do you really love her?" asked the colonel, in an anxious tone, as though sympathizing with me.

"No matter what my feelings are, sir," I answered, crustily. "I respect the lady; and I wish I could say as much for the father."

With these words I left the cabin, and went on deck, followed by the colonel, whose lameness and feebleness increased in a surprising degree as he prepared to join his daughter, who was still enchanting Soulé by the witchery of her eyes and smiles.

I found Bowmount smoking, and mentally speculating on the prospects of running the blockade with a load of useful articles; so I lighted a cigar, and took a seat by his side; but not a word did I utter respecting the events of the evening; and when I was ready to seek my berth, I looked over the papers which had been taken from Soulé's carpet bag, and found them of the utmost importance.

They contained information respecting the number of soldiers in the field; the men to be raised without delay; the naval ships that were building and fitting out; a long list of names of parties who were to be relied on as ready to assist the South with sympathy, money, or by engaging in blockade running. I saw some prominent men on that list; but it will not do to mention them, as they are, at the present time, all good patriots, and, according to their own assertion, have been so from the first.

Among the papers I found letters addressed to Jeff Davis, to General Lee, and others; and all told the same lying story of admiration for the South, and contempt and detestation for the North.

I almost sickened at the baseness that was exhibited; but nevertheless folded the papers, and put them in a secure place where no one would have thought of looking, and then turned in, and went to sleep.

The next morning at the breakfast-table, the burly Englishman who commanded the steamer, after rapping on his plate, said, —

"Gentlemen, somethin' serious 'as 'appened on board the steamer."

All the passengers dropped their knives and forks, and looked as though prepared to rush on deck at a moment's notice.

"Lor', captain," cried Miss Rhett, with a pretty little giggle; "I hope the vessel is not on fire."

"No, ma'am; there's no fire except what you 'ave kindled in the 'earts of the passengers;" and the red-faced captain put his hand upon his breast, and grinned like a sea lion with the toothache.

Miss Rhett giggled more than ever; and then, as a matter of course, finding all eyes were directed towards her, blushed scarlet, and looked a little uncomfortable.

I suspected what was coming, so braced myself for the shock, and assumed as innocent and independent an air as an impudent man could put on.

"Gentlemen," said the beef-eating captain, when the titter had subsided, "one of the state-rooms was entered yesterday, and a lot of papers stolen from it."

"Valuable papers?" asked Colonel Rhett, with an air of much concern.

"They was waluable, sir," responded the captain, in an emphatic tone. "So waluable, in fact, that I don't think the gent what lost 'em would have sold 'em for any money."

"Who lost them?" was the general cry from those at the table.

"Gentlemen," said the captain, after a moment's thought, "I'll let the person what lost the property speak for himself."

7

I knew what was coming, but assumed an air of deep concern, as Soulé, with sullen looks, said, —

"Some one has entered my state-room, and stolen a carpet bag containing valuable papers. If any one did it as a joke, it has gone far enough; if with criminal intentions, I can assure the thief that the papers are worth more to me than to any other person."

"If there are thieves on board, it is time that we knew something of it," remarked Colonel Rhett, banging his fist down on the table, and looking around on his fellow-passengers with an angry scowl.

"Now, papa, do be quiet," pleaded the daughter. "You must not get so excited on the subject."

If I had not seen the colonel enter and leave the state-room, and if I had not taken charge of the papers which he secreted under the sofa cushion, I should have been deceived by the manner in which he attempted to throw suspicion from his own shoulders. His face wore such a virtuous look, that I knew no one would question his honesty.

"You have lost papers," Bowmount said, during a pause, after Soulé's explanation. "Now, if any one took 'em for a joke, they'll say so, and so end the matter. But, as no one says so, we must conclude that they have been stolen. Shucks! what must we do? Just this: Let some one search our state-rooms, and see if he can find the carpet bag and papers. Here is the key to mine."

We all followed his example, and threw our keys upon the table.

"Who'll do the searching?" some one asked.

No one answered. The colonel, in a modest manner, as became one of the first families of Virginia, looked on his plate, then whispered to his daughter.

"O, no, papa. Let some one younger than you undertake so painful a task. Do not think of it."

Of course, after such an expression, all hands declared that the colonel was just the person to undertake the mission; and I must confess that I joined in the general cry with much satisfaction, while at the same time I thought the Virginian the most arrant hypocrite I had ever seen, and I longed to tell him so; but, recollecting that I was also acting a part, and a very deceptive one, I concluded to restrain my virtuous indignation until I could appear in a new light.

So, in a few words, it was settled that the old colonel should overhaul the passengers' baggage, and report as soon as possible.

"He's to do it, is he?" asked Bowmount, as we moved from the table.

"Yes; all hands seem to decide for him."

"Well, then I'll just move some bills of exchange from my trunk, and put 'em in a safe place. Come and see me do it. Shucks! there shan't be no cheating; only I don't want strangers overhauling my money matters."

The Kentuckian uttered these words in a low tone, but the Virginian heard him, and would have made an angry rejoinder if I had not checked him with a look; for it was not for my interest to provoke a discussion at that time. I feared the colonel in his rage would involve me in a row, and that was just what I did not desire. As long as I remained quiet, and did not wound the prejudices of my fellow-passengers, I was called a clever fellow, and all that; but I knew that it would not endure if I was conspicuous.

We lighted our cigars, and went on deck, while the colonel commenced his agreeable task of overhauling the passengers' luggage — looking into their boots, handling their soiled linen, and doing other things which were of a light and agreeable nature to a man who was disposed to exercise a general supervision over the affairs of others.

But, long before the colonel had concluded his investigation, there was a cry of "Land, ho!" and the island of New Providence was in sight — low, flat, but still inviting to those who had experienced the horrors of sea-sickness.

Our passengers were enthusiastic as we approached the town, passing several long, low, fast-looking steamers, on our way to the inner anchorage; all from England, all painted lead color, and all waiting for dark nights so that the blockade could be run, or attempted with less risk of detection than on moonlight evenings.

Floating from the peak of each steamer was the confederate flag, and from the fore, the English flag; the latter in compliment to British neutrality. As we slowly steamed past the vessels, our passengers cheered in a lusty manner, and pretty Miss Rhett clapped her hands, and declared that it was the prettiest sight she had ever seen; while her father, the gray-headed old colonel, who belonged to one of the first-family tribe, took off his hat, and waved it in such a hearty manner, that I suspected he must have money invested in the blockade-running business, and was afraid he should lose a portion of it unless he was enthusiastic.

At last the captain touched a bell, the wheels were stopped, the anchor dropped, and into the shore-boats we tumbled, and landed at Nassau.

"Come," growled the Kentuckian, after we had acknowledged a cheer for the Southern Confederacy, "let's go to the Royal Humbug Hotel, and see what kind of quarters we can obtain."

And off we started for the best hotel in town, followed by a crowd of dirty little boys, each anxious to show the way, and earn a piece of silver.

It was not difficult to find the Royal Humbug Hotel. A dozen people, after learning that we were not Federals, that we belonged south of Mason and Dixon's line, were glad enough to point out the spot where the house was located, and, in course of half an hour after we landed, we were registering our names on the books of the hotel; while, at the same time, we were surrounded by a dozen or more young men, all eager for news, and laying claim to the most rabid secession principles, as though there were some doubts as to their patriotism.

Finally the gong sounded for dinner, and there was a rush from all parts of the building equalling anything that I had ever seen in a New York hotel. Bowmount thrust his arm through mine, and in we went to dine, where I noted the confeds as they flocked in to the table. There were about fifty of them, male and female; and, while the former were inclined to be a little reserved, surrounding themselves with a haughty exclusiveness, the latter, although equally proud, were as chatty as so many parrots, and during the exchange of remarks I noted that the Yankees caught it most unmercifully. Heavens! how those women did revile them, and stamp on them with their pretty little feet, and tear them to pieces, and stab them with their tongues! and all the while the men seemed to enjoy it, and listened in approving silence.

But at last I saw that Bowmount, who had drank enough to feel independent, and as bold as a Kentucky tobacco-raiser usually is, had his attention attracted by something that one of the pretty little females uttered. His dark eyes glared, and his heavy face lighted up as if by inspiration, as he swallowed a glass of wine, and then addressed the lady who was nearly on the opposite side of the table.

"You don't like the Yanks, mum?" he asked in a loud tone, so loud that the attention of all at the table was attracted.

"No, sir, I don't!" with a snarl, and a curl of her thin lips.

"You never seed much of 'em, did you?" continued the impudent Kentuckian.

"No, sir; and I don't want to. The miserable Yankees are not fit associates for a Southern born and bred lady."

A murmur of applause was heard up and down the table on the part of the females present, and those who applauded the loudest attracted the most attention. Among the most vehement applauders of the sentiment I noticed Miss Rhett, the daughter of the gray-headed colonel.

She caught my glance, and smiled a friendly recognition, as though she did not want the friendship to end, now that we were on shore.

"O, they ain't fit associates, eh?" continued Mr. Bowmount, sipping his wine.

"No, sir. I dislike everything that belongs to the Yankees. They are an impudent race — a scheming set of savages, without refinement or manners. Our slaves are far better."

"Just so, mum," the Kentuckian remarked; "but, before I agrees to all what you says, let me ax you a few questions."

"As many as you please, sir, if it is for the purpose of proving the Yankees the meanest race on the face of the earth. But first let me know whom I am addressing?"

"My name is Isaac Bowmount, mum, and I was colonel of the Ninety-ninth Regiment of Kentucky Cavalry. I served a year in the confederate army, and left when my time expired. You won't accuse me of being a Yankee — will you?"

He smiled as though to invite her confidence, and the announcement of his rank was enough to secure it. She bestowed a keen glance upon the Kentuckian, and so did the owners of other bright eyes.

"Yes," said Bowmount, in a musing tone, but loud

enough for all to hear, "I has fit against the Yankees, and I must confess that I don't like their style of fightin'."

"There! there's good testimony to what I have said," cried the Southern girl in triumph. "Just hear what the colonel says."

"Yes," continued the Kentuckian. "I don't like their style of doing things. When the Yankees fight, they seem to be in earnest about it, and don't care if they do kill all who stands before 'em. I have been in several fights, and, in all but one, the Yankees licked us. We started 'em at Bull Run, but they touched us up in Western Virginia and Tennessee; and I must confess, that, when the cusses come at us with fixed bagonets, our men was allers inclined to run, and hang me if some of the officers didn't lead the way!"

"More shame for them!" cried the indignant young lady on the opposite side of the table; and the gentleman who sat by her side — her husband or brother, I could not just tell in which relation he stood — seemed to coincide with her.

"Yes," resumed Bowmount, in a dogmatical manner, after glancing along the table, and seeing that all present were listening; "it was a shame for Southern-born men to run at the sight of Yankees; but you know that, unless some of us had took to our heels we shouldn't have been here eatin' turtle and drinkin' claret. In fact, I think it more honor to try and fight and run away, than not make any appearance of fightin', but skulk out of the country as soon as a shot is fired!"

This was a hard hit, and I saw some of the young fellows squirm; but they looked as though they were not troubled, and continued to sip their wine. To my surprise, the lady on the opposite side of the table seemed to agree with the Kentuckian.

"If I were a man," she remarked, "such a charge should not be brought against me."

"No, I s'pose not. You women has more spunk than the men. But that ain't what I was comin' at. I want to talk with you about the Yanks."

"They are a mean, deceitful people. There is no gallantry, or refinement, or courage about them."

This sentiment met with universal applause from the ladies.

"Let's see about that," said Bowmount, with a mischievous smile. "Whar was you edicated, mum?"

"At the South, sir," returned she, with a glow of pride.

"Very good," continued he. "At a boardin'-school?"

"No, sir; my father employed a governess as teacher."

"And whar did that 'ere governess and teacher come from?"

There was a moment's silence.

"Shucks!" continued the Kentuckian. "No backin' out. Honor bright. Come up to the scratch."

There was another pause, when she replied, hesitatingly,—

"I think she came from Massachusetts."

"And whar did the piany that you played on come from?"

"Boston," she said, in a low tone, after a moment's hesitation.

"And whar was the books printed that you learned from?"

"I have forgotten."

"Honor, now."

"You are pressing the lady in an offensive manner," said the man who sat by her side, noting her hesitancy.

"Never you mind," retorted the Kentuckian. "It's our fight, and we mean to keep it up till one or the other of us cries out enough. Now, then," turning to the lady, "whar was the books printed?"

"O, 'they were Yankee books!" was the reluctant confession.

THE KENTUCKIAN'S QUARREL. — Page 105.

"And your father had his house nicely furnished — didn't he?"

"Yes, sir."

"And whar was the furniture made?" continued the persistent Kentuckian.

"In New York," replied the lady, in a more sullen tone.

"And now," cried Bowmount exultantly, "you pretends to despise the Yankees for the want of refinement and courage; and yet you have just showed that all the articles of luxury and larnin' that you ever heard of or knew anything about come from the land of the Yankees! That's jist about as much sense as some o' you Southern women has got."

The young lady looked her rage, and then turned her glance to the man at her side as if appealing for protection.

He answered it in the usual Southern style — without thought or consideration, or without a care as to who was right and who was wrong. Filling a glass with claret, he suddenly lifted it from the table, and dashed both the glass and its contents into the face of the plain-spoken Kentuckian.

The surprise was so complete, that for a moment I almost fancied that I was the party insulted, for a few drops of the liquor touched my face; but all doubts on the subject were set at rest in an instant; for Bowmount sprang to his feet with an angry oath, and, seizing the claret-bottle that stood near him, dashed it full at the head of the young fellow who had so grossly insulted him.

The bottle struck the Southerner squarely in the face, and shivered into atoms; and with the thousand pieces fell the young man, apparently lifeless.

Then there was a scene in the dining-room of the Royal Humbug Hotel that had seldom been equalled since the Southerners took possession of it.

As soon as Bowmount had sent the claret-bottle on its

way, he prepared to follow it right across the table, and thus fall upon the senseless man and complete his punishment, just as though the fellow had not been sufficiently dealt with.

But I saw the movement of the Kentuckian, and, despite the hilt of the bowie-knife which I noticed in his pants, caught his arm. In an instant the man had his hand free of my grasp, and whipped out his weapon.

As soon as he found his hands free, the infuriated man once more turned his attention to the prostrate Southerner at the other side of the table. By his side was kneeling the young lady whose free speech had caused all the trouble. By the words which she uttered in her despair, I saw that she was a wife, and that the person that she was so tender of was her husband.

As Bowmount gathered his forces for a rush, I hastily glanced around to see if any one was disposed to lend me a helping hand. To my surprise, no one stepped forward. Even the colonel retained his seat; but his amiable daughter was mounted on a chair, so that she could command a good view of the fight, and bestow applause where it belonged.

I had time to see this much, and no more; for my attention was turned to the Kentuckian, who sprang on a chair, and was just about to leap over the table, when I caught hold of his coat-tail, and pulled him back. He turned suddenly, to see who was opposing him; and, just as he aimed a blow at my head with his formidable weapon, I overturned the chair, and down the brawny fellow fell with a crash, carrying dishes and a portion of the table with him.

Before Bowmount could gain his feet, I had his knife, and was holding him down by main force. He struggled violently, and I thought it necessary to be rude.

I put the knife to his neck, and said, in a determined tone,—

"If you don't keep quiet, I'll cut your throat as sure as you live."

This threat astonished him. He ceased his struggles, and looked at me as though to note if I was in earnest.

"Do you mean it?" he asked.

"Yes; and I'll do it, too, unless you listen to reason."

"I didn't think this of you," the Kentuckian said, after a moment's silence, during which he remained quiet.

"Perhaps I could return the compliment. A man who makes a cut at me with a knife don't deserve much consideration."

"Wall, I didn't mean to do it; so forgive me, and let me up."

"Will you promise to behave in a quiet manner?"

"Yes. Keep the knife as security that I'll do right. Shucks! don't bother a feller now."

"I think he's still dangerous," muttered one of the Southerners.

"He should be given in custody without delay," continued another; but, without listening to such remarks, I released the Kentuckian, and allowed him to rise.

"Humph!" he growled, as he gained his feet, and shook himself, "you couldn't have done it, old feller, unless you had played me a trick. I can throw you with a fair hold, and make nothin' of it."

"We won't discuss the matter at the present time. One of these days I'll give you a trial."

"That's all right. What do you want by pressing round me so — eh?" and Bowmount turned on the crowd that was near him, all of them wearing threatening looks, and appearing as though half disposed to assault him.

The chivalry retired a short distance, for they feared that the Kentuckian would resort to some of the bottles on the table, and break their heads in regular order.

"Keep quiet," I said. "You have done mischief enough

for one day. I think you have killed the man on the other side of the table."

"And serve him right if I have. What right had he to shove in his oar, and throw wine in my face? I tell you, Barnwell, if that feller gets on his feet again, I'll have another peck at him — you see if I don't."

"And if he don't shoot you at sight, I will," returned the lady, who had been kneeling by her husband's side. "O, you brute! You deserve to be kicked by Yankees for your conduct!"

"Shucks! and what does the feller deserve for throwing wine in my face?" indignantly demanded the Kentuckian.

"I believe he is a base Yankee spy," some one said; and, looking for the person, I found that it was Miss Rhett who had spoken.

The idea was seized upon in an instant, and passed from one to the other; and then the fair dames scowled at the Kentuckian more vindictively than ever, and there were some threats of shooting the man on the spot; but at length I managed to get him out of the room, just as an English surgeon arrived to attend to the injured person.

"Now go to your chamber, and remain there until to-morrow," I said, as we closed the dining-room door. "You have raised a confounded row, and I must do the best I can to end it."

"Tell 'em," said the Kentuckian, as he laid one of his heavy hands on my shoulder, "that they are a set of confounded sneaks, and that I'll fight the whole of 'em, one at a time, whenever they wants me to. Shucks! Talk about mean Yankees! Why, them fellers is ten times meaner than the worse Yankee that I ever seed. A Yankee don't pitch wine into your face, and then cry baby 'cos you knocks him down. But there's no use talkin'. Come to my room, and let's have a bottle of wine."

I refused to accept his proposal, but it made no difference

in the man's feelings. I left him, and entered the dining-room, where I was received with a chorus of approbation from the dark-eyed women who were assembled there — every one of them rank little rebels.

"O, Lieutenant Barnwell!" said the lady whose husband was injured by the bottle which Bowmount threw, "how can I thank you for what you have done? You have saved my husband's life by your courage and conduct. That brutal man would have killed him. I don't know but that he will die, as it is, from the effects of his injuries."

As I moved along the room to the spot where the Southerner was lying, I was congratulated on all sides, and suddenly found that I was quite a hero in their eyes. Even Mr. Newton Fudge, the confederate agent, a native of Tennessee, — the same man whose head Parson Brownlow had threatened to punch for cheating in selling negroes, or some shrewd election trick, — came to me, and extended his hand.

"Lieutenant," he said, "I have all along thought that you was nearly destitute of snap and spunk, and that you was leaving the South to avoid fighting. But now I know different."

"It was well done!" cried Colonel Rhett, hobbling towards me. "I never saw but one thing that equalled it. At the battle of Bull Run, a Federal officer made at me with a sabre in one hand, and pistol in the other. I —"

I never heard the fate of that Federal officer, for I passed on. I had no doubt in my mind, at the time, that Colonel Rhett escaped from the fury of that Federal officer by the speed of his horse, or else he used his legs to good purpose.

When I gained the side of the injured man, I found that a surgeon was busily engaged in binding up his wounds; and bad enough some of them were. The bottle had broken when it touched his face, and the sharp edges of the pieces had lacerated the skin in a terrible manner, so that much blood had flown, and the man really looked in a dangerous condition.

He was in no mood to talk; so, when informed by his wife that I was his "preserver," he merely pressed my hand in token of his thanks; and then I advised an immediate removal to his room, where he could no longer be annoyed by the crowd, and where his injuries could be attended to in a proper manner.

"We shall never forget you, sir," the wife said, and gave me her hand to prove it.

I gave it a little squeeze to show that I appreciated her favorable opinion, and took an admiring glance at her face.

Perhaps Mrs. Anthony Gowen, of Augusta, Ga., noted that look of admiration, and was not disposed to feel offended at it, for she blushed a little in a coy manner, and once more held out her hand, while the servants and a few friends were helping Mr. Gowen up stairs to his chamber.

"I shall always be grateful to South Carolina for sending such a brave son to our aid," she remarked, with a tiny pressure of her hand. "When Southern gentlemen from other States stood aloof, fearful of danger, you risked your life to save my husband. South Carolina is honored in owning such a son."

"That is what I say!" cried the Virginia colonel, who it seems had been standing near, listening to all that was said, without my knowledge.

"Lieutenant Barnwell," cried the colonel, who seemed reluctant to allow me a moment's conversation with the Georgia lady, "you should be thanked for what you have done this afternoon — you should indeed."

"But I desire no thanks, sir."

"It is because you are too modest, sir. That is the reason. I never saw more heroism, even at Bull Run, than that displayed by you this day."

"Shall I offer you my arm, and assist you up stairs?" I asked Mrs. Gowen.

I saw that there were many men in the hall, and that they were inclined to block the way.

She laid her hand on my arm at once; and then, with a bow to the colonel and his daughter, we went up stairs towards her room, whither her husband had preceded us.

"Will you come in?" the lady asked when we arrived at her door.

"No; not at present."

"You will call in the course of the evening, sir?"

"If I find time, I shall be pleased to."

She seemed satisfied with this answer; and, with a bow and look of gratitude, the lady entered her apartment.

I went to my own room, entered, and locked the door. I then waited for darkness, so that I could leave the house unnoticed; for I was determined to have an interview with the American consul that night, and place in his hands the valuable papers which the colonel had stolen from Soulé, and which I had secured by a little stratagem. I also had other information to impart, and desired to receive some light on important points. In fact, I had no doubt but that the consul and I could pass a half hour quite pleasantly, and for the benefit of our government.

At nine o'clock, it being dark enough to move without fear of detection, I rolled up a bundle of sailor clothes, — blue shirt and pants, — and then removed some of my superfluous clothing, together with my watch and money, locked them up in my trunk, so that when I made my toilet in the open air, I should not be embarrassed by fear of losing what little property I had. Then, watching my opportunity, I dropped the bundle in the yard near the corner of the hotel, and stole down the back stairs. Fortunately I was unobserved; and taking my bundle, I retreated to the shadow of a tree some distance from the house, changed my clothes, rolled my citizen's dress into a ball, and, hiding it in the branches, started for the American consul's, a jolly-looking sailor to all appearances.

CHAPTER IV.

AN ENCOUNTER. — THE STREETS OF NASSAU AT NIGHT. — THE AMERICAN CONSUL. — A ROW. — A FOUL BLOW. — ON A BLOCKADE RUNNER. — AN IMPRESSMENT. — A FRIEND IN NEED. — THE SUSPICIOUS STEAMER. — A SIGNAL. — HARRY BLUFF AND HIS STATION IN LIFE.

THE night was dark, and the city of Nassau is not particularly brilliant with gas and candles; so I was compelled to feel my way, in a measure, as far as the sidewalks were concerned. Which way to move, or what direction I should steer, was more than I could tell. I had not the faintest idea where the American consul had located his office or house, so determined to inquire of the first person I encountered. For five minutes I walked on in silence, and then came to the harbor, where there was light and more people. I singled out a sailor, and asked him if he could tell me where the American consul resided.

The blue-jacket looked at me in surprise, and then raised his voice, and shouted in Jordey-like tones, —

"Eh! here be a South Spain prig, what takes the bread out our mouths. Let us duck him."

The fellow attempted to lay hands on me, but I dropped him with a blow that made him see stars.

Before any of his shipmates, all belonging to one of the blockade runners, could interfere, I was off, and, although they followed me for a distance, shouting out that I was a Yankee spy, yet I managed to evade them, and once more considered what I should do to find the person I was in search of.

By this time I was aware that I had secured a reputation, and felt that it would not answer to extend it; but how to find the consul, unless I asked for him, was a question that puzzled me.

For a while I stood on the corner of a street, and thought the matter over; and while I was thus thinking, two persons stopped near me.

"Well," asked one, "you think that you will sail to-morrow, do you?"

"Yes; if we have wind enough. I am tired of remaining in this cursed secesh hole."

"Ah!" returned the other, with a sigh, "what do you think of my position? Insults and defiance are what I have met with ever since I have been stationed here. I have to submit to many things which nearly drive me frantic, and yet there is no help for me."

"I can imagine some of the hard things which you have to bear; but have patience and courage. The time will come when all of these things will be remembered and paid for. The wind will not blow in one quarter for a lifetime."

"I hope not; and now good night, for I must hasten home."

The parties separated, — one walking towards the water, and the other towards the centre of the town. The latter seemed to be the man I wanted, so followed him as rapidly as possible, keeping close to his heels, until he suddenly noticed my movements, turned, and, to my surprise, presented a revolver close to my head.

I must confess that I stopped quite suddenly when such a threatening demonstration was made; and, when I was about to ask the cause of it, the person I confronted remarked in a quiet, confident manner, —

"If you follow me another step I'll put a piece of lead through you."

"I should be extremely sorry to have you do anything of the sort. Cold lead is unpleasant, and not to be trifled with."

"Who in the devil's name are you?" asked the man with the revolver, still keeping his pistol on a level with my head.

"Don't you see that I'm a sailor?"

"Yes; I see that you are dressed in a sailor's rig, but that don't make you a sailor; so keep at arm's length until we've had a better understanding, or I swear to you that I will blow your brains out."

"Nonsense!" I cried. "If I had brains, I should not be here. Put up your pistol, and don't fear me."

"Do you belong to a blockade-runner?" the stranger asked, and slowly lowered his pistol, so that it no longer covered my head, for which I was thankful, for the man before me was of a nervous temperament, and a little too active to suit an inquiring mind like my own.

"No; I am not in that line of business."

"Who are you, then?"

"A sailor, without a shot in the locker, anxious to find the American consul."

The man before me seemed to meditate on the subject, as though debating as to the amount of reliance to be placed on what I stated. At last he said, —

"I am the American consul. Come to my office to-morrow morning, and I will listen to your wants."

He was about to turn away, but I detained him by my words.

"I must talk with you to-night, or not at all. I can't see you at your office in the daytime."

"Why not?"

"For good and sufficient reasons."

"Let me hear one of them."

"Convince me that you are the American consul, and I will convince you that I have something worth listening to."

"You are not a common sailor;" and I saw the consul raise one of his hands in a slow, cautious manner, and make a sign that I instantly recognized.

I had been waiting for that demonstration; and now that I was satisfied a United States officer stood before me, I returned the sign, and saw that it was comprehended immediately; for the grand secret-service signal was given, and answered as soon as made.

"I am glad to welcome you to Nassau," said the consul, as he held out his hand, and received the proper grip.

"And I am glad to find you, for I have had enough trouble in so doing."

"You have news for me?" asked the consul.

"Yes; important news."

"Did you arrive in the steamer from New York?"

"Yes."

"Then you are just the one I want to see. My letters tell me that a large number of secesh and blockade runners would take passage for Nassau. You can give me some important information, I have no doubt. Come with me to the house, and have a glass of wine; and then we will compare notes, at the same time drink success to our cause."

As we walked along, I related to the official some of the incidents which I had encountered during the evening; and if the consul had been a mirthfully inclined man, he would have laughed and enjoyed the thing as much as I did; but Mr. —— had suffered so much while in office, that it was rare to see a smile on his face. He appeared to regard jokes something in the same light that he regarded blockade runners, — things to be dealt with in a severe manner, and put down without delay.

I saw his disposition for thoughtfulness, and rallied him a little on it; but it was useless to force him from a beaten path, so I let the matter drop, and we walked on in silence until we reached his house and entered.

The consul conducted me to his library, where we could be alone, ordered some wine, pulled down the curtains so that no one could look in, glanced under the sofa to see if any one was concealed there, and then announced himself ready to hear all that I had to offer.

"And let me entreat of you to speak low," said the consul. "I am surrounded by spies; all my actions and visitors are watched and reported to the select circle at the Humbug Hotel, where blockade runners and confederate agents make their headquarters and revile the North. Hark! what was that?"

We listened for a moment. All was quiet.

"It might have been the wind stirring the bushes and trees in the garden," the consul said, looking as though he hoped I would confirm his suggestion; but I could not, for, unless my ears deceived me, I had heard a footstep under the window.

We waited a moment for a repetition of the sound, but all was quiet.

"Well," said the officer, "I suppose you may as well go on. Perhaps I was mistaken; but you don't know what the people who track me and annoy me are capable of."

"Yes, I do. I have seen several specimens of the chivalry during my life, and rare specimens they were. I will enlighten you regarding my companions on board the steamer. In the first place —"

I stopped in my narrative abruptly; for, as sure as I sat in a chair, I heard the breaking of twigs beneath the window, as though some one was approaching very cautiously for the purpose of listening to our conference.

"I knew that I was not mistaken," the consul said. "Some one is hovering around the house, hoping to hear something, having seen us enter the building."

"Have you any objections to my slipping my cable, and crowding sail in chase?" I asked.

"It would be useless. Before you could get out of the front door the scamp would be off."

"Yes; but I don't propose to leave the house by the front door. Does that window move easy?"

"Yes. A light touch will open it."

"Then allow me to remove the fastenings, and do you pull up the curtain when I give the signal."

"But the sneak may fire at you. Blockade runners are capable of anything."

"Do not fear for me. A man detected in an act of meanness is not apt to possess much coolness. I will run some little risk for the purpose of rebuking one of these sneaks."

The face of the consul glowed, and he seemed to enter into the arrangement with more spirit than I anticipated. He removed the fastening of the window, arranged the curtain so that it could be pulled aside at a moment's notice, and, when all was ready, I gave the official the papers which Colonel Rhett had stolen from Soulé, and which I had obtained possession of through a ruse; also related all that had transpired while on board the steamer and at the hotel, and requested the consul to forward the facts to the Secretary of the Navy as soon as possible, in case I were unable to write out a detailed account of all that had transpired.

During my narrative, more than once had we heard footsteps under the window, but we pretended not to notice them, for I was desirous of concluding my remarks before I attended to other business. But I spoke so low that there was no danger of being heard by the listener, whoever he was; and although one of his ears, I had no doubt, was glued to the window-pane, yet he was no wiser when I had concluded than when I commenced my yarn.

"Now," I whispered to the consul, "I am ready to overhaul the fellow outside."

"Had you not better think twice of the matter? There is no occasion to give chase of such a sneak as is in the garden."

"We can see who he is and what he wants," I replied. "Ah! he is growing impatient. Now, then, I am ready, if you are."

The consul nodded, and up went the curtain and the window at the same time, giving a momentary glimpse of a dark and surprised-looking face; for the change was so sudden that the eavesdropper had no time to dodge out of sight.

As I put my hand on the window-sill to spring out, the spy vanished amid the bushes; but the next instant I had alighted on the ground, and was in close pursuit; vaulting over roses and other shrubs, stumbling and dodging amid the branches of fruit trees, but still keeping the form of the spy in view, until I found that I should break my neck if I kept on, and then I called on the fellow to halt.

"Stop!" I said, "or I'll fire."

He only made more exertions to escape; and I soon saw that he had the best of me, as far as heels were concerned. Determined that he should not get off without some little damage, I drew my revolver, and taking a rapid aim, fired.

The party I was pursuing uttered a fearful yell, which was an indication that I had hit him; but the cold lead seemed to act just the same as a steel spur acts on a horse, causing him to bound higher and run faster; and at last, after I had nearly knocked my brains out against the boughs of trees, I was compelled to give up the chase, and return towards the house.

I met the consul in search of me. He had heard the report of a pistol, and it had alarmed him. He feared that I had been shot at and wounded, and he also feared that the noise of the revolver would draw a large crowd in the vicinity of his house, and that, through Southern influence, a row would ensue, thus complicating matters for the United States and England; a row between the two countries being just what the confeds at Nassau most earnestly desired, so that independence could be secured through such a result.

"I am glad that you are uninjured," the consul said, as soon as I had answered his questions; "but I am sorry that you fired your pistol. Hark! already the alarm has been given, and in a few minutes a crowd will collect around the house. I must go in and put out the lights. Will you come with me, or make your escape while there is time?"

"Let me go with you, and share your danger," I said.

"There is no danger, unless some one throws a stone through one of my windows. That is about all that will be done. The work is just brave enough for some of these Nassau people.

"Who are pirates in disposition, and sheep in courage," I said.

The consul did not reply. The murmur of people collecting in the streets became more audible; and it was evident that they were nearing the house on an errand of investigation.

"You must now leave me," the consul remarked in a cool, calculating way, as though he was accustomed to such sounds and scenes. "I must hasten to the house, while you had better return to the hotel at once. We will meet again in a few days, and compare notes. Good by."

He left me just as a crowd of noisy men and boys halted

in front of his house, and shouted and groaned as though endeavoring to raise their courage sufficiently to commit some act of an aggravating nature.

"Come out, you representative of a brutal and tyrannical government!" yelled one voice, which I had no trouble in setting down as belonging to a Southerner. "Let us see your flag, and if you dare to face this enlightened crowd of freemen."

"'Ear! 'ear!" roared a score of Englishmen.

I jumped over a wall, crossed the street, and, by the absence of light, soon managed to join the crowd without exciting remark.

I saw that there were about fifty men near the house: two thirds of them were people of Nassau, who engaged in little piratical ventures, such as robbing wrecks, running the blockade, and anything to earn an honest living; and the other third was composed of Southerners who had joined hands with the pirates and the sons of pirates for the purpose of humiliating the flag of our Union and the country that gave them birth.

"Let the man wot shoots at men show hisself," roared an English cockney, stooping down and feeling for a stone; and it was lucky for the consul's windows that but few stones could be found in the streets of Nassau, sand being the principal substance.

"Say, Yankee! why don't you shoot at some of us?" roared a bold individual.

"Yes; let him try it on if he wants to. Come, fire at us. We are ready for you."

Then all hands yelled, like a lot of fiends as they were; but still the consul did not show a light, or give any indication that he was awake.

"O, he can kill people when there are no witnesses," one young ruffian said, and raised his arm to throw something; but, just as he was about to launch a shot at the windows, I gave the scamp a push, and sent him headlong to the earth.

"Who did that?" he asked, in an indignant tone.

No one paid the least attention to the question, for just at that moment the consul appeared at the door, and asked, in a loud tone, —

"Gentlemen, to what am I indebted for the honor of this visit?"

A hoot of derision was the answer; and some of the Southerners, in their zeal and rage, hurled sand at the consul, while others searched for missiles; and lucky it was for the official's head that they could not find what they wanted.

"Gentlemen," said the consul, in a quiet tone, "I shall complain of this outrage to the government."

A shout of laughter was the reply to this threat, and more sand was thrown; but just at this moment some one cried, —

"The sojers are coming!"

The crowd started on the run down the street, and scattered in all directions. I went with some of the swiftest towards the water; for I thought that, with the harbor for a guide, I could find my way back to the hotel without trouble.

So I ran, with some half a dozen others, until I was within sight of the water, and then, just as I was about to stop and take breath, I was struck a savage blow on the head, and down I tumbled insensible."

When I began to recover I heard some terrible shouts of laughter, and songs, and harsh words; and when I was enabled to see, found that I was lying in a berth in a steamer's house, and that the crew were seated on their chests, on their clothes-bags, and on kegs, with tin pots in their hands, drinking and carousing, and singing the joys and pleasures of the sea.

For a few minutes I remained quiet, and endeavored to comprehend all that had passed during the night; but I was so weak and faint that I found the effort almost impossible; and when I raised my head to speak, and ask how I happened to be where I was, found that the motion was a little too much for me, and settled down with so much pain that a groan escaped me.

"Hullo!" cried one of the youngest and liveliest of the men. "Our new shipmate is swinging with the tide. He begins to feel his helm, like a seventy-four in a close-reefed-topsail breeze. What cheer, old feller? How goes it?"

He left his seat on the chest, and came towards me, while his companions stopped their singing for a moment. But the lull was only for a moment, for they almost immediately recommenced howling for the success of some noted steamer that had run the blockade many times, and bidden defiance to all the ships in the Yankee navy.

"Well, shipmate, what cheer?" asked the sailor, as he bent over me.

"Give me a little water," I said. "I feel faint and thirsty, and my head pains me dreadfully."

"Won't a little brandy do better?" asked the young fellow.

The very thought of touching liquor made me shudder.

"Well, well; don't kick. You shall have the water; but some of the crew wouldn't believe it if I should tell 'em that you liked it better than grog."

He left the house for a moment, and returned with a quart pot of water from the scuttle butt, so that it should be fresh.

"Here you are, shipmate. Let me help you raise your head. So; that will do. Now down with it."

The water was warm; but it tasted good, and refreshed me a little.

"Now let me look at your calabash. You must have been awful swipsey to fall and damage your figure-head in that way! Run afoul of a stone, didn't you? for you have a devil of a cut here just aft of the ears."

"No; some one struck me with a slung-shot, I suppose."

"Then the mean sneak was a coward, what didn't dare to stand up, man fashion, and give and take. How did it happen?"

"I don't know."

"Well, some of our crew brought you on board, by order of the 'old man.' They said they found you on the beach. But here you are, and here you must remain, 'cos we trip anchor to-morrow."

"For where?"

"That's only known to the skipper and the chaps on shore. Lord! they don't let us coves into the secret, 'cos they fear we should prove a little leaky, and then Uncle Sam's boys would get wind of the matter, and gobble us up. But cheer up, matey; in a few days you'll be all right, and eatin' your reg'lar 'lowance like the rest of us."

This was far from satisfactory to me, and so I made an impatient gesture, and attempted to sit up; but my head ached so severely that I could not, and was forced to lie down again.

"I want to see the captain of the steamer," I said. "I must be set on shore. I'll have satisfaction for this outrage."

The young sailor smiled.

"The 'old man' has company, and won't notice you. You'd better make the best of it. Take what is offered you, and think yourself lucky for it."

I made no reply; and the young sailor, seeing that I did not rally at his words, continued, —

"You jest keep still, and I'll go aft and ask the surgeon to come for'ard and look at yer head."

In a few minutes the young sailor returned with the surgeon of the ship, — an old Scotchman who was on his way to the Southern Confederacy to offer his services. He hoped to do wonders in curing diseases and amputating limbs, and receive his pay for doing the same in cotton at the rate of fourpence a pound, intending to sell the same in Liverpool for about four shillings.

The Scotch surgeon's name was Donald MacFearson, and he came from Glasgow.

MacFearson, on the night that he was called to attend me, had been drinking success to the Southern Confederacy with half a dozen of the chivalry, who were on their way to the seat of the rebellion; and consequently he was not so clear-headed as he might have been.

"Here he is, doctor," said the young sailor, by way of introduction, as he appeared at the side of the berth with the Scotchman.

The doctor approached and bent over me, holding on to the berth with one hand, and said, in his broadest accent, —

"Weel, mon, what is the matter with ye? Who ha' been and hurted ye?"

As he spoke, he was sober enough to turn my head, and examine the wound. He then continued, —

"Ah! a moughty bad whack, mon. Some one hit ye that meant it should tell. I will do the best that I can for ye till I am a bit fresher; for the punch to-night was unco good, and there was much of it. Here, hold the light, young Harry Bluff, and let me see if I can cut away some hair, and put on a plaster."

"Nonsense!" cried the young sailor who was called Harry Bluff; and he laughed as he steadied the doctor, and kept him on his feet. "Do you go aft, and get the plaster, while I nick off the hair. You'll stick the scissors in his head, as sure as fate, if you attempt it."

"Weel, lad, perhaps ye are right. Do you do the rough

MRS. GOWEN INTERFERES. — Page 124.

work, and I'll do the fine; and, as a reward, I'll give you a stiff dose of punch."

Off the doctor went, and Harry Bluff trimmed the hair from the wound with as careful and tender a hand as a woman's; and, just as he had finished, the steward entered the house with some plaster and the doctor's compliments, and hoped that Harry would finish the work, for he had resumed his old seat at the cabin table, and was drinking whiskey punches as though on a wager.

"Never mind," whispered Harry Bluff, in a soothing tone, as he bent over me. "I know a little of surgery, and will attend to your wound. Keep up your spirits, and you will come out all right, like the sun after a rain squall on the equator."

He put on the plaster, bound up my head, and then went aft and obtained an opiate of some kind for me, which made me feel easier, and put me to sleep in spite of the noise and confusion around me. I slept soundly through all the uproar of getting under way; for, when I awoke, I knew, by the rolling of the steamer, that we were at sea, and that the crew were washing down decks. I almost groaned as I reflected that all my clothes and valuables were on shore at the Royal Humbug Hotel, and that they were lost to me forever.

I was aroused from this disagreeable reflection by the entrance into the house of Harry Bluff, with a pot of hot coffee in his hand.

"Come," he said, "rouse and shine; you're worth a dozen dead men. I've blarneyed the cook into giving me a pot of coffee; and you and I will share it."

The coffee was so reviving that I was enabled to raise my head and sit up; and then I concluded to go on deck, have an interview with the captain, and see what he meant by such treatment as I had received.

"Is the captain on deck?" I asked.

"Yes," replied Harry.

I at once determined to seek him before any of the passengers were stirring.

"What is his name?" I inquired.

"Captain Pooduck; and this is the steamer Pet. She's the fastest and most successful blockade runner that ever bothered a Yankee gunboat. This is her fourth trip."

With the assistance of Harry Bluff, I cleansed the blood from my face and hands, arranged my hair, and then left the house, where the starboard watch was snoring, and went on deck, where the larboard watch were washing down.

The sun was up and shining brightly, the air was clear and pure, and the water looked blue and crisp as the waves dashed against the steamer or rolled after her as if anxious for an embrace. The fresh air inspirited and strengthened me; but, for all that, I was compelled to sit down and rest, I was so weak.

The captain of the Pet was walking the quarter-deck, cigar in mouth, and hands in his breeches-pockets, meditating on the profits of the trip in case he escaped, when I crept aft and accosted him.

At first the captain did not hear me; but at last he allowed his eyes to fall on my face, and then he stopped and asked, —

"Who are you, and what do you want?"

"I want justice," I replied.

"You be d—d! Go forward and get sober, and then go to work. You have been drunk and fighting."

He was about to resume his walk, but I was not to be turned off in that manner. I knew quarter-deck etiquette too well for that.

"Captain Pooduck," I said, "I was knocked down last night, and, while insensible, brought on board of your vessel. It was an outrage that I am determined to resent as soon as I have an opportunity."

"There; that will do for the present. Now go forward, and do your duty."

"I shall do no such thing. I am a Southern gentleman; and when we reach a Southern port, I'll make you smart for this treatment. I have been kidnapped, and you had a hand in it."

"I'll have a hand on your throat, if you don't start your stumps for'ard," Captain Pooduck responded, and made a motion as though he would kick me. But I did not move; so he said, —

"Look a-here, young feller; I found you on the beach last night, with a big cut on your head. I told the men to bundle you in the boat, and take you on board; and they did so. Here you are, and here you must remain till we reach some port. Now go for'ard."

"I shall do no such thing," I remarked, in a quiet tone, "unless you tell me who struck me, and how I happened to be here. There is some secret connected with the affair, and I am determined to know it."

"Not from me, you won't, that I can tell yer."

As the captain spoke, he threw off several coils of a rope from a belaying-pin, so that he could work to advantage, and then came towards me, rope in hand.

The crew of the steamer, who were washing down decks, dropped their buckets, and crowded aft, anxious to see the row; for most of them had witnessed too many shots and blows to be afraid of a quarter-deck breeze. Foremost in the ranks that pressed aft was young Harry Bluff; and although I could not think of assistance from the men, yet I did hope that Harry would prove a friend in case I had to fight for my life.

"Stand back, Captain Pooduck," I said. "If you offer to strike me with a rope, you are a dead man."

As I spoke, I drew my revolver, and levelled it at his head; and if ever there was an astonished man, Captain Pooduck was the one.

He stopped, and no longer threatened with the rope; but, although baffled for the moment, did not despair of carrying out his plan.

"Bring handspikes, some of you," he said, " and knock him down. Kill him! Throw him overboard!"

The mate of the steamer, as in duty bound, made an attempt to carry out the captain's benevolent designs; but before he could snatch a capstan-bar from the rack, a new actor appeared on the scene,—one who seemed quite surprised at what she saw, for it was a lady, who left the cabin, and came on the quarter-deck. She gave vent to her astonishment, by exclaiming,—

"Mercy, Captain Pooduck! what is the matter?"

I turned, and saw, standing near me, Mrs. Margelia Gowen, the wife of the Augusta cotton-broker, the man who had been knocked senseless the day before at the dinner table.

The instant she caught sight of my face, she knew me, and, with a pleasant smile, held out her hand, and came towards me, saying,—

"Why, Lieutenant Barnwell! how glad I am to know that you are on board!"

I put up my pistol, and was really glad to see the lady; for she was the means of preventing bloodshed, and perhaps had saved my life.

At the time I escorted the handsome Mrs. Gowen up the grand stairs of the Royal Humbug Hotel, she had not even intimated that she was to leave Nassau in a hurry, but had urged me to visit her as often as I could make it convenient during my stay at the hotel; and now she appeared like a ghost, and just at the time she could serve me most. In truth, I was very glad to see her, for she was a handsome woman, a wilful one, and accustomed to always have her own way.

"Barnwell," she asked, as she took both of my hands, after I had put my revolver out of sight, "what is the meaning of this masquerade? What are you doing here, and how does it happen that you and Captain Pooduck are quarrelling? Come, sir, answer me. I'll have no evasion."

The master of the steamer Pet dropped the rope's end, and looked as though he had been detected in committing simple larceny, with a prospect of being arraigned before a police court, and having his name published in the papers. He shoved his hands in his pockets, and whistled softly.

"Captain Pooduck and I were having a slight discussion relative to the manner in which I came on board," I replied. "Some personalities have passed between us; but I think we now understand each other."

"If Captain Pooduck offends or insults a friend of mine, he will hear from me," Mrs. Gowen remarked in a haughty tone. "I have some influence in the confederacy when I desire to exert it."

The master of the Pet instantly exhibited all the craven, mercenary qualities of a Yankee blockade runner, and became as humble as a cabin-boy after tasting of rope's end; for he well knew that the cotton which he expected to receive for the merchandise on board must come with the consent of the rebel powers, and a handsome woman had influence with Jeff Davis and his cabinet.

"I hadn't the slightest idea that he was a friend of your'n," the captain replied. "I thought I was doin' him a good service when I took him on board last night; I wanted a hand or two, you know, and he was dressed like a sailor."

"Yes, yes, I see! Tell me how it happens that you have those clothes on?" queried Mrs. Gowen.

9

"A freak of mine," I replied. "I did not wish to mingle with the people as a gentleman, and so I put on this toggery."

"I see. Men will be men. But I will not reprove you, because I don't know that I have the right.

"Captain Pooduck," the lady said, in some such tone as she would have used had she been addressing her negro overseer, "let Mr. Barnwell have a state-room,—one of the best in the ship. He must change his clothes, and reassume those of a gentleman. My husband has a trunkful of new articles of apparel, and they will just about fit you."

I remonstrated and pleaded, but without avail. The lady was determined. She said that I had proved myself a brave man, and she loved brave men. I had saved her husband's life at the peril of my own; and I must not think she was ungrateful, for she was not. She should recollect me as long as she lived. And a great deal more was said to the same effect.

"State-room all ready, sir," said the steward; and then I entered the cabin, wondering at the great change that had taken place within half an hour, and querying how it would end.

In the mean time the crew had finished washing the decks, and were wondering what it all meant, but it got reported round that I was some great confederate officer whom the Yankees had endeavored to kill, and that I was on my way to Richmond to take charge of the James River fleet.

My toilet was soon made, and then I returned to the deck, and found my patroness waiting for me.

"You have been expeditious," she remarked, as I joined her.

"Who would not be, when so agreeable a lady was waiting to be thanked for all her kindness?" I replied.

"Nonsense! you don't think me agreeable, or even handsome."

"I dare to think both, but not to express my thoughts."

"What do you fear?"

"I do not fear, but I remember."

"What do you remember?"

"That you are a wife."

The thin, red lips curled, and the large dark eyes flashed, while a scornful smile passed over her face.

"Yes, — a wife without a husband."

"How? Mrs. Gowen, you are disposed to laugh at me."

"I never was more serious in my life than I am at the present time. Come! it is luck, on some accounts, that we have met on board this steamer. I can make a confidant of you."

"I shall feel honored with so proud a trust," I said.

"Will you really? Well, then, listen to me with all your attention."

She glanced around the deck to see that no one was within hearing.

She then assumed a more confidential air, laid one of her small but brown hands on my arm to secure my attention, and said, —

"You are surprised at seeing me on board the Pet?"

"I am pleased at seeing you on board," I whispered.

"Why should I not be pleased, when your presence saved bloodshed, and perhaps my own life?"

"I shall be happy if I can think so," she said, and then continued, —

"When we parted last night, I had no intention of leaving Nassau; but that odious brute of a Kentuckian drove us from the place. O, if I had been a man, this should never have occurred. You know how badly my husband was injured by a blow from the bottle? He cannot see at all; his face is disfigured for life, and all his spirit is gone. I think that it was near nine o'clock," Mrs. Gowen continued, when a note was brought to the door of our room. It was for my husband, — a challenge from the Kentuckian. He insisted upon an immediate meeting, and swore that he would enter the room and horsewhip Mr. Gowen unless he complied with his demand. My husband was weak, and blind, and suffering, and became terrified at the prospect. Not being able to see, he knew he could not avoid the Kentuckian, and so insisted upon immediate flight. I begged and prayed Mr. Gowen to wait and meet the brute, or else let me attend to him; but he was too much under the influence of fear: so he left all his business with an agent, and we took passage in the Pet. And that is how we happen to be here. I implored Mr. Gowen to wait till I could consult with you on the subject; but he refused to listen to me; and so that brute of a Kentuckian can boast that he has driven from the town one of the first families of Georgia."

I started with surprise. Gracious! were there first families in Georgia as well as in Virginia?

Just at that moment one of the lookouts stationed at the fore masthead uttered a yell that brought everybody to their feet, and every spy-glass into requisition.

"Sail, ho!" shouted the lookout.

Captain Pooduck was in his state-room, brushing up for breakfast; but, hearing the cry, he came on deck at a bound, and glared around the horizon like a hungry tiger in search of a dinner.

"Where away?" yelled Pooduck; and he had hardly asked the question before all the cabin passengers were on deck, some of whom had not yet slept off a drunken debauch of the previous night.

There was alarm on many faces, and anxiety on all. The Scotch doctor, who had drank nearly a gallon of punch the night before, made his appearance with a scalpel in one hand and a boot in the other, laboring under the impression that he had got to fight or travel, and perhaps both.

"Eh, weel!" he growled, "it's unco hard if the Yankees grab us this time. Gi' me but a chance, an' I'll na let their coffee rest on their stomachs."

The lookout reported that the sail was two points off the weather bow, and standing on the same course as the Pet.

Captain Pooduck tucked his glass under his arm, and went up the fore rigging, for the purpose of getting a fair sight of the stranger; while the cabin passengers mustered their opera-glasses, and took wonderful observations of the vessel.

For half an hour Captain Pooduck refused to answer all questions relating to the steamer; for it was easy to see that it was a steamer, and standing on the same course as the Pet: but at the end of that time a long line of black smoke began to be noticed in the wake of the stranger, and then we saw canvas spread, and noticed a gradual edging away, as though a nearer acquaintance would be desirable on the part of those on board the steamer.

"Well, is it a Yankee gunboat, or is it a blockade runner like ourselves?" asked Mrs. Gowen, who manifested not nearly as much alarm as some of the Southern heroes on board, and who talked fight continually, though they had never been in a battle.

"A blockade runner wouldn't want to speak a stranger," remarked Captain Pooduck in a thoughtful tone.

"Then it is a Yankee," Mrs. Gowen said; and, as she spoke, I saw many a cheek pale at the idea of seeing the inside of Fort Lafayette or Fort Warren.

Captain Pooduck did not answer the last remark until he had placed his glass to his eye, and taken one more long and strong look. Then he touched a bell that connected with the engineers' room, and the result of that signal was a volume of smoke that poured out of the funnel, black and heavy, caused by mixing coal with pitch and tar, and kept separate from the rest of the fuel, so that it could be used in such an emergency as this.

The effect was soon manifested by an increased number of revolutions of the wheels, by the fierce hissing of the steam, and by the rapid speed of the Pet. Yet the course of the steamer was not altered; and, consequently, every knot that we made only brought us nearer to the stranger, until at last we could see her hull, painted a dull lead color, as sober as a Quaker arrayed for a quarterly conference, and not a sign of war or strife to be observed. All seemed to be at peace on board of that craft; yet Captain Pooduck was a Yankee, and not to be caught by a fair exterior.

"Keep her off two points," said the master of the Pet to the man at the wheel.

By altering our course, we headed in the same direction as the stranger, so that she could not cross our bows or near us without edging away.

We were not more than five miles apart, the stranger to the windward, a little forward of our beam, and apparently disposed to remain in that position, although we could tell by the bearings that we were gradually drawing ahead of the lead-colored craft, and that we sailed nearly three knots to his two, while we had only our fore and aft sails and our foretopsail set.

"Not a single port-hole to be seen," muttered Captain Pooduck, as he once more put the glass to his eye. "Confound him! if it is a Yankee gunboat, he is well disguised. Only half a dozen men on deck, and some of 'em in red shirts. That don't look much like a man-of-war,— does it, Mr. Barnwell?"

Since Mrs. Gowen, the rich Southern heiress, had taken

me under her protection, the master of the Pet had grown very attentive and polite.

"Uncle Sam would not tolerate red shirts even if his men were freezing," was my answer, although I knew very well that the lead-colored craft was a Yankee cruiser, disguised as a blockade runner.

"Show him our buntin'," Pooduck remarked to the mate; and up to the peak went an English flag, while at the same time the stranger showed similar colors.

"Cuss him! now I know he's a cheat," muttered Pooduck; yet there were many on board who thought the captain mistaken, and contended that one of our gunboats would not dare to display the Cross of St. George unless authorized; which precious nonsense the master of the Pet treated with the most perfect contempt.

"Do, Mr. Barnwell, put an end to this dispute," Mrs. Gowen remarked, as she laid one of her hands on my arm. "Come, you are a sailor, and should know the character of yonder fellow. Oblige me by giving an opinion."

"But I am too weak to climb the rigging, or look through a glass."

"True. I am selfish. I had forgotten your injured head."

At this moment my eyes fell on young Harry Bluff, who had shown me so much attention, and cared for me the night before. He was near the quarter-deck, and engaged in swabbing it dry, apparently paying not the least attention to the conversation that was taking place; yet he could not have failed to have heard all that passed.

As Mrs. Gowen spoke, Harry completed his task, and was about to leave the quarter-deck; but as he walked forward, he gave me such a friendly, peculiar glance, that I could not help saying, —

"Harry, drop your swab, and take the glass aloft."

He threw the swab forward, seized the glass, and started

up the main rigging as active as a monkey, while I followed slowly so that I should not disturb my head, and set it to aching.

Harry reached the cross-trees, handed me the glass, and then seated himself on the topgallant-yard, and chatted on matters and things in general, in his usual lively manner.

The stranger was not more than four miles to the windward, for he had edged away a little, and was now heading directly for Great Bahama Island, while our course was more to the westward, and would carry us between Florida and the Island. Land was in sight off our weather bow, and off our larboard beam, Abaco Island bearing about east-south-east, while off our larboard quarter were the little keys that helped form the Strait of Florida.

While I was looking at the lead-colored steamer, Harry was at work on the gasket of the topgallant-sail; and, through carelessness on his part, the bunt of the sail and the leash escaped from his hands, and shivered and slatted in the breeze, shaking the blocks and clew-lines so roughly that Captain Pooduck's attention was attracted, and so was mine.

It was one of the secret signals of Federal service, and the shaking of that sail was intended to convey valuable information to Uncle Sam's Navy.

But I did not have time to speak or draw conclusions, for the sharp, fierce voice of Pooduck was heard from the quarter-deck, shouting, —

"What do you mean by taking the gasket off that 'ere sail? Who told you to do that, and be d—d to you?"

"Sir?" answered Harry, letting the sail flap for the purpose of paying proper respect to the quarter-deck.

"What did you cast that sail adrift for?" the master of the Pet yelled.

"I didn't do it. The gasket was all chafed, and when I attempted to secure it, parted."

And as Harry spoke, he commenced gathering up the fluttering canvas, and stowing it on the yard, and then suddenly releasing, shouting to those on deck,—

"Sheet home!" just as though he had received orders to once more loosen the sail.

The rage of Captain Pooduck was frightful, and not even the presence of Mrs. Gowen was sufficient to prevent him from uttering some very original oaths.

"Come down, you lubber!" yelled Pooduck, "or I'll shoot you where you are."

"Why, didn't you order me to let the sail drop?" asked Harry, with an expression of genuine terror such as I did not think he could show. "I understood you to say let it go. Mr. Barnwell, in the cross-trees, he heard you say so too,—didn't you, Mr. Barnwell?"

In the mean time the sail was flapping in the fresh morning breeze, and the sharp eyes on board the United States cruiser could not help noticing the signal, and understanding it, while Captain Pooduck and his mate were damning the tarry toplights of Harry, and then turned and damned his eyes by the way of variety.

"They're having a jolly time on deck," Harry remarked, as he looked down at the raging officers. "I 'opes, Mr. Barnwell, they won't turn that Blakely gun on us what they carries amidship. They seems more than half inclined to do so."

"Main-topmast cross-trees," yelled Pooduck.

"Sir," replied Harry.

"What are you doing with that sail?"

"Nothin', sir. I'm waitin' to see what you wants done with it."

"Then overhaul the clew-lines. Sheet it home, men! I'll settle with that fellow when he lays down."

"Well, Mr. Barnwell, I s'pose I'll catch it," remarked young Bluff, after the sail was sheeted home, and the yard hoisted. "I don't relish a pounding at the hands of such a slab-sided Yankee; so I hope you will stand my friend."

"Yes, I'll do that, of course; and, if I can't ward off the danger, I'll get the lady to try her hand. Here, take the glass. I have squinted long enough at that Quaker-looking gentleman."

"And what do you make of him?"

"O, it's one of Uncle Sam's cruisers, I suppose."

The boy's face flushed, and I thought he looked a little disappointed. But he soon rallied, and continued, with affected carelessness, "Well, she's a slow old tub, at any rate, and we can move two fathoms to her one. There's no fear of her dropping alongside of us — is there?"

"No; I should think not. We are leaving her every moment."

Then, just as I was about to move from the cross-trees, I looked in the young fellow's face, and remarked, —

"How does it happen that you can talk grammatically, all ship-shape and Bristol fashion, at one moment, and the next you bring out the fo'castle lingo in lively style? Come! overhaul your thinking log, and you'll find that my position is correct."

The young fellow laughed, blushed a little, but did not hesitate long before he said, —

"Well, the fact of it is, Mr. Barnwell, I've seen better days. Family misfortunes drove me to sea. Poverty is a great curse, sir; and my father was afflicted with it: so I undertook to earn my own living, and here I am. That's the reason I uses one kind of lingo at one time, and another kind of lingo when I'm in the fo'castle. There's nothing wrong in it, is there, sir?"

"No, my lad; but some people might suspect you of being above your station, unless they understood all the circumstances of your life."

With these words of caution I left the cross-trees, and descended to the deck, Harry following me.

"Well," asked Pooduck, "what do you think of her?"

I was just as well aware that Pooduck knew the stranger was a Federal cruiser, as if he had told me his secret thoughts; so I considered it useless to disguise my real opinions, and suffer in the estimation of the master of the Pet. In answer to the question, I said, —

"O, the fellow is Yankee all over, from keel to truck; but we can laugh at him, for we have heels and he has none."

"Jist as I thought," he said. "Keep her off a p'int;" to the man at the wheel. "We'll see if he wants to follow us to the Gulf of Florida.

The lead-colored cruiser did not seem disposed to take further notice of us, for she kept on her course, and gradually dropped off the quarter; but there she hung, neither gaining nor losing, the whole of the forenoon. This puzzled Captain Pooduck and myself: but we settled the matter by agreeing that the gunboat must have a favorable current, while we were compelled to stem it, and that the difference was equal to two knots per hour.

But long before such conclusions were arrived at, Harry Bluff had been pardoned by the captain, at my solicitation, the mistake being explained, and the passengers were summoned to breakfast. This meal consisted of regular hotel fare, — turtle from one of the sand-keys, fruit from Nassau, coffee from Java, and delicacies from Liverpool, where the Pet was partly owned.

As none of the passengers were sea-sick, they did justice to the good things on the table, and then adjourned to the deck, where they could smoke, talk treason, laugh at Uncle Sam's slow-sailing gunboats, and indulge in dreams of the future Southern confederacy.

As we arose from the table, Mrs. Gowen signalized that

she wanted me; so I waited until the rest of the passengers had left the cabin.

"I want you to see my husband," the lady said. "He desires to speak to you, and thank you for what you have done. His face is terrible; but you will not see much of it, covered as it is with a plaster. John," she continued, turning to a smart-looking mulatto, a servant and slave given to the lady by her father when she was married, — "tell your master that Mr. Barnwell is about to visit him."

The slave bowed, and entered a state-room.

"How did you dare to take that young fellow to Nassau?" I asked. "Did you not fear that he would leave you?"

"No: John is a slave, but he would not take his freedom if it were offered him. I have no fear of his leaving me. We were brought up together."

"Is it possible," I thought, "that I have seen one slave who has no aspirations for independence and freedom? Such must be the case; for, if he had desired freedom, he would have taken it when on English ground."

I entered the state-room, and found the Scotch surgeon dressing the face of Mr. Gowen. The injured man put out his hand, and gave me a friendly welcome, and then said something complimentary; but his nerves were all unstrung, and he appeared little better than a wreck. I went on deck, and took a survey of the situation. We were steaming through the Northwest Channel, with Berry Island and Stirrup Key off the larboard quarter, and the Great Bahama off the starboard bow, while the head of the Pet was pointed in the direction of Florida, — Captain Pooduck preferring to take this exposed and open course to running close to the Keys, on account of the Federal gunboats, which cut off the usual route, or at least rendered it more dangerous than when simple merchantmen were in sight.

"You see," says the master of the Pet, "that we steam three knots to the Yankee's one. By to-morrow mornin' she'll be out of sight."

Mrs. Gowen came on deck just at this moment, with a smile on her face and a dangerous light in her eyes; I knew she was bent on mischief. But the nature of that mischief I could only guess; for as I approached her, she whispered, —

"Leave me with that odious, renegade Yankee a short time, for I want to pump him, and learn how it happens that you are on board."

I informed her that she would confer a great favor on me if she could obtain the truth; and then I left her to beguile the skipper by her blandishments and smiles, while I went forward to smoke a cigar, and make friends with some of the passengers.

There were ten of them. One was a gentleman who had just returned from Europe loaded with despatches for the Southern Confederacy. He talked loud, and swore the new republic would be acknowledged in less than two months by both France and England, and that those nations would combine to break the blockade.

In the course of an hour or less, Captain Pooduck concluded his conversation with Mrs. Gowen, and went to his state-room to look at his charts and take a dose of whiskey, of which he was rather fond. As soon as he had left the deck, I hastened to join the lady, whose eyes welcomed me as I took a seat by her side.

"Now," she said, "I can tell you all that the master imparted to me. Listen and wonder at what I relate. It seems that Colonel Rhett had some grudge against you, or else fancied that he had. At any rate, he met Captain Pooduck last evening on board of this vessel, and informed him that you were a man the confederacy wanted at home, and that a hundred bales of cotton would be given to the person who delivered you to any Southern provost-marshal. Then he bargained that Captain Pooduck should take charge of you, and give you up on arriving at Wilmington. When the trade was concluded, the parties went on shore to find you, and concoct some scheme for inducing you to visit the Pet. Fortune favored them; for just as they landed, the colonel, who was disguised, saw you on the beach, and knew you in spite of your sailor clothes. They altered their plan in an instant. One of the sailors was sent to strike you senseless with a slung-shot, and the villain performed the work to the satisfaction of those who watched the result."

"I hope I shall live long enough to pay the gentlemen for their attention," I remarked.

"I hope you will," was the reply. "Count on me to assist you." Then she continued: "While you were insensible, the captain ordered that you should be taken on board the Pet, and placed in the forecastle as one of the crew; and there you would have remained until the vessel reached port had I not been on board. The captain knows that I have influence, and he dare not offend me. But I am thankful that I saved you some rough treatment: and that's the end of my story. Now what do you think of such rascality?"

"I think that Colonel Rhett and Captain Pooduck will one day repent of their share in the transaction."

"But why should that boasting Virginia colonel plot against you?"

"Because I detected him stealing on board the Growler."

"What! one of the first families of Virginia?" and the lady laughed. "I knew some were mean enough for most anything, but I supposed they were sufficiently shrewd to escape detection when thieving."

I then explained why Rhett did not like me, and the lady was astonished at what I said; and in talking and laughing, reading and smoking, the first day on board the Pet passed off rapidly, and at night we saw the Great-Isaac Light, while the Federal gunboat, at eight o'clock, was more than five miles astern, but still holding her own in a wonderful manner.

CHAPTER V.

THE CHASE. — A SIGNAL. — A RESPONSE. — A SURPRISED MASTER. — AN APPARITION. — MORE TROUBLE FOR THE PET. — THREE MORE STEAMERS IN SIGHT. — POO-DUCK'S BLOOD IS UP. — A MEETING. — A TIGHT SPOT. — A PRIZE TO THE STINGEREE. — A BLUFF CAPTAIN. — A SURPRISE. — HARRY AND OLD BEN IN NEW PARTS.

As soon as night set in, the captain of the blockade runner commenced making preparations for throwing the Federal gunboat off the track; and to do this it was necessary that all our lights should be extinguished, and the course of the vessel changed.

"I needn't tell you that I is bound for Wilmington," said the captain, as we walked the deck after the lights were all extinguished but the one in the binnacle, and that so screened that its rays could not be reflected. "It can do no harm to let out that much. I has a valuable cargo under hatches, and if I runs it in my fortune's made; so you see I has no wish to take risks. In the mornin' we shall be clear of that fellow what is astern, burnin' out coal for no use at all, 'cos we can out-steam him as easy as rollin' off a log."

Just at this instant the chase threw up a rocket, that burst after it was many fathoms above the water, and showed hundreds of green stars in all directions.

"What in the devil does that mean?" demanded Captain Pooduck.

The question was one that I could not answer; so remained silent when the captain spoke, and pretended to be as much surprised as he was.

"Can the cuss mean that he wants to speak us," continued Pooduck. "He must be green if he thinks I'm goin' to allow myself to be drawn under the range of his guns."

Just at this moment, while the captain was indulging in a quiet chuckle at the thought of such stupidity, we heard a whizzing sound, and then a bright light flashed over the deck, and away up in the heavens sped a red-colored rocket, with sparkles that resembled drops of blood.

Some one on board the Pet had answered the signal of the Federal gunboat.

For a moment Captain Pooduck was speechless with astonishment. He could hardly believe his eyes or his ears; but, as the light of the rocket faded away, he recovered his senses, and, drawing a revolver from his breast, rushed forward to shoot the man who had dared to answer the gunboat's signal.

"Who did that?" he demanded in a loud tone.

No one answered the question. The men were apparently as much astonished as Captain Pooduck. I feared that my young friend Harry Bluff had committed the act, and, if detected, I knew that I could not save him this time; but as I glanced around the deck, I saw the dashing and reckless little sailor curled up on the fore hatch, his head on a huge coil of rope, and apparently sound asleep.

"Who sent up that 'ere rocket?" again yelled Pooduck; and he flourished his revolver in so nervous and reckless a manner, that I feared he would shoot the first one who spoke. But all the men clustered on the forecastle and around the fore hatch seemed as much astonished as the master of the vessel; and one old salt, a grizzly fellow with a red nose and a hard and weather-beaten countenance, grunted out, —

"We don't know who sent that 'ere rocket up; but I knows if I could pick him out, he would walk a plank in short order."

"Haven't you any idea who sent it up?" Pooduck asked, still trembling with rage and fear lest some one should escape his vengeance.

"No, sir," old Ben replied. "I was at anchor here on the windlass, and Jimkins was spinnin' a yarn about the last trip he made with yer, when all at once we heard a whiz and whirl, and up went the rocket."

"Turn up the hands!" cried Pooduck. "Turn up the hands, Mr. Cringle," addressing the mate. — a fat, red-faced Englishman, with a pair of shoulders like an elephant. "Call every one of 'em, and let's see what we can make out of it."

The starboard watch, which was turned in, mustered on deck; and all of the larboard watch, excepting the lookout and the man at the wheel, was collected. Not a sailor was missing. Harry Bluff had been roused from his sleep on the fore hatch, and was as much surprised as the men who were below respecting the rocket.

"Well, men," said Captain Pooduck, as soon as all hands were mustered, "I have called you up to see if any of you knows anything about that rocket what was fired from the forecastle."

There was no response.

"We was snoozin', sir," at last the starboard watch responded, with almost one voice; "so we can't know much about it."

"That is true, sir," old Ben said, touching his cap. "They was all turned in, 'cos I'm sure of it, havin' been in the house but a few minutes afore to light my pipe. At that time, sir, some of the chaps was snorin' as though they was makin' steam very fast, sir; and as for the chaps on deck, there was Harry — he was calkin' the fore hatch; and Bob — he was on the lookout; and the rest of us was spinnin' yarns around the windlass. So I don't think, sir, that any one for'ard did it; and it's my opinion, sir, that some one who belongs aft did the job. That's what I thinks."

This was a stunning surmise, and it almost took away Pooduck's breath.

"So none of you know anything of the matter?" the master said.

Not one of the men would acknowledge that he could give the least information on the subject of the mysterious rocket; and at length Pooduck turned to me, and asked me to walk aft a short distance.

We talked the matter all over for half an hour, and then were unable to settle on any person in the cabin who would be likely to aid the Federals; but at last we arrived at the conclusion that one of the men had sent up the rocket merely for the fun of the thing, and not in the hope of warning the gunboat, or of signalizing to her our course. As soon as Captain Pooduck arrived at such a conclusion, in which I joined him of course, his mind was more at ease, and he could even laugh at the incident without displaying any temper.

"I must have frightened the scamps," the master said, as he lighted a Cuba cigar, "when I p'inted my pistol at 'em."

Hardly had these words passed the captain's lips, when we again heard a familiar whiz, and then saw the peculiar light of a rocket. Up into the air it went, soaring until it burst and scattered stars in all directions; and, as they fell towards the sea, Captain Pooduck awakened to the fact that signalizing by rockets was no longer a joke.

He uttered a terrible oath as he rushed forward in hopes of detecting the person who had dared to trifle with his orders. Mr. Cringle and I followed as fast as possible, and reached the forecastle just in time to find the master laying about with a rope's end, hitting every head that he could reach and see, and swearing like a genuine Nassau pirate who had been disappointed in running the blockade. The sailors were not such fools as to stand and be pounded; so they jumped out of the way with all the agility of young salts, and various were the remarks made at the unexpected assault.

"Blast my bloody eyes!" said Ben, who was on the topgallant forecastle, and had escaped the end of the rope. "But what does this mean? Do you think that we are niggers, to be beat over the head in this way?"

"Rascals!" roared the master, "who sent up that rocket? Tell me, or I'll clap you all in irons. A hundred dollars for the name of the man what did it."

"Avast a bit with the rope's end, cap'n," said Ben, and we'll try and work the thing out by dead reckonin', as we was doin' when you comes for'ard."

The master dropped his rope and prepared to listen, although he was in a terrible rage, and could hardly keep still long enough to hear what was offered.

"I tells you what it is, cap'n," the old salt said, with an uneasy glance over his shoulder, as though fearful that he should see something, "them 'ere rockets was not sent up by any of the Pet's crew. No human hands done it, sir, I'm sure. Spirits, sir, is at work with us."

Sailors are superstitious, and always attribute to unearthly agency matters for which they cannot account; so I did not wonder that Pooduck for a moment was startled at the suggestion of the old salt. But the captain soon rallied.

"You fool!" he shouted, "ghosts don't throw up rockets, and cut up like that. Ghosts ain't such blamed fools. That yarn won't go down with me."

"Well, sir, perhaps not; but if people from the other world didn't do it, who did? I has had my weather-eye upon all the watch, and I hasn't seen none of the Pet's crew figurin' with rockets."

"I don't believe a blasted word of ghosts or spirits," the master muttered. "There's some cussed spy on board, and he wants the gunboat to foller us all night. Now I tell you, men, that if I can lay my ten commandments on him, he'll never send up another rocket, or make another signal to a Yankee cruiser, you can bet on that."

"Ah, sir! the works of spirits is wonderful," murmured Ben, with another glance over his shoulder. "I has been a sailor for twenty-five year, man and boy; and I has seen some strange things in my time. I could tell you of matters what would make your hair stand right up on end, like the bowsprit of a Dutch galliot, or a man-of-war's yard a-cockbill."

"Shut up, you blasted fool!" roared the master, who saw that the crew were becoming affected with Ben's superstition. "All the spirits what you ever saw were in a tin pot or a black bottle."

"Yes, sir; but I've seen some come right out of their hammocks, arter they had been sewed up and launched overboard with a round shot at their feet. I knowed one — she was the wife of Bill Birch, a marine — what was on board the Asia, — a eighty-gun ship, sir, — and she was buried in a coffin on shore, all shipshape, as the land lubbers do that kind of things. She was a good and pious woman, sir, and used to take on bad when Bill swiped it rather rough; and arter she was dead, she'd come to him all in her coffin, and tell him what she thought of him; and once or twice, when he cut up bad, she appeared to him, and scratched his face with her ten commandments; and when Bill got over his horrors, he used to tell just how she worked him, and how she looked."

Before any one could speak, Harry Bluff, who seemed to take much interest in the yarn which Ben had spun, suddenly looked over his shoulder, and exclaimed, with chattering teeth, "What's that?"

All eyes were turned in the direction of the heel of the bowsprit, where Harry pointed.

Slowly, and with many ominous motions of head and arms, a tall, white figure arose in the very eyes of the steamer, apparently depending upon one of the catheads for a foothold; and there it rested for a second or two, and then vanished, disappearing as suddenly as though it had fallen overboard.

With wild cries of alarm all rushed aft. Captain Pooduck was borne by the rush to the quarter-deck; and when I joined him there, I saw that he was as much puzzled at what had occurred as any man on board, although he had too much Yankee common sense to believe that a ghost had visited the Pet, even if it had frightened all hands into convulsions. We made another search, but could not trace the source of the signals, or find the figure in white, so gave it up for the time.

By six bells, or eleven o'clock at night, all the passengers had turned in, leaving the deck to the watch. Tired, and rather weak from the effects of the wound on my head, I soon fell asleep, and remained unconscious till next morning, when I was awakened by a tremendous commotion on deck. The loud roar of Pooduck's nasal tones, the slapping of canvas, the cries of the men as they pulled and hauled on ropes, — all convinced me that something unusual had occurred. I turned out, dressed as quickly as possible, and started for the deck.

In the cabin I met John, the mulatto slave, with a cup of coffee in his hand, intended for his mistress or master.

"What's the trouble on deck?" I asked the servant.

"Heap of trouble, sir," was the grinning answer. "No less than three strange steamers in sight, sir."

"Well, that is no unusual occurrence," I replied.

"No, sir; but it happens that they are all heading for this vessel."

"The devil they are!"

With this somewhat profane expression, I went up the cabin steps, and found Pooduck raving like a madman, stopping every few minutes to look through his glass at the strange vessels. When he did this, he ceased swearing; but being fully convinced that the three steamers were Union men-of-war, and that they were making great efforts to overhaul the Pet, his rage knew no bounds.

There was a large gunboat not more than three miles astern of the Pet; and, from the rig of the craft, we had no doubt but that it was the one we had seen the day before. This was the first vessel Pooduck called my attention to; and he uttered rare oaths when he pointed to her.

"Look at the blasted Quaker," he said, "with her drab sides and cat-like air! We thought the Pet could steam three knots to her two; but you see she has hung on to us all night, and now she is doin' her purtiest to come up to us."

It was evident that the gunboat was making an effort; but the speed of the Pet had been tested in many a trial, and never found wanting; so that, as far as the craft astern was concerned, Captain Pooduck had no great fear. But he did gnash his teeth, and swear oaths which I must not repeat, when he seized my arm, and told me to look in another direction.

"Damn 'em!" he muttered, "they have spread a net, and think they will make a haul; but the Pet has heels, and will show 'em what she can do."

He touched a bell, and signalized for more steam.

Soon a dense volume of smoke poured out of the stack, smelling strongly as though pitch had been thrown upon the fire to enable the engineer to comply with the demand.

Pooduck then pointed to the southward and westward; and there, just off our larboard-beam, was another steamer, — lead-colored, low in the water, clipper-looking, but appearing as demure as the fellow astern.

"This looks serious," I remarked, as I examined the drab-colored gunboats, and noticed that dense volumes of smoke were issuing from their funnels.

"I should think it did," said Pooduck, in a dry tone. "But, blast it! that ain't the worst. Look there!"

In the direction indicated was a third steamer, — lead-colored like the rest, clipper-built, with three masts, and yards and sails, like a three-masted topsail schooner; and this one was just ahead of us, lying apparently motionless, with no smoke issuing from her stack, and no white water near her paddle-wheels. She was under easy sail, and standing on the same course as ourselves.

There was but one way to escape, or one way that promised hope of success. This was to furl all sail, crowd on steam, and dash through the line that enclosed us. There was a prospect that success would crown a bold effort; but all would depend on the speed of the Pet. If she could steam three fathoms to the gunboats' one, we might escape, unless a shot from a Parrott gun overhauled us, and damaged our machinery.

On the other hand, if we edged away, we should run on a sand bank, and have the pleasure of being taken from the wreck by Uncle Sam's officials; and, as I wanted to put as much money in their pockets as possible, I advised the latter course.

"No, we'll have a race, and be darned to 'em!" muttered Pooduck, as he touched the bell leading to the engine-room, and gave orders to the man at the wheel to starboard his helm so that the head of the Pet was pointed just astern of the steamer off our beam.

The reader should bear in mind that the steamer astern was not more than three miles from us, while the one off the starboard beam was about five miles distant, and that we were to attempt passing between them.

The Pet began to tremble as she was forced through the water under a full head of steam. She moved so fast that sometimes she did not have a chance to rise when a heavy swell met her, but ploughed right through it, splitting the wave like a wedge, and flooding the deck with water.

"Now we move," said Pooduck, and a cold smile passed over his haggard face. "I think we shall do the trick."

In fact there did seem a prospect that such would be the case, for the gunboats did not appear to notice the change, but kept on their course; but hardly had the smile passed from the master's face, before I saw the steamer to the windward of us wear short round, turning on her heel like a marine on parade, and then point her nose so as to cross our bows, while the craft that was astern vomited a cloud of black smoke, and then luffed up some six points, rolled up her canvas as if by magic, braced her yards sharp up, started men aloft to send down topgallant yards and masts at the same time, and in five minutes all this work was accomplished, and the gunboat was standing along nearly the same course as ourselves.

"Cap'n," said one of the hot-headed Southerners, the bearer of despatches to the confederates, all of his papers being in a lead box which he was to throw overboard if capture seemed imminent, "do you mean to let the Yankees get us? 'Cos, if you do, we want to understand it, that's all."

"O, go to the devil!" retorted the perplexed master. "Don't bother me at the present time."

"But I mean to understand this 'ere thing. I have a 'sponsible position, and can't afford to trust to the mere word of a doubted Yankee,—I can't. I'm a Virginia gentleman, I am, and belong to one of the first families; and you can't come no Yankee trick on me."

Pooduck looked wild with rage, but self-interest kept him within bounds. He thought of the gold he was to gain by running the blockade; so he submitted to the despatch-bearer's insolence, in hope that it would soon end.

We had run so close to the gunboats that we could make out their hull without the aid of a glass. It was evident that we could not pass between the two without receiving such a fire as would send us to the bottom in short order; for the Union ships were nearing each other so rapidly, that, if we kept on, they would soon be within half a mile of us. I was delighted, as a matter of course, with the position of affairs, hoping that we should soon be captured; but I could not understand what Pooduck meant by being so rash; and while I was silently wondering, the rest of the passengers had urged the despatch-bearer to once more assail the master of the Pet.

"Do you mean to betray us, sir? Answer me that," the Virginian cried, with all the arrogance that he could assume.

Pooduck turned on the man like a wounded lion, all of his Maine blood boiling with rage and insulted dignity. He forgot the dreaded confederate government, his blockade-running profits, cotton and tobacco, and other articles that commanded high prices.

"You damned Southern dog!" the Yankee howled, and with one blow of his hard, bony fist struck the despatch-bearer on the face, and down he fell, thumping the deck with his head, and leaving stains of blood on the white planks.

"Curses on you, son of a dog!" the Yankee renegade said; and he spurned with his foot the body of the man lying before him.

This was more than the chivalry could endure, and, true to their instincts, they thrust their hands in their pockets, and produced revolvers and bowie-knives. They could not look on and see one of their number maltreated by a low, money-making blockade runner, who should be classed as one of the "poor whites," and therefore of no account.

"Let the gentleman alone," the dark-eyed Southerners said, as they crowded towards Pooduck, weapons in hand.

The master of the Pet did not shrink from the encounter. He did not appear to take the least notice of the threatening attitude of the passengers, his whole attention and fury being concentrated on the prostrate man, the fellow who had dared to insult him on his quarter-deck in the presence of his crew.

As the despatch-bearer, rather humbled, attempted to rise from the deck, Pooduck gave him a kick that sent him sprawling once more; and no sooner had he inflicted this last indignity upon the representative of one of the first families of Virginia, than one of the passengers, mad with rage, raised his revolver and fired, aiming at the captain's head.

The bullet whistled past the right ear of the daring Yankee; but he did not even flinch. His blood was up, and he cared no more for the men who surrounded him than he would have cared for a party of mutinous sailors, all demanding more grub and less work.

"You miserable cowards!" the master howled, "do you deal in murder, you sneaks? Not bold enough to face a Yankee in line of battle, you must shoot at him when his back is turned, and when he has no weapon in his hands.

Wait a moment until I can send for a pair of revolvers, and then see how quick I will clear you out."

The master of the Pet had called to the steward to bring his revolver from his state-room, and then shouted to his mate, who was in the waist waiting for a call.

"Mr. Cringle, arm the crew with capstan-bars and handspikes, and send them aft. Be lively about it. We will see if these fellows are to take possession of the ship."

"Cut him down! Shoot him!" were the cries heard from the passengers.

I must confess that I expected the man would be killed before I could interfere; and this I intended to do at the proper time, although I knew that each moment of delay was of vital importance if I desired to see the Pet captured by the Union gunboats.

"Put up your weapons," I said, and walked into the midst of the crowd.

Just as I spoke, the air was stirred by a loud report, and a hundred-pound Parrott shell burst just under the stern of the Pet, and threw water all over the quarter-deck.

At the same moment, the crew, firemen and all, came tumbling aft, armed with pokers, handspikes, and capstan-bars; and foremost among them were young Harry Bluff and old Ben the sailor.

"Down with 'em!" roared old Ben the grizzly, and flourished his capstan-bar as though he was handling a cutlass.

"Drive them over the traffrail, my bully boys!" yelled Harry Bluff. "Down with the traitors, and up with the flag."

I could not help laughing at the little fellow's actions, he was so eager, fearless, and excited; but I thought his words a little out of place in the midst of so many confeds.

"Avast there with yer noise," growled old Ben to Harry, as though the young fellow needed a check. "Don't you take the word out of us able seamen's mouths. We men must settle this muss."

I had thrown myself between the captain and the passengers, and thus far had kept them apart, and that was all; but at the instant when it needed only a word from Pooduck to renew hostilities, and cover the deck with blood, a loud report startled us, and then a shell burst but a few fathoms from the starboard-beam of the Pet.

I glanced at the two gunboats, and saw that they nearly had the range with their Parrott guns. We were running into a sack from which we could not extricate ourselves.

Pooduck saw his danger in a moment. He had not calculated on the speed of the Union gunboats. They were faster than he had anticipated; and, having a less distance to run than the Pet, were likely to reach the angle quite as soon.

"You fools!" shouted the master. "Do you see the jaws of the lion, and the teeth ready to crush you?"

The Southerners did look, and saw, without the aid of glasses, the American flag at the peak of the gunboats, fluttering gayly in the wind as though aware of its mission.

Pistols and knives were concealed in a hasty manner, and the Southerners shook and turned pale at their danger. All thoughts of vengeance had disappeared from their minds, and now they only desired to be kept from the rude grasp of the Federal authorities.

"Save us!" they cried in chorus.

"Into the cabin with you!" roared the master of the Pet. "Leave the deck to me and my men. That's all I ax of you jist at this time. Go!"

The terrified representatives of the South slunk into the cabin without a murmur. The Yankee renegade had triumphed over pride and passion.

One more look did Pooduck cast at the gunboats. The captains of the latter were so certain of their prize, they now forbore firing at the blockade runner, fearful that the shot would injure her, and damage some of her cargo. The shrewd captains had an eye to prize-money. At that date the New York prize courts had not learned to take the oyster, and give the sailors the shells. That game was successfully played until beggars rode in carriages, and thieves were made rich.

The master of the Pet placed his hand on the knob of the bell that led to the engine-room. He made the signal for more steam, at the same time waving his hand to the man at the wheel. The helm was put hard up, the head of the Pet was gracefully turned from the direction in which she had been steered, and then steamed away in an exactly opposite course, so that the Union gunboats were enabled to look at the stern of the beleaguered steamer instead of her bow.

"Away aloft, men, and loose every rag. Be lively, lads! It's our only chance."

The men sprang into the rigging, and cast off gaskets and overhauled clew-lines and bunt-lines in a manner so truly man-of-war-ish that the Pet was covered with canvas in a short time, and we were bowling before the wind with all of the square-sails filled and doing good service.

Then Captain Pooduck gave one glance at the Federal gunboats before he strode to the speaking-tube that communicated with the engineers' room.

"Crowd on all the steam that you can get!" he shouted. "Keep down the safety-valve by fifty-sixes, pile rosin and tar in the furnaces, and, by thunder! let her rip!"

An answer was returned by a rush of black smoke, by the hissing of steam as it attempted to escape, by the increased speed of the Pet, and by the manner in which she trembled as she cut through the water, dividing the waves like a sharp knife. The gunboats had taken the hint, and were after us with full head of steam, and with canvas spread wherever it could catch a breath of air.

By standing on the course we had, we were the means of compelling the gunboats to near each other, thinking they were to cut us off; and it was evident that the Federals had not the least idea that the Pet would wear round and show her stern, when she was almost under the guns of her foes, and when a broadside of well-directed shot would sink us. But Pooduck had calculated on the desire of the Federal officers for prize-money, and knew that they would not injure the hull of his steamer if there was any prospect of effecting her capture in any other manner. For a while we kept on our course without molestation, each craft being tested to the utmost for speed. For the first ten minutes there did not seem to be any difference in point of sailing; but as our steam increased, and the engines got warmed up, I rather feared that we were leaving the gunboats, although I did not say so. But Pooduck soon made the same discovery, and rubbed his hands with satisfaction as he noted the result.

"Throw the log," the master said to the mate, who was chewing tobacco at such a rate that it seemed as though his jaws were trying to keep pace with the revolutions of the wheels.

Mr. Cringle called one of the lads to hold the reel, while the master held the second-glass. The log showed that we were making fifteen knots an hour.

The gunboats seemed to have discovered that we were moving rather fast, for one of them pitched a shell at us; and over the steamer it went, and struck in the water, without exploding, some forty fathoms ahead of us.

"A good line-shot," muttered Pooduck. "A degree less elevation, and we should have been plugged."

Bang! went a gun from the other steamer; but the shell dropped astern, and was not even in range.

The gunboats were about two miles astern, straining boilers and engines to overhaul us; but it seemed as though we must escape, unless some fortunate shot disabled our machinery; for I did not believe that the United States owned a vessel that could move as lively as the Pet was then doing.

I had just whispered as much to Mrs. Gowen, when young Harry Bluff came to the break of the quarter-deck, apparently to coil up a rope; and while he was about it, the lad made a sign that he desired to speak with me.

"Mr. Barnwell," he said in a whisper, as soon as I had joined him, "if you have any valuables, you had better stow them away about your person."

"Why?"

"Because, sir, in less than six bells, one of those gunboats will be slap aboard of us."

"Nonsense! We can out-steam them, and run back to Nassau. The Pet is too lively for Uncle Sam's crafts."

"Don't you believe it, sir," persisted Harry. "The craft that is astern of us can sail as fast as we can. It is the Stingeree, sir; and when they fire up under all her boilers, she will come up to us hand over hand. You will see, sir, shortly."

"How do you know this, Harry?"

The boy blushed and stammered for a moment, as though he had not thought that such a question might be put to him; but at last he managed to explain.

"I have seen something of blockade running, sir, during the past six months," he said; "and I know most of the Federal ships. I am familiar with all the slow tubs and the clipper steamers. Take my advice, and stow away all your private and valuable swag before Uncle Sam can clap his paws on it."

"Thank you, Harry, for the hint," I remarked, with a

laugh. "But you know my condition when I came on board, and consequently can imagine that I am not possessed of many private effects."

"But I didn't know but you might have some papers," hinted the young fellow.

"Not a line."

Harry was about to go forward, when I laid a hand on his shoulder, and detained him.

"Look you, my lad, you mean well, I've no doubt, but you must be cautious how you warn people on this steamer. What are you, and who are you?"

He smiled, as he answered, —

"One who has seen better days, sir."

"Poor boy!" I answered; "I have no doubt of it."

I was just about leaving him to rejoin Mrs. Gowen, when old Ben, the red-nosed, called the lad, and in harsh tones scolded him for lingering near the quarter-deck, where he did not belong and had no business.

"What did the young fellow want?" asked Mrs. Gowen.

I told her, in confidence, what Harry had said to me.

"Do you believe it?"

"The lad was positive."

"Then I had better make preparations. We have ten thousand dollars in gold in our state-room. The Yankees shan't have that. I'll toss it overboard first."

"Better stow it about your persons. The Federals won't interfere with private property."

"You don't know them as well as I do. But I will take your advice. Come to our state-room, and assist us in concealing the treasure."

She led the way to the cabin; but, just as I was leaving the quarter-deck, I saw the lead box which the confederate despatch-bearer had placed on one of the hen-coops, so that it would be handy to throw overboard in case the steamer was captured. It was not larger than my two fists; but, small as it was, looked desirable, and I thought would form valuable additions to the literature of the Navy Department.

I glanced over the deck to see if any one was regarding my motions. The master was watching the movements of the two strangers in chase, while the crew were discussing what they should do if captured. No one seemed to care for me. It was but the work of a moment. I seized the lead box, opened the door of the hen-coop, threw the valuable prize in among the chickens, closed the door, and rejoined Mrs. Gowen.

The cabin passengers were in a terrible state of alarm at the prospect of capture. Mr. Gowen said that he knew the Federals had no mercy, and that he was a marked man; while the despatch-bearer felt of his throat as though dreading the touch of a hangman. Such a number of pallid faces I had never seen before on the water.

"Mrs. Gowen informs me," the husband remarked, as I entered the state-room, and closed the door, "that you will assist us in securing what little gold we have. You have already rendered us so much service that I fear to trespass on your kindness."

The gold was removed from a trunk, and stowed about our persons; and, after we had accomplished that part of our business, I went on deck, and took another glance at the pursuing gunboats.

I could no longer doubt that the Pet had found her match in sailing and steaming. All three gunboats were in pursuit; and, in spite of our most desperate efforts, we could not throw them off, as anticipated. They held their own, and even gained on us, — the Stingeree leading her consorts in the race.

In the mean time, the breeze which had blown quite strong gradually died away. This was favorable for the Pet; as she did not spread as much canvas as the gunboats, and the latter had spread every rag, and even wet the sails to catch every breath; but, now that the wind had died away, we noticed that we held our own, and I feared would escape.

Pooduck began to rub his hands when he found there was still a chance for him.

"If I can only edge away from 'em till I get in sight of neutral shore," the master said. "A few more hours, and we'll be in English waters; and then we'll dare the Yankees to take us."

As though the commander of the Stingeree had heard the words, and was ready to show that he knew a trick worth half a dozen such as Pooduck had planned, he gave us a shot that fell a few fathoms off our starboard-beam, and even threw several buckets of water on our deck.

"Barnwell," the master said, "them 'ere fellers is in earnest."

"I should think so," I replied.

I saw the smoke of a gun from the Stingeree, and then a dull, heavy report, and directly over our heads was a whizzing sound, and then a sharp crack, and on our deck were scattered two or three pieces of shell, tearing up the wood-work, and creating much consternation.

Mrs. Gowen was the first one to leave the cabin after the shell had burst over us.

"Are you hurt?" she demanded in a tone of alarm.

"No."

"Then come out of danger. Do not remain on deck. My husband wants you to do so."

Even before she had finished her remarks, the confederate despatch-bearer rushed on deck, looking terribly excited.

"Give up the ship!" he yelled. "I order you to surrender. You will sink us, and every person will lose his life. I shall lose mine, and it's worth a dozen vessels like this. Where are my despatches? Stop the engine."

Pooduck turned on the man, seized him by the shoulders, and with a vigorous kick sent him flying off the quarter-deck. He struck on his hands and feet, crawled to the cabin-door, and disappeared, too much frightened to utter one-word about despatches or his lead box. Some of the crew laughed at the display which the fellow made ; but before they had time to laugh long, another shell burst over our heads, sending every one to cover, tearing through the deck, chipping a piece of wood out of the foremast, cutting some of the ropes, and causing the men to lose all heart and hope of escape ; for as soon as the pieces of shell had performed their allotted parts, the crew, headed by old Ben, came surging aft to remonstrate with the master against any further resistance.

"Cap'n Pooduck," said old Ben, who appeared to be the spokesman of the crew, "we don't think it's any use to hold out any longer. If we does, we shall go to the devil, or Davy Jones's locker, in less time than it takes to stow a stay-sail in a net."

The master of the Pet looked at the crew for one moment, and then he put his hand in his breast, and produced a revolver, which he deliberately cocked, and pointed at the sailors.

"Men," he said, "as long as I have life, I'll command the Pet, and surrender when I please, and do as I please. Go forward, and attend to your duty, and I'll attend to mine. Move!"

The crew hesitated, and some of them shrank back, as though fearing to face a revolver ; but, as I glanced over the line of sailors, I saw that old Ben and Harry Bluff maintained their positions, and did not quail at the sight of the weapon. They acted as though they had seen such things before.

During that moment of hesitation, the Stingeree once

more ventured on a shot from her midship-gun. The shell burst just over the stern of the Pet, and one of the pieces passed over the quarter-deck, striking Pooduck in the back, and then, glancing and cutting one of the shrouds of the main rigging, dropped into the water without further damage. As Pooduck fell, he managed to gasp out, —

"Pile on more steam. Don't give up."

Two of the mates ran to pick the master up. Already were the planks stained with his blood; and, as the officers of the steamer raised him, I saw a gaping wound just below the shoulder-blade, where the piece of shell had torn out flesh and muscle, pieces of bone and strong sinews. The poor fellow did not again speak, although he made one or two attempts to do so, as though even in the agonies of death he had some thought to save the steamer.

At that instant there was a sudden jar of the machinery of the Pet, a crash as though some of the iron work had gone through the bottom, and then the paddle-wheels ceased their motion, and the steamer was at the mercy of the gunboats.

"What is the matter?" I asked.

"Some traitor has played a trick with the machinery," one of the Southerners replied. "An iron bolt has been thrown among the works, and the result is a smash."

"Do the engineers know who did it?"

"No; and we have no time to investigate. See, the cussed Yankee is within half a mile of us. Escape now is impossible."

"Mr. Barnwell," said Cringle the mate, with a peculiar hitch of his trousers, "I'll surrender the command up to you, if you'll take charge."

"No, I thank you," I replied. "I have no desire for a trip North."

The mate looked glum enough; but, not satisfied with

my refusal, he attempted to induce one or two others to assume the command, but none of them would listen to the suggestion; and by the time poor Cringle had made up his mind that he would have to take the responsibility, the Stingeree, Captain Switchell, was close off our starboard-quarter, and the gallant Switchell himself standing on the hammock nettings, trumpet in hand, hailing us.

"What is the name of that steamer?" the captain asked in a stern tone.

"She hain't got any name," answered Cringle, and, as he spoke, he dropped a box overboard, which sank immediately.

The action did not escape the sharp eyes of Captain Switchell.

"I suppose you have just thrown all your papers overboard. But that will not avail you. I know you, and all about you; and I can tell just how many boxes of rifles, how many bales of cloth, how many casks of liquor, and how much powder you have on board. But where is the master of the Pet? Where is Pooduck?"

"He is dead, sir. One of your shells tore his back all to pieces."

"Indeed?" with an air of the most supreme indifference. "I thought he would live long enough to be hanged as a pirate."

The captain waved his trumpet, and then the first-cutter was piped away, and pulled towards us, with three armed officers in the stern-sheets, and eight seamen, with cutlasses and navy revolvers in their belts.

The boat came alongside, and the officers touched their caps as they reached the deck, and bowed low when their eyes fell upon Mrs. Gowen, who was leaning on my arm, her curiosity overcoming her repugnance at the sight of Yankees. The officers were astonished and delighted at a vision of so much female loveliness; but their politeness and low bows did not soften the heart of the Georgia beauty, and not even a gracious nod of her stately head welcomed the enemies of the so-called Southern Confederacy.

"One thing," I whispered to the lady. "Do not lisp that I belong to the confederate navy. If you do, I shall be held as a prisoner of war."

She pressed my hand to show that she understood; and then her dark, expressive eyes followed the movements of the Yankee officers with some curiosity, mixed with a little share of disdain, that added much to her peculiar style of beauty.

"Gentlemen," said one of the officers, a smart-looking young fellow, — a lieutenant, so his shoulder-straps denoted, — "I am happy to inform you that your vessel is a prize to the United States steamer Stingeree, Captain Switchell."

"But are we prisoners?" demanded some of the most rabid passengers.

"For the present you are. If any of you belong to the confederate army or navy, you will be likely to go North; but if you are all civilians, I have no doubt but Captain Switchell will land you on some of the keys, so that you can get home before the war closes. Lieutenant Barnwell, of the confederate navy, you will please report on board the Stingeree to Captain Switchell."

"Who gives me that rank?" I asked.

"I do," answered one of the passengers, — a mean little fellow from North Carolina. "You are known on board as a confederate naval officer; and there is no use denying that you are on your way to Richmond to take charge of a ship."

"That will do," responded the lieutenant. "I see that Mr. Barnwell and I understand each other. Now for the information you can pocket a hundred dollars in gold.

Here men, push off, and bring back what help I want as quickly as possible, or we shall have the crews of the Bouncer and the Ballywhack on board; and if once they step foot on deck, it is precious little prize-money we shall make."

Captain Switchell, of the Stingeree, was walking his quarter-deck, and mentally cursing the two gunboats which were steaming towards him. He received me on board with a scowl and the following salute: —

"Who are you, sir? A d—d rebel, I know. Don't answer me, sir; I can see it in your looks. Now, sir, what were you sent on board for? No evasion, sir."

I was about to make a reply, but just at that moment the lieutenant on board the Pet hailed us.

"Captain Switchell, that gentleman, I am told, is a confederate lieutenant; and he was on his way to Richmond. One of the passengers gave me the information."

"Ah!" growled the captain, in a tone like that of a huge sea-lion, "I suspected it all along."

The captain glared at me as though he was debating what punishment he should inflict. But I looked him full in the eye, and raising one of my hands, made a certain sign.

"Eh? what?" demanded the captain; and he rubbed his little gray eyes in astonishment and bewilderment.

I still looked at him, and waited for an answering signal. At last it came, but in such a manner that it proved to me the captain was almost inclined to believe I had made a mistake, and blundered on one of the secret-service signals.

I gave the second signal promptly, and then the captain's face was a study.

"Blast it! who are you?" he asked, in a whisper.

As he spoke, he came a step or two nearer, scanning me closely.

"Perhaps we had better retire to your cabin," I remarked, "and have a little conversation in private."

"Yes, we will."

"But," I continued, "you must recollect that I am a rebel."

"Why, didn't you just give me two of the secret signs? This beats all my wife's relations. Blast me if I know what you mean!"

"Understand me, Captain Switchell," I said. "To you I am a Union man, and an officer of the United States Navy; but to all others, I am a rebel."

"Ah! I understand you now, my hearty," he said, his countenance clearing up. "You have more work on hand?"

"Yes; and you must help me do it."

"Of course. I will put myself out to give you a lifting hand."

The captain led the way to his cabin, and the first thing my eyes rested upon, after entering, was the lead despatch-box which I had secreted in the hen-coop, and missed when I went to look for it.

"Halloo!" I said, "here is something that has turned up most unexpectedly. I thought to place this in your hands."

"Well, it's all right, I suppose; but you see some one got to the wind'ard of you," chuckled the captain.

Seeing that I still looked mystified, the captain touched a bell, and the steward made his appearance.

"Request Mr. Swivel and Mr. Reefpoint to come here," the captain said.

In a few minutes two officers in uniform entered the cabin, and I had no difficulty in recognizing both faces. One belonged to the frank, good-looking Harry Bluff, and the other represented the weather-beaten features of old Ben, red nose and all.

"This is Mr. Swivel, the master's-mate of the Stingeree," the captain said, nodding to the one I had known as Ben. "And this young gentleman is one of my midshipmen — Mr. Reefpoint; although for the past few weeks he has been known as Harry Bluff — an English lad, a hater of the Yankees, and all that."

I must confess that I was taken all aback, as the sailors say, at the introduction. I had suspected that Harry Bluff was not so rabid a confederate as he wished people to think: but that he was a United States officer had never entered my mind; and now, when he stood before me in uniform, with his laughing eyes and smiling face, I could readily understand how it happened that he talked grammatically at one time, and forecastle lingo the next.

"You are a little surprised?" asked Captain Switchell.

"Yes; I confess it."

"Perhaps the gentleman was more surprised when he seed the rockets go up last night," said the master's-mate, with a grin that lighted up his mahogany face for a moment, and even made it look interesting.

"Captain Switchell," I cried, "I wish to thank this young gentleman for his kindness" (and I laid my hand on the midshipman's shoulder) "to me when I was taken on board the Pet in an insensible condition. I really wish you would recommend him for promotion."

"Well, I will; but I have some thoughts of sending him off on another trip. How would you like it, Mr. Reefpoint?"

"If you think I had better go, sir, I am ready," was the modest answer.

"Well, I'll think of the matter. Keep out of sight for the present, and put on your sailor togs. Don't let the people on the Pet suspect who you are."

"But have you no fear that this gentleman will know too much?" — and the young rogue pointed to me.

"O, no. He won't blab."

"The Bouncer and the Ballywhack are nearly alongside, sir," reported the officer of the deck.

"I'll be up in a minute. Now, Mr. Constant, what have you to say about your future operations?"

We were alone in the cabin, for the master's-mate and the midshipman had gone on deck.

"Simply that you must land me, and two or three whom I shall designate, at Nassau, while the rest of the people on board the Pet had better make a journey North, and await the pleasure of the government."

"Well, just designate whom you want for company, and I'll set you on shore in the course of the week."

"Thank you; but you must be persuaded to adopt this course by the entreaties of a very handsome woman."

"Humph! I don't understand you."

"The lady thinks that I am a rebel. If she supposed that I was a Yankee, I should be treated like a dog. By her aid I can learn all that is worth learning in Nassau, or at any Southern port which I may stop. I shall tell her that I am a prisoner, and must go North. She will entreat of you to let me remain with herself and husband. After a little hesitation, you can consent."

"A married woman, is she?"

"Yes, sir, — a handsome one."

"Bah! you talk about beauty. You never saw my wife and daughter. Well, I'll consent."

We went on deck, and found that the two gunboats were ranged alongside; and after mutual congratulations, Captain Harnesscask — a stout, fat, tub-looking sailor — asked.

"I say, Captain Switchell, what will you do with her?"

Captain Switchell was the senior captain, so had control of the prize.

"Send her to New York, I think," was the answer.

"Send her to ——," was the blunt answer. "I sent a schooner in there, loaded with molasses and sugar, sir,— think of that, sir, — and, by ——, sir, if the sharks didn't sell all, and brought me in debt to their infernal courts, sir."

"Well, I think that we shall have to send her to Boston," responded Captain Switchell.

"Boston and Philadelphia give a man a chance for his life. They don't take the oyster, and give you the shell; but even in Boston they hanker like the devil for poor Jack's prize-money. But, halloo, Captain Switchell, you are to have a visitor, and a petticoat at that!"

The captain waved his trumpet, and we saw one of the cutters of the Stingeree leaving the Pet, with Mrs. Gowen in the stern-sheets.

"My eyes, but she's a beauty!" muttered the captain, who was looking at her through his glass. "Almost as handsome as my wife and daughter. Pipe the side, Mr. Compass. We'll receive so handsome a woman with all the honors. It may soften her rebel heart to see that she is appreciated."

The side was piped, and up the steps came Mrs. Gowen, radiant in colors and beauty, causing the most profound admiration among the crew.

CHAPTER VI.

MRS. GOWEN AND THE CAPTAIN. — A SPECIAL PLEA. — A RELEASE. — HARRY BLUFF AND I JOIN FORCES. — A ROW AT NASSAU. — " UP, STINGEREES, AND AT 'EM." — A RECONCILIATION. — I AM WELCOMED BY COLONEL RHETT. — A LITTLE QUESTIONING. — A CHANGE OF SCENE.

SEVERAL of the officers stepped forward to assist her; but the haughty woman waved them off, as though fearing they would soil her garments if they approached too near.

" I wish to speak with the captain of this steamer," the lady said, in an impatient manner, as though she were addressing some of the slaves of her father's plantation.

With a firm step she walked towards the quarter-deck, and said, —

" Captain, I wish to speak with you for a moment."

The rough old sailor's cap was raised in an instant, and he answered, gallantly, —

" I am proud to give some of my time and attention to so handsome a lady, and hope that I shall be able to grant her any favor."

Mrs. Gowen smiled, but it was a smile of disdain.

"I suppose that I must consider myself a prisoner, captain?"

" Why, yes; I am afraid that you will be called such."

"Sir, I am a poor weak woman, and my husband is ill. To be sent North would kill him. Will you land us at Nassau? We are not dangerous people. We have done nothing to provoke your folks. We are plain citizens, almost neutrals."

"To be sure I will. I cannot surely wage war against a man who is sick, and a woman who is so amiable and lovely."

Mrs. Gowen bowed her thanks.

"But I have one more favor to ask," she continued.

"Another one?"

"Yes, captain."

"Well, broach it, and we will see what it appears like."

"Mr. Barnwell is a dear friend of my husband's. He saved the poor man's life. Without each other, they are miserable."

"Whew! is that so?"

"Yes, sir; I assure you that it is."

She began to appear a little nervous and anxious for the first time during the interview with the bluff old sailor.

"But, madam, I am informed that Mr. Barnwell is a confederate naval officer, and that he is on his way to take charge of a queer kind of craft your folks are building at Wilmington, North Carolina. I don't state this as a fact, madam; but it has been hinted to me by more than one."

"O, sir, you are mistaken, I assure you. Mr. Barnwell is a civilian, and has no idea of taking part in this war."

"Well done," I thought. "Even a lady can tell a lie when she is disposed to."

"Will Mr. Barnwell reel off such a yarn to me?" demanded the captain, with what was meant to be understood as a very suspicious glance.

The lady did not reply; but she turned to me, and, laying her hand upon my arm, whispered hurriedly, —

"I have told a falsehood on your account, Mr. Barnwell. Now tell one for yourself, and be saved."

I looked at her flushed face, and saw what a terrible struggle she had had with her better feelings before she were able to utter the words she did.

"Remember, for your sake and the sake of my husband, you must go with us."

"Well," cried the captain, in a pretended tone of severity, "what does the gentleman say about it?"

"He says the same as myself," cried the lady, in a hasty manner.

Captain Switchell seemed to enjoy the pantomime, and would have continued it had I not motioned to him that matters had gone far enough.

"O, well," he said, "I am willing to take your words. I will land such dear friends at Nassau. In a short time we shall be under way for that port; so both of you had better return on board the Pet, and pack up your traps, and bring them here. One of the cutters is at your disposal."

Then the lieutenant in charge of the Pet received his instructions, and was ordered to Boston, with intimations that he must keep an eye on all his prisoners, and prevent them from being mutinous, and iron them if they were uneasy. Twenty men were sent on board, while most of the crew of the Pet were transferred to our deck, and four of them joined the Stingeree in less than ten hours after they were under the shelter of the old flag. With a full head of steam, the Pet started for the North, while the three gunboats separated. The Stingeree steered direct for Nassau, with as jolly a crew as ever assembled on the deck of a man-of-war.

Mrs. Gowen and her husband were provided with a state-room in the captain's cabin; I was turned over to the ward-room; while John, the mulatto, was made to fraternize with the captain's servant, — a smart black fellow, on whom John looked with perfect contempt, considering him one of the free trash that he had heard so much about.

When we entered the harbor of Nassau, and dropped anchor, almost as soon as it touched bottom a notice was sent on board warning the Stingeree to leave the place in the course of twenty-four hours, because it was wrong to shelter a belligerent in a neutral's port longer than that time; yet within half a cable's length of the gunboat were lying three blockade runners, draped with confederate flags and British ensigns. All this increased the ill feeling which our men entertained for the pirates of the place; but the officers of the gunboat were not allowed to exhibit the least temper, or to appear to notice the many insults they received.

"The time will come," whispered Captain Switchell, "when we can repay these barbarians for all their feeling and partiality. Some day the United States will send a fleet of ships down here, and shovel the blasted sandhills into the sea; and that will be the end of the place. But patience, old fellow. Keep cool. Help me capture one of those saucy fellows lying so near us, and we'll laugh at Nassau neutrality."

"I'll do what I can to aid you," I remarked. "Keep outside, near Hog Island, and I will manage to communicate with you in a day or two. But you must let me have Mr. Reefpoint, or rather Harry Bluff, for he must be known by that name. I need his help."

"You shall have him. I'll send him on shore to-night, and tell him to desert. You can pick him up on the beach, or pretend to. Keep the lad a little in hand, and he'll play his part well. I have no more advice that I know of. Pipe away the first cutter, Mr. Compass, and see that Mrs. Gowen's dunnage is stowed away in the boat."

I shook hands with all the officers, and was rowed on shore in company with Mr. and Mrs. Gowen; but it was not until we landed that the lady appeared to breathe as though she was free.

"O! 'ere's a lot o' Yanks a-comin' on shore," cried a number of beach-combers and loafers. "Let's pitch 'em in the drink. They is tyrants, and is fightin' agin' the freedom of the South."

Just at that instant one of the cutters from the Stingeree, containing some ten smart sailors, with two officers in the stern-sheets, touched the beach. The loafers saw the landing, and leaving us, rushed towards the cutter, satisfied this time that they had hit upon a party of Yanks, as they called the Federals.

While the sailors were landing the baggage which Mr. and Mrs. Gowen owned, I watched the operations of the mob. They clustered around the boat, and for a short time contented themselves with calling the sailors hard names; but, as the men of war took but little notice of such conduct, the rabble threw a few stones, and then sand, and with the latter some hard words, just enough to awaken the indignation of the boat's crew. The officers who had landed hurried up town with orders to the cockswain to wait a few minutes for their return.

"Shall we stand all this?" cried one of the crew of the cutter.

"Up, Stingerees, and at 'em!" yelled the cockswain; and, boat-hook in hand, he leaped ashore, right into the midst of the pirates.

"Let go, and haul!" the young fellow yelled; and down upon the head of one man fell the boat-hook.

"Stingerees, show your sting," was the cry; and oars were raised, and boat-stretchers were flourished, and in the midst of the crowd the Yankee tars charged, laying about to the right and left, knocking down the loafers without mercy, or regard for life or limb.

"Yanks! Yanks! Yanks!" yelled the Nassau pirates.

It was the beach-combers' war-cry.

From all parts of the beach the Nassau people hastened to the rescue; and, thus reinforced, the pirates commenced driving the sailors.

"Shall we stand that, shipmates?" demanded the crew of the cutter, who were unloading Mrs. Gowen's traps.

The response was a rush for the scene of the fight, the men armed with boat-hooks and stretchers.

Thus re-enforced, the tars compelled the Nassau beach-combers to give way in confusion; but just as they were about to run, a lot of sailors belonging to the blockade runners lying in the harbor issued from grog-shops in the neighborhood, and turned the tide of battle in favor of the shore people; but not until half a dozen loafers were stretched on the beach almost lifeless.

Just at this moment the two officers from the Stingeree rushed down to the beach, and with drawn swords attempted to separate the belligerents.

But they might as well have called upon bulldogs to cease fighting; for the sailors were determined to avenge some of the insults that had been heaped upon them; while the Nassau pirates were desirous of annihilating those who were interfering with their bread and butter. But, discouraged at the influence of their officers, the sailors began to give way, causing the others to press them all the harder; and just as I thought the tars would turn and run for their boats, a new actor appeared on the scene, — one whom I was much surprised to see.

"Shucks, you d—d cowards! fight three to one, will you? Count me in. Old Kaintuck forever! Whoop!"

It was Bowmount, the blunt Kentuckian, — the very man who had damaged Mr. Gowen with the glass bottle.

I saw him tear off his coat, draw a two-pound bowie-knife, and rush into the thickest of the fight.

"Bully for the Union!" he yelled. "Whoop! Kiyi! Give 'em shucks! Bah!"

Heaven only knows whether it was the formidable knife, the unearthly yells, the horrible imprecations, or the threatening appearance of the Kentuckian, whose eyes and face looked murderous, that struck fear to the hearts of the pirates; but it is a fact, that no sooner did they hear his war-whoop, and see the flash of his bowie-knife, than terror took possession of them.

"A knife! a knife!" was the cry from all quarters.

They instantly gave way, and began fleeing in confusion. At this moment Mrs. Gowen whispered softly to me, —

"You see my husband?"

"Yes."

"You notice that he trembles?"

"He appears agitated."

"You can imagine the cause?"

"Perhaps the row he has just witnessed has disturbed his nerves."

"Partly. But there is something else. The sight of that rude brute, that Kentuckian, has recalled the scene at the hotel, and the threats he made to kill him."

"I think there need be no fear on that account."

"With you, there would be none; but Mr. Gowen's nerves are not like yours. Come, now; have pity on me, and do us a favor at the same time."

"Willingly. What shall it be?"

"Go to that wild brute, and tame him. Make him give you guarantees that he will not harm Mr. Gowen, or even speak with him. If he does not promise, I shall have to defend my husband with my life."

I promised, and instantly started to confer with the Kentuckian, and also to remove him from the beach, for he was liable at any moment to arrest for assault with a dangerous weapon.

The officers of the Stingeree understood the matter; for as they glanced along the landing, and saw some dozen cracked heads lying on the sand, they determined to reach their ship as soon as possible, and thus escape all dangers from a court of law, — where prosecution would be rigorous, and conviction sure, especially if the parties arraigned were Federals.

They left Bowmount standing near the landing, unconscious of all that was going on; for as I approached him, he muttered,—

"The purtiest little fight I've seen this side of Old Kaintuck; and not a man of 'em dared to stand up and face me. Shucks! Dog on 'em! what's the reason they couldn't give a man a chance to have a little fun?"

"Well, old fellow, how are you?" I asked, as I laid a hand on his arm.

The Kentuckian started, and once more placed his hand on the knife he had sheathed beneath his vest.

"Bowmount," I continued, "how are you? Couldn't keep out of the fight — could you?"

"Ah, I didn't think it was in you to do as you have done," was the reply. "Shucks! didn't I put more trust in you than in any other man?"

"Well, suppose you did? How have I betrayed that trust? Come, old fellow, speak quick. or you will find a squad of police down here after those who were engaged in the disturbance."

"Well, it wouldn't grieve me so much to be took as to know that I has put confidence in a man what turns agin me."

"What do you mean?"

"That's what I mean."

There was a look of defiance in the Kentuckian's face, as though he were "mad all through," and nearly inclined for another fight.

"You are laboring under a mistake," I said, "or else you want to quarrel with me. If the latter be your object, I shall not gratify you until I am satisfied that you have grounds for your complaint."

"You South Carolina chaps," was the answer, "is pe-ert — mighty pe-ert; but old Kaintuck's as good as any of 'em, now I tell you."

"Never mind that," I remarked. "You come with me to a place where there will be no danger of arrest, and then I'll talk with you."

Bowmount followed me, in a quiet manner, to a part of the landing where we would be screened from observation. To be sure he muttered, in a low tone, some grievance that he had at heart; but I could not detect what he meant until I turned on him, and said, —

"Now, free your mind, Bowmount. What have I done?"

"I shouldn't have thought it of yer, dog on it!"

"You have said that several times already." I said.

He turned on me like a panther, and replied fiercely, —

"I knows it; and I'll say it several times agin, if I wants to."

"No, you won't," I answered, "at least to me; for if you are disposed to continue it, I shall take an early opportunity of leaving you to talk to yourself."

"You South Carolinians is pe-ert; but, shucks! we is pe-erter. Old Kaintuck won't back down for any of you."

"No one wants you to," I responded. "But if you can't explain what the trouble is, I'll leave you."

I was about to move off, when Bowmount remarked, —

"What did you cut and run for, jist when I wanted yer to help me?"

"Is that the trouble?"

"Yes, it is. Where has you stowed yerself the last few days? Why did yer leave me all alone with none but the mean sneaks at the hotel to talk to? Why couldn't you have said to me, 'Bowmount, I'm tired of your rough ways. You like to fight too well for my money. I don't take any pleasure in your company, so I'll quit you at once?' Yer might have done that, and no one would have gin yer a more tough shake of the hand than me, a dog-on-'em sort of a feller what likes fair play and square sort of men."

"And that is what you have in my disfavor?" I asked.

"Yes; and enough it is for any man."

"Well, suppose I should prove to you that I had to leave in opposition to my own wishes?"

"How's that? I'd like to see the man what could make me leave unless I wanted to."

"You are a brave man," I said, "and a strong one; but even you might be taken by surprise, and forced to surrender."

"O, a sneakin' cuss might hit me on the head when my back was turned. Of course all men is liable to that sort of thing."

"Well, old fellow, that is just the manner I was served. See," and I removed my hat, "where a slung-shot struck my head, and almost fractured my skull."

"Shucks! so it did. How did it happen?"

"Well, that is more than I can tell. I was on the beach, after I parted from you, some one struck me, and it was the last that I knew until I awoke on board the blockade-runner Pet, on her way to Wilmington."

"The devil! you don't say so!"

"I'm telling you the truth."

"I know you are. Don't think I'm the man to dispute yer. Shucks! it's jist like a romance. But how comes yer here? That's the question. If yer was on the Pet, why ain't yer thar now? It's a long ways from here to Wilmington, and a vessel don't move like a swaller."

"I'm only too thankful that I am not on board the Pet, for she is bound North, in charge of a prize crew; and I'm here, a free man, and not a prisoner."

"Was she took?" demanded Bowmount, with a surprised look.

"Yes; and there lies her captor, the Federal gunboat

Stingeree, — the crew of which you assisted a few minutes ago."

"Whew! the devil I did!" whistled the Kentuckian, with a peculiar expression on his red face. "What a cussed fool I am — ain't I? But never mind that just now, old boy. We'll talk of that matter some other time. What I wants to know is how the Yanks come to let you up."

"By the aid of a handsome woman."

"O! is that the lay? Well, who is the woman that did all that for yer?"

"One whom you have injured."

"O, shucks! golong. I don't know any woman what I have injured. I wouldn't hurt the hair of a woman's head. Name her."

"Mrs. Gowen."

"Dog on it! you don't say so? How come she on board the Pet?"

"You frightened her so badly that she compelled her husband to leave in a hurry."

Bowmount looked a little guilty, and tried to change the conversation, but I wouldn't let him. I held him to the mark.

"After I left you, on the evening of the row, you sent a challenge to Mr. Gowen."

"Yes, I s'pose I did."

"You promised me that you would do nothing of the kind."

"I know; but you see you left me all alone, and I began to think that the d—d Georgian would boast that old Kaintuck had no courage for a fair fight; so I jist sent him a letter, and I worded it pretty strong. Then I went to sleep; and when I woke up in the mornin' you warn't to be found, and Gowen had cut and run for it. I didn't know what to think; so I put you all down as mean sneaks what didn't understand civilized ways."

"Do you still think so"

"There's my hand, Barnwell. I won't lift it agin yer, nor agin any man what is yer friend."

"O! I'm not alarmed on my own account. I was thinking of Gowen and his wife."

"I'll be like a lamb to 'em," the Kentuckian cried. "Only don't you go back on me — will you?"

"No, — not if you will come up to the mark like a man, and offer your hand to Mr. Gowen."

"I'm a man, and will do it."

"Then come with me."

The brawny Kentuckian put his arm through mine, and we walked to the place where Mr. and Mrs. Gowen were waiting for a carriage to take them to the Royal Humbug Hotel.

Mr. Gowen looked uneasy and felt uneasy when he saw the Kentuckian approach; but his wife drew up her well-proportioned form, flashed her eyes, and ruffled her plumage like a royal eagle annoyed by the approach of some mean bird or sneaking hunter.

"Mr. Gowen," said the Kentuckian, "thar's my hand. We have had a fight, and you got the worst punishment. If you don't mind that, I don't, I'm sure. Shall we be friends, or shall we be enemies?"

"Friends, by all means," was the eager reply. And they shook hands.

As soon as this was accomplished, I hurried Bowmount from the beach, and we reached the hotel in safety.

I once more dressed myself in my own apparel, and descended to the veranda of the hotel. The first man I met there was Colonel Rhett, the Virginian, — the same old scoundrel who had been instrumental in having me carried on board the Pet after I had been struck senseless by a slung-shot in the hands of a sailor working under his directions.

"Ah, lieutenant!" said the colonel, giving a sudden hobble as he spoke, as though requiring considerable support from his stick, — for he seemed lame by spells, as though his rheumatism was troublesome, — "I am glad to see you to-day."

The old rascal extended his hand as though he was sure of a warm welcome. I took his proffered hand, and squeezed it; for I did not mean to let the old cheat know that I was aware of his treachery. I meant to pay him in his own coin at some future time.

"Where have you kept yourself for the past few days?" the colonel asked, in a soothing, confidential tone. "My daughter has inquired for you several times. Have you been sick?"

"It seems that you have not heard the story of my adventures."

"Adventures? No, indeed. Pray tell me what kind of adventures."

I wanted to rave at the old scoundrel; but restrained my feelings, thinking the time would come for a sweet revenge. I had to fight such a man with his own weapons. So, in as composed a manner as possible, I related how I had been knocked down, and then carried to the Pet, and all the particulars of her capture, &c.

The gallant old colonel listened (I wanted to knock the hypocrite heels over head) with all the marks of astonishment that he could command; and, when I had concluded, he swore that an outrage had been committed, and that I should apply to the governor for redress, and that, "if some notice was not taken of it, the Southern Confederacy would look after the affair when the proper time arrived."

"Bah!" I replied, with an expression of contempt. "The governor could do nothing; and, as for the confederacy, it has as much as it wants to attend to at present."

"That's so," replied the colonel, in so hearty a manner that I looked at the man in astonishment.

He noticed my surprise, and attempted to explain matters; but while he was uttering some commonplace remarks, full of Virginia's peculiar dialect, Miss Rhett, the old gentleman's daughter, made her appearance, looking as lovely as she appeared on the first day that I saw her.

"O, Mr. Barnwell!" she cried, in a gushing tone, tripping towards me, both of her little hands extended in the frankest, freest, most amiable manner. "O, how pleased I am to see you?" she continued, as she put her little white fingers in my hand, and allowed them to remain there for the space of a minute. "You are a naughty man to keep away from us for such a length of time."

"I didn't think Miss Rhett would miss me when she had so many polite gentlemen to entertain her," I said; for I remembered how she had favored Soulé on the passage to Nassau.

The young lady smiled, and glanced at her father; and the old gentleman seemed to take the hint, for he said,—

"Come to our room, Mr. Barnwell, and have a social glass of wine, and a quiet smoke."

I should have refused, but the young lady laid her hand on my arm, and whispered,—

"O, do come."

Her eyes looked too inviting to decline such an invitation, so man-like I went.

When we arrived at the room, wine was placed on the table, and Miss Rhett insisted that I should light a cigar, and smoke in company with her father, just for her gratification. She did like the smell of cigar smoke; and gentlemen took so much comfort with tobacco, that it seemed a pity to deprive them of it. She was sure she should want her husband to smoke cigars, and she should not object if he used a pipe. But then she never expected to be married, so what was the use of talking on that subject. Then she laughed, and appeared a little annoyed, as though she had overstepped the bounds of maiden modesty.

Colonel Rhett did not check his daughter. He seemed so accustomed to her child-like ways, that he did not appear to notice her prattle, or think that it was necessary to reprove it; but, while I was listening to the young lady, the colonel all of a sudden espied some one on the grounds of the hotel, and he must have desired to see him very much, for he turned to me, and said, —

"Remain here ten minutes, won't you, while I speak to Richards. I'll be back in that time. Entertain him, Magnolia."

He was gone before I could remonstrate.

Hardly had the door closed, before the young lady drew her chair nearer to mine, and said, —

"I'm glad he's gone."

"Why?"

"Because I can now have a pleasant chat with you. I feel, Mr. Barnwell, so much interest in the fate of the confederacy,.that I want to talk to you on the hopes and prospects of the South. You know all that is going on, or, if you don't, you should; and I want you to tell me what is your candid opinion of the condition of things."

"You can read and use your eyes," I said. "Look towards the harbor, and see the fleet of blockade runners loaded with supplies for the South; glance over the Northern papers, and see how despondent they are. All show that the end is not far off."

"O, how glad I am to hear you talk in that manner! You give me such encouragement."

Yet in truth the girl did not look as though she were delighted.

"Do you know the names of all the blockade runners in port, Mr. Barnwell?" the lady asked.

"O, yes! there are six of them."

"And is it possible that you know what is on board of each? How singular!"

"It is not so very singular if you think of the matter for a moment. I am a sailor, and take an interest in such matters."

"True, true. I didn't think of that. Now, shall I test your knowledge?"

"Yes."

"I don't believe you know, but I have a good mind to ask the question. Papa will never talk with me on matters that interest all noble-hearted girls."

"Well, put my knowledge to the test," I said. "Ask me any question that you please, and see if I don't answer it to your satisfaction."

"Now," the lady said, with a pleasant smile, "tell me what is on board of the Saucy Jane."

"There are on board the Saucy Jane two batteries of guns, ten thousand rifles, and some medicines and wine."

She clapped her hands in glee.

"O, how I hope she will run the blockade in safety! Do you know when she will sail?"

"Some time to-night."

"Indeed. So soon?"

For a moment she was thoughtful, as though making some mental calculation; and then she looked up and asked, —

"Do you know what is on board the Spitfire?"

I didn't know, but replied, —

"Powder, guns, boots and shoes, and confederate gray."

"And when does she sail?"

"On Sunday, I think, unless there is some Yankee vessel outside."

"And the rest of the steamers, — do you know when they will start?"

"Just as soon as their agents, Alderny & Co., say the word."

Just at this moment there was a sharp knock at the door, and who should enter the apartment but Mrs. Gowen, the Georgian heiress.

I am certain that I had done nothing to provoke her wrath, even if she had possessed a right to control my actions; so I was much surprised when the Georgia lady, after entering the apartment, and closing the door, turned full upon Miss Rhett, and, with scorn and rage depictured in every feature, said, —

"Here are pretty goings-on, I am sure. A nice little party this, with the stern papa left out for some purpose or other. I am not as blind as a bat, I would have you to know; for I can see into a private arrangement as far as the next person. This I consider as highly improper."

"May I ask to what you allude?" demanded Miss Rhett.

This young lady's first emotion, on seeing the proud Georgian, was that of pleasure, simply because a haughty woman likes to receive a call from another.

"It is evident enough."

The flashing eyes were turned on me, but only for a moment. Then they were directed to Miss Rhett, as though she were the culprit on whom all the scorn and indignation should be concentrated.

"I do not understand you, Mrs. Gowen."

"Then it would be improper for me to explain all that you should know. Good day."

She turned, and was gone before I could utter a word in reply. Miss Rhett and I looked at each other in silence for a moment, and then laughed. We could not help it, the scene had been so ludicrous.

"Well," said the dark-eyed Virginian, with some little signs of embarrassment, "I suppose that I shall have a dreadful name for my wickedness; but I shall look to you for vindication."

"We have had a pleasant chat," I returned.

"Yes; I am sure that we have. You don't know how much you have instructed me. And all for the love of our dear South."

She gave me her hand as she spoke. At that moment Colonel Rhett returned. Hardly was he in the room before the door flew open without a warning knock, and in rushed Soulé, the rebel despatch-bearer.

He was so eager and joyful that he did not notice me, but ran straight to Miss Rhett, caught her in his arms, and showered several kisses upon her face before he was aware of my presence.

Perhaps I was astonished more than the colonel; for the latter simply said, —

"Mr. Soulé. I am surprised at your extraordinary conduct."

"My dear sir," was the answer, "I am so happy that you need be surprised at nothing. Miss Rhett will forgive me for what I have done, when I tell her that McClellan has been defeated in front of Richmond, and his army not only broken up, but a great part of it destroyed. The fate of the Southern Confederacy is now certainly assured."

I was confounded at this statement, and could not believe that it was true; but if I looked for a moment the dismay that I felt, the Rhetts certainly were overwhelmed with joy; for they could not speak, but gazed at each other in silent amazement, while Soulé gave vent to his joy by throwing up his hat and cheering most extravagantly.

. "Is this certain? Is the news from an authentic source?" I demanded, after I had crushed the agony that tore at my heart-strings.

"A steamer has just arrived from New York," replied Soulé; "and our friends in that city have sent us the most reliable information. Whoop! The military power of the North is destroyed, and the South is free. My dear Miss Rhett, do allow me to shake hands with you on the strength of it. We shall now belong to one of the first nations in the world."

"The North won't give it up yet," remarked the colonel, after a long silence.

Then he looked at his daughter with a wearied air, as though he was too much elated to cheer at the tidings he had heard.

"But it must give it up," was Soulé's reply. "The North is bankrupt, and men can no longer be driven into the army, or hired to volunteer. I have travelled all over the country, and know what I state. The last army the North can raise is crushed in front of Richmond."

The enthusiastic young man rushed towards Miss Rhett to take her in his arms, and once more embrace her; but the young lady dodged in an adroit manner, so that the young fellow missed his prize, and with a laugh left the room to impart the information to others as deeply interested as himself.

I then bowed myself out of the apartment, and found Mrs. Gowen near the head of the main stairs, where she seemed to have been waiting for me.

"O, you mean, deceitful man!" she said in a vindictive manner, and with a look that showed how angry she was.

"For Heaven's sake, what have I done?" I demanded.

"Done?" she repeated in a tone of supreme contempt. "What haven't you done?"

"Hollo! here's a jolly row."

Mrs. Gowen heard the dreaded Kentuckian's voice, turned and fled precipitately, leaving me to explain matters to Bowmount.

"What's the matter, my boy?" he asked.

I explained to the Kentuckian that Mrs. Gowen was fretful. Just at that moment some one came along, and said something about the "glorious news from Richmond;" and it started Bowmount on another track.

"Shucks!" he said. "You fellers go crazy over a victory, and think that the war is ended because one of the Northern armies is drove back. I tell you another army will spring up, and take its place. You fellows don't know the North as well as I do; and some of you don't know the South, though you have lived there all your nateral days."

Here some one, flushed with the news, and not having the fear of Bowmount's bowie-knife before his eyes, intimated that the Kentuckian was no true Southerner.

"Perhaps I'm not," was the reply. But it was made in good-nature, much to my surprise; for I expected he would fall into a terrible passion. "I am so good, though, that I would have prevented this war if I could, and would have hung every infernal scoundrel that attempted to urge it on."

There was a murmur of indignation at this, and one or two hostile demonstrations; but the Kentuckian replied calmly, —

"Let's argue the p'int, and see who is the best friend of the South."

Unfortunately Bowmount just at that moment placed his hand in his breast-pocket. Although I am confident that he meant nothing by the action, yet it appeared that all dreaded an explosion; for there was such a sudden retreat, that in a moment the Kentuckian and myself were left together.

"What's the meaning of this?" demanded Bowmount, looking around in a puzzled sort of surprise.

I could not help laughing, the man was so astonished at the sudden flight of those who had been listeners.

"It means," I answered, "that your friends expected a shot instead of an argument. They can stand your words, but not the contents of your revolver."

"Shucks!" he exclaimed; "is that so? I hadn't the least idea of drawin' on the cusses. If I had, they wouldn't have got away with whole skins, now I tell you."

I left the Kentuckian marvelling at the suspicions of his Southern friends, and passed down stairs, where I mingled with the crowd, heard the comments on the Virginia news, drank with some of the more moderate of the confeds, talked with others, and then retired to my room, and slept till luncheon.

After luncheon, I lighted a cigar, and walked out, hoping that I should have time to exchange a few words with the American consul without being observed by the rebels who thronged the island.

As I strolled along, regretting the bad news I had heard, some one touched my arm.

"If you please, sur, will ye be kind enough to give me a shillin' to prevent me bein' choked to death?"

It was a rich brogue that saluted my ear, and the owner of the same was a young fellow dressed in the garb of a sailor — blue shirt, pants, and a Scotch cap, with a leather belt and jack-knife attached.

I could not get a full view of the lad's face (for he appeared to be but a lad) on account of the cap which he wore, having drawn it over his eyes in an unsailorlike fashion.

"Have you an idea of hanging yourself?" I asked.

"No, yer honor. Why does yer ask?"

"For the simple reason that you said you intended to choke unless you had a shilling."

"Ah, yer honor; but 'tis for the want of whiskey I suffer. A small coin will now save me from a terrible death."

"Why, you impudent vagabond," I replied. "A young fellow like you should be above begging."

"I know, yer honor; but what is a buy to do when he has nary a shot in the locker, and is terrible dry?"

The impudence of the scamp amused me. I handed him a shilling, and was about to pass on, when the rogue gently touched me on the arm.

"If you plase, sir, couldn't you add anither one to it? I'm awful when I'm dry."

"You impudent scoundrel!" I said. "If you don't take yourself off, I'll keelhaul you!"

The young man chuckled, and I passed on. I had walked but a few paces when I found that the persistent beggar was following me; so turned on him with a regular quarter-deck air.

"Didn't I tell you to crowd sail and be off?" I demanded.

"Yes, yer honor."

"And will you mind me?"

"Certainly, sir. That's what I was sent on shore for."

The youngster raised his hand and brushed away his cap as he spoke, changing his tone entirely from rank brogue to good English.

"Why, Harry! is this you?" I demanded; for I saw before me Harry Reefpoint, the young midshipman of the Stingeree.

"Yes, sir; here I am, with orders to report to you."

"I did not recognize you, and should not have noticed you."

"No, sir; I hope not. My brogue, sir, I trust, was perfect. It was put on for effect, like sky-scrapers to a merchant-ship. But I'll take any character you like, from a Yankee tar, disgusted with the North, to an English jolly and drunken devil of a sailor, more anxious for a swill at the grog-tub than a haul at the purser's stores.

Tell me what to be, and I'm all that your fancy painted me, although I'm not lovely or divine, according to a man's acceptance of the term."

"Well, what are you according to a woman's idea on that point?"

I could not repress a smile at the blush that mantled his handsome face, and glistened in his speaking eyes.

"Recollect, sir, that we gentlemen and men of honor are commanded, by all that we hold sacred, not to divulge the secrets of a lady. A sailor is too chivalrous to think of such a thing."

"Very well answered, Harry, and I hope that your modesty will last through life; but I fear not. But now to business. When did you land?"

"An hour or two since."

"And the Stingeree is ready to sail as soon as the twenty-four hours expire?"

"Yes, sir."

"That is right. I am in hopes that we shall find work for her before long."

Harry glanced over his shoulder, and then looked all around before he said, —

"I've already heard something that is of interest, sir."

"Indeed! What is it?"

"To-night the crew of the Spitfire is to be shipped."

"Well, can we prevent it?"

"No, sir. I wouldn't try to. She is a bouncing big steamer; is crammed full of guns, rifles, and all that the South wants. If she should run the blockade, there would be great rejoicing in Dixie, and mourning in the North."

"Is the Spitfire fast?"

"Yes, sir. She beat the Pet in a race out of Liverpool. I think that even the Stingeree would have to keep in her wake, although the gunboat can do pretty well alongside of the fancy sailers."

"Harry, I must think of this matter, and see if we can't earn a little prize-money."

"Yes, sir."

"You know where the men are to be shipped?"

"Yes, sir; at Bucknor's."

"If we could get a dozen or twenty of the Stingeree's crew on board, there would be little trouble in making a capture," I suggested.

"Can't we do it, sir?" the lad asked with a smile.

"Can you get a note to Captain Switchell?" I inquired.

"Yes, sir. He is on shore now, and at the consul's house."

"Well, wait here until I return. I will write to the captain, and detail my plan; and if he approves it, then I will make any attempt on the steamer. Keep close until I come back, and recollect that you are Harry Bluff, the English lad."

"Yes, sir; I am anxious to make a few shillin's by cheatin' the bloody Yankees."

Harry would have willingly given me some more specimens of English marine humor, if I had waited and listened; but I was too much hurried, wishing to write the letter, to stop and hear him.

I returned to the hotel, and found that all the boarders were singing songs, and that "Maryland, my Maryland," was one of them.

"Come and have a drink, Barnwell," roared the Southerners as I hove in sight.

"I'm in a hurry just at this moment."

"The man who does not drink on such an occasion as this deserves to be called an abolitionist," roared one young fellow, who had left the sunny South for the purpose of escaping conscription, and serving in the army.

"That's so," yelled half a dozen of the most drunken. "You must drink with us, or be called a Northern nigger-lover."

A roar of laughter greeted the remark; and to prevent suspicion, I joined in the merriment, and went towards the bar for a glass of iced punch.

"Who says a man what don't drink with you is a nigger-lover?" asked a deep bass voice, which I knew quite well.

It was Bowmount, the Kentuckian, who seemed determined to make his presence known just at times when his Southern friends wished him to the devil.

There was no response to the remark. Even those who had been most noisy but a moment before were silent now, sipping their liquor, and smoking their cigars, as though to occupy their time, and not for pleasure.

Bowmount was more than half intoxicated. I could see that, and also noticed that he was determined to quarrel with some one, or even with all in the room, if occasion was given him.

"I won't drink with your d—d cowardly party; and I ain't an abolitionist, nor a nigger-lover. Who says I am?"

There was no response to this.

"Who'll invite me to drink? Don't all speak at once. Shucks! dog on yer, what is yer afeard of?"

"Take a glass with me," I said, and passed a champagne bottle to him.

"No, sir; I won't drink with you. But I'll liquor with these cusses what called me a nigger-lover. Whoop!"

With a yell like that of an Apache, the Kentuckian sprang towards the nearest rebel; but the latter went out the window head first, landing in the garden.

"Whoop! Wake, snakes, and give 'em ginger!"

The crazy-headed man made a rush for a second rebel — a fat, pursy, wheezy little man, bald-headed and near-sighted.

The little man had but a moment before declared that

BOWMOUNT EXPLAINS. — Page 197.

a warrior's death was the death he preferred to all others; and he had intimated, glass in hand, that he should like to die several times for the benefit of the Sunny South.

When the man whom Bowmount first attacked bolted from the room head first, the little greasy, fat fellow had looked upon the whole thing as a good joke, and had laughed until his sides shook like a jelly; but the noise which he made attracted the Kentuckian's notice. The fellow had better have shaken a red cloth in the eyes of a mad bull than to have thus called down upon his head the wrath of that drunken man.

"Whoop! yaw!" roared the madman; and, waving a heavy champagne-bottle in his right hand, charged ferociously upon the little bald-headed genius.

"Run, little one," I yelled, fearful that the man would be brained and killed.

He started from the table at which he had been seated, and gazed with dismay at the Kentuckian. He seemed incapable of moving, appearing as one fascinated with the wicked eyes of a serpent.

"Run, you cussed fool!" some one shouted to him.

But the warning was not heeded.

On went the Kentuckian, uttering powerful whoops and yells.

"Jump out of the window," I said.

But the words were not noticed.

"Wake, snakes; for you is wanted," howled Bowmount.

Raising his bottle as he spoke, in a moment more it would have fallen, and perhaps crushed the skull of the little rebel. But luck favored the man who desired to die on the field of battle. His legs, stout and fat as they were, gave way beneath the load that pressed them down, and his whole person collapsed, and went under the table, as though struck down by a flash of lightning. As the little fellow fell, he also overturned the table, — a marble-topped one, — and, as it fell, struck the Kentuckian's toes, skinned his shins, and finally tripped him up, falling headlong, and carrying with him to the floor half a dozen of the confeds who were near.

"'Now I lay me down to sleep!'" cried the little fat man as he arose, repeating portions of the first prayer that came to his mind. "'May all good angels guard me and mine evermore!' Cuss such a man. He's drunk. Take him off. Save me. Glory to the Highest. Good luck about that table, now I tell you. Kill him, some of you. He's a pretty Southerner. Bah!"

With these words and this salutation, the fat man rushed from the room, and sought that quiet in his chamber he could not find in the bar-room.

"He's a disgrace to the house, and should be made to leave it," said some one — a testy old gentleman who didn't understand such Kentucky fun.

Bowmount heard this remark as he raised his battered form from the floor.

"I'll teach you civility, you mean old cuss!" roared the rash man.

Grasping his bottle, he prepared for another rush; but the children of the Sunny South did not wait for the charge. They turned and fled as though they feared broken heads and bloody noses; and in a few moments no one remained in the room but the Kentuckian, the barkeeper, and myself.

As soon as the room was cleared, the Kentuckian brushed the coarse hair from his eyes, and gazed around like a wild bull that had been maddened and baffled.

"O, my God!" he said, with a sort of sob. "To think that out of ten men not one of 'em would stand before me even for a minute! This is hard luck, hard luck. It's not so in old Kaintuck. Thar, if you make a motion or even p'int a finger at a feller, he'll strip for a fight. Ah! I long for the old times and the old State."

I saw that it was useless to argue with him; so, making an excuse to get him to his room, I left him in the enjoyment of a nap, while I hurried to my apartment, and wrote a letter to Captain Switchell, asking for twenty reliable men — sober fellows, who would obey all orders, and not ask a question. They were to land in the course of the day, and report to Harry, or old Ben, on the beach, one at a time, and there receive instructions.

After writing the note, I hurried out, and found the midshipman, who was waiting most patiently for me, and who promised to see that Captain Switchell received the letter in the course of an hour or two. I then explained to Harry my plans for the capture of the Spitfire; and the lad was kind enough to say that he was delighted with them, and thought they would succeed.

"Very well," I answered. "Be on hand promptly this evening, and we will make an attempt even if it fails."

I turned away, and through the trees caught sight of Colonel Rhett and his daughter sauntering in the shade.

I pushed Harry behind a thicket of bushes, and waited for the Virginians to pass; for I did not want them to see me just at that moment in company with the middy.

Colonel Rhett and his lovely daughter appeared to be engaged in an earnest conversation, so that Harry and I had no trouble in secreting ourselves. They did not notice us, or appear aware that we were near.

They were soon lost to view in the shadows of the trees and shrubbery. The young midshipman and myself then stole from our place of concealment, and walked in an opposite direction.

"Faith, she is a pretty one," said Harry.

"In fact," continued the good-looking youngster, "she reminds me of my Boston cousin — one of the handsomest girls that ever walked Washington Street."

"Indeed? Who is she?"

"O! no one that you ever heard of," was the careless answer.

"Perhaps not," I insisted; "but tell me her name."

"Hatty Blank."

"Hatty Blank?"

"Yes, sir—the daughter of my uncle Pemberton Blank, a wealthy and aristocratic East India merchant."

"Is it possible that that young lady is your cousin?"

"Yes, sir. Did you ever see her?"

"Yes."

"Isn't she a stunner for good looks? Did you ever see a clipper that would equal her for all that's neat and taunt, alow and aloft?"

"She is a lady, and a very beautiful one. In fact, it is seldom we meet with a more lovely face."

I spoke in a warm tone; for I recollected that I carried the young lady's photograph near my heart, and that her bright face and coquettish airs were still as fresh in my mind as the day I saved her from insult on Pennsylvania Avenue, in Washington.

Just at that moment I heard footsteps on the gravel walk. We dodged behind some bushes, and waited to see who the stranger was. In a few seconds the pursy form of Captain Switchell, of the Stingeree, approached. He was mopping his face with his pocket-handkerchief, and growling audibly at some subject that lay on his mind.

"Captain, you are just the one I want to see," I said, as I stepped from the bushes.

Captain Switchell, who entertained an idea that Nassau contained more pirates and robbers to the square foot than any country under the sun, started, and laid his hand on a revolver, under the impression that murder was contemplated; but, as soon as he saw my face, his features relaxed their scowl, and good-nature appeared.

"Damn me," he said, "if I didn't think that you was after cotton, and the gold lace on my coat."

"Can you spare me a word, captain?" I asked.

"Yes — a dozen of them. Only be lively; for the scoundrels have ordered me off."

We withdrew to the shade, and then I laid my plans before the captain for the capture of the Spitfire. Captain Switchell bit his thumbs while I was relating the plans, and at last he exclaimed, —

"Blast it, you know that it is clear agin national law."

"Who ever heard of law when capturing or breaking up a nest of pirates?"

"I know all that; but, darn it! the thing might be brought home to me, and then I'd be broken as sure as fate."

"But there is no need of it. I assume the whole responsibility. Give twenty of your men a chance to leave the ship for a few days, and no questions asked. You need to know but little of the matter; but, after the Spitfire is outside, your trouble is over. Take her three leagues from land, and what a prize you will have! and no other ship to share it."

"How my wife and daughter would rejoice to see me rolling the shot into my locker!" remarked Captain Switchell, his eyes protruding at the anticipation.

"Of course they would. Why should they not rejoice at your prosperity? If you have fair treatment by the prize courts, you can count on ten or twenty thousand dollars as your share of the Spitfire."

"Damn it! you know it is a little irregular. We are in a neutral port."

"Yes; and see how they show their neutrality, by ordering you to leave the harbor in twenty-four hours after you have arrived."

"Blast 'em!" muttered the captain. "A set of bloody pirates as ever lived. The whole bloody place had ought to be sunk in the ocean."

"Then you'll lend me the men?"

"No; I'll do nothing about it."

I looked my disappointment; but the captain winked with one of his pig-like eyes, as he added, —

"No; I'll have nothing to do with the affair. But I'll just hint to Mr. Swivel that I can spare him and some twenty of the best and most reliable men in the ship. He can take the hint or not; but from what I know of the man, I rather think he will."

"We shall want an assistant engineer to start the engines in case we don't find one on board."

"Well, I'll hint as much to Mr. Swivel. He's a sly old fox, and won't miss a chance if he can help it."

And with these words we parted company, — the captain bolting in one direction, while Harry and I drifted in another.

"Now, my lad," I said, when we had stood on one tack as long as we thought proper, "we must part company for the present. I will meet you on the beach to-night; or if anything of importance occurs between now and then, let me know. Come to the hotel in your character of an Englishman, and speak to me."

There was the sound of more footsteps on the gravel. Harry heard them, drew his cap over his eyes, and scampered off towards the harbor, while I sauntered towards the hotel, yet in the direction of the approaching intruder.

"Hollo, Barnwell!"

The Kentuckian stood before me as sober as on the day he was born; and yet I had left him, two hours before, half crazy drunk, and lying on his bed with a prospect of having a long nap. I saw, though, what had sobered him. His dripping hair and damp shirt collar showed that he had dipped his head into a pail of iced water, and kept it there until the liquor had been driven from his brains — a result obtained through a species of strangulation that was emphatically Kentuckian in its nature.

"I thought you were asleep," I remarked, as soon as I could recover from my surprise at seeing the man.

"Asleep? What made you think that? What do I want to go to sleep for at this time of the day?"

"O!" I laughed; "I didn't know but you would be tired."

"Shucks! I've other things to think of jest at this time."

"What occupies your thoughts that is of so much importance?"

"Well, I've been tryin' to make it out whar I've seen that woman's face."

"What woman?"

"Why, the Georgia woman — that 'ere Mrs. Gowen."

"And have you solved the difficulty?"

"I think I has."

"Will you give me the information? although, for that matter, I know all about her."

"O! you does, hey? Well, then, 'tain't much use to tell you all I knows; so I'll keep quiet for the present. Besides, I ain't certain, arter all, that I'm jest right."

In spite of all that I could say, the Kentuckian would not open his lips to answer my question; so in silence we returned to the hotel, and separated to dress for dinner, which took place at five o'clock.

CHAPTER VII.

A SUDDEN ATTACK. — A RESCUE. — ON BOARD THE SPITFIRE. — A CAPTURE. — JOHN BULL MAKES A DISCOVERY. — A CHASE. — A RECOGNITION, AND WHAT CAME OF IT.

IN consequence of the disturbance that had occurred during the day, the tables were far from being crowded, some of the brave Southern exiles preferring to take their meals in their own rooms to appearing in the public hall, and encountering the terrible Kentuckian. Miss Rhett was present, as fascinating as ever, and full as liberal of her smiles, while Mrs. Gowen appeared, dressed with exquisite taste, with flowers in her hair, and displaying a pair of shoulders that were faultless in their proportions.

She gave me a smile, and poor crushed Miss Rhett a frown, and then applied all her great talent to the task of mastering the details of her dinner, which I noticed she ate with great relish, while, to aid digestion, she did not scruple to pay frequent attention to a bottle of iced claret that had been placed at her right hand.

I did not have much time to linger over the dessert; for I recollected that I had business to occupy my attention; so, as soon as possible, I left the table; but, as I looked back I saw that Miss Rhett and Mrs. Gowen had their eyes on me, as though suspicious of my movements.

At the bar I shook off Bowmount, having first enticed him to enter into a discussion with an English officer on the relative positions of the North and South. I knew that he would talk, smoke, and drink all night if any one would keep him company; so I felt sure that he would not interfere in my movements; but just as I was passing down the entrance steps, who should come forward, and put his arm through mine, but that abominable wretch, Colonel Rhett!

"I am so glad to have company for an evening walk!" the man said, not taking the least notice of my expression of disgust. "Gently, my friend," he continued; for I had hoped to shake him off by a little rudeness. "You forget that I am lame. That Bull Run wound will follow me to the grave."

We walked on for a moment or two in silence. At length I asked,—

"Have you any particular business with me, Colonel Rhett?"

"No; I don't think I have."

"Will you walk by yourself, and release my arm?"

"Certainly, if you wish it."

But still he retained his hold on my arm, and walked along with me in the most composed and confidential manner.

"Colonel," I said at length, in an abrupt manner, "who in the devil's name are you?"

"Colonel Rhett, at your service, sir."

We walked on in silence towards the beach, where I was to meet Harry and some of the men from the Stingeree. The shades of evening began to fall, and conceal objects that were close to us; yet still the colonel stuck close to me, and I began to suspect a second abduction, so kept my eyes open, and watched all the fellow's movements.

At last I saw Harry and two sailors standing near an overturned boat on the beach; so I strolled towards them, and yet appeared to take no notice of the party.

Still the colonel clung to my arm, and manifested no

intention of relinquishing it. I began to get nervous and angry, wishing the man to the devil.

"Have you an appointment with any one here?" I asked.

"No."

"Then you had better run home, and take care of your health. The dew is falling fast."

"I don't fear it, and I like your company too well to part just at the present time. See; isn't one of the steamers firing up?"

"Yes; I think so."

Just at that moment, four men strolled past us. The colonel gave them a keen glance, and then cried, in a tone that was intended to attract attention, —

"If she is firing up, it is full time."

The men stopped, hesitated for a moment, and then came towards us.

"Yes," cried the colonel, in a peculiar tone, and with a little manifestation of impatience. "It is full time, for the steam is up."

The men continued to edge towards us.

"What in the devil's name is the matter with you?" I asked the colonel. "Can't you keep still for a few moments?"

"My wound," he said, "troubles me. Let me lean on you a little heavier."

He clasped my right arm so tight that I began to suspect the old fellow had more strength than I had given him credit for.

"What are you about?" I asked. "Let go your hold."

"I can't, for it is time," he answered in a loud tone, clinging to my arm with renewed energy.

Just at that moment the four men who had been edging towards us made a rush, and almost before I was aware of the fact, I found that they had piled on to me. One big fellow seized me by the throat, seeming determined to choke the life out of me, while the hero of Bull Run made vigorous efforts to thrust something into my mouth to prevent my calling for help, at the same time clinging to my arm as though he was drowning, and needed considerable assistance.

I struggled desperately; but five to one, all strong men, tells in a short brush; so was not surprised when I found that the assailants had lifted me from my feet, and were throwing me to the ground, so that they could handle me to greater advantage. But by a mighty effort I freed one of my feet from an embrace, and with a force that must have told, planted it in the colonel's stomach, just below his digestive organs.

"O!" he yelled, releasing his hold, and placing both hands where my heel had struck; and he did this while sailing stern first, like a Dutch droger.

But the others did not let me up; and although I struck to the right and left, and inflicted some hard blows, drawing blood and curses at the same time, the four men got the better of me, and down upon the soft sand I was thrown. Then I thought it full time to use my voice, or what there was left of it.

I shook the man's paw from my mouth, and shouted, —
"Harry! to the rescue!"

"Away, boys! away!" the lad shouted, dashing towards me, followed by two of the Stingerees, old Ben being of the number.

They had been watching the struggle since its commencement, and awaited orders. They supposed me to be indulging in a little skylarking with some of my friends, and had no idea that the affair was serious until they heard me call for assistance.

"Board the bloody pirates!" roared old Ben, the master's mate.

And then down upon the scamps they came, and in so

ferocious a mood that the ruffians were compelled to drop me, and look after their own heads, in spite of the old colonel's command to hold on to me at all hazards.

"Whack!" I heard somebody hit; and over went one of the pirates, — a slung-shot in the hands of the master's mate producing the result.

"Down with 'em!" yelled Harry, making a spring at the biggest of the party.

But the fellow dodged, and ran like a hound, the middy after him. In the mean time, the rest of us were not idle. We had pitched in to the right and left, and soon finished the remaining assailants; and then I had time to turn my attention to the Virginia colonel.

The old fellow had seen how the battle ended, and was endeavoring to creep off on his hands and knees; but when he found that it was impossible for him to escape, stopped, and raised a new cry.

"Give it to 'em, Barnwell," he said. "Don't let 'em up. They begun it, and must suffer the consequences."

"Why, you old traitor," I exclaimed, "what do you mean by such conduct?"

"Yes," the old rascal whined. "It's mean enough the way they used you. If I hadn't lost my foothold, I think we two would have beaten them off; don't you?"

As he spoke, he attempted to get upon his feet; but just as he was in a proper position, half stooping and half standing, I raised my foot, and gave him a most unmerciful kick on a not over sensitive part of his body.

He went forward with a lurch, like a foundering ship in a heavy sea, and once more stretched his full length upon the sand. I left him, and went to the scene of the conflict to look over the list of killed and wounded.

By this time Harry had returned, flushed with the exercise of running.

"It is time that we were on the way to the shipping-office," whispered Harry. " Some of our fellows must be there already. We must hurry up, or we shall lose the trick."

" But what shall we do with these loafers ?" growled Ben, pointing to two of the insensible pirates, whose heads had suffered from the effect of a slung-shot.

" Let them alone, and regain their senses the best way they can," I replied. " But as for the leader in this affair, we will take precious good care that he does not trouble us for the third time. Come and look at him."

We went to the spot where I had left the colonel insensible; but he must have regained his senses very soon after I departed; for the old wretch had disappeared, and no trace of him could be found. We spent ten minutes looking over the beach, in hope of running the fellow down, but found that it was a waste of time.

" It is useless to look for the old rat," I said, when the men returned from their unsuccessful search. " He is housed long before this. Now for the shipping-office."

" And here is something to make a tar of you," Harry cried, stopping by a boat that was overturned on the beach, and producing a blue shirt and a pair of duck pants. " I suppose we must keep up appearances. You can leave your shore toggery here till such time as you want to resume it."

In a few minutes I was dressed as a sailor; and then away we rolled towards Bucknor's shipping-office, where we saw some twenty men lounging about the door, as though awaiting the arrival of some one.

On inquiry, we found that Captain Duncan of the Spitfire had not yet arrived; but almost before the information was imparted to us, the master made his appearance; and to my great satisfaction, saw that he had been dining, and had drank more wine than was wholesome for a man about to sail.

"Well, b'ys," said Duncan, with a strong Scotch accent, "ye want to ship in the Spitfire — do ye?"

"Yes, sir," replied the Stingerees with one accord.

As they spoke, they commenced working in pairs towards the master, so that those not in the secret would be pushed to the rear, and stand but a poor chance to be shipped.

"An' ye dinna ken where ye is to go?" asked the master.

"No, sir," was the blunt answer, "and don't care."

"Faith, then ye is the b'ys for me; so come in, and I'll take twenty of ye. And be lively about it; for we must be in blue water afore light in the mornin'."

We crowded into the office, and had the shipping-papers laid before us. By shrewd management, we succeeded in keeping from the documents all those who were not in the secret; but while Ben was looking out for this, we found that the required twenty sailors were booked, and Ben was not among the number.

"There, men," said Captain Duncan, "I have all I want. Now cut stick for the ship as soon as ye loike."

"But," cried Harry, as ready with a yarn as midshipmen usually are, "here's a man that must go. He's my uncle, and a better sailor or gunner never walked a ship's deck."

He pushed Ben towards the table to attract the captain's notice.

"I ha' enough," was the master's answer; "an' ye ken, my boy, that enough is as good as a feast."

"But he's a thorough-built sailor," pleaded Harry.

"There's but little for a sailor to do on board the Spitfire."

"But there's no gunner in the harbor that can compare with him. He served ten years in the English navy."

"That's somethin' in his favor," muttered the master. "Would ye be feared," he continued, addressing Ben, "to crack at one of the Yankee gunboats?"

"I should think not," chuckled Ben. "Jist give me a chance, and you'll see."

"Then I'll take ye," said the captain; "for there's no knowin' what may happen. Can ye write yer name?"

"No, sir."

Most all of the men had confessed that they were unable to sign their names, so that they could the better sustain the characters they had assumed; for it is well known that many of the great mass of foreign sailors cannot read or write, owing to a defective education.

Ben put his fingers to the pen, after the master had made a mark; and then we were informed that we must go on board immediately, as the steamer was to sail in an hour or two, and off we went.

We were pulled to the Spitfire, and mounted the lead-colored sides. At the gangway we were received by the mate — a burly Englishman, who had been drinking quite freely; wishing success to the voyage, probably.

The man had drank too much to notice that we had but little dunnage; so we went to the forecastle, where we found some eight or ten dirty fellows — a cross between coal-heavers and deck hands, without the generous characteristics and neatness of sailors.

They did not welcome us, or show the least sign of pleasure at our appearance. They sat on their chests, and smoked their dirty black pipes, and drank some grog that they had managed to get hold of, without asking us to freshen our nips, or to share the forecastle, like good messmates. In fact, but one of them spoke to us; and he was black and filthy enough for a Jordey.

"Ah!" he muttered, "where does all of these 'ere South Spain boggies come from, — a tumbling in here as if they owned the ship?"

"Where do we come from?" repeated one of the crew of the Stingeree — a splendid specimen of a sailor, broad-shouldered and stout as Hercules. "We come from the shore. Where the devil do you think we come from? Hey?"

He struck the fellow, as he spoke, on the back with the flat of his hand, intended as an introduction; but the blow was so severe that the Jordey was almost knocked off his chest.

"Damn, man, don't do that 'ere," cried the dirty-looking fellow, as he righted himself. "If ye does, we'll ha' a fight."

"Will we?" asked Hercules; and with the utmost coolness he reached over, seized the black bottle that contained the grog, put it to his mouth, took a long swig, and then passed it over to his shipmates, who helped themselves, and returned the empty bottle to the Jordey, who sat sullen and silent, not daring to make an effort to secure the liquor from the hands that had taken it.

Just at this moment Harry whispered to me, —

"The Stingeree is under way, and poking her nose out of the harbor. Shall I make a signal that thus far all is right?"

"Yes; but be careful how you manage it."

"All right, sir."

Harry went on deck, where I followed him, leaving the men to pick out the bunks which each required, and make a great show of stowing away their clothes.

I found that the engineers were getting up steam on the Spitfire. I looked into the engine-room, and saw half a dozen coal-heavers stripped to the waist, and heard an officer, apparently half drunk, giving orders about the machinery. I was satisfied that we should not encounter much opposition in the engine-room, so turned away, and found Harry in the bows of the steamer.

"I made the signal," he whispered, "and the quarter-deck answered it. There's anxious hearts on board the Stingeree just at this time. The captain is more nervous than ourselves, I'll warrant."

"Which is the engineer from the Stingeree?" I asked. "I want to speak with him."

"I'll bring him to you. His name is Clark. He's the third assistant, and a devilish smart fellow. He'll make his way through the world; for he knows all about a boiler and steam, and such things, and thinks more of his engines than he does of the hull of the ship. You shall see him."

Harry returned to the forecastle, and came back with the third assistant — a modest-looking little fellow, with a coal smooch over his eyes as a designating mark. He was full of pluck and ambition, and just such a man as I needed.

I led Mr. Clark and Mr. Reefpoint into the very eyes of the steamer, so that no one should hear us converse, and then asked the former if he was certain that he could take care of the engines, and start them when steam was up.

"If the engines are in order, I can take full charge of them. If they are out of order, which is not at all probable, I can put them in order if you will give me time."

"That is something that I cannot do. We must start to-night, or all is lost."

"Then let us commence operations at once," whispered Harry. "Steam is nearly up, and it is past ten o'clock."

I took a brief glance over the harbor. All was quiet. On board the British steam sloop of war Amazon, the sentry had just struck five bells, and all the blockade-runners in the harbor had followed suit. The last boat had left our ship, and the officers but waited for the master to come on board to give the orders to man the windlass. Most of the crews of the steamers lying near us had gone to sleep, after several noisy fights, the effect of liquor and liberty combined; so that even if we had a slight struggle, it would attract but little attention.

"It is time," I said. "Pass the signal to Ben; and then we will go aft, and operate on the quarter-deck."

Harry went to the house door, and struck three distinct blows with a handspike.

"It is time," he said, and then closed the door, so that no noise could reach the after part of the steamer.

Just at this moment, the third mate came forward to call the hands on deck. We could hear the struggle going on in the forecastle, and knew that, if the officer should notice it, he would raise an alarm.

As the mate passed the foremast, we looked at each other and at the officer.

"It is time," I said, throwing an arm around the mate's throat, garroting him so effectually that not a single cry escaped his lips.

Clark and Harry lent their assistance in holding the man; and when we judged that he would remain quiet for a while, we laid him on deck, stuffed some oakum in his mouth, and lashed his hands behind his back with stout marlin. We had no more than concluded, before one of the crew of the Spitfire dashed off the house door, uttered a wild yell expressive of horror and fear, and then jumped on to the rail of the ship, and went overboard.

"Damnation!" I muttered. "What shall we do now?"

"Do nothing," answered Clark. "Keep quiet, and swear that the man is drunk."

The noise that the man made was sufficient to attract attention; so we were not surprised at hearing the chief mate sing out from the quarter-deck, —

"What's that row there for'ard?"

"One of the new men is overboard," I answered.

"Is he boozy?"

"Yes, sir."

"The cussed fool! Let him stay there till he's sober. He can sink or swim, just which he likes."

When the officer had arrived at this state of feeling, old Ben emerged from the forecastle, looking as anxious as a marine.

"Whar is he?" whispered the master's mate, referring to the fellow who was in the water.

"Overboard."

"Glad of it. Hope the fool will drown, and be d—d to him."

"What did you let him escape for?"

"Cos we didn't know he was in the house. He was a snoozin' in one of the bunks; and, when the row roused him, he makes a rouse, and dives out, and, the fust we knowed of him, he was a turnin' flukes, and pipin' like a landlubber."

"But the rest of the men are secured, are they?"

"Yes; they is all flat on their backs, with pieces of their shirts stuffed in their mouths, and their hands tied, and their eyes lookin' wonderfully astonished at the treatment what they have received."

"Now let us make all secure aft," I said, as soon as Ben had finished his yarn. "Call up the men, and we will proceed to work at once."

The men came on deck obedient to the call, and then we commenced preparations for securing the first and second mates. But, just as we were going aft, the sailor who had jumped overboard, and who was swimming for the shore, found that he had over-estimated his strength, and that he needed help to prevent him from sinking; so he uttered some lusty cries, which could be heard all over the harbor, and which caused us to fear, that, unless the salt water soon filled his mouth, our plans would be discovered, and the project fail.

Even the mate of the Spitfire could not help making an effort to save the poor fellow; so he called from the quarter-deck, —

"Jump into the boat, three or four of you, and pick that man up."

"And bring him on board to have him blab, hey?" muttered Harry. "We don't see it that way."

We made no answer to the summons, and remained quiet.

"D'ye hear?" roared the mate.

"Yes."

"Then move lively; or I'll come for'ard, and help you."

The second mate came towards us; but he had no sooner passed the mainmast, than he was seized, gagged, and thrown helplessly upon the deck.

Once more we waited patiently the next move. It soon came. The chief mate, enraged at the slowness with which his orders were obeyed, came forward, swearing like a sturdy Englishman.

"You lazy hounds!" he said, "I'll start you with a rope's-end if I get among you. I'll stir you up when we git in blue water; you jest see if I don't."

"Bah!"

Some one uttered the bleat in mockery; and it was enough to drive the Englishman mad. To be bleated at like a sheep was more than he could endure, and he sprang angrily towards us; but, before he could use the pin he had snatched from the rail, a dozen strong hands were laid on him, and the man was a prisoner almost before he was aware of what had happened to him.

"I'll murder some of you for this," the mate muttered.

But these were the last words he uttered for some time; for, as he opened his mouth, a quantity of oakum was thrust in, and his speech stopped.

The man's limbs were lashed together; and then he and his brother officers were thrown into the house, and two men placed as guard over the whole party, while the rest of us proceeded aft to search the cabin, and the engineer went below to secure the firemen and those who had charge of the machinery.

All this was accomplished in a short time, and the vessel was ours — unlawfully, I will admit; for we had no legal right to capture even a pirate in Nassau; but still, right or wrong, we had possession; and that was something. But hardly had we congratulated each other on what we had accomplished, before we heard the sound of oars; and the next moment a boat touched the side, and up the steps came the master of the steamer, followed closely by some half a dozen or more passengers.

"Gentlemen," said the master, speaking to the passengers, "the stewards will show you your state-rooms in case you want to stow away your traps. We shall be under way in half an hour. Mr. Fid, is the steam up?"

"Yes, sir," I answered, giving as beery a tone to my voice as possible, in imitation of the mate.

"Then man the windlass immediately."

The passengers had entered the cabin, following two of the men, who represented stewards, the night being so dark that it was impossible to distinguish them a fathom distant.

Mr. Reefpoint and Ben looked to me for the next move. For a moment I hesitated, but the next I gave the signal. The master of the steamer had turned his back to us, and was about to enter the cabin, when an arm was thrown around his neck, and strong hands seized his limbs. He was a stout fellow, and made good use of his arms; but numbers were too much for him, and down to the deck he went, uttering, as he fell, one wild cry for help. Then all was silent.

"What's the row?" asked a familiar voice, as a head was protruded through the open cabin door.

It was my old friend Colonel Rhett, with whom I had a long score to settle. The treacherous scoundrel had come on board with the master, but for what purpose I was at a loss to understand.

"What's the row?" repeated the colonel, stepping on deck.

He could not see us distinctly, on account of the darkness, and also because he had just come from the light. In asking the question, he put his face close to mine, as though determined to see who I was. It was not my purpose that the man should see me on board the Spitfire; so, to prevent it in a measure, I just hit him on one of his eyes; and down he went, all in a heap.

"Murder!" yelled the old villain. "Mutiny! murder!"

We soon had the fellow's mouth stuffed with oakum, and his hands secured behind his back; and we were none too quick in doing the work; for hardly had we stowed away our prisoners in the cabin, than we heard the long, steady strokes of men-of-war as they dipped their oars in the water, and urged a cutter over the bay.

"The devil!" growled old Ben. "Here's a pretty mess of fish for us to cook. A boat from that d—d John Bull is pulling towards us. What shall we do?"

"Do?" repeated Harry, with the boldness of a lion. "Why, take 'em prisoners, and carry 'em to sea. That's what we can do."

"That's spoken like a boy," said the old salt, with a sneer. "No able seaman would give such advice as that."

"I give such advice as I think would be beneficial in an emergency like this," cried the midshipman, with a haughty gesture.

Old Ben was about to make a cutting remark; but I stopped him.

"Avast," I said. "This is no time for yarning. All now depends on coolness. A single mistake, and we are lost."

"Give your orders, sir, and we is ready to obey 'em," remarked Ben, with a snap of his strong teeth through a plug of tobacco.

I glanced over the rail, and saw that an eight-oared cutter was near us, and bound to come alongside. An officer had undoubtedly been sent to the Spitfire to investigate the cause of the loud cries which had been heard all over the harbor.

"There is no occasion for alarm," I said to my subordinates. "The ship is not yet lost, and will not be if you keep your weather eyes open. Go forward, Harry, and see that the men man the windlass. Ben, look to the cabin, and the prisoners there. Tell those who are stationed over them to crack their skulls if the least noise is made. All must be quiet, although I don't care if the crew forward do get up a smart row, just to show that they have been bowsing up their jibs rather lively. Now, then, away you go to your duties. Set the men to work, and then return aft. Be lively and cautious."

I spoke in a tone of assumed confidence for the sake of assuring the two officers that there was no danger; but I did not feel at ease, by any means; and, when the cutter came alongside, I would have sold out my share of the prize-money of the Spitfire at a very small sum. As the boat touched the paddle-wheel, an officer seized the man-ropes, and came on deck, followed by four of his men; and I noticed that all of them were armed.

"Where is the master of this steamer?" demanded the officer — a lieutenant, I judged.

"You are addressing him, sir," I answered in a quick, curt tone, just to show John Bull that I did not tremble at the sound of his voice.

"You have had considerable noise on board, sir," the officer remarked. "What is the meaning of it?"

"I should suppose that you had been in Nassau long enough to know that the liquor which is sold to seamen, by the sharks on shore, is fighting proof."

"Yes; I am aware of it."

"Then there is no reason for me to explain that some of my men are drunk, and have had several knock-downs during the evening."

The officer turned to one of his men, and said,—

"Send that man on deck."

What man did he mean? I had not the least idea; so, while the command was being obeyed, I pretended to be occupied with matters that related to the ship. In a minute or two, over the rail crawled a dirty-looking sailor, who seemed to have been soaked in water, and then wrung out to dry.

"Do you recognize this man?" asked the lieutenant, turning to me, and holding up a lantern.

"Perhaps I should if some of the dirt was washed from his face," I answered, wondering what he was driving at.

"Tell your story, Bobbins," commanded the officer, as though he was not to be trifled with.

"Vell, yer 'onor, I vos down below, and had beaten my supper, and vos a smokin' of my pipe, ven a lot of coves comes in the forecastle, and they takes the grog out of our mouths, and then punches our heads, and puts marlin on our 'ands. I seed it all, and I jist cuts and runs, and jumps overboard, and I should have been drownded if it vos not for the boat vos picks me up."

"You hear the story, sir," remarked the lieutenant, in a tone that showed he wanted an explanation.

"Yes; I hear it. Have a cigar? It's one I brought from Havana, and a fair one. Steward, a light. Yes; I hear the man's story, and I'm sorry you picked up the drunken cuss. He had ought to have sunk in the harbor, and remained there. Blast him! he's given me enough trouble already."

"Vy, this ha'n't the skipper of the steamer!" cried the sailor, quite dismayed at the manner in which I talked about him.

I did not pretend to notice the remark, but continued, —

"Ever since the fellow has been on board, he has been drunk and quarrelsome. In fact, two thirds of my men have been drinking and fighting, so that at times I have had to employ all the sober ones to take care of those intoxicated. Such a crew I never saw before. Just come and look at the rascals."

Now, if the lieutenant had taken me at my word, all would have been lost: for the true state of the case would have been discovered; but the officer had seen enough drunken men not to desire to look at a fresh lot; so he excused himself, and declined to enter the forecastle.

"I tells you I vos sober as I'm now sober," cried the sailor, who was somewhat excited at my yarn.

"You are sober now, I hope," I answered in a severe tone. "If you are not, I'll find a way to sober you when we are outside. Go forward, and man the windlass. Mr. Swivel," speaking to old Ben, who was within hearing, "see that this man is set to work. If he don't stir his stumps, lay a rope's-end over his back."

"Ay, ay, sir," was the answer; and before the cockney could recover from his astonishment, or the lieutenant remonstrate, the fellow was bundled forward, and placed at the breaks of the windlass.

So far we had succeeded to perfection; but, just as the officer was about to leave the deck, some one confined in a state-room got the gag from his mouth, and shouted, —

"Help! murder!"

The lieutenant started, and seemed a little surprised. Then he listened most attentively; but no other sound greeted his ears.

"What is the meaning of that cry?" asked the officer.

Before I could answer, Harry approached, and said, —

"Captain, the crazy man is awake, and is as violent as ever."

"A crazy man on board?" asked the lieutenant.

"Yes," I answered, with a cool lie. "One of the passengers lost all he was worth by the capture of a blockade-runner. His friends are sending him home, where he can be taken care of; for, since he lost his fortune, he has also lost his reason."

"Ah! a hard case. He has cause to curse the Yankees. Is he violent?"

"At times. When he sees a person whom he suspects of being a Yankee, his ravings are shocking. I wish that he was on board of some other vessel, for it's not pleasant to have the company of a lunatic."

"I agree with you. Can I look at the poor fellow?"

Now it struck me that the officer made the inquiry in a sarcastic manner, just as though he did not believe me: so I was at my wit's end to substantiate my word. If I refused to exhibit the lunatic that I had spoken of, the officer would insist upon entering the cabin, and searching; in which case the game was up, and we were all prisoners for breach of neutrality. But, while I was hesitating, Harry touched my hand, and whispered, so that none but I could hear, —

"It's all right. Let him enter."

"You seem to have some objections to my looking at your patient," the British officer remarked.

"O, no! But I was thinking that the sight of your uniform might injure the lunatic. Come, sir, and see how the Yankees are hated."

We followed Harry to the cabin. All was quiet, and the doors of the state-rooms were closed, so that no slight sound could escape from them. A dim light burned in the centre of the cabin, and threw its feeble rays on one or two men who acted the part of stewards or jailers, sailors or fighters. They started up as we entered, but, on a sign, appeared to take no further interest in our movements.

"This is the state-room, sir, that the poor fellow is confined in," said Harry, as he opened a door.

The room was dark; but no sooner was the door opened, than the most frightful oaths greeted our ears.

"O, you cussed Yankees!" howled the poor fellow. "Capture my vessel, will you? All cotton, and lots of money to be made running the blockade. Ha, ha! I'll cheat 'em yet. All's lost. They've got her. One, two, three. Three shots, and all miss. Up with the steam. Pile on tar and rosin. We must out-steam the Yankee. He don't gain on us. Now, then, one more mile, and we shall be under the guns of the fort. Bang! We are hit. All's lost."

A loud, wailing cry closed the rambling remarks. The lieutenant had heard enough. He retreated in some haste.

"Won't you have a light, and look at the men?" I asked.

"No, no; I've seen enough. What misery this civil war has produced!"

"Yes; and we are not to blame for it. The Yankees forced it on us. We wanted peace."

"So you did, and you will have it if you fight but a little while longer. The Yankees are about tired of it."

"Let me out of this. Help!" roared one of our prisoners, who had removed the gag from his mouth.

"Poor fellow! I shall have trouble with him before we reach Wilmington," I remarked, as we reached the cabin door.

The officer seemed to notice that the voice was a little different; but he appeared to think that it was the effect of lunacy. I must confess that I felt relieved when we once more reached the deck, and Ben came to me, and reported that the anchor was clear of the bottom.

I touched the bell to let on steam — a strong hint for the lieutenant to take his departure; but just at this moment the Englishman laid his hand on my arm, and said, —

"It won't do, Mr. Yankee. Run the ship under the guns of Her Majesty's ship. The trick was well planned, but it has failed."

The Englishman had discovered who we were, and all seemed lost.

"Yes," said the lieutenant, after a significant pause. "Your Yankee trick won't go down this time. I suspected you all along, but thought I'd wait and see how far you would go in your peculiar business. It was well played, Mr. Yankee; but John Bull is fully as sharp as you are. Run the steamer under the guns of the Amazon."

"You have won," I said, more for the purpose of gaining time than anything else. "I thought that I had a sure thing; but it seems that I had not. You Englishmen are smarter than I gave you credit for being."

The Briton chuckled, and assumed important airs immediately.

"Yes," he said; "we are the boldest and most venturesome race in the world. There is nothing we do not dare to undertake, however reckless."

"Yet I doubt if you would have undertaken such a job as this."

I tried to laugh as I spoke; but the effort was not successful.

"Pooh! this is nothing compared to what a Briton is

capable of doing. If we were at war with you Yankees, not a ship in your harbors would be safe from our boats. We should cut them out, sir. We could do it, and we should, sir."

Suddenly, while I was listening to the Englishman's blast of complacency, a mouth was placed close to my ear, and a whisper said, —

"Keep him yarning as long as possible. There is yet hope."

It was Harry's voice. He had stolen aft in the dark, and communicated with me without the least suspicion on the part of the lieutenant, who was leaning against the fife-rail, smoking a cigar, and boasting of his smartness.

"Come," I said, "and take a glass of something. We have time enough, for we shan't be under the guns of the ship for some time."

But the fellow fought shy on the liquor question, fearing some Yankee trick.

"No," he said. "I shall remain on deck until the steamer is anchored under the guns of the Amazon. No Yankee tricks on me, Mr. Violator of Neutrality."

As he spoke, I saw two of his men leave the cutter that was alongside near the steps of the wheel-house, and pass forward.

"You are still suspicious of us," I remarked for the purpose of continuing the conversation, glad that the lieutenant saw nothing.

"Yes; I have to keep a weather eye open for people of your stripe."

Two more of the cutter's crew passed over the rail, and walked forward.

"I am sorry that you don't feel confidence in us," I remarked. "What can we do to inspire it?"

"Jump overboard," was the insulting answer. "Such people as you ain't much better than pirates."

Two more of the English sailors came up the steps, and jumped to the deck. They were careless, and made so much noise that the lieutenant's attention was attracted.

"Hollo!" he said, as soon as he saw the men. "What are you doing on deck? Go back to the boat, and don't you leave it again till I order you to."

To my surprise and the lieutenant's consternation, the men made no answer. They merely hesitated for a moment, and then walked forward.

"By St. George!" exclaimed the enraged lieutenant; "but I won't stand such damned insolence. Come back, you beggars; or I'll make you."

He started to follow the men; but they disappeared in the darkness, and the baffled officer returned aft, and looked eagerly over the rail into the boat.

"Brown! Jones! Riley!" he cried.

There was no answer.

"Hollo!" he continued impatiently. "Are you all asleep?"

Still there was no response to the officer's demand.

"If I come down there," he cried, getting decidedly angry, "you will talk and walk rather lively."

No attention was paid to the threat. This surprised me; for I certainly supposed there was at least one man in the boat.

The lieutenant could endure no more. He sprang to the rail, and went quickly down the side steps.

No sooner had he disappeared, than Harry touched me on the arm; and turning, I saw the youngster with a broad grin on his mischievous face.

"It's all right, sir," he said. "We have 'em, sure."

"What do you mean?"

"I mean that we have played them another Yankee trick, and that the steamer is still in our possession."

"Explain. And be lively about it; for the Englishman is cursing like a pirate, and will soon be on deck."

"Well," said Harry, "we enticed the fellows forward on the plea of having a drink; and after they had swallowed about a gallon of whiskey, it was not hard to put them under hatches, where they are, safe and sound."

"And now we must deal with the lieutenant," said I, in a low tone. "Hark! here he comes, tearing mad."

"What is the meaning of this?" roared the Briton as he touched the deck. "My men are all gone."

"It means that you are a prisoner. Give up your pistols and sword."

The officer started back, and laid a hand on a pistol; but old Ben and Harry clapped their paws on him, and held him fast, in spite of struggles and oaths.

"Do you dare to lay your hands on me?" demanded the Briton.

"Yes, and shall keep them on unless you are civil. Realize your situation. You are a prisoner for the present. Resistance is useless; so don't compel us to be rough."

I stepped to the tube that connected with the engineer's room, and gave orders to go ahead at moderate speed.

While I was speaking with the engineer, the lieutenant broke away from Ben and Harry, and ran aft, and before we could prevent him, had hailed the Amazon, which was lying about a cable's length from us.

"Amazon, ahoy!" he cried; but before he could utter another word, Ben's huge hand was upon his throat, and for a time his breath was stopped.

"Hollo!" came the answer back from the sloop of war.

I knew that some answer must be returned, or suspicion would be excited. There was no time to lose. Imitating, as well as I was able, the Englishman's voice, I shouted, —

"The steamer is all right, and will proceed."

"Very well," came back in surly tones, as though the officer of the deck wondered what in the devil's name was the use of hailing to convey such information.

"You shall suffer for this," our prisoner gasped, as soon as he could recover his breath.

"Perhaps we shall; but we will take good care that you keep quiet, nevertheless."

All this time we were slowly leaving the harbor and vessels astern of us. We were steaming along at the rate of five knots an hour,—just such a rate as would not attract attention, or make the officers of the Amazon think that we were over-anxious to leave their company,—and just as we supposed we were all clear, the dull report of a gun from the spar-deck of the gunboat startled us.

"What does that mean, Ben?" I asked; for the old master's mate stood near me, helping me pilot the steamer out of the harbor.

"It looks like a signal to get under way, sir, and a recall of the cutter at the same time. We had better turn the officer loose, and let him shift for himself in the boat."

"But the crew who accompanied him. What shall we do with them?"

"Let 'em be on board, sir. They is all asleep, primed with whiskey; and it would be a pity to disturb 'em. When they wakes up, they will be satisfied, I'll warrant you."

We disarmed the lieutenant, and in spite of his remonstrances, made him enter the cutter, and then cast off the painter, and the boat dropped astern.

"Give our love to your shipmates," I said. "The next time you want to get ahead of the Yankees, you must look out for their tricks."

He cursed us in great shape, and the last thing that we

heard was a solemn, vow to overhaul and sink us before we got clear of the shoals.

"Now, then, what will you do?" asked Ben, as the cutter disappeared from sight. "Can't you go along with us?"

"No, Ben," I said. "I can't go with you just at present. I must return to the shore, and thus save myself from suspicion. You know what to do with the steamer as well as I. Keep on until you sight the Stingeree. She is lying near Hog Island, somewhere, on the watch. Steam on until you are out of neutral waters. Then a round shot or a blank cartridge can stop you. But above all things, don't let the Bull Dog overhaul you. Burst the boiler before you permit such a thing."

The steam was shut off, the dingey hauled up, and once more I shook hands with the officers, and then descended the side.

Just at that moment I heard the discharge of a gun, and saw by the flash that it came from the English sloop of war.

"Clap on steam," I shouted. "The Bull Dog is after you."

"Ay, ay; but he must catch us afore he crows too much!" growled Ben; and with the words the painter was cast off, and away the steamer went at the rate of twelve miles an hour.

"A stern chase is a long chase," I muttered, as I lay on my oars, and followed the course of the two vessels. Then, recollecting that the hour was late, I once more applied myself to work, and pulled in shore, working along the beach until I gained a good landing. After stepping from the boat, I gave it a shove, and sent it out into the tide-way, where it met the current, and drifted seaward, thus destroying all evidence of my complicity with the seizure.

When I set foot on land, it was about eleven o'clock, and all was quiet on the beach. I met but few persons as I walked towards the town; and none of those spoke to me, for the reason that I was dressed in the garb of a sailor, and did not present a very promising aspect to those who made Nassau their headquarters, and who would have hanged me like a dog if they had known the business in which I had been engaged but an hour before.

When I reached the hotel, I found that about all the guests had retired for the night, so that no one noticed me as I stole up stairs, and went to bed, tired with the fatigues and adventures of the day.

I dreamed of Englishmen, blockade-runners, Mrs. Gowen, Hatty Blank, Colonel Rhett, and the amiable daughter of that Virginia hero; until the gong sounded for breakfast, and down to the dining-room the guests flocked, eager for their coffee and fresh fish.

On the stairs Bowmount seized my arm.

"Wan't I a little tight last night when I went to bed?" he asked.

He didn't know of my absence from the hotel during the evening, it seemed, by the question.

"Well, you were a little over the bay," I remarked.

"But not noisy, you know. I wasn't in an argufying mood, now was I?"

"No; I think not. You seemed to enjoy your liquor in a rational way, and didn't want to fight but one man during the evening."

This was a guess on my part, and it seemed that I was correct; for the Kentuckian said in an apologetic manner, —

"But, ye see, the fellow would run down the Yankees, and I kept tellin' him to stop. A man what drinks my whiskey, and don't agree with me, had better cut than stay round and kick up a row with a peaceable man like me. I told the bloody fool to stop ; but he wouldn't. But you seed it all, and knows that I wasn't to blame ; now don't you?"

"Not so much as you are sometimes. But no harm was done."

"No. Shucks ! didn't the coward run and leave us ?"

I pretended to acquiesce in this statement, for the reason that I might want the Kentuckian as a witness to prove that I was in his company all the evening, in case any one should assert I was on a "cutting-out" expedition the night before. Little did I think, when such thoughts passed through my mind, that I should need just such assistance, before long, as Bowmount could render.

We sat down to the table, Bowmount on my right, and a fat little fellow from Charleston on my left. He had escaped from South Carolina to avoid the conscription ; although, according to his own story, he was helping his government by picking up items that would be beneficial to all concerned.

Just opposite to me was a vacant chair, and I hoped that Miss Rhett or Mrs. Gowen would take possession of it. But neither lady liked the location ; so they gave it a wide berth, when they saw the Kentuckian.

I had just ordered my breakfast, and was sipping my coffee to see if it was to my taste, when some one entered the dining-room, and took the vacant chair. As he made considerable noise in seating himself, some attention was attracted ; and in looking up, I saw, to my surprise, that it was the English naval officer who had boarded the Spitfire the night before, and who had been turned adrift in his own boat, after he thought he had matters his own way.

There was a peculiar feeling in the region of my heart when I realized how near I was to danger. But it was only for a moment. I soon regained all of my coolness, and awaited an attack with becoming resignation, and faith in my supreme impudence to repel it.

The storm burst in less time than I had anticipated.

The naval officer had just sweetened his coffee and taken one glance around the table, when his eyes fell on my face.

I could hear him breathe hard as the fact became impressed upon his mind that I was the same person who had played him such a Yankee trick the night before.

In the mean time I had assumed one of my most indifferent looks, and appeared to be eating my breakfast as though I enjoyed it, while I pleasantly chatted with the Kentuckian and the little fat Charleston fellow, who was only too glad to have me notice him.

"I beg your pardon, sir," said the Englishman, speaking across the table, and turning very red in the face, while he breathed as though laboring with an asthma.

"Did you speak to me, sir?" I asked. looking at the victim in an inquiring manner, as though surprised at being addressed.

"Yes, sir; I did."

"O! Well, what do you require?"

"When did you come on shore?" asked the Englishman.

"Let me see; when did we land here, Bowmount?"

I turned to the Kentuckian as though I had forgotten the day.

"Two weeks ago yesterday."

"So it was. Do you hear, sir?"

"I mean, sir, at what hour did you land this morning from the Spitfire?"

I looked at the Kentuckian as though demanding an explanation.

"What the deuce does he mean?" I remarked.

"Cuss me if I know. Throw a cup at his head, and see if it won't bring him to his senses."

This was said in a whisper. I did not follow the advice, for the time had not yet arrived for honest indignation.

"My meaning, sir," said the lieutenant, in as calm a tone as he could assume, considering the importance of the accusation, " is quite simple to a man of your sharpness."

"Do you intend to cast any reflections on me, sir?"

"I simply want an understanding, sir."

"Well, sir, you can have it; only be lively about it; for I want to eat my breakfast in peace."

"Did you ever see me before, sir?" demanded the Englishman.

"I should think not, and you will excuse me if I add that I have no desire to see you again."

Some of the people at the table, who heard the answer, laughed quite heartily, and among them was the little fat fellow from Charleston. It seemed as though he would choke, he appeared so pleased.

"It is useless to return any such answers to me, sir, because I know you."

"That's more than he does himself when he has finished six whiskey-punches," put in Bowmount with a growl, that produced another laugh; but the naval officer did not smile. The subject was too serious for him to exhibit much mirth.

"What have you on your mind?" I asked, as soon as the laugh had somewhat subsided. "Come; speak plainly, and let me know."

"Were you on board the blockade-runner Spitfire last night?"

"No; were you?"

The lieutenant did not relish the answer; for he raised his voice, as he said, —

"You can't deceive me. I recognized you. You were

on board the Spitfire last night, and helped capture her in the harbor, and set me adrift in a boat after getting my men drunk."

"O Lord! but that must have been a Yankee trick," roared Bowmount. " Cuss 'em! they is capable of most anything. We isn't safe in our beds. Afore we knows it, they'll hitch on to this bloody island, and tow us in one of their harbors; and then we shall wake up prisoners in Fort Warren, or some other place. If the English ain't no cuter than they has shown themselves, they won't have a ship left by the time the war has finished. Shucks! but I wish it was John Bull we was fighting, instead of our own flesh and blood."

This remark was followed by a slight hiss from some of the Southerners; and the sound excited the Kentuckian, as I knew it would. In an instant he began to grow ugly.

"This bluster won't turn me aside," remarked the officer. "I know both of you now. You each performed a part on board the Spitfire. Both of you are pirates."

Before he had a chance to utter another word, Bowmount had hurled coffee-cup, saucer, and hot coffee, full at the head of the Englishman; and all three of the articles struck where they were aimed.

The naval officer was rather surprised at being saluted in the manner that Bowmount had chosen to adopt.

His first attempt was to clear the coffee from his eyes, and to brush the crockery ware from his hair; and after he had performed those operations, he turned to Bowmount, and in a voice that was tremendous with rage, said, —

"You and your friend shall suffer for this. I know both of you."

"Well, I'm d—d sorry for the information; for I don't want your acquaintance. I'm particular on that p'int if I ain't on others."

"You've committed a gross outrage, sir, and shall suffer for it. I'm in her majesty's navy, sir."

"Shucks! I don't care if you is in it or out of it. In Old Kaintuck, we settle such things in short order. There is few words; and what there is of 'em, is sharp, and to the p'int. You will know where to find me when you wants to see me."

"Mr. Bowmount," I said in a firm tone, "I shan't allow this to go any further. If there is any quarrel, this gentleman and I must be allowed to settle it."

"No you don't," was the reply. "I hain't had a real fancy fight since I left Kaintuck, and I don't mean to be disappinted now."

As we passed out of the dining-room, Mrs. Gowen stood in the door of the ladies' parlor, and beckoned to me.

I entered the apartment, and the lady led me to the farther end of the room, and said in a low tone, —

"You must leave the island. If you remain here another day, you will be arrested and imprisoned. Do not delay, but go at once. You have no time to lose."

"Who is to arrest me?"

"The British officer whom you quarrelled with a moment since."

"I didn't quarrel with him. Bowmount was the one."

"No matter for that. Both of you are marked for imprisonment. I overheard the officer tell another Englishman that he was going to lodge a complaint against both of you for being concerned in the cutting out of the Spitfire."

"I only laugh such an absurd accusation to scorn."

"But there is trouble in the charge. Go you must. I shall go with you. I have business in Georgia. My husband can remain here, and look after his affairs."

Just at this moment, into the parlor came Bowmount.

"Shucks, Barnwell!" he said; "but they is arter us,

and no mistake. What do you think they accuse us of? Of piracy. That Britisher says we is on it. I call it cussed uncivil to talk that way about a man what is engaged to fight a duel with yer; now ain't it?"

"It is hard."

"Yes; and what is worse, I don't believe the feller will see me. I has just been told to run for it, 'cos they is goin' to take us both for cuttin' out the Spitfire. It's little we knows about her. Cuss the chap! if I gets a crack at him, I'll make him feel it for life; now you see if I don't."

"But what shall we do?" I asked. "If we remain, and are arrested, who will go bail for us?"

"Hang me if I know. I s'pose the fellers would be glad to see me under lock and key out of their sight."

"Yes; but as far as the Spitfire is concerned, we can prove that we know nothing about her. But the question is, will they listen to us until they get ready to hear what we have got to say?"

"Of course they won't," muttered Bowmount, perplexed.

"Then don't remain here," cried Mrs. Gowen, with all the nervous excitement of a Southern woman. "Leave Nassau as soon as possible. A steamer sails at noon."

"Yes," slowly muttered the Kentuckian; "we can go in her jest as well as not, 'cos half of her belongs to me."

"Why, I didn't know that you had been speculating," I remarked, in a somewhat surprised tone.

"'Cos I wanted to startle yer. While ye thought I was drunk, and full of fight, I was at work. Yes, sir; I owns half of the steamer, and most of the cargo. She's called the Belle, and she's purty enough to be called so."

"Is she fast?" I asked, as I thought of the Stingeree.

"Wal, I don't think the Yanks has anything in their navy that will touch her. But keep mum. I has a plan to propose. I wants a captain for my steamer. The one what I had is down with some kind of sickness. You must go and take charge of her."

"Perhaps Mr. Barnwell is not quite proficient enough to take charge of a steamer," the lady remarked, in a tone that was intended to be kind; but I thought it a little sarcastic.

"Don't you believe all that," was the reply of Bowmount. "He knows all about a ship. Weren't we passengers together, and didn't he tell what I didn't know about? I ain't afeared to trust him with my vessel, I ain't. If he says he'll go, we'll give 'em the slip in no time; and afore they opens their eyes, we'll be out of sight."

I still hesitated, but the Kentuckian continued: —

"If we gets in all safe, it puts ten thousand dollars in gold in your pocket, and a hundred thousand in mine. There's risks to run, but we can't make money without some venture."

There was no way that I could escape without enraging the Kentuckian, and endangering my own safety; so after a moment's more reflection, and thinking what excuse I could offer to the navy department, I agreed to take charge of the steamer, and try a trip to Charleston, which I knew was pretty closely blockaded, and therefore capture, I was almost certain, would follow.

"I take all the risks," the Kentuckian said. "If we is took, there's so much money out of our pockets. If we is lucky, there is so much money in. Pack up, and pay your bills, and then go on board. As for me, I must steal off the best way I can."

"Leave me to take care of your baggage," said Mrs. Gowen. "I will bring it off with me."

"Then you insist upon being a passenger?" I asked.

"Yes; I must go to Georgia. I am needed there."

"A state-room is at your service," Bowmount said.

He did not appear in the least surprised at the determination.

"Your husband will remain here, will he?" was the only question asked.

"He will."

"Then I will leave you to see that our traps is on board, while I tends to other things. You see we ain't no time to lose."

The Kentuckian pointed out of the window. Coming up the gravel walk, we saw six police officers, and at their head marched the naval officer whose face had been baptized in coffee.

"I think I could lick 'em all," growled the Kentuckian, as he rested his hand on the formidable bowie-knife that reposed in his bosom. "Is it best to tackle 'em?"

"No. Discretion is the better part of valor just at present. Mrs. Gowen, will you be kind enough to pay our bills? We must leave."

Bowmount leaped from the piazza to the ground, and I followed.

We met no one belonging to the hotel until we were near the street that led to the harbor. Then we came plump upon Soulé, with a despatch-box under his arm.

"Where are you fellows going?" he asked.

"Not far."

"Then I will join you. I want to put these despatches for the confederate government on board a steamer that is to sail in a day or two."

"Do you mean the Belle?" Bowmount asked.

"Yes."

"Hand them here. Don't say a word, but we are going on board that steamer. Don't mention that you have seen us."

The Kentuckian snatched the box from the spy's hand,

and walked off before the fellow knew what to think of the matter.

"We don't want him poking along with us," Bowmount said; and Soulé appeared to think the same thing, for he stood looking after us for a moment, and then walked towards the nearest billiard-saloon, to compose his feelings by knocking about the balls.

We found one of the steamer's boats at the mole; and without waiting a moment tumbled in, and ordered the men to pull us on board.

Luckily the sailors knew Bowmount as one of the new owners of the Belle; so they made no objection to obeying orders.

As we pulled past the English sloop of war Amazon, the companion steamer to the Bull Dog, we turned away our heads to prevent the officers on the quarter-deck from recognizing us, as they would have done had they seen our faces.

In a few moments the boat was alongside the blockade-runner, and I had a fair view of my charge. She was a snaky-looking craft, painted lead color, set low in the water, with a stem like a razor, and run like a yacht. She had paddle-wheels, and was rigged like a brig forward and schooner aft, with patent caps and fids to her masts, so that they could be housed in ten minutes in case of a head wind, or if it was necessary to make as little display of top-gear as possible.

We went forward, and found two ten-pound Whitworth guns and several small swivels secured to the rail; but they were evidently more for show than use, as the Belle meant to show her heels to a foe, and not her teeth.

The cabin was small, but neat, with six good-sized state-rooms, and one for the master, which was extra large, and lumbered with charts and all the instruments needed to define a ship's position at sea or near the shore. From the cabin we went to the engine-room, where Bowmount introduced to me the engineers, both of them natives of New York. Smart-looking fellows they were; but it was evident that they thought more of gold than they did of the country that claimed them.

"I found 'em in Nassau, and took 'em in preference to Englishmen," whispered Bowmount. "They'll keep up steam, or bust the darned b'ilers; you see if they don't."

"Are they to be trusted? Are you sure of them?"

"Yes; 'cos they have made two trips already, and piled up the profits, now I tell you."

I was compelled to believe the men honest as far as their work was concerned.

"Now let me tell you one thing," said the Kentuckian, as we returned to the cabin, after seeing that fires were started under the boilers. "I has put my all in this venture. I bought out the captain's half, ship and cargo, and paid him the cash for 'em — in gold, Barnwell; all in gold. If we gets her through, I shall make something handsome. If I returns with cotton, a fortune is mine, and I need run no more risks."

"But what does the cargo consist of?"

"O, arms, cloth, and some other things what will sell, and be useful to the confederates."

I could hardly prevent groaning at the position in which I found myself. I did not want to ruin a man who placed so much confidence in me, and yet I did not like betraying my country.

"What's the matter?" asked the Kentuckian, who noticed that I looked thoughtful.

"Nothing; but I am sorry that you have placed all your eggs in one basket."

"But, if they should hatch, I shall have some glorious chickens."

"Yes," I sighed; "if you are successful, the chickens may pay you for your trouble."

"Well, Barnwell,"—and the man extended his heavy, dark hand,—"I trust to you. Do the best you can for me, and you shan't lose anything."

"Yes; I'll do the best I can for you," I answered, determined to trust to luck, and stand by him.

Just at that moment the mate put his head in the cabin, and said that a lady was coming alongside. I went on deck, and saw that it was Mrs. Gowen, and her mulatto servant John.

"Shall we move as soon as steam is up?" I asked Bowmount, who came on deck to see what was going on.

"Yes; I'm all ready. Let her rip when you are."

I gave the order to man the windlass, and in a short time the chain was all in, the anchor catted, and the Belle steaming out of the harbor.

CHAPTER VIII.

AT SEA. — A STRANGE STEAMER. — COLONEL RHETT TURNS UP AGAIN. — HIS STORY. — A STERN CHASE. — A RUN FOR CHARLESTON. — RUNNING THE BLOCKADE. — THE SIGNALS. — A HAIL. — A CLOSE SHAVE. — A RUSE. — MAKING SIGNALS. — A CROSS ADMIRAL. — COLONEL RHETT AGAIN IN TROUBLE. — INSULTING AN ADMIRAL. — COLONEL RHETT EXPLAINS. — AN INVITATION, AND WHAT CAME OF IT.

DURING the evening, Mrs. Gowen, who had kept close to her state-room, came on deck to inhale the cool air, and enjoy a few moments' conversation with the master of the vessel. The instant Bowmount saw her, he prepared to sheer off, and give her quiet possession of the quarter-deck; but I saw his intended movement, and stopped him.

"Why do you crowd on sail, and run for a harbor, the instant that lady shows her signals?" I asked.

"Because," was the blunt answer, "she don't care for me. Yer see I ain't gentle enough to suit a woman like her; so we had better keep a good ways apart."

"But recollect you have not told me the mystery connected with the lady."

"Hain't I?"

I thought the man showed an inclination to chuckle.

"No," I said, decidedly. "You know that you have not."

"Well, the time hasn't arrived yet for me to open my mouth. You is contented as you is; and what's the use of yer tryin' to pry into darkness?"

Then, with a laugh that sounded a little malicious, the Kentuckian walked to the waist of the steamer, and looked out upon the waters, which sparkled like myriads of diamonds in a carpet of green.

Mrs. Gowen was assisted to the poop-deck by her servant John, the light mulatto, who seemed as attentive as a lover, and as careful as a father. She took a seat on a hencoop, and then dismissed the slave. The fellow left the quarter-deck rather reluctantly; and I thought he cast an ominous look at me as he did so, as though I was the cause of his misfortune in being separated from a beloved mistress.

"You have managed to keep yourself secluded during the day," I remarked, taking a seat by her side.

"I had a motive in not appearing on deck, Barnwell."

"Will you confide it to me?"

"Yes; because I trust you. Has Mr. Bowmount told you one word concerning me, past or present?"

"Not a syllable has he lisped respecting you or your welfare."

She seemed to utter a sigh of relief.

"Yet you have spoken to him about me?"

"Yes, several times. But he shakes his head, and the conversation ends."

"I had no idea that men had so much curiosity."

A little later Mrs. Gowen returned to the cabin. I remained on deck until past twelve; and then, finding that the night was clear and calm, and that nothing was in sight except sand-keys, I retired, and went to sleep, and was not disturbed till morning. Then the mate touched me on the shoulder, and I was awake in an instant.

"Beg pardon, sir, for disturbin' yer afore six bells; but there's a steamer jist off our starboard-bow."

"Ah! What does it look like?"

"A Yankee, I think, sir. Looks like one o' them 'ere new gunboats. She's got steam up, but is lying quiet, like, as though waiting for us."

"How far are we from land?"

"One of the keys is about ten miles from us."

"Well, we will run into neutral waters, and see if we can shake him off in case he is hostile."

I went on deck, and took a look at the stranger. I did not have to glance through the glass a second time to convince myself that I had once more encountered the Stingeree, and that she was waiting for us. For a moment I hesitated, and argued if I had not better give up, and surrender the ship to those authorized to make such captures; but when I reflected, that, if I did, I should no longer be useful as a secret agent, that I should probably lose my life at the hands of the enraged Kentuckian or some of the men, and finally that I should forfeit all confidence on the part of Mrs. Gowen, who had learned to look upon me in the light of a brother, — when I thought of all these considerations, I decided on doing all that remained in my power to save the vessel. So I altered the course of the steamer, intending to hug the shore, and get within neutral waters, where the Stingeree would not be likely to venture; but, even if she did, I was satisfied that the Belle could, by the aid of her speed, keep out of the reach of long shot or broadside guns.

Just as I altered the course of the vessel, the Stingeree hoisted a white flag, and fired a gun to leeward.

"That means, 'I want to speak to you,'" I said to Bowmount, who had turned out, and come on deck.

"He's a Yankee, ain't he?" growled the Kentuckian.

"Yes."

"And he's got a white flag flying?"

"Yes."

"Well, then run towards the feller. I'll trust a Yankee with a flag of truce where I wouldn't trust some other people."

He might have meant the confederates; but he did not say so.

"If we put our heads in the lion's mouth, you must bear the responsibility," I remarked. "I will not."

"All right. Shucks! I ain't afeared to trust the Yankees. They'll ginerally keep their word. Run towards him, and see what he wants. I take all the risk."

"You hear, Mr. Thimble, what the owner says?"

"Yes, sir."

"Very well. Remember I'm not responsible for accidents."

The Kentuckian laughed, and lighted a cigar; while I gave orders for hoisting a white rag, and changed the course of the steamer. Then I slipped into my state-room, and put on a pair of white whiskers, and a wig that was venerable on account of the number of gray hairs it contained. I had no idea of allowing Captain Switchell to see my face, and recognize it.

"Hollo!" said Bowmount. "What do you mean by that rig?"

I gave an excuse that was satisfactory; and it pleased the Kentuckian so much, that he resolved to disguise his own face and head. He found the materials with which to work in some mysterious manner: but I asked no questions; for just then we were alongside of the Stingeree, and I saw Captain Switchell standing on the hammock nettings, speaking-trumpet in hand.

"What steamer is that?" he asked.

"The English steamer Belle."

Captain Switchell laughed in an ironical manner, as he said, —

"Of course you are bound to some neutral port."

"Yes; perhaps Key West or a market."

"I thought so. Well, I have a favor to ask of you."

"Will you please to name it?"

The captain did not recognize my voice or form, and neither did the officers nor crew, who were looking at us with wishful glances, as though mentally calculating how much the Belle and cargo were worth in a prize court, where the marshal would not seek for two thirds of the net proceeds, and his assistants the other third.

"Well, you see I have on board a confederate gentleman, who was captured the other day in a steamer. He is a civilian, and a feeble old man, not capable of harming any one. I have concluded to send him to some Southern port, and I really wish that you would help him. He will pay for his passage, and not only that, but bless you for doing a deed of charity; for he is anxious to join his friends, and die in the bosom of his family."

"Let him come," said Bowmount, who could not withstand an appeal to the heart. "Let the old fool come on board. We will give him a passage. It won't hurt us, and will do the old man some good. Tell them to bundle him on board; and be in a hurry about it."

"We'll take him, captain," I said; "but I hope you

won't be compelled to receive him again before we find a port to suit us."

"I shall do what I can after you are at a proper distance from us."

"What do you call a proper distance?"

"Say ten miles; just twice as far as you were from us when I signalled you."

"That is satisfactory. We have a pair of heels."

"And so have we," remarked Captain Switchell, in a significant tone. "We are not fast; but there are few vessels that can show us their sterns."

I made no reply to the remark. The boatswain of the Stingeree piped his shrill whistle, the first cutter was lowered with the rapidity, precision, and care that distinguishes man-of-war life, and then I saw an aged man pass down the steamer's side, and enter the boat.

It was cast off, and pulled for the Belle. Just at this moment, Mrs. Gowen sent word that she wanted to see me; but it was simply to ask a question or two, and to chat for a minute on some indifferent subject; and then I returned to the deck, and was in due form introduced by the Kentuckian to my new passenger. I was somewhat astonished to see before me Virginia's favorite son, the gallant Colonel Rhett, more gray and decrepit than ever.

If I had seen the President of the United States, I could not have been more surprised than I was to meet face to face with Colonel Rhett, whose right eye still bore traces of the blow which had sent him to the deck on the night we cut out the Spitfire.

However, if I was astonished, the colonel was not; and for a moment I wondered at it; but then I recollected that I was disguised with beard and wig; so it was not surprising he did not recognize me immediately.

"Captain," the old fellow said, "I am proud to think

that I once more stand beneath the flag of the free — old England's Cross; which, next to the confederate bunting, is the proudest in the world."

"Shucks! what gammon!" interrupted Bowmount. "But you allers was some on the highfalutin, colonel, like most of you fellers from the fust families of Old Virginny."

"You know me, then?" asked the astonished old scamp.

"I should rather think I did," was the reply of the Kentuckian.

As he spoke, he threw off his false hair and beard.

"O!" said the colonel, in a tone of great surprise. "I guess I'll return to the Stingeree. I won't trespass on your kindness."

It was too late. As soon as the colonel touched the deck, the engineer had put on steam, and we were heading on our course, already a mile from the man-of-war, which still remained quiet, with the flag of truce flying, waiting until we were ten miles apart, as was promised, before pursuit was commenced.

The Kentuckian gave a hearty and uproarious laugh.

"Why, you old fool," he said, "you is as safe here as on board one of Uncle Sam's crafts. What more do you want? We'll land you in a Southern port in less than three days."

But the colonel looked far from being satisfied, and glanced at me most suspiciously, as though he feared danger in my quarter; so, not to keep him in suspense, I just threw off my disguise; and, when he saw who I was, he felt worse than ever.

"You d—d scoundrel!" I remarked, in a quiet tone, "do you remember heading a gang of ruffians on the beach at Nassau, and making an assault on me?"

"There must be some mistake here," the old man said, with the most unblushing impudence. "If you will recollect for a moment, you will call to mind that I was badly injured in endeavoring to assist you. I was kicked very severely in the stomach."

"Yes; I did that when you urged on your party, and attempted to assist it."

"I am sorry you labor under such a great mistake," the colonel continued, as bold as a lion, yet appearing as honest as a man could appear when he knew he was telling a lie. "I attempted to help you all I could; and, in doing so, I was taken prisoner, and carried on board the Spitfire."

"What a romance!" I remarked, in a sneering tone.

"Yes, sir," was the reply, quite unmoved. "But the most wonderful thing is yet to come. I was thrown into a boat, and carried on board the Spitfire; and, when she was just ready to up anchor, a party of Yankees cut her out, and made off with her. But I fought them as well as I could; and you see the result in this black eye. I was floored by a blow; and, when I returned to consciousness, we were many miles out of the harbor."

"Go on. What next?"

"Well, sir, the next morning a Yankee gunboat ran alongside, and threatened to sink us unless we surrendered. The threat wasn't repeated; for the flag came down, and the Stingeree took possession. I don't say that it was a contrived plan, but I think so."

"And how did you manage to persuade the captain of the Stingeree that you were of no account?"

"By concealing my military rank, and relating how I had left my daughter in Nassau without a lawful protector, and with but little money to support her in my absence. Captain Switchell, although he is a Yankee, has a heart that can feel for the misfortunes of others. He saw that I was eager to join my sweet child, and knew that I could do so by taking passage on board of some swift blockade-runner. The Stingeree has no idea of touching at Nassaw for some time to come, fearful that an investigation would be ordered."

"Well, colonel, you can see as well as any man I ever saw. But we are now quits. Go and get your breakfast, and behave yourself hereafter."

As soon as breakfast was over, Mrs. Gowen made preparations to retire to her state-room, while the male portion of the passengers lighted their cigars, and went on deck.

The Stingeree had not gained on us. In fact, I thought that we were dropping her; and in the course of an hour our more, this surmise proved correct. The entire hull of the gunboat disappeared from the horizon, and then all that was left to mark the place where a steamer still ploughed through the waters of the channel was a line of dark smoke that floated upwards, and assumed fantastic shapes as the light wind carried it leeward.

Of course Bowmount chuckled at this evidence of the superiority of the Belle. He even asked the Virginian to drink whiskey — an invitation that was accepted with most wonderful alacrity. So bottles and tumblers were brought on deck, and a gay time the Kentuckian had, bluffing the colonel when he was disposed to enlarge on his valuable services at the battle of Bull Run, and talking sharp when he abused the Yankees.

We were well through the North-east Channel, and had left Great Abaco far astern, before we lost all sight of the Stingeree, and were alone upon the ocean, steaming along at the rate of twelve knots an hour, and calculating how soon we should be in the midst of the blockading vessels, which were as thick as locusts in Egypt off Charleston and Savannah. It was night when we ran for the harbor of the former place.

At dark I put all the lights out except the one in the binnacle, and shaded that one in such a manner that its rays could not be seen. The engine-room was covered with blankets, the steam was raised to its highest point, and with a full pressure we dashed towards the land.

Bowmount was on deck with me, and so was Mrs. Gowen; but the Virginia colonel did not seem inclined to leave his state-room, while John kept out of sight.

The Kentuckian did not appear in the least excited, and, for a wonder, did not touch liquor. He was more subdued than I ever saw him, while the lady was inclined to be a little hysterical, calling the Yankees hard names, and uttering little gasps as she hoped we should escape their vigilance.

Two hours passed, and still there was no sign of the blockaders. We were going through the water at the rate of fifteen miles an hour; for I judged it best to put on nearly all speed, and pass the gunboats with a dash, if it were a possible thing.

I began to congratulate myself upon the probability that we should meet none of the Union cruisers, when a rocket was sent up from some vigilant gunboat about two miles off our starboard bow. It was green and red, signifying that something suspicious was in sight, and to be on the lookout for it.

Hardly had the bright stars grown dim, and the stick which guided the rocket struck the water, than a second one was thrown to the air; but this one came from our larboard bow, and was a significant reminder that Uncle Sam's men were on the alert.

Still we steamed on; but it seemed as though it was to certain capture; for just ahead of us, right in our course, illuminating the water for many fathoms, was a burning blue-light, revealing the grim hull and battery of a sloop of war.

To go on was certain capture or destruction; for it was evident that the officers of the national vessels saw us, and suspected our mission; for hardly had the blue-light burned out, than three lanterns appeared in the steamer's rigging, in the form of a triangle, — a red one at the top, and a white and a green one at the bottom.

"What does that signal mean?" whispered the Kentuckian.

"It asks, as plainly as words can express the question, 'Who are you?'"

I altered the course of the vessel, and headed towards Folly Island, hoping to run into Light-house Inlet, and find shelter under the guns of the batteries which the Charleston soldiers had erected all along the shores of Morris Island. We shut off some of our steam, and moved along as silently as possible; but our paddle-wheels would beat the water; and as the night was calm, the noise could be heard for some distance, and I feared would lead to our detection.

For a few minutes we kept on our new course; but the gunboat that we were edging away from had no intention of letting us rest, or allowing us to slip by in peace. All at once we could see showers of sparks and black smoke issue from her smoke-pipe; and then there was a flash, and the deep report of a Parrott gun. The shot struck the water some ten or twenty fathoms from us, and sent it foaming in the air like a waterspout.

"That fellow means business," muttered Bowmount, lighting a fresh cigar.

"Yes, confound him! he will wake up the whole fleet."

"Steamer ahead," shouted the lookout on the topgallant-forecastle.

I made a signal to the engineer to stop the engines; but we were close upon a black, heavy hull before we could slacken our speed. We were so near, in fact, that we could make out a long row of ports, and by the aid of our glasses see the muzzles of some black-looking guns.

"It's a ship at anchor," whispered the mate. "The

fellow is not awake; and I'm glad enough of it, for he carries some devilish ugly-looking barkers."

In thinking the lookouts were asleep, the mate was mistaken; for hardly had he concluded, than a sharp hail was heard from the quarter-deck of the anchored vessel.

"What steamer is that?"

As the question was asked, a dozen replies passed through my mind; for on one of them depended the fate of the steamer and all those on board.

Before I answered, I took another look at the anchored vessel, and rapidly formed an idea of what she was. It was a sailing frigate, large and comfortable — just such a vessel as the admiral of the station would select as his home as long as the weather was such that he would not have to get under way to keep from the shore, sending out the steamers to do the light and heavy work, while the commander took his all-night in, and made himself generally comfortable over his claret and whiskey-punch.

All these thoughts passed through my brain very rapidly; but even then, before I had time to answer the pointed hail, there came another sharp and quick, —

"Steamer, ahoy! What steamer is that?"

And with the words there was a flashing of lights on the deck of the frigate: and then I could hear the alarm sprung, and the sudden roll of a drum beating to quarters.

I did not answer the pointed question, and the one that my interrogator was so anxious to know; for, as the lanterns took the form of a private signal, I bellowed back, —

"I was sent to inform the admiral that a blockade-runner has made her appearance, and attempted to run in. We may have headed her off, but are not certain. The Straddlebug (I did not know but she might be on the station, as I had heard that she was to sail for Charleston) "got a shot at her; but I don't think it took effect."

"Why the devil don't you answer the private signal, instead of chattering like a marine?" cried the officer of the deck, who was in a rage at the idea of being so unceremoniously disturbed in his nap.

"Because I supposed that you cared more for the news than you did for signals. We have signalized the flagship for the last hour, and devil of a reply could we obtain. Captain ——" (here I mentioned a name that I knew the officer could not understand) "thought you were all asleep, or else gone ashore for a lark."

"We are much obliged to Captain ——. What name did you say?"

This question was asked in a deep-toned voice, calm and powerful, as though the owner knew his position, and was bound to be respected by all under his command.

It was the admiral of the fleet, who had turned out to see what was the matter, and had taken the subject of hailing into his own hands.

"Captain ——."

Once more I pronounced a name that the devil couldn't have understood, even if he were familiar with both the Russian and the Polish languages.

"O, yes!" responded the admiral, who did not care to spend time in asking more questions. "Request the captain to see me in the morning. I shall have some business with him."

"Ay, ay, sir. I will tell him. Have you any further orders?"

For a moment there was no answer. They were precious moments to me, and I dreaded the silence that prevailed. At last a voice abruptly asked,—

"What do you mean by waving your lanterns in that manner?"

Now, I had not the slightest idea what was meant by the waving of lanterns on board the Belle; but I knew that it would not answer to show my ignorance to an admiral; and, as bold as a lion, I replied, —

"It is the signal which I agreed to make to the fleet as soon as I had ascertained that the blockade-runner had not passed this way."

"Then why in the devil's name don't you signalize in a shipshape manner, and not in that blundering style?" roared the admiral, who began to lose his temper under the combined influence of loss of sleep, and the prospect of losing some prize money by the escape of the blockade-runner.

"I'll see that it don't happen again. sir," I answered, in the faint hope that a soft answer would turn away wrath.

"Why, sir, you are doing it all the time," yelled the admiral, on whom meekness was entirely thrown away. "What do you mean, sir?"

I took time to glance over the deck, and to run forward as far as the waist, near the house, in the hope of discovering the cause of the admiral's displeasure.

For a few moments I saw nothing. Then, just as I was about to return to the quarter-deck, and attend to the hailing department, I saw Colonel Rhett issue from the house used by the men as their sleeping-quarters, and wave a lighted lantern over his head.

"You old scoundrel, what do you mean?" I cried, seizing him by the nape of his neck, and throwing him to the deck, while at the same time I jerked his lantern from his hand, and extinguished it.

Bowmount heard the scuffle, slight as it was, and hastened towards me.

"What is the matter?" he asked.

"Matter enough," I answered. "This double-faced traitor" — and I shook the colonel until his teeth chattered in his head — "has been making signals to the frigate."

"Overboard with him," the savage Kentuckian cried. "D—n him, don't have any mercy on the cuss."

"What is the meaning of this, gentlemen?" demanded the colonel. "What have I done?"

I did not have a chance to reply to that interrogation; for just then came a sharp hail from the flagship, and it needed my attention.

"Give him to me," whispered Bowmount "I'll settle his coffee. Shucks! don't I know what to do with just sich vipers?"

"You won't kill him?" I asked.

Bowmount laughed in a low and threatening tone.

"If this 'ere ship is captured, I'll give his carcass to the fishes jest as sure as I'm a man. If it is the last thing I does in this world, I'll have that satisfaction out of the varmint."

"For Heaven's sake, gentlemen," begged the colonel, "spare my life on account of my daughter. I've done nothing to merit this treatment. I'm one of the members of the first Virginia families, and a rebel clear through to the back-bone."

"Steamer, ahoy!" roared the admiral from the flagship, in a towering rage at the idea of not securing prompt answers.

"Go and speak to the old nanny-goat," cried Bowmount, "or he'll butt his jolly old head agin' somethin'; you see if he don't."

"No violence," I whispered, as I relinquished my hold of the prostrate man.

"All right. Shucks! don't be afeard of me."

I reached the quarter-deck just in time to hear the admiral roar, —

"What do you mean, sir, by not answering me? What is the trouble there?"

"There is no trouble, sir. I saw a commotion on the

outer station, and I thought the blockade-runner might be captured. I can't make out by the aid of my glass."

By this time we had drifted astern of the ship, and towards the shore; for the wind was blowing in that direction. We were just in a position most favorable to prevent receiving a shot or broadside from the frigate in case she should discover our true character. I longed to give the engineer the signal to start, and make a run for it, but feared that an unlucky shot would disable us before we could get out of range, or hide ourselves in the darkness.

Just as I was thinking of these things, I heard the sound of paddle-wheels, and then a dark mass hove in sight, and signalled with lanterns that she was all right, and desired communication with the admiral.

"Flagship, ahoy!" roared the new comer.

"Yes; what is it now?"

"I have been sent to inform you that a blockade-runner has attempted to enter the port. She passed some of the fleet, and disappeared."

"How many more steamers are to be sent to me with the same information?" growled the admiral, who began to think that all of his captains were mad or drunk. "If some of you had remained on the outer station, and looked as hard for the blockade-runner as you have for the flagship, we should all have been a few thousand dollars richer by this time."

This was the peculiar way which the admiral had of "bearing down" on those under his command when things had not gone to please him.

"I was not aware that another had been despatched to convey the news," tartly responded the captain of the steamer.

"No, I suppose not. But if you had kept a bright lookout, you would have brought me a prize instead of bad news."

"There's arrogance for you," muttered Mrs. Gowen, who had stood by my side all through the hailing.

"It's about time to move from this 'ere location, or it will be ter hot for us," muttered the Kentuckian, who, having disposed of his prisoner, the colonel, was now ready to join me in all that related to the success of the project.

"I know it. In a few minutes the admiral will make his quarter-deck too hot to hold its officers."

We were about forty fathoms from the stern of the frigate, just near enough to hear all that passed, and to understand when it was time to think of real danger.

The chief engineer of the Belle was near me, ready to communicate with his subordinates in the engine-room at the least sign from his superior.

"Can you set the wheels in motion, so they won't attract attention, and allow us to draw ahead?"

"Yes, sir; I think I can."

"Do so, then; but be careful how you work."

The engineer left me to communicate the orders, and I once more turned my attention to the admiral and his captain. The former was pacing his quarter-deck, and wondering if he should utter some more sarcastic remarks, or let the latter up.

All at once it entered the wise noddle of the commander of the fleet, that he had not treated the captain of the first steamer (meaning the one I commanded) to a little sensation in the way of sharp words; and he prepared to give me a dose.

"Steamer, ahoy!" he yelled, just as our paddle-wheels commenced moving.

"Ahoy, the fleet, sir!"

"What in the devil's name are you doing there?"

"Waiting for orders, sir."

"Waiting for orders!" in a sneering tone. "Don't

you know that your services are needed on the outer station? I can take care of the inner station."

"I'm glad to hear it, for it is all news to me," I retorted; for I could not help taking the Tartar down a little.

"Hey? What's that?" was the cry.

We were moving off in a slow but precious sure manner, the paddles making but few revolutions, yet enough to obtain steerage-way. We were headed, owing to the drift, direct for Sullivan's Island, where several batteries were erected, and where I could find shelter in case we were pursued.

Even as the admiral spoke, his ship began to grow dim and indistinct, a black speck on the water.

Before I could return a suitable answer, the Kentuckian took the words from my mouth, and yelled, —

"Say, old fuss-and-feathers, do you want to see a blockade-runner?"

There was a moment's indignant silence on board the flagship, and in the mean time I had a chance to remonstrate with Bowmount.

"For Heaven's sake, keep quiet till we are out of danger. A few minutes more, and we shall be all right."

"Come on board, and report yourself under arrest," roared the admiral.

"I'll see you d—d first," bellowed the Kentuckian, who, to save even ship and cargo, could no longer keep still.

"Put on all steam," I cried to the engineer. "Port your helm a little. We will still keep in the wake of the frigate."

The vessel sprang through the water under the influence of steam; but before we could vanish from sight, two stern guns were brought to bear on us, and two thirty-two pound shots were sent flying over our heads.

"Let her rip, old addle-head," roared the Kentuckian; and with this parting salute we vanished from the sight of the frigate.

Then we altered our course, so as to keep out of the range of the guns, and, with a full head of steam, ran for Sullivan's Island, while the admiral's ship kept up a running fire for five minutes, in the hope of hitting us. But they were somewhat disappointed; for we felt our way in, and by private signals were enabled to anchor under a confederate battery, where we remained till daylight.

"O, Mr. Barnwell," cried Mrs. Gowen, taking both of my hands, the next morning, as soon as she knew that we were safe, "how can I thank you for your coolness in escaping from those mean Yankees! I'll make a hero of you by the manner in which I shall report your exploits."

"In the name of Heaven, don't do that!" I cried, more and more convinced that I should be ruined through the injudicious kindness of friends. "Let what I have done pass without special notice."

Just at this moment the Kentuckian appeared on deck with the Virginian, Colonel Rhett, who had passed the night in irons, and in the run of the steamer, where he had no chance to do mischief, being waited upon and guarded by John, the slave.

The representative of the first of Virginia's families looked a little the worse for the treatment he had received at my hands, and at the hands of Bowmount. He exhibited marks on his face that told of rough usage; for the enraged Kentuckian had taken the opportunity to hit him once or twice, as soon as I had gone aft to attend to my duty the night before.

"There he is, Barnwell," said the Kentuckian. "What shall we do with him? He won't make no more signals to the Yankee fleet, — not if I has my way, he won't."

"So help me God," the colonel cried, "I was not making signals to the fleet."

He looked and spoke as though he meant the truth. There was an air of sincerity on the man's face that was almost convincing.

"What in the devil's name did you mean by waving a lantern?" I demanded, in a stern tone.

"I was not aware that I was waving it," was the confident answer.

"How came you with the lantern, anyhow?" the Kentuckian asked. "Didn't you hear the orders for all lights to be dowsed?"

"No, I didn't."

The man looked us square in the eyes as he answered. I began to think of his daughter, and to wonder if he was not innocent of evil intentions.

"What were you doing with the lantern?" I demanded. "If you were not signalizing the enemy, how did it happen that you had a light?"

"I can explain all in a few words, sir; because I see that I am in as bad a predicament as I was at Bull Run, when I cut my way through—"

"O, damn Bull Run!" snarled the Kentuckian. "Go on with the story. Shucks! let's hear how you got hold of the lantern."

"In a moment, sir. I was in the cabin, suffering in my mind for fear the Yankees would capture us, when John, the servant of Mrs. Gowen,—the nigger, you know,—came to me, and said he'd lost his watch, and he feared some of the poor white trash for'ard had taken it; and would I oblige him so much as to take the lantern, and hold it while he searched the house on deck. Without thinking a moment, I said that I would; so away we went on our mission."

"Did you find the watch?"

AN EXPLANATION. — Page 261.

"Yes: we found it hanging on a nail at the head of the cook's bunk; and then John recollected that he had lent it to the cook to boil some eggs; so there was no theft, after all."

"But how happened it that you waved the lantern?" I demanded, "as though signalizing the fleet?"

"I was not aware that I was doing an injury. I was so much amused, that I laughed; and between my laughing and the rolling of the ship, I suppose the lantern moved back and forth, and up and down."

"Eh?" sighed Bowmount, "you is bound to trick us, arter all. But we'll see what John says. Come on deck, you specimen of milk and 'lasses, and let's hear what you has to say on the subject."

John came from the cabin, and appeared surprised at the summons.

"John," said the Kentuckian, "I feels good-natured, and wouldn't hurt a mouse this 'ere mornin'; but by ——! if you goes to come any of your dodges, I'll hang yer like a dog. I means it now. I'm not to be trifled with."

John did not look in the least alarmed. He listened to the threats without flinching, or appearing apprehensive of injury. Once he glanced at the colonel, but the Kentuckian snapped him up for it.

"You jist keep yer eyes fixed on me till I gets through with yer, or I'll make that back of yourn a little sorer than it ever was."

"I will answer all your questions, sir," John replied, and looked full at the Kentuckian, as though he knew the man, and knew he was not to be played with.

"Did you ask Colonel Rhett to hold a lantern for you, last night?" Bowmount demanded.

"Yes, sir."

"For what purpose?"

"To help me search for a watch that I thought had been stolen from me."

"That will do. Return to your duties," and the Kentuckian dismissed the slave.

"You see that I was right," exclaimed the Virginian, in a tone of triumph.

"Yes, I see that you was. But it seems to me that I'd ruther have it established by some other way than by a nigger's evidence. You is let off — aquitted; and if we has hurt your feelings by our treatment of you, we must be forgiven. That's all."

The Kentuckian turned away as though he did not half believe Colonel Rhett was innocent, and for my part I was of the same opinion; but still we had no evidence to show that treachery was intended, except the swinging of the lantern, and that the colonel declared was an accident. If he had signalized the fleet, it amounted to nothing; for we had nipped it in the bud, before the Federals suspected anything: so no great harm was done. We could not hang the man just on suspicion that he meant treachery, and yet I really believed that he did intend to deceive us. In the course of the forenoon, Colonel Rhett left the steamer for a hotel; but he promised to look at us once a day, if not oftener — an act of kindness on his part that was not appreciated by us. But the ship was entered at the custom-house, and Bowmount found an agent to purchase the entire cargo, and pay cotton for the same; and towards nine o'clock the Kentuckian felt his way to a state-room, and turned in, large doses of whiskey soon sending him to sleep. Just as he began to snore, John, the mulatto slave, entered the cabin, and informed me that Mrs. Gowen was waiting to see me at her residence.

"I hope that your mistress has comfortable quarters," I said to John, while preparing for the visit.

"Yes, sir. You will think so when you see her."

"And how did you manage to pass through the streets without being stopped?"

"I have a pass, sir, that serves me at all hours of the night."

"Let me see it," I said.

The slave hesitated, and I was compelled to speak the second time before he made a show of feeling in his pockets for the document. Even when he had found it, he did not hand it to me until I had spoken quite sharply, and as though I was to be no longer trifled with. I looked at the paper, and saw that it was signed by Colonel Rhett, and that it spoke of John as though he was the Virginian's property, and on business of importance.

"What does this mean, John?"

The fellow hesitated only a moment, and then replied, —

"Colonel Rhett gave me the pass because he thought I might want to use it while here, as I have friends in Charleston."

"Then you have no pass from your mistress, Mrs. Gowen?"

"No, sir. I showed her this one, when she spoke of writing a pass, and then she said it would answer full as well as though she gave it, and save her trouble."

It was not an improbable story; but at the same time I wondered that Mrs. Gowen, who hated the sight and name of Rhett, should care to allow her slave to use a pass signed by the colonel. But I supposed it to be one of her freaks, and so handed the paper back to John with the remark, —

"It is very singular."

John made no reply, and I continued to think until dressed, and ready to leave the ship.

"I shall return some time in the course of the evening," I remarked to the mate, who was on deck smoking his cigar. "Keep an anchor watch; for, if we don't have one or two men on the lookout, the thieves will carry off our anchor and cables before morning."

The mate promised compliance, and up the wharf I went. At the head of it I found a close carriage in the care of a negro coachman. He was a giant of a fellow, and black as coal-tar, sitting indolently on his box, where he seemed to have waited quite patiently for the arrival of myself and John.

"It's all right, Sam," said John, opening the carriage door, and motioning me to pass in.

We passed through the most populous parts of the city; and by the aid of the dim lights that flashed from stores and houses, — for the streets were not lighted, — I could see the gray uniforms of the confederate soldiers, as they thronged the streets, some of them shouting and singing, and apparently enjoying themselves after a fashion of their own. In a few minutes we had left the city some distance behind us, and entered the country, where all was darkness — not a light to be seen. I did not feel in the least alarmed at this, but thought it a little singular that Mrs. Gowen should be so far from the city, when she had intimated that she was to stop with some friends in Charleston; but, after going on for ten minutes, I knocked on the window, and attracted John's attention. He lowered the front window, but did not stop the carriage, to ask what I wanted; and I fancied that the fellow was a little impertinent in his tone.

"Where are you taking me, John?" I asked. "It seems to me that you are steering a wild course out here in the dark, with not a light-house to mark the channel."

"We shall be there in a few minutes. Don't you be alarmed just yet."

"Alarmed, you milk-and-water colored vagabond? What should I be alarmed at?"

"Nothing yet, sir."

Then up went the window, and I heard John and the coachman laugh. It aggravated me so much, that I was almost resolved to get out and kick both of the slaves, and then return to the city, and wait until Mrs. Gowen sent a more civil messenger to conduct me to her retreat. But I smothered my wrath when I recollected that in a few minutes I should come to the end of my journey, and then my annoyances would be brought to a close. And, sure enough, my predictions were verified; for we soon turned from the road into an avenue lined with trees, but dark and sombre, with not a light to be seen. Through this avenue we rolled for a few minutes; and then the carriage stopped, and I heard whispering, John leaving the box to carry on the conversation. Once more I let down the window, and asked impatiently, —

"What is the matter now? Are we on the wrong road?"

"No," was the snappish reply. "We are on the right road."

"Then why don't you drive on?"

"We will when we are ready," was the impudent reply.

"You milk-and-molasses scoundrel!" I exclaimed in a rage, "I have a great mind to kick you for your impertinence. I shall report it to your mistress."

"Yes," was the cool, insinuating reply; "I expect you will."

And then John and Sam laughed in concert, as though some joke lurked beneath John's insolent words. I drew my revolver from my breast, and cocked it. It made some noise, the sharp click being heard quite distinctly in that silent avenue, with not a breath of air to disturb the heavy leaves overhead. The slaves, and the people with whom they were whispering, heard the ominous cocking of the pistol, and knew what it meant; for, when John next spoke, his tone expressed much more civility.

"Don't be impatient, sir," said he; "for a surprise is intended you."

"And one is intended you," I replied, "unless you keep a more civil tongue in your head. You have been insolent, to-night, and if I see any more of it, I'll blow your black brains out, as sure as I'm a Southerner."

"I am sure, sir, that I did not intend to be rude; and I'm sorry for the offence."

"If you are, don't repeat it; for I have lost all patience with you."

"I hopes massa will put up his pistol now dat we has shown dat we don't mean nuffin but what is good for him," whined Sam, the black, giant coachman.

"Mrs. Gowen will have a hearty laugh when she hears that you suspected us of being unfriendly," added John. "I do assure you, sir, that everything we have done to-night has been according to orders."

"Dat's so, massa," grunted Sam. "We's only 'beyin' orders."

"Well, then, I will trust you. Drive on, and let us reach the house some time to-night."

The coachman walked his horses, and in a few minutes' time we drew up in front of a door. I could see a light in the hall of the house, and a light in one of the rooms; but the building did not present a very lively aspect, although the night was so dark that I could not judge what kind of a house it was. It appeared to me like the residence of a planter.

"Here we are, sir," said John, opening the carriage door, so that I could step on the veranda that ran around the house.

"Yes, sah, here we is," chuckled Sam, the coachman, as he got off his box.

"But where are all the people?" I remarked. "There appears to be no one here to receive me."

"O, yes, there is, sir," answered John. "There are plenty here; only you don't see them."

"Well, then, I would like to; for a darker place than this can't be found in South Carolina."

"The gentleman wants some light," the mulatto cried.

"Well, den, let 'em hab it. O, dear, yes! let 'em hab light by all means."

And Sam laughed as though he had just heard a good negro joke.

There was a scraping of matches, and brief and uncertain flashes of light, revealing dark faces and woolly heads, and then there suddenly blazed up some twenty torches, held by slaves of all ages, from the impulsive negro of twenty years to the veteran of sixty. They were arranged with some degree of order, forming a lane through which I had to pass as I walked to the door of the house. As the light flashed over the dark faces that surrounded me, I took a quick survey of them, and noted the almost stony sternness of their countenances. There was not one expression of pleasure or joy to be detected on a single face, young or old, which I regarded as something wonderful; for the negroes of a plantation generally take much pleasure in welcoming the guests of their masters, receiving one with grins and even somersets of delight when all other marks of approval failed them. As I took a step towards the door, the torches, composed of light, resinous wood, giving out dark and smoky flame, were advanced, as though to get a good view of my face. The act was so sudden and solemn, so peculiar and unexpected, that I stopped, and started back a pace or two.

"Are you afraid of a few negro slaves?" asked John, in a tone so like a sneer, that I turned on him, and would have struck him if he had not been the favorite slave of a lady whom I respected as much as I did Mrs. Gowen.

"I am afraid of nothing," I answered in a firm manner; "not even of a dozen or two slaves, who tremble at the frown of a white man."

"The day for such trembling is nearly past," quietly responded John.

"Nearly past — glory to God!" cried the slaves with one accord, and without changing a muscle of their faces, so stern and grim.

"De day is breakin'! glory, hallelujah!" screeched one old fellow, nearly bent double with rheumatism and hard work in the rice and cotton fields of South Carolina.

"De day is breakin'! glory, hallelujah!" cried the others in chorus, and with a wave of their torches and a flash of their eyes.

I did not feel alarmed at the scene before me, yet I thought it wonderful and strange that a planter should allow his slaves to show such religious fanaticism near his house when receiving a strange guest. It was so unusual that I could not help commenting on it to John.

"What is the matter with all the slaves to-night?" I asked. "Have they been attending camp-meeting?"

"Yes, sir; one kind of camp-meeting."

"One kind, bress de Lord," chorused the negroes.

"Ah! what is that?"

"The camp-meeting of freedom. We are slaves no longer. Strike! Down with the slave-driver!"

I must confess that I was surprised; so much so that I had no time to draw pistol or knife. Sam, the coachman, a negro of giant strength, threw himself upon me, and pinioned my arms to my side, while, at the same moment, two other negroes, whom I had not seen, came up behind me, grasped my feet with their hands, and down I tumbled.

"Take away his pistol and knife," cried John, the treacherous mulatto, who had not yet laid a hand on me, but who appeared to direct all the movements.

"Yes," chuckled Sam. "Take dem t'ings away, 'cos dey is dangerous. If de knife should go into dis chile's belly, he wouldn't feel like eatin' gumbo for one while, now I tells yer. Yah! yah! yah!"

"Don't you be afeard, Sam," one of the others cried, pulling a revolver from my pocket, and coolly placing it in his own — an operation that caused Sam to show the whites of his eyes in an alarming manner.

I found that struggling with three or four stout men, who were determined to succeed in their purpose, was quite useless; so I lay still, panting under the compression of the negroes, and wondering what had induced them to attack me, who had never injured them in word or deed.

"Suit yourselves, gentlemen," I said, at length. "Only please to get off my breast; for it is difficult to breathe; and Sam is rather fat, and smells none too sweet."

"What dat you say?" cried the giant. "I's as sweet as you is, you blamed, gol-darned old rebel."

"De Lord be praised, de day ob jubilee is comin', comin', for de children of Israel," chanted rather than sang the blacks, who still held the torches, and still remained in line, interested spectators of the struggle that was going on between their colored brethren and myself. While the slaves were chanting, the rest of the scamps, with Mr. John to lead them, were overhauling my person, and taking such articles as they could find in my pockets. I began to ask a few questions of John, who had stood looking on.

"My Christian friend," I asked, "will you please to tell me the meaning of this outrage upon me?"

"He calls this an outrage, boys," the mulatto cried,

speaking to the blacks who were holding the torches. The slaves, in response, uttered a dismal groan, as though they did not see matters in that particular light.

"Yes," continued John; "a man who has beaten us, sold us into slavery, and parted husbands and wives, and mothers and children, now calls such a trifling and paltry thing as this an outrage."

"You treacherous scoundrel," I said, addressing John, "you know that I never sold a human being into slavery, or ill-used the blacks. Tell me the meaning of this."

"You belong to South Carolina — don't you?" demanded John.

For a moment I hesitated, but only for a moment. There was too much risk to be run in acknowledging myself to be a Northern man. I did not dare to trust the negroes so soon after running the blockade.

"Well, what if I do belong to South Carolina?" I asked.

"Then you are an enemy to the Yanks; and being such, you are our enemy."

"Then I understand you to say that you are in favor of the Yankees?" I asked, astonished at what I had heard.

"We is de Yankees' friends, bress de Lord! bress de Lord!" howled the negroes, waving their torches, and swaying their bodies back and forth, and only with the utmost restraint refraining from dancing at the same time.

"You have your answer," John said, as soon as the slaves had ceased their chant, and quieted down.

"Yes, I see that the answer has come; and I am astonished at it. But let me ask why you have singled me out for a victim, when there are so many who are much more prominent than myself."

"Because I hate you," hissed the mulatto between his teeth.

"Indeed! I was not aware that I had given you any cause for such feeling."

"Listen to him, boys," cried the mulatto, addressing the slaves. "He runs a vessel past the blockading squadron, and cheats our friends the Yanks."

Then came another howl from the negroes, and they chanted, —

> "May de debbil nab him!
> O, may de debbil nab him!
> O, may de debbil nab him!
> At dis time o' night!"

And once more they planted the soles of their flat feet upon the boards, until it sounded like rain beating against a tin roof.

"Is that all?" I demanded, as soon as the noise subsided. "Come! let me know the whole of my sins. I am getting quite impatient to learn them."

"You shall," the mulatto answered, in a voice that trembled a little with rage.

"Well, go on, for I'm tired of remaining here."

"The place to which you will be removed from here is not a paradise; and you had better enjoy the open air while you can, and not hurry us. There is time enough before the men who surround you will be compelled to take to the swamps. At the first glimpse of daylight, they will be off."

"I have no objection to their leaving immediately, if they are so disposed," I remarked, insinuatingly.

"They will remain until I bid them depart," answered John, haughtily, with a proud wave of his hand.

"Just as you please. Drive on with your yarn, and let me know why you are detaining me."

"I have told you: because you are an enemy of the North."

"So are thousands. Mr. Bowmount and Colonel Rhett are enemies of the North, and hate the Yanks."

"But they are not dangerous, like you. They could not have run past the blockaders, and answered all their signals, the same as you did last night. We take only the leading ones, and leave the ignorant rabble to be shot by the Yanks."

This started the negroes to howling again, and their voices mingled in chanting,—

> "O, bress de Nothern marksmen!
> For dey can shoot de guns,
> And make de cannon rattle,
> And drive —"

"Silence!" roared John, who found that the chorus was likely to be longer than he desired, and therefore interfered with his oratory. "Silence, you black scamps. Do you want to bring the patrol down on us?"

"No fear of der comin' to dis house," chuckled an old white-headed negro, with a face like an intelligent ape's. "Dis house ain't de kind ob house for white men to look arter in de night time. Yah! yah! Why, bress de Lord! dar lots of peoples ready to swear dat dey has seen old massa trampin' round de rooms wid ebber so many little debbils punchin' 'um wid forks, 'cos he was cruel to his slaves, and cruel to all his white relations. Ah, a berry hard man was old massa."

As the negro seemed to be an oracle with the slaves, all listened to him in silence, and one or two, with that peculiar superstitious feeling that will overcome the best of us at times, when near a ruin reputed haunted, rolled their eyes in all directions, as though their owners were attempting to obtain glimpses of matters in the rear, where the dark woods moaned with the sighing of the night wind, and the croaking of frogs blended with the dismal notes of some lonely whip-poor-will anxious for a mate.

"When I t'inks of de time when old massa cut 'em

throat from ear to ear," continued the venerable ape, who seemed to like to hear himself talk, "I almost see 'em now, wid de blood pourin' out ob de gash—"

There was a visible sensation in the ranks, and many torches trembled, and heads could no longer be controlled. They had to turn and look towards darkness, as though their owners feared something would jump on them, and clasp them in a clammy embrace. If it had been possible for the slaves to turn pale, they would have done so; but, as it was, the darkest looked several shades lighter than their natural color.

"Yes," continued the white-headed oracle, "when I t'inks ob dat mornin', I feels quite lively; 'cos I knew dat de slaves ob dis plantation had escaped a plague, wusser dan Goliah in de lions' den. Yes: I can see old massa a lyin' on de floor, wid his troat all open-like. and de razor covered wid blood, and his eyes wide open. Dar—"

"Whar?" yelled a dozen voices, the slaves wrought up to the highest pitch of excitement at the details of a horrible domestic tragedy that had occurred some ten years before.

"Thar," I shrieked, springing to my feet, and pointing with one hand, with all the dramatic action that I could command. "Thar he comes, razor in hand."

Some half a dozen torches were dashed down, and some half a dozen negroes ran howling from the house; but, to my regret, those who were nearest to me did not move, though they were shaking in an awful manner. I thought I might break through the circle; and perhaps I should have done so had it not been for John, the mulatto, who had received a good education, and was not so superstitious as his companions. He saw at once through my designs, and frustrated them; for just as I meant to jump and run for the woods, trusting to luck and superstition

18

to enable me to escape, he caught me by the arm, and shouted to Sam, —

"Don't be a fool, you big coward. Take hold of the captain, or he'll run for it."

The negro followed his directions. Once more he seized me with no gentle hand; and when the others saw a slight scuffle, in my attempts to escape, their courage returned, for they had something else to think of besides ghosts. The scoundrels forced me on my knees, and there held me until those who had the torches could throw a little light on the dark scene; and, by the best bower that ship ever carried, there was need enough of it; for some of the faces that surrounded me were darker than coal-tar, and as the night was warm, and the torches were hot, the holders of the same smelt worse than bad beef.

John enjoyed his triumph, and so did the rest of the negroes; for they uttered a shout of derision, and that yell was answered by one in the avenue. Once more the shout was repeated, this time nearer the house. It was answered by one of the negroes; and then the clatter of horse's hoofs was heard, and into the light that the torches shed around, rode two horsemen, one of them as black as the forest at the back of the house, and the other I made out to be a white man. They dismounted and came towards us; and when within a fathom or two, the slaves, who had circled around me, opened to admit the new comers.

"Ah, John!" cried a familiar voice, "you have him fast, I see."

I looked at the man's face, and, to my surprise, saw Colonel Rhett before me.

"Ah, colonel!" I cried, "you are just in time to aid me. I never in my life was more glad to see you."

"You be d—d for a rebel and a traitor," was the brutal answer of the insulting and arrogant Virginian.

The old colonel lighted a cigar by the aid of one of the

torches, and then, insolently puffing a cloud of smoke towards me, coolly and deliberately said, —

"Nary a helping hand do I lend you."

He laughed as he said this, but did not continue the conversation; for John, who had entered the house for a moment, now returned, and the white man and the slave whispered together for a few moments. While they were thus engaged, I was allowed to stand on my feet, but so closely guarded that escape was impossible. At length the colonel and the mulatto closed their conference.

"Lead him on!" said the latter.

Whereupon two of the negroes butted at me in such a manner that they were as resistless as Federal rams, and I was compelled to move on or go down.; but just as I ranged along in line with the colonel I manifested a little resistance, enough to provoke the ire of the slaves. They thought they would settle me with one grand combination butt, that would send me end for end like a spar in a hurricane. I watched their motions with a wary eye. I saw them bend their bullet-shaped heads, stiffen their bovine necks, and huddle closer together, as they made preparations for the plunge; and then, when they rushed forward, I stepped hastily to one side. The darkeys passed me with a grunt and a snort, and struck the Virginian just under the line of his belt in front. The result was what could be expected. The colonel went over as though struck by a thirty-two pounder; and the slaves, unable to stop their career, fell upon the warrior, and nearly crushed the life out of his body. The sight was so ludicrous, that even John was compelled to laugh; and that was the signal for the rest of the slaves to join in.

"Yah, yah!" roared the negroes. "By golly, Pete and Sam butt de wrong one dat time, and no mistake. Dey jest like bulls, — shet 'em eyes, and away 'em goes. O, de Lord! to see dem nigs roll ober!"

The colonel managed to gain his feet; but he could not speak for some time, owing to the blows which he had received in his stomach. He held on, with both hands, to that portion of his anatomy, and gasped for breath. When he did find his tongue, he swore some bitter oaths; and his temper was not improved when I told him I was one of the blessed, having given him that which I should have received.

"None of your d—d blockade-running jokes on me," gasped the victim, with both hands on his stomach. "I wish the niggers had killed you."

"The same to you, my valiant friend. Your loss would have been but little in the great cause."

"Curse you and your cause. O, how my insides ache! The niggers' heads are harder than cannon-balls."

John saw that the colonel was all doubled up with pain and rage; so he composed his face, and motioned for me to move on. The slaves gave me a hustle forward, and on I went, John leading the way. He pushed open a stout oak door, snatched a torch from one of the negroes, and, waving it over his head, showed me the cell I was to occupy. It was not an inviting-looking place. It was close, dark, and damp, with a tomb-like smell that was sickening. There was no window to admit light or air: only the earth could be seen, wet and unwholesome, with great drops of water issuing from the soil, slimy and green —just such a place as snakes love to revel in. In one corner of the cell I saw several toads, — big fellows, with white breasts and black and yellow backs, — venerable chaps, which sat upon their hind legs, and winked in the most confidential manner, when the light of the torches flashed in the cell, and awoke them from their slumbers.

"Here," said John, with a sardonic smile, "you can remain comfortable until such time as you are wanted. It is useless for you to think of escaping or calling for help.

One of the colored gentlemen will always stand at your door, but no noise that you make can be heard beyond the building. You will live on bread and water, and none too much of that."

"Thank you, John. Have you anything more to say?"

"No."

"Then be kind enough to leave me and the toads and other reptiles together. We can dispense with your company for the present. The time may come when I shall request a longer interview."

"Well, you are a cool hand, ain't you?" the mulatto asked.

"Yes; I think I am. Good night, and don't lie about me to Mrs. Gowen more than you can help."

"Your interests in that quarter shall be attended to."

With this remark, the door was closed, locked, and barred, and I was left alone in the cell, with the bloated toads and spiders.

CHAPTER IX.

A PRISONER. — A NEGRO LEAGUE. — A FELLOW-SUFFERER. — BOWMOUNT IN A TRAP. — HE FINDS A CHISEL. — AT WORK TO GET OUT. — THE KENTUCKIAN ESCAPES. — SOME OLD FRIENDS APPEAR. — A MOMENT OF PERIL. — TIMELY ARRIVAL OF THE KENTUCKIAN. — THE TABLES TURNED.

It was some moments before I could realize that I was a prisoner in the custody of escaped slaves, who were doing all that they could to weaken the South and help the North. They had selected a deserted mansion house as their head-quarters during the night, knowing that its reputation for being haunted would keep people at a distance; while, in the neighboring swamps, to which they fled in the daytime, they were secure from attack, even from men or dogs; for the former feared to venture near them on account of snakes and desperate negroes, and the latter could not scent their prey over spongy ground and stagnant pools of water.

So the negroes were safe from pursuit. For food, they depended upon contributions from the hands of dark-skinned allies, and sometimes foraged a little on the plantations from which they had fled some months before. They knew, to a chicken, how large a number of fowls were kept on the several places; and, what was better, they could tell where to put their hands on the fattest, even in the darkest nights — an advantage of which the slaves often availed themselves when out prowling. The men were communicated with by couriers from the city, who brought word when their services were required on any particular night; and the dark brotherhood never failed to attend in a body on every such occasion, prepared to do all the honors required. John had put himself in communication with the gang the instant he had landed. He had even gone to the house, in company with Sam, the coachman, who was one of the chief conspirators, and, in connection with some dozen others, attended to the Charleston department. John had told the slaves what a dangerous and desperate character I was, and what a good thing it would be if I was out of the way.

This was the whole history of the gang, — some of them desperate and bold, and others arrant cowards, unfit to do the hard and bold work of their superiors. They seized upon all prominent confederates whom they could reach, or get into their power, and sold them to the Union forces as prisoners of war, or else quietly made way with them in the dreary cellar of that dark and lonely house. Those who were silently conveyed to the Union fleet were sent North, and refused exchange until the war was closed up. This was done at the special request of the slaves, who knew that if one of their prisoners should return to Charleston, and expose the secret of his capture, their rendezvous would be broken up, and all slaves in the vicinity be subjected to cruel treatment until some revelations were made. Of course I did not learn all these particulars for some time; but I had plenty of opportunity to think of many things, and to study out the designs of the slaves, while lying in their dungeon; for, in spite of the damp earth and my unpleasant companions, I was compelled to lie down to rest my weary limbs. But, for the first two hours after I was locked up, I remained on my feet, not daring to move for fear of stepping on a toad or some other obnoxious thing. But after a while I grew tired, and wanted a change; so I yelled out at the top of my voice, —

"Corporal of the guard?"

I knew no other method of attracting attention, and did not just understand how I was to call my captors. There was no response to my first hail; so I shouted again, —

"Corporal of the guard?"

This time I pitched my voice in so high a key that it echoed through the cellar, and even startled me, it sounded so unearthly. Presently some one began slowly descending the steps, and when about half way down, stopped, and asked, —

"What de debbil you mean by makin' dat ar' noise, and callin' arter de corporal ob de guard? Dar ain't no such nigger here."

"Then what do you call yourself? If you ain't a corporal, what are you?"

"I's Sambo Hayes; dat's what I is. Now what you make dat noise fur?"

"Come close to me, Sambo, and I'll tell you. I want to speak to you in a low tone."

"Look 'e here, sah," cried the slave, in a threatening manner; "none o' yer damned blockade-running tricks on me; 'cos I won't stand 'em, yer see."

"Don't be afraid. You know that I am unarmed."

"I ain't afeard of yer, white man. Don't yer t'ink I is. It would take a bigger white man dan you is to make me afeard."

"I have no doubt of it, Sambo. Now, come close to the keyhole of the door, so that I can whisper to you."

"Don't yer be playin' any of yer tricks on dis nigger, now I tells yer."

His voice sounded as though he was both frightened and angry.

"What is the matter?"

"I tells yer what it is, white man, yer can't skeer me. Yer may groan as much as yer likes; but I's got lots ob spunk, I has. O, de Lord! what dat?"

I did not wonder at the slave's concluding exclamation; for as distinctly as ever I heard a sound, on shipboard or on the land, came a most unearthly groan floating through the dull, stifling air of that cellar, and die away in a low, sigh-like moan, that did sound most ghostly, and caused me to wish myself out of that den and in the open air.

"Don't yer do dat agin," cried Sambo, with chattering teeth. "White man, I tells yer to stop it. If yer don't, I leaves yer to yer own fate."

"I have done nothing," I said. "Let me out, and I'll prove it."

"N-o — n-o," was the stammering answer.

Then for a moment there was silence; but I could hear the teeth of the negro chattering as though he had an attack of fever and ague. Once more a groan, like that produced by a person in the last extremity, — low and gurgling at first, then rising higher and higher, until the sound resembled the sob of a sick-room. Then it died away like the sigh from the bosom of a dying consumptive.

"O, de Lord!" cried the negro. "Jesus hab mercy on dis nigger, for ebber and ebber, amen. What de debbil does it mean? Do you does dat, white man? Speak and tells me."

"Sambo, it is a warning for you to release me," I said, in as solemn a tone as I could assume. "Unless you throw open the doors, and set me free, you will be haunted for life."

"Den," cried the negro, with the most wonderful alacrity, "dey don't haunt dis child in de dark, now I tell yer. I'se off like a rigger, I is."

He ran up the stairs, and slammed the door after him; and that was the last I heard of Sambo for the night: but the groans did not cease, for they were as dismal and frequent as ever, until at last I was forced to call out, and ask if flesh and blood produced such moans, or if they were forced from some unhappy ghost, who had walked the earth until tired of such sport, and now desired to enter the silent tomb, and take some rest.

I called out three or four times, but no answer was returned. A deep groan was the only response; and at last I became satisfied that some human being was a prisoner, like myself, in that dreary cellar. I was superstitious, but not enough to believe that the groans were produced through unearthly agency; so I kept on talking and hailing.

"Groans, ahoy!" I cried. "Just give us a different signal from that; for I am tired of it. Try some other key, and see how you will succeed."

This remark seemed to attract some attention, for the dismal sounds ceased.

"That is right," I remarked. "Now vanish or go to sleep like a decent person; or, if you can't sleep, let others."

For a minute there was a profound silence, during which time I kicked at several toads that were hopping around my feet as if to claim acquaintance, for mutual protection. Just as I was about to sit down on the cold ground, with my back to the wall, a feeble, shaking voice, coming from a distant part of the cellar, startled me.

"Who are you who calls so loud?" it asked.

"That is a question that I would like to ask you," I replied.

"I am a poor, unhappy woman," was the response.

"And I am unhappy also because I'm a prisoner, and unable to assist you," I said.

"What! do you know who I am?" the shaky voice asked.

"I haven't the slightest idea."

"Then why do you take such an interest in me?"

"Because 'a fellow-feeling makes us wondrous kind.' I'd like to get out of this den. Wouldn't you?"

"Alas! yes."

"So should I; but I don't see any prospect of it just at present."

"Neither do I, unhappy me."

"How came you here?" I continued.

"Before I answer that question, let me inquire, who you are? A negro?"

"No; a white man."

"Thank God! You are a confederate?"

"Am I not in South Carolina?"

"True; you must be a friend."

"I hope that I am the friend of all women, and especially the friend of those in distress. Now, tell me how long you have been here, and how it happens that you are a prisoner."

"I have been locked up in this damp and filthy cell for three weeks. During all that time I have not seen daylight, anything but the black faces of my jailers, who have thrust a little unwholesome food into my den, and then retired. Can you wonder that I am nearly dead, or that I groan with anguish, or that I am half insane?"

"Why did the negroes meddle with you, a lady, who would harm no one?"

"Because I was active in the cause of the Confederacy. I have crossed the lines a dozen times, and brought information to our rulers."

"Ah, a spy!"

"Yes," in a tone of triumph; "and I was called the best one in the whole South. I know all the public men in Washington and Richmond, and in both places they trusted me. My services were so valuable to Mr. Davis and his cabinet, that they kept me constantly employed on my missions."

"Missions of peril," I remarked.

"No; far from it. The Yankees never harmed me, or offered to. The wretches have enough self-respect to abstain from insulting an unprotected female."

"I am glad to hear so good an account of them," I remarked. "They will grow wiser in time."

"Before that happens the South will have secured its independence."

"Perhaps so. You are a bold woman. But there is one thing you have not told me. Why did the negroes molest you?"

"I know not, unless it is with the intention of cutting short my usefulness; for I believe the wretches are more in favor of the North than the South."

"It would be just like them," I remarked, in a dry tone. "They seem capable of most anything."

"Yes; but if I was free, I would pay them for such treachery."

"I suppose you would," I simply said.

Then the female spy, overcome by her feelings, uttered several dismal groans in succession, which so exasperated one of the negro guards, that he opened the upper door, and swore he would "come down dar and choke her if she didn't shut up her head;" while, in spite of groans, toads, spiders, dampness, and the peculiarities of my situation, I sat down on the cold ground, and went to sleep.

I think that I slept several hours; for I was tired and worn out with the excitement of the previous night. When I awoke, I found several toads nestling on my breast, where they had sought refuge for the purpose of sharing the warmth of my body. I did not shake them off with the disgust which I had previously manifested. I began to look on them as companions, not agreeable ones, but to be endured because we were in the same cell, and could not escape, or obtain that freedom which I at least so much desired, even if the reptiles did not wish to see the sun, or even a glimmer of daylight, once more.

Hour after hour passed. I paced my cell until I was tired, and could hardly stand; and then I lay down, and went to sleep. I was wakened by a war of words, an outcry, a struggle; and jumping to my feet, the toads hopped to the right and left as I started up. Light was entering the chinks of the door of my cell, but none of the cracks were large enough to permit me to see what was going on. I listened attentively, and heard a struggle as the negroes attempted to force some one down stairs. For a few minutes it was carried on without words; but at length the slaves lost all patience, and I heard them threaten as though they were in earnest. Then a familiar voice replied to the intimidations, —

"Shucks! Do yer think ye kin frighten me, yer black devils? Look 'e here; I've licked a dozen jest sech niggers as you is afore breakfast, and never thought much of it. Don't roll up the whites of yer eyes to me, my boys; 'cos I ain't in the least afeard of yer. You has me in a trap; but dog on me ef I ain't Kaintuck enough to break out of it if yer give me a chance, now I tell yer."

"But we don't 'tend to let yer out, sah," replied one of the negroes. "We means to hold on to you; dat's what we means. You is too waluable, old man, to let loose and run round most anywhar."

"You black dogs!" was the angry rejoinder, "ef I had yer in Charleston, I'd pay yer for this; dog on me ef I wouldn't, now; though thar ain't a man in old Kaintuck what treats his niggers as well as I does, and would be more glad to git rid on 'em, forever and ever, amen; for we has been cussed enough with yer."

"Den why don't yer stop it?" asked one of the slaves. "Dat am de question."

"'Cos we is obstinate people, Cuffee. We don't like to be driv. Don't yer shove me that way. Hands off, yer black scoundrel. What! yer will, hey?"

Then followed the sounds of a desperate struggle; and curses and blows were scattered quite freely. I knew that the Kentuckian would make a desperate fight, and had my fears that the slaves would kill him; but it seemed that they did not desire to take his life; for they used no weapons except their hands, but those quite recklessly and freely.

But numbers got the better of Bowmount. He was overpowered and crushed; and then the negroes lifted him up, and pitched him into the cell next to the one that I occupied. The door was slammed to, bolted and barred; and then the slaves began comparing damages, and at the same time taunting the Kentuckian with what he had done.

At last the Kentuckian became speechless in his rage;

and then, when the negroes found that it was useless to taunt him further, they departed, in high glee at the success of their little scheme.

For half an hour all was quiet in the cells. I did not speak, fearing that one of the negroes was posted on the watch for the purpose of listening to what passed between Bowmount and myself. The Kentuckian would recover from his fit of anger, but still gave no sign that such was the case.

All at once, without previous warning, the female spy, who had remained remarkably quiet during the struggle, as though she rather enjoyed it than otherwise, commenced uttering some of her extraordinary groans, the peculiarity of which I have before alluded to. Twice she sounded her notes of warning before Bowmount roused himself to make a response.

"Shucks! what's that?" he growled, wonderingly.

Another groan was the answer.

"Look 'e here!" he fairly yelled; "if you niggers is up to some more of your tricks, just shut down on 'em; 'cos I tell yer they won't go down with me. I know 'em, and don't care for 'em. All the niggers in old Kaintuck can't fool me a mite."

A more terrible groan was the response.

I had become satisfied that none of the darkies were listening, and so spoke to Bowmount in a whisper; but, to my surprise, he seemed to regard it as another device of the enemy, and roared out, —

"To the devil with you, you black son of a gun! Don't bother me now that I'm caged and disarmed. You've trapped me, and that ought to satisfy you."

"Hush!" I cried. "Listen to me. You know my voice — don't you?"

"You black scamp! if I had hold of you for a second, I'd — "

"Bowmount? Don't be a goose. Hear me a moment."

"Who is it?"

"It's Barnwell."

"My God! you don't say so! Is it possible that you are here?"

"Yes. I was trapped and caged in a simple manner."

"But I warn't. They told me that you was sick, and wanted to see me. I said, 'Show me where he is, and I'll have him cured if money can do it.' Then I put a bottle of A No. 1 whiskey in my pocket, and got into a carriage John said had been sent for me."

"And they drove you here."

"Yes; that whitewashed nigger John, and a big black cuss they called Sam. And he took my watch, and be damned to him."

Just then, the woman, who had been silent for some time, uttered a dismal groan, as though she sympathized with the Kentuckian in his misfortunes.

"Ah! no wonder you grunt," cried the practical Kentuckian.

"O, my dear good man!" cried she, utterly ignoring Bowmount's remark, "can't you get me out of this?"

"Humph," muttered he, "I'd like to see myself gittin' out, or else gittin' a drink of whiskey. If you'll open my door, I'll open yours; and then we'll help one another."

"I wish I could," was the dismal response.

"So do I, with all my heart. If wishes had any effect, then I'd have a bottle of old rye in the twinkling of an eye."

I heard my eccentric friend kick at the toads, so that he could clear a place and lie down, and in a few minutes, by his deep breathing, knew that he was asleep. I thought that I could not do better than follow his example; and much, no doubt, to the gratification of my companions, I soon afforded them a resting-place, for when I awoke I found toads roosting on my breast, as contented as toads are supposed to be.

I removed them as gently as possible; but Bowmount was not so forbearing when he awoke. He hurled the harmless things across his den, uttered some frightful growls and oaths, and then arose and shook himself like a wild beast.

"Did you have a good sleep?" I asked.

"No. How in the devil is a man to sleep on the ground? Bah! I'm all cramps and cold. A bottle of whiskey would now be worth a fortune. O for one good pull at a flask!"

Then for a few moments he thrashed round the den, to circulate his blood; but soon stopped all noise, and seemed to meditate over some project. Presently he whispered, —

"Barnwell, old feller!"

"Yes; what is it?"

"Darn me if I ain't found a chisel in my cell."

"Is it good for anything?"

"Yes; quite stout and sharp."

"Can you work with it?"

"Work with it? Why, man alive, I could open half the jail doors in old Kaintuck with it."

"Never mind Kentucky. Can you open your door, and then mine?"

"Shucks! I'll try it, dog on me if I don't. You jest lay low, and look out for ducks. If them nigs will give me a chance to work, I'll go through the door like a dose of corn-juice."

I was willing to put trust in his promises, so waited patiently for him to commence operations.

"Now, then," he said, after he had made a brief examination of the cell, "you just whistle or sing, and I'll work. If that woman could groan a little, I wouldn't object. It might help us some."

I commenced the task assigned me, and Bowmount went to work with vigor, yet did not make noise enough to attract the attention of the negroes who were on guard just above us. After an hour's labor, I ventured to ask how he was succeeding.

"Bully," was the reply. "Keep whistling. I'm doing well."

I recommenced, and went through all the tunes that I knew, — Dixie, Yankee Doodle, and Hail Columbia, coming in for a share ; the two latter causing the confederate spy to utter some dismal groans, as though in remonstrance at such wickedness. At length the Kentuckian tore off a piece of the oak door with less caution than usual ; and the noise drowned my music, and attracted the attention of the negro who stood at the head of the stairs.

"What dat you do dar, hey?" he demanded, opening a door.

We returned no answer.

"What noise dat I hear?"

"I want something to eat," I said. "I am hungry. Give me a hoe-cake, or I'll whistle all night."

"Can't do it now, sah," replied the negro, in a tone that was far from brutal. "Yer see the nigs is all off on a stealin' raid, and only me and one oder is here to look arter you fellers. If I had de grub, you should hab it. De best dat I kin do is to gib you water all round, and dat'll have to do yer till the nigs comes back wid some dings."

"We don't want water. We have enough of that."

The door closed with a slam, and for half an hour Bowmount remained silent, fearing to work, thinking that he might be overheard by the sentinels. But, when we supposed that our vigilant colored guard was asleep, the chisel was once more called into use. The Kentuckian then labored with such vigor, that, in an hour's time, he announced, with a mighty effort suppressing a shout of

19

exultation, that his door was open, and he had free run of the cellar.

"Now what shall I do?" he asked. "Shall I pitch into the niggers single-handed, and kill 'em; or had I better help you out first, and then join forces?"

"Help me out, and then we'll see what can be done."

"The chisel is dull, and my hands are bleeding."

"Then why not escape without delay, and return with a force strong enough to rescue me?"

"Thar is somethin' in that," muttered the Kentuckian.

"There is much in the suggestion that will meet your views when I tell you that it is the only course that will save your life and my own. Of course you cannot hope to liberate me for an hour or more."

"That's so, Barnwell. Dog on the chisel! it's so dull."

"Well, suppose the negroes should enter the cellar while you were at work; wouldn't they see that you had operated on the door?"

"Shucks! of course they would. If they had eyes, they'd see the splinters. How could they help it?"

"And, as soon as they made the discovery, we should be shot, or ironed in a secure manner, with no hope of escape."

"Yes; the nigs would light on us like June-bugs."

"Then see if it is not possible to escape before the raiding gang returns."

"But, shucks, Barnwell! I can't leave you here all alone."

"I shan't be alone. Don't you know that the groaning lady will keep me company until you return?"

"Yes; but dog on sech company as that. It's wusser than none."

"Then I have my toads."

"The warmints."

"They will prevent me from growing rusty. Do as I request you. Leave this place, and come back and rescue me."

A STRUGGLE IN THE HAUNTED HOUSE.—Page 291.

"If I thought that you wouldn't think hard of me, old fellow."

"Not a hard thought shall cross my mind. I tell you that it is the only safe plan. Lose no time, but leave at once. Crowd sail, and be off."

"I will, old feller. Good by till I sees yer agin. I'll come back, unless they lets daylight into me."

He then moved from the door; and I could hear him feel his way to the stairs, and ascend them in so soft and quiet a manner, that I knew he had taken off his boots, and was proceeding in his stocking-feet. I listened in breathless silence for the result of the Kentuckian's venture, uncertain how he would proceed. Presently I heard a light tap on the door, as though produced by the foot of an impatient cat, anxious to escape from the cellar. It did not arouse the negro sentinel, however; so the tap was succeeded by others, until, at last, the slave unbarred and opened the door, growling impatiently, —

"What is all dis about?"

He had no time to utter more; for the wiry Kentuckian at the instant seized him by the throat, hurled him down the stairs, and closed and bolted the door. The slave struck on his head, and so was not injured in the least. He appeared to rub the parts that came in contact with the stones and boards, and I could hear him muttering to himself, —

"What de debbil does all dis mean, I'd like to know? How come dis chile here?"

As no answer was returned to this pertinent question, the negro, after a moment, continued to soliloquize: —

"De fust t'ing I knows, I was down here when I oughter be up dar. Bress de Lord! if I don't b'lieve dat wild bull of a Kentuckian is out and off. Is you in dar, old Kaintuck?"

There was no answer. I thought it best to pretend sleep.

"Blame me if I don't t'ink he's gone. What de debbil will I do? How can I get out, and go arter him? What kind ob a way am dis to treat a man? What will de udders say when dey comes back? By de Lord! but dis do beat eberyt'ing."

The slave continued to grumble until even the female spy could not stand it; so she uttered a deep groan, expressive of her disgust. This started the negro on a new topic, and he exclaimed, —

"Stop dat nonsense, will yer? What de debbil yer mean by makin' such a noise as dat are? Don't yer know dat I don't like it? If yer must do so, jist wait till dis chile gits out ob de way. O de Lord! who dat?"

I had spoken to him; but such was his terror, he was not disposed to think my voice a human one.

"Don't be alarmed, Sambo," I said. "Nothing will harm you."

"I ain't alarmed a bit, massa," he replied, his tone a little shaky yet; "but yer did rudder gib me a start, now dat am a fact. I t'ought you hab gone wid dat wild Kentuckian, dat we had so much trouble to git here. I's glad dat I has you and dat groaner left to show de nigs dat I has had my eyes open."

I talked with the slave for an hour, for I was glad of the opportunity; and, without revealing my true character, gave him some hints as to the intentions of the Yankees. Finally the door of the cellar was unbolted, and some one asked, —

"Sambo, is you dar?"

The answer came rather ungraciously.

"Yes; I be."

"What de debbil you doin' dar? Who tole yer to go down, and den bolt yerself in?"

"Nobody."

"Den wot yer do it fur?"

" 'Cos I couldn't help myself. Dat am de reason, you ignorant nigger you."

" Will yer 'splain about it ? "

" Well, den, while you was gone, dat wild bull of a Kentuckian bust t'rough de door widout any warnin', grab me by de neck, chuck me down de stairs, and den bolts de door, and cuts and runs. I is here ; but where de debbil dat Kentuckian is, I don't know. Dat's all about it."

The slaves uttered a howl of indignation, and would have vented their spite upon Sambo if some one had not interfered, and put a stop to the row. Who it was I had no means of learning ; but he seemed to have some power over the negroes ; for I could hear him order Sambo from the cellar, and bid the slaves close the door, and talk less, — all of which was obeyed. It was a white man who assumed charge, and he made those around him obey like a person who was accustomed to discipline.

All noise ceased. If there was any discussion, it was carried on in subdued tones, so that I could not hear it, much as I tried to ; but, after waiting an hour or more, a gang entered the cellar, and opened the door of my cell.

" Come," Sambo said ; "you is wanted."

" Who wants me ? "

" Never yer mind dat. You jist come along, and don't ax questions. Now, den, no tricks on us; 'cos we is ready for wiolence of any kinds."

I could see, by the torches which the slaves carried, that all the men were armed, some with pistols and knives, and others with knives and no pistols. As there was no doubt in my mind but that the negroes would use their weapons in case of necessity, I concluded to accompany them, the more readily because I was anxious to leave the den where I had been confined for so many hours.

" Sambo," I said, "I would like to know if I am to come back to my cell."

" What for you want to know dat."

"Because I have some companions in here whom I wish to take leave of if I am not to see them again."

The slaves thought I meant human beings; for they jumped back, and laid their tawny hands on their pistols and knives, fearing a Kentuckian-like attack.

"Whar am dem companions what you speak of?" Sambo demanded.

"Those three or four toads which you see in the corner."

The negroes peered at them by the aid of their torches, and then laughed, while Sambo remarked, —

"You don't take dis t'ing berry hard — does you?"

"No; why should I?"

"Well, massa, dat is for yous to find out. You isn't a bad rebel, I reckon, even if you is a South Carlinian; so I'll do what I can for yer; but blast dat Kaintuck! he's de debbil and all. We has no mercy for white trash what forces a colored gemman down stairs when de gemman don't want to go."

The colored guards closed around me, marched me up the cellar-stairs, Sambo leading the way, a pistol in one hand, and a long, sharp knife in the other. His companions carried the pine torches, the smoke from which was dense and black enough to suffocate one, causing the female spy to utter the most dismal groans, much to the enjoyment of the slaves, who appeared to have but little sympathy for her sufferings.

Into the large room, on the ground floor, I was marched; and there I found some ten or twelve other slaves, with only one settee for the entire party; consequently the apartment was not so full of smoke but that I could breathe, although but little air entered the room, on account of the windows being boarded up on the outside.

"You jist stand dar!" cried Sambo, who seemed to rank as sergeant, and to have recovered the ground which he had lost through the escape of Bowmount.

He pointed to a corner of the apartment, the one farthest from the door and windows, as though he feared I would make a flying leap, and disappear from their sight. I assumed the station allotted to me.

"Now tell 'em that we is ready," Sambo commanded in a pompous tone.

One of the slaves left the room; and, while I was wondering what was up, he returned, preceding two white men and half a dozen negroes. Among the latter I recognized John, the mulatto; but his white companions I did not know, their faces being concealed by slouched hats, and coat collars turned up.

"This is the rebel I spoke to you about," John said, stepping forward as master of ceremonies. "He is one of the most dangerous men I ever saw. He is bold and unscrupulous to such a degree that no one is safe who ventures to differ from him. He is a great prize, and must be taken care of."

I saw one of the white men start, as he looked me over, as though surprised at seeing me; but as I kept my eyes towards the person, interested in his movements, I noticed that the slouched hat was partly removed, just enough to show me the handsome and boyish face of Mr. Harry Bluff, *alias* Reefpoint, *alias* English Harry, *alias* English seaman, the Yankee midshipman on board the Stingeree, Captain Switchell. A 'finger was laid on the lad's lips as a token of silence, or I should have uttered an exclamation of astonishment.

"Bah!" said the midshipman, in a tone of contempt; "he don't look dangerous. The Yankees could walk through a million such men, and not exert themselves."

"You don't know him!" cried the mulatto, in an eager tone. "He is one of the most dangerous men in the rebel states. A person who can bamboozle an admiral, run his ship past the entire fleet, and laugh at the whole Yankee forces, is one to be looked after."

"But where is the other character? Where is the rebel Kentuckian, the owner of the steamer Belle? He is the desperate one, I should suspect. Trot him out. Let us look at him. If he is as desperate as you say he is, we'll take care of him, and give him safe quarters."

The negroes remained silent. Mr. Reefpoint's companion, who I saw was a young petty officer of the Stingeree, intimated that, if it was not too much trouble, he should like to see the Kentucky roarer.

"We had trouble enough with him," said the mulatto, gnashing his teeth; "but, in spite of all our precautions, the rascal has escaped from our clutches."

Then the negroes yelled in chorus, —

> "Hallelujah! hallelujah! see him run,
> Run, run, run!
> May de debbil catch him,
> Catch him, catch him,
> And jerk him to kingdom come,
> Come, come!"

A relic of their plantation days, when all hands were compelled to listen to the preaching of one of their own number, and sang extempore songs in praise of Him whom they worshipped in their rude way.

"Tell your friends to stop that howling," said Mr. Reefpoint. "I don't want a squad of confederate soldiers coming down on me like a thousand of brick. The less noise we have about this business, the better."

"There is no fear, sah," replied an old negro. "Dis house am haunted, and no white man come near it in de night time. De more noise we make, de less dey come here."

John looked at my watch, — for, by some means or other, the rascal had obtained it from Sam, — and announced that it was time to make a movement of some kind or other.

"It is three o'clock," he said. "In a few minutes we shall have daylight; and then the men will have to take to the swamp, and keep concealed till dark. You should be on your way unless you intend to remain with us until to-morrow."

"Which course is the safest?"

Mr. Reefpoint pondered this question in a careless tone, as though he was rather indifferent on the subject.

"My advice," John replied in a decisive tone, "is to leave at once."

"What is there to fear?"

"That escaped Kentuckian is more to be feared than you suppose. If he clears the swamps, he will bring a squad of soldiers down upon us. Then our secret is discovered, the house taken possession of, and a hound-like hunt for our gang. You must get out of the way of all danger."

This caused a sensation in the negro ranks; and several dark looks were cast at Sambo, who had been on guard when Bowmount made his escape.

"That would be awkward," Mr. Reefpoint remarked. "I have no desire to see rebel soldiers so far from salt water. Put the darbies on the prisoner," said the midshipman, addressing the petty officer at his side. "We must make all safe."

When the slaves heard the click of the irons, they were inclined to be jubilant, and hardly knew whether they had better dance or shout in chorus. Already had they commenced shuffling their feet, and began to throw back their heads, for the purpose of expressing their joy, when Mr. Reefpoint interfered, and checked the outburst.

"None of your confounded noise at this time of morning," he said. "Wait till I'm out of sight before you put on steam. Come; we must start. Let the pilot lead the way, and we'll follow him."

A young and vigorous negro stood forth as the person who was to lead us to salt water. He had a knapsack on his shoulders, and a revolver and bowie-knife in his belt. He looked just like a person who would endure much toil and privation to maintain a principle; so I was not surprised to learn that he was the regular guide for those adventurous Yankees who landed on the coast, and penetrated to the interior of South Carolina, for the purpose of holding consultations with the negroes, and receiving important prisoners whom the slaves had captured.

"I am ready," said the young black, opening the door.

"Now, Mr. Rebel," cried the midshipman, "will you go along peaceably, or will you be led?"

"Peaceably," I replied.

"On your honor?"

"On my honor, I will make no effort to escape unless you approve of the same."

"I'm satisfied."

Then, turning to the mulatto, he said in a louder tone,—

"Good by, John. Let us hear from you, as soon as possible, in relation to the subject I spoke to you about."

It was not until we had left the broad avenue, nearly overgrown with grass from utter neglect and disuse, and struck across the country, that the midshipman spoke to me; and then it was in a whisper, so that the negro pilot could not overhear him.

"I found you in a bad fix, Mr. Barnwell," he said.

"Yes," I responded eagerly; "but it might have been worse."

"Egad, I don't know about that. Are you aware that those fellows hain't much conscience when a white rebel is concerned?"

"So I should suppose; but I was not in the least alarmed for my safety."

"The devil! Will you tell me who you are, sir? for I don't know for certain if you are loyal or rebel."

"Certainly. I am an officer in the confederate navy."

"Gammon! Excuse me, but I don't believe it."

"Just as you please. Now let me ask you a question."

"Fire away."

"Well, how does it happen that I see you on such duty as this? I supposed you were on your way north in the Spitfire."

"O, Captain Switchell said that I was very useful to him; so transferred me to the Stingeree. We chased a blockade-runner as far as Fort Sumter; and then I received orders to land, and follow the lead of this black pilot. Barnes and I had a sweet time of it, last night, riding through swamps and jungles, cruising around hills to avoid the rebs, and getting shot on suspicion that we were a parcel of darkies on a raid."

"You'd better believe it," muttered Barnes, the petty officer. "It was awful cruisin'-ground, and a feller had to feel his way."

"Or else run the risk of feeling lead," remarked the middy, as though he cared but little for danger, provided he could share some excitement.

"You are a rash boy, and Captain Switchell should have known better than to have sent you on such an expedition," I said.

"O, I don't know about that. Some one had got to go, and I as well as another. I suppose that my neck is no more precious than Barnes's, and yet Barnes volunteered to accompany me."

"Of course I did, Mr. Barnwell. I likes a lark as well as the next one, and I guess our prisoner does too, 'cos I think I has seen his face on board the Stingeree."

"As a prisoner," I remarked.

"Well, sir, you can call it what you please; it don't matter to me. Only I saw you there."

"Well, I hope that you won't see me again in a hurry,"

I remarked; "for I must leave you in a few minutes. Be kind enough to take off the darbies."

"What! ain't you going with us?" asked the middy, in a tone of astonishment.

"Not this morning. You must return to the ship without me. Come; remove the irons; for I have worn them long enough to accommodate you." .

"But what shall I tell the pilot? He'll think it devilish strange."

"Perhaps so, after he discovers the loss; but you'll notice that he does not turn his head very often to look in this direction; and, besides, it is dark; so I can slip away quite readily, and be in Charleston by sunrise."

"But the admiral and captain will grumble if I don't tow them a prisoner. They expected two big ones, you know."

"Give my compliments to Captain Switchell, and tell him that I prefer land to water just at present."

"Yes, sir; I'll do so."

Then off came the irons that had graced my wrists. Just as they were removed, we crossed a road, and then the noise of ringing muskets saluted our ears, and the words, uttered as though in earnest, of, "Who goes there? Halt."

Our negro pilot gave one look, a bound, and then landed in a clump of bushes, and disappeared from the scene. Half a dozen shots were fired; and the bullets struck the bushes, cutting off twigs, and scattering them to the right and left, as though distributed by a whirlwind.

"Look after that nigger," shouted a commanding voice. "Capture him, dead or alive."

Half a dozen men, dressed in gray, sprang from their ambush, and dashed after the runaway pilot; while I could see that enough soldiers remained to take care of us. I think that, while I was waiting for further commands, I counted no less than thirty musket-barrels; and all of them were pointed in our direction, ready to speak if we moved in opposition to commands.

Even in this moment of confusion I had time to ask Mr. Reefpoint and Barnes a question.

"Have you on your person," I asked, "a single article which will prove that you belong to Uncle Sam? Speak quick, and don't deceive me."

"Not even a button," the midshipman replied, as cool as the day we met in Nassau.

"Are you sure?"

"Quite sure. We took care of that when we left the ship."

"Then be guided by me, and I'll try to save you. Know nothing of the Yanks. You are common sailors, — nothing more, — and here on a lark."

"Do you surrender?" roared an officer, who now appeared in front of his line.

"Of course we do, and devilish glad to find the chance," I replied. "We are unarmed, and incapable of making resistance, even if we desired to."

"Remember, let me do all the talking," I cried, in a low whisper, when I saw the soldiers order arms, and then advance to surround us. "You belong to the blockade-runner Belle, Captain Barnwell, now in the port of Charleston. You came out to look for me, and to have a lark. Not a word more, as you value your neck."

"All right," both of my companions replied.

Then they commenced whistling Dixie, in regular sailor style, careless and free. Some thirty men — dark, long-haired men, with dirty gray uniforms, rough beards, and reckless manners — surrounded us before we had time to exchange another word.

"Who are you, and where do you hail from?" demanded the officer who commanded the company.

"They is Yankee spies; that's what they is," two or three of the confeds shouted, giving us a push, so that they could see our faces and examine our persons.

"If they are Yankees, a rope and a tree will make short work with them," the officer said.

"Let's hang 'em fust, and try 'em arterwards," was the cry.

I did not know but that such a course would be adopted; still I did not manifest the least impatience or fear.

"I reckon some of you fellers never faced the Yanks, or you'd know them better when you saw them," I remarked, in a bantering tone. "But I don't intend to quarrel with you on that account. I'll just tell you who I am, and see if it won't satisfy you."

The soldiers leaned on their guns, and the officers on their swords, all waiting to hear my yarn, and all prepared to disbelieve it, no matter how closely I stuck to the truth.

Just at this moment, the six scouts, who had gone in pursuit of the negro pilot, returned and reported that, although they had failed to capture the runaway, they had secured his knapsack and blanket, and that in the former they had found a bottle of whiskey.

"Show it," was the cry that went up from all hands.

"Here is the bottle," cried one, holding it up.

"And the whiskey?"

"We've drank it."

A chorus of groans was the response to this exclamation; and one fellow, who seemed to feel especially aggravated, uttered an emphatic hope that the liquor would "pizen the selfish cusses what swallowed it."

This little episode over, the soldiers prepared to listen to what I had to utter in explanation of why we were there.

I commenced by telling the truth. I informed them

that I commanded the blockade-runner Belle, and that the negroes had enticed me away from the vessel on the ground that some one desired to see me on business, and they had kept me confined in a house until within a few hours, when an opportunity offered to escape, and that I had met a negro, who had agreed to take me to the city, and while on the way I met the two sailors, who had come in search of me, being also on a " lark " at the same time.

As soon as I had finished speaking, there was a moment's silence; and then the captain of the company asked, —

" And you expect us to believe all you have said ? "

" I certainly do."

" Why do you ? "

" Because it is the truth."

The soldiers uttered a shout of derision, and some of them laughed in a scornful manner at the idea of their swallowing such an improbable yarn.

" Look here, my friend," said the captain, as soon as the noise subsided; " we have heard just such yarns before ; and when I tell you that I don't believe it, I but express my convictions. We have often heard of Yankees landing on the coast, and penetrating inland, for the purpose of acting the part of spies. In fact, it was only last night we were informed that a party had come on shore from one of the gunboats ; and so we were on the lookout for you, with orders from the general to string you up as soon as we captured you."

" On the supposition that we are the ones who came on shore ? "

The captain bowed, and lighted a home-made cigar.

" Do I look like a spy ? " I demanded with dignity.

" You don't look like anything else," was the consoling reply.

" And you won't believe the yarn that I have related ? "

"I can hardly take it in. It looks too improbable."

"Name one thing that looks to you unreasonable."

"A dozen, if you desire so many. In the first place, do you think that a South Carolinian would believe that a party of slaves dared to play such tricks at the present time? They are too faithful for that; but even if they desired to aid the Yanks, they have no chance; for a constant watch is kept on their movements. They cannot stir unless it is known to the patrol."

"Haven't you missed some of your prominent men within a month or two?"

"Two or three of them have stepped out; but we can guess where they are, without thinking that they have been kidnapped in such a way as you suggest."

"It is no use," whispered Reefpoint. "We can't pull the wool over their eyes. Save yourself, and let us meet the fate they intend for us."

"Never," I replied. "We will all go clear, or we will all hang together. Even to the last, stick to it that you are confeds. We must pull through."

"I think," remarked the captain, " that you had better get ready for a swing from the limb of some tree. You have played your trump card, and it isn't large enough. Now we'll play ours, and see if we can't euchre you."

"I have no doubt but that you can," I said; "for you hold the right and left bowers; but if you proceed to extremities, you will find that even the winner of the game had better have lost."

"Look 'e here," cried the captain in a confident tone; "if you are innocent, as you try to make out, what made your guide, the nigger, cut and run for it?"

"I haven't the slightest idea."

"Another question. Why was you heading towards salt water, across the country, instead of making for the city?"

"Haven't I told you that the negro said he knew of a short cut, that would save us several miles?"

"Gammon!" roared the men, laughing at the absurdity of the story.

"Our South Carolina niggers," said the captain, "are not up to such games as that. They have too much respect for a white man to deceive one."

"I think you are mistaken, and believe that the negro guide meant to lead us astray; but of our honesty you can be assured by returning to the house where I was confined, or else taking us to Charleston."

"It would be a waste of time. We have proof enough of your guilt, and so don't care to add to it."

With this remark, the captain glanced in the direction of the stout limb of a palmetto tree that grew near by.

Some of his men took the hint; and with a yell that sounded fiendish and cruel, they stacked their arms, and produced three ropes, which were made of Manila hemp, were small and new, and which looked as though they were kept on hand for special cases, just like the one now presented.

Up the tree went one of the soldiers, reaching the stout limb with the agility of an ape; and there the fellow sat, and waited for his comrades to throw the ends of the ropes up to him, so he could make them secure.

Once more little Reefpoint appealed to me, in the hope that I would save my life at the expense of his own.

While we were looking at the ropes, and wondering what we should do next (for I had not given up all hope), some of the more adventurous of the soldiers, recollecting that we had not been searched, thrust their hands in our pockets, and went all over us in so expeditious a manner as to prove that they were accustomed to such business. But they found nothing that was calculated to establish either our innocence or guilt.

While this was going on, I asked the captain to give me a moment's private conversation. After a minute's hesitation, he complied; and I had an opportunity to speak to him without being overheard.

"Captain," I asked, "do you really mean to hang us?"

"Such is my present intention," the officer replied, once more lighting a cigar, and having the politeness to offer me one.

. As it seemed to be the last time that I should have an opportunity to taste tobacco, I accepted the present, and lighted the cigar from the captain's smoking weed.

"You had better think twice of the matter," ·I remarked. "You will be sorry if you carry out your intentions."

"Perhaps I shall. If I am, I'll let you know when we meet in the next world."

"There's not the slightest prospect of that," I replied.

"Why not?"

"Because, while you will go to a hot place, I shall go to a more agreeable abode."

"Then I'll send word; although I'm not sure but our positions may be reversed."

The captain was a good-natured man, and did not take offence. From this I had great hope. I thought I might joke him into a reprieve until I could get word to my friends in Charleston. But I soon saw that the scamp could laugh and smile, and still be willing to inflict capital punishment upon parties whom he supposed unfriendly to the Confederacy.

I was just about to make a last tender, to offer a large sum for my life and the lives of the other two, when we heard the sound of horses' feet; and then down the road came two men, mounted on stout cobs.

"Hollo! whom have we here?" muttered the captain.

"Perhaps some one whom you know. If so, call him as a witness."

The horsemen approached with much confidence, until they were near enough to show me the venerable face of Colonel Rhett and the dark countenance of John the mulatto — two men whom I could not expect would act a friendly part.

"Here are two persons," I said, addressing the captain, "who will prove me a true friend to the Confederacy, provided they speak the truth."

"What makes you think they won't do the right thing by you?" asked the captain.

"Because both of them were concerned in my imprisonment. They belong to the gang of negroes I spoke to you about."

The soldier laughed in a careless, incredulous sort of manner, as though he was not to be deceived by such shams.

"You are a victim to persecution," the captain said. "I have met just such people before."

"So much the worse for me. But call them, and hear what they say."

"Bring those men here," the captain ordered.

His soldiers had surrounded the new arrivals, and were asking a few questions. These were important in some respects; for all the interrogations commenced with whiskey, and ended with tobacco — two articles which the confederate defenders desired above all things.

As Colonel Rhett seldom travelled far from home without whiskey and tobacco, he was in a measure enabled to supply a small stock of each to the men; which was received with growls that it was not more, and disposed of in a few swallows and some twenty chews.

The valiant Virginian and the mulatto had consulted together for a moment, while the whiskey and tobacco were being shared; but that moment was enough to enable them to settle on their plans; for one or two adroit questions to the soldiers had revealed the fact that we were prisoners, captured as spies, and about to be executed as such.

As bold as impudence could make them, the colonel and John presented themselves to the commander of the company.

"Who are you?" the latter asked.

"I am Colonel Rhett, of Virginia," the white-headed old wretch answered. "I perceive that I am speaking to a gentleman of the rank of captain. I am happy to meet you, sir. I was at the battle of Bull Run, sir; and I am proud to say that I did my whole duty on that glorious day. Gods! how we made the Yankees take to their heels! I laughed until I cried at the panic."

"I should like to have been there," the captain remarked. "But I was at Sumter."

"Another great triumph for our arms, sir. We struck for liberty the day the Yankee flag was lowered from that fort. I should have been pleased, sir, to have lent my aid on that occasion. But it was impossible. Virginia did not lead this time, but left it to a more noble state, South Carolina, to reap all the laurels."

"Who is your companion?" asked the captain, pointing to John, and seemingly anxious to cut short such a torrent of compliments.

"A slave belonging to a Georgia lady, a Mrs. Gowen."

"The wife of a cotton agent?"

"The same."

"I am acquainted with her and her husband; but I thought they both were at Nassau."

"Her husband is, but the lady is in Charleston. She arrived only a few days since in a blockade-runner. I have the honor to rank as one of her friends."

The colonel raised his hat, as though he could never sufficiently honor the lady for allowing him such claims.

"If Mrs. Gowen has a particle of friendship for you, it is a sufficient guarantee of your honesty and respectability," the captain remarked. "I know her peculiar fastidiousness, and her zeal for the cause."

The colonel rubbed his hands, and bowed, while the soldier was speaking.

"The slave, having nothing to do, is permitted to act as my groom," Colonel Rhett added, in explanation of John's presence. "Mrs. Gowen loans him to me to ride out in my company, on account of my health being so poor."

"This person," said the captain, pointing to me, "intimated that you can prove him loyal to the South. Can you do so?"

"O de Lord! just t'ink ob dat, massa colonel!" cried the mulatto John, suddenly assuming the tone and manner of a happy but rather ignorant negro; and then the fellow roared with laughter.

"Silence, John," thundered the colonel, with all the fierceness that so well becomes a military man. "How dare you, John?"

"O de Lord! but I couldn't help it, massa colonel, when I t'ink ob dat man sayin' dat he is ob de South."

"Well, well," remarked the colonel, somewhat mollified; "don't be too forward, even if Mrs. Gowen does pet you too much. Recollect in whose presence you stand." And the Virginian pointed to the captain.

"Yes, sah; I'll remember 'em well."

But still the slave giggled and grinned as though he had discovered a magnificent joke.

"Do you know this person?" asked the captain, pointing to me.

The colonel took another look, and then shook his old addled head, as though he was dodging balls at Bull Run.

"O! don't massa colonel know 'em well! dat am a fact," ejaculated the slave.

And he once more chuckled in a quiet manner.

"John," mildly remarked the colonel, "won't you be quiet?"

"Yes, sah; I'm dumb as a turtle, sure."

"As John says," continued the colonel, in a benevolent tone, "I do know the man, and it pains me to add that I don't know much good of him. A more precious rascal does not exist on the face of the earth."

"Dat's so," muttered John, as though to clinch the assertion.

I did not answer them, but still smoked my cigar, and listened to the comments of two of the most lying scoundrels in South Carolina. I saw that they were determined to make an end of me, if such a thing was possible; and all that I had to hope for was, that they would contradict themselves, and thus give me a chance.

"What do you think of your witnesses at the present time?" asked the captain, turning to me with a peculiar smile.

"O, I'm not in the least surprised at what they say; you know that I told you I was uncertain how they would testify."

"I'll be bound the fellow invented some cock-and-bull story respecting us," the colonel remarked.

"No; he merely said that both of you could help him if you desired, but that he had some doubts on the subject."

"Is that all?" and the colonel's face looked the relief he felt.

"Wal, dat is a wonder, sure," John had the pleasure to utter.

"But he told me some other things which rather surprised me," the captain said; and then related my yarn as to how I was trapped by the negroes, and kept a prisoner.

"I hope, for the honor of your profession, that you will not believe such an improbable story," Colonel Rhett cried, in a scornful tone.

"De niggers ob South Carlina is faithful to de palmetto tree. Dey be faithful to de last," the mulatto said, in a confident manner. "I knows dey is."

"We are all glad to hear it, John," the colonel remarked in a tone that he meant to be patronizing. "We have done enough for the people of your color to make them fast friends."

"Dat you has, colonel, and we is grateful for it, all ob us."

"I don't see but that I must hang you three gentlemen, much as I dislike the job," the captain said, turning to me and my two companions.

"On what charge?" asked the colonel and mulatto in an eager tone.

"As spies."

Rhett and John seemed a little astonished, and the rascals looked at each other as though they could hardly believe their ears.

"As spies?" they muttered.

"Yes; Yankee spies."

"If that's what they are, jerk 'em up. I reckon they deserve it. I don't have any sympathy for a man who serves his country in that way."

"Hang 'em, sah, as quick as you can," the mulatto cried, taking his cue from the colonel.

"But I want a little more proof," the soldier maintained.

"Proof, sir! you have ample proof," Colonel Rhett cried in an eager tone.

"I don't see it just yet;" and the captain, who was rather a good-natured, humane fellow, looked his perplexity.

"You want more proof — do you?" demanded the colonel in an eager tone. "I didn't intend to say one word about it, but will on account of the position in which you are placed. It is painful to my feelings to thus speak, but justice to my country prompts me. That man" — and the colonel pointed his long, bony finger at me — "I met at Nassau. He lived for some weeks in the same hotel with myself and daughter. We went to Nassau in the same steamer. On the sea or on the shore I never knew him to be regarded in any other light than that of a Vandal or damned Yankee spy. As such, he was shunned and despised."

"I knows dat," John said, with a grave shake of his head; "'cos one day, master, he pint to dis feller, and say, 'John, dat one of dem cheap white trash dat lib Norf. He spyin' round here in hope of pickin' up some news; but de Southern peoples all know him, and I tink he no get much here.'"

"And the other two — do you know aught of them?" the captain asked, pointing to Harry and the petty officer Barnes.

The colonel hastened to speak. He probably knew that Mr. Reefpoint and Barnes were on a mission regarding me, so considered that he was in duty bound to save them if such a thing were possible. For this purpose he took a long and careful look at both faces, and then rendered his judgment to the captain.

"These young men I've seen in Alderny & Co.'s store, at Nassau, and they were pointed out to me as blockade-runners, and successful ones at that. I'll stake my life that they are all right."

"Sergeant, remove them, and keep them in custody for the present," commanded the captain; and off Harry and Barnes were marched, not being allowed to exchange a word with me.

"You have done one good thing in saving the lives of those men," I said, addressing the colonel. "Now tell the truth about myself, and you will fare better for it."

"I have told the truth, young man," the colonel remarked in a tone of great severity. "I wish that you were as Christian-like and sincere as myself."

"I don't see but that I must hang you," the captain cried. "It's hard, I know; but still I must do it. You won't mind it after all is over. In fact, I rather think you will like it."

"You're a pretty good fellow, even if you do want to hang me," I said. "Now just take my advice, and carry me to Charleston, and you'll see how I'll turn the tables on these fellows, and what a laugh we'll have at their expense."

The captain shook his head.

"I wish I could, but my orders are imperative."

I had no time to utter more, for some of the soldiers approached me, in obedience to a signal, and laid their hands on my shoulder.

"Come," they said; "the rope is ready, and awaits you."

"Is there no hope?" I asked, and once more turned to the captain; but the soldiers had faced to the right, so that the captain could not hear my appeal.

I was about to walk towards the tree where the ropes were suspended, when I caught the sound of horses' hoofs on the road that led to Charleston.

The soldiers who were conducting me halted for a moment on hearing the noise, and receiving no sign from their captain, remained in a stationary position.

"On with him!" cried the colonel, fearful that something would happen so that his vengeance could not be satisfied. "To the tree! to the rope!"

"We take orders only from our captain," a corporal replied.

By this time, some twenty-five horsemen appeared in sight, clad in the gray uniforms of the Confederacy. But there was one man who rode a powerful animal, and who led the advance, plying whip and spur; and he, I noticed, was not in uniform, nor did he wear any of the emblems of military life. A slouched hat concealed his face, and there was no way by which I could distinguish it; yet my hopes arose when I thought that it might be the Kentuckian leading a party of soldiers to the house in the hope of effecting my release.

"Whom have we here?" muttered the captain. "They ride as though blooded stock was abundant, and oats cheap, in the Southern Confederacy."

"Can't you string him up before they reach here?"

The colonel betrayed such intense eagerness in this inquiry, that the captain replied, —

"Do you want the show all to yourself, that you are in such a hurry? If we must hang, let the others have a chance."

"Whoop!" shouted the man who rode in advance of the cavalcade. "Wake, snakes, and give 'em ginger!"

Then off went his hat; and to my joy, I saw the rough, dark, stern face of Bowmount, for it was now daylight.

"This is very unmilitary," muttered the captain; "but what can you expect from the cavalry as a body where every private owns the horse that he rides? Of course all discipline is lost. The infantry is the arm for service, after all the talk."

While the captain was thus consoling himself, the Kentuckian was uttering any number of Indian war-whoops; but whether from the effects of joy or whiskey, I could not tell. However, one thing I noticed — that my two particular friends, Colonel Rhett and John, manifested symptoms of uneasiness at the approach of the Kentuckian; and by the manner in which they glanced over their shoulders, I judged that they wanted to retreat before all communications were cut off.

"Don't let those fellows escape," I said to the captain, the instant I noticed they were disposed to edge away. "We will now prove who is right, and who is wrong."

"Sergeant," said the captain, "keep your eye on those men, and don't let them leave the grounds until I order their release. Colonel," he continued, addressing the Virginian, "I am astonished that you should wish to take up your line of march just at this time, when proof of your assertions is so near at hand. Now we can have a full and fair hearing; for I see that General Rampage is at the head of the cavalry. He isn't a man to be trifled with, and can sift truth from falsehood, as well as the smartest city judge."

I saw a look of terror and dismay on the faces of Colonel Rhett and the mulatto. Then the cavalry checked their horses, and the men dismounted.

The Kentuckian threw his reins to a corporal as he touched the ground, and then came running towards me, his arms widely extended, and his face expressing joy and several large doses of whiskey.

"Shucks! man alive, what are you doing here?" roared the Kentuckian, throwing his stout, muscular arms around me, and hugging me like a gorilla. "Damn it! why ain't you in the house, in the cell, all locked up, keepin' toads and other varmints company, not to speak of the groaning woman, what is never easy unless at it hard? Speak — can't you? How did you get out? Damn me ef I ain't glad to see you, and no mistake!"

It was impossible to answer all these questions, much as Bowmount would have liked me to do so. I only hugged him in return, and swore that I was never so glad to see a man in all my life.

But, while I was thus assuring my friend of my affection and joy, the Kentuckian's eyes were at work, and fell on the military captain. A smile passed over Bowmount's face as he advanced towards the soldier with outstretched hand.

"Shucks, captain," cried the Kentuckian, "but I'm jolly glad to see you, dog on me if I ain't, and no mistake. I ain't seen yer since we was in Tennessee together, a cuttin' up the Yanks' supplies."

The two shook hands in the heartiest manner, as though they were old comrades, as indeed they were; for when Bowmount commanded a regiment of wild Kentuckians, all mounted on blood horses owned by their riders, the captain was a lieutenant in the same body of men, and had received some favors at the hands of the colonel, establishing a lasting friendship between the two.

Just at this moment Bowmount's eyes fell upon Colonel Rhett and the slave.

"Hollo!" he said, with no friendly glare; "how does it happen that you are here? Shucks! I was in hopes that I should never see your two faces again. Dog on me if I ain't tired of 'em.

"Do you know the colonel and the slave?" asked the captain, who was so ambitious to hang me a moment before.

"Well, I reckon I do know 'em."

"Then your arrival is most opportune, for you can tell me which party is worthy of the most confidence."

"Why, haven't you found out yet?"

"No."

"Well, dog on me if that ain't good," roared the Kentuckian. "Why, a man what has been two minutes in the company of 'em couldn't help noting who told the truth, and who told lies."

"That there has been lying I am ready to admit," the captain remarked; "but I want to know who tells the lies. I have arrested your friend as a spy; and, by George, I was about to hang him as a spy when you came up."

"Hang him! Spy!" roared the Kentuckian. "If you had, there'd been murder committed in this state afore long, now I tell you."

"There is no occasion for excitement on this subject," the captain remarked in a quiet tone, as though he knew the Kentuckian's temper and peculiarities. "We'll talk it over in a quiet manner, so that justice shall be done."

"That's all we want. Rampage, you'll see justice done here won't you?"

"That's what I came for," was the general's answer.

"Now," continued the captain, pointing to me, "tell us who that person is."

"Why, he commanded my blockade-runner, the Belle. Shucks! but you should have seen him rush her past the fleet, and talk right pert with the admiral, just as cool as a cobbler well supplied with ice."

"And you can vouch for his loyalty to the South?"

"Shucks! a man what does that don't need no vouching for — does he, Rampage?"

The general thought that it was good evidence of patriotism.

"You have never seen anything to make you believe he's a Yankee spy?" continued the captain.

"Known him for months, and never heard such a thing," was the prompt answer.

"So far, so good," nodded the captain. "Now, do you know of his being trapped by a party of negroes?"

"I reckon. Shucks! dog on me! but wan't I took the same way, and put in a pen not fit for a hog?"

"This grows interesting," remarked the captain. "Who trapped you? Can you point out the parties?"

"Well, I reckon. Do you see that light-colored nigger, what is getting a little shaky in the kneepans?"

"Yes."

"Well, he's one of 'em."

"Do you mean it? Mrs. Gowen's slave engaged in such business as kidnapping?"

"Sartin. He's a cuss."

"A what?"

"A cuss. I reckon I know him by this time."

"But how does it happen that you escaped from the slaves' clutches?"

"Well, you know jails never held me a great while; and when I found myself in a pen, jist set to work to git out. I did escape, but I couldn't take my friend with me; but I promised to return for him as soon as I could, and here I am, with half a company of dragoons to back me."

"You see, captain, that my story holds good," I remarked.

"I see it does, and feel ashamed that I did not rely upon your word. What interest could those men have in telling such a falsehood?"

"Ask them, and see."

"Colonel Rhett," the captain remarked. "you and the slave are in a bad position. You have made false statements. Can you explain matters? You have a chance to do so."

The Virginian did not want for a lie. He stepped forward, as bold apparently as ever, and commenced his defence.

"There's some mistake here," he said, "and I'm glad it's rectified in time to prevent bad consequences. We certainly were led to believe that Captain Barnwell was a notorious Yankee spy. Acting under that impression, John concluded that it would be a good thing to cut short his career. So he imprisoned him, and attempted to obtain all his secrets, under the impression that he could sell them to the Confederacy, — not for money, but renown, — and to show that the slaves of the South are for the South. If he has made a mistake, I suppose that he is sorry for it."

The treacherous old scamp was attempting to screen himself at the expense of the slave. He did not care what punishment was inflicted upon John, if his own neck escaped.

The Kentuckian had listened to the whole yarn with but few expressions of impatience; but I saw by his eyes that he was getting enraged very fast, and when he roared out an oath and several ejaculations, I was not surprised.

"You miserable specimen of a Bull Runner!" he yelled to the terrified colonel; "you remnant of the first families of Virginia! you cringing dog, you lying colonel, what do you mean by tellin' sich yarns as that for, when you know that I was took in the same way that Barnwell was, and locked up next to him, like a sojer arter a drunk? Answer me that, you miserable specimen of another age. How dare you lie so in the presence of a gentleman like myself?"

The unfortunate colonel seemed to have forgotten that the Kentuckian had been treated the same way as myself; so, for a moment he seemed overwhelmed at the evidence of his rascality; but he rallied, and once more attempted to throw the blame upon the slave, who as yet had not uttered a word in his own defence.

"As for Mr. Bowmount's detention, I know nothing about it. If he was trapped, it was done by John for some purpose that was unknown to me. I am sorry that he should have been put to such inconvenience, and I am astonished that John should have interfered in the movements of so valiant a defender of the South. Had I known that Mr. Bowmount was a prisoner, no one would have aided him quicker than myself."

The mulatto stood and heard all this, sullen, and with his eyes cast to the ground. The white man, with his oily tongue, smooth words, his plausible stories, was casting all the blame upon the slave, and, to all appearances, was believed as implicitly as though in a court of justice, and sworn upon a Bible.

But the Kentuckian, while he listened with patience, did not credit all that was said; and when the Virginian had ceased speaking, he sprang forward, caught Rhett by his throat, and then slapped his face several times with his open palm, while, at the same time, he shook the old fellow until his teeth chattered in his head, and his hair promised to take its departure from the scalp, and fly away in the direction of Fort Sumter.

"You damned old scoundrel!" shouted the irate Kentuckian, "don't I know you, and your tricks and excuses? Didn't you try to have me captured by the blockading fleet? Didn't you swing lanterns, and be hanged to you? You're a sweet one. Shucks! I'm almost minded to break your neck."

"Blast him," said General Rampage. "If he has conducted in the manner you state, why not hang him as an enemy of the South?"

"That's it. Up with him to the very tree that they intended to devote to Barnwell. The rope is all ready. You shall swing for it, you false-hearted, lying devil."

The gallant colonel showed more spirit than I had anticipated; for he did not commence begging for mercy, but appeared to meditate upon the difficulties of his position, as though he were asking himself if all hope and expedients were gone. Once or twice he glanced towards the mulatto; but the latter did not return the look, or appear in the best of spirits. No doubt he was thinking of the baseness of the colonel, and wondered why the man had not possessed a little more honor, even if it had to be shown at the expense of a slave.

At last the Bull Runner turned to me, as though he knew I was the most tender-hearted man in the crowd, and would be more likely to befriend him than any other man present.

"Captain," he said, with an assumption of frankness that was quite refreshing after his late conduct, "if I have seemed harsh, you must pardon me, for I have only the good of my country at heart. Now that my eyes are open — "

"By the Lord Harry! if he ain't as cool as the Mammoth Cave of Old Kaintuck," muttered Bowmount. "Damn me, what is the fellow made of — ice or stone?"

For the first time, John cast a look of scorn at his companion. He appeared to feel that the colonel was making desperate efforts to save his own life at the expense of somebody's else, and he thought it mean to thus shirk the responsibility.

"Will you, gentlemen, hear me for a moment?" asked John, after he looked his scorn at the colonel.

"Say what you has to say, and be done with it in quick time," the Kentuckian remarked. "We can't wait all day, when we know breakfast is ready."

"I have but few words to utter, and those shall be true," John remarked. "I was engaged in trapping these two white men, and I did so because I thought that both of them had injured me. Other people helped me, and encouraged me; but you may tear my heart out, black as it is, and I will not give you the names of the parties, or blame my companion, now that I have been detected."

"Quite right and proper," the Virginian muttered,

21

with an approving nod of his head. White men first, the world over."

There was something rather noble in the mulatto's character, after all. Had I desired his instant destruction at that time, it would only have been necessary for me to repeat his confession, and in ten minutes he would have been dangling from the limb of a tree. But I was too good a Unionist to wish the destruction of a man who was likely to serve the North, even if he had played me some tough tricks while laboring under the natural impression that I was a very determined and active rebel.

"We have stumbled on some kind of a nest," General Rampage said, after a moment's pause, and one that seemed terrible to all present. "We have traitors in our midst, and must make short work with them, or they will buzz around our ears like hornets. Up with both fellows at once."

"A just decision. Lay hold of them, men. Be lively, for I'm in a hurry to get my breakfast."

The soldiers, in obedience to the order of the captain, came forward, and laid their hands on the two prisoners, and commenced dragging them towards the tree, from which dangled the ropes that were intended for myself and party.

"Look here," cried the colonel, with a slight struggle; "this isn't the thing, you know. I'm a defender of the South, and loyal to the back-bone. You will suffer for this outrage."

"Not near as much as you will," answered the Kentuckian. "Swing lanterns, will you?"

As to John, the mulatto, he said not a word, and required but little urging. He seemed to think that, as his companion was to be treated the same as himself, it was not worth while to make a fuss.

I did not think that the two men deserved death, even

if they had treated me in an outrageous manner, while laboring under the impression that I was a zealous rebel. I wanted to save them, but how to do so I could not imagine, until I happened to glance at General Rampage's face, and thought that there I saw tokens of pity.

CHAPTER X.

A PLEA FOR MERCY — A FLOGGING FOR HANGING. — ON THE BELLE. — A CAROUSE. — HARRY UNDERTAKES AN EXPEDITION. — THE CHARLESTON IRON-CLADS. — I SEE SOME OLD FRIENDS, AND AM SURPRISED AT MEETING THEM. — HARRY AND HIS UNCLE. — VALUABLE PAPERS, AND WHAT I DID WITH THEM. — SAM IS PENITENT.

"GENERAL," I said, approaching him, "do not let them hang those two fellows. They have hardly earned such a fate."

"Can you forgive their treatment of you?" demanded the general in a cold tone, and with a searching look.

"No; I can't forgive: but still I don't demand the extreme penalty for such conduct. Let them be tried before a regular court, which will decide their fate."

"A waste of time and money. I'm satisfied that the scamps are spies. Their fate is death; still I don't know but that —"

"You will save them; but you must be quick about it, for the soldiers are putting the ropes around their necks."

"That John is a sprightly nigger, but rather pert," said the general, in a musing tone.

"Yes; he is all that," I cried, in an eager tone.

"He might be made to do right, I should think," continued the general.

"I have no doubt of it. But you see, general, that the ropes —"

"Ah, yes; I see. Bowmount, hadn't we better save that nigger's life? He represents so much capital, you know."

"He's worth two thousand dollars, if he's worth a dollar," replied the matter-of-fact Kentuckian.

"Then don't hang him. Give him a good thrashing, and put him in jail. The court will order him to be sold, and I can buy him for a trifle."

"What do you say to that, Barnwell?" asked Bowmount.

"I'm willing. I think that it is the best course you could pursue. But you must treat Colonel Rhett in the same manner."

The Kentuckian would not agree to that for a minute or two, but consented just in time to save the old humbug's neck, much to my gratification, and his own, I have no doubt.

"Look 'e here, you rascals," Bowmount said; "you're indebted to Barnwell for your lives, and to me for a thrashin'. Tie 'em up, men, and give 'em a dozen apiece, and then lodge 'em in jail. We'll let the courts take care of 'em."

"You will carry out the orders," the general said, turning to the captain, "and then join us on board the Belle, where we are to have breakfast."

"But what shall I do with the two sailors who were captured with our friend?" asked the captain.

The general and the Kentuckian did not know what he meant. They had not seen Reefpoint and his companion, who were to convoy me to the United States ship.

"O," I said, in a careless tone, "two of my men left

their ship and wandered off on a spree, pretending that they were searching for me. They are of no account. Send them back to their ship, or let them have their blow out, and then I'll warrant that they'll return to the Belle."

"Let me see the scamps," the owner of the Belle cried. "I don't object to a man getting drunk; but, damn it, he has no business to leave his ship without permission."

I felt some anxiety for the result, as Bowmount had an eye like a hawk, and could see as far as most men. If he had ever noticed the crew of the Belle, he would know that Mr. Reefpoint and companion were strangers, and that I had deceived him; but if he had not paid much attention to the men, I had no fear but that the midshipman and petty officer would give a good account of themselves.

At any rate, while the soldiers were occupied in stripping the clothes from the back of that old scamp who called himself Colonel Rhett, and the mulatto John, we went to the place where Mr. Reefpoint and companion were guarded by half a dozen soldiers to prevent their leaving until permitted.

As we approached the lad, he took a pipe from his mouth, and touched his slouched hat in true English sailor style, frank and hearty as one could desire. Bowmount looked the two over with a sharp eye.

"You belong to the Belle — do you?" he demanded.

"Yes, sir," both answered.

"What are you doing here? Don't you know enough to get drunk and keep on board?"

"No, sir;" and there was another salute.

"Where do you belong? North or South?"

"We is Hinglish, sir," replied Harry, with a genuine John Bull twang.

"And devilish willing to make an honest penny by blockade-running, like all Englishmen. I recollect your faces now. Do you keep sober for the rest of the day, and come on board at night. I hate drunkenness in man or boy."

An hour later we entered Charleston, and steered for the steamer, where all the officers of the party were to eat breakfast at the invitation of the Kentuckian, the owner of the vessel, whose liberality was not restrained by any considerations of dollars and cents; for when he opened his heart, he opened his hand at the same time.

Breakfast awaited us; and glad enough most of the party were when they saw it on the table. I had an opportunity to slip into my state-room while the military were brushing the dust from their clothes, change my dress, and remove some of the stains from my hands and face, contracted while lying in the cell at the haunted house.

The breakfast was protracted till past the dinner hour. The military drank till their faces flushed with the potations which they swallowed. They toasted each other, the cause which they served, their chiefs, and made such bombastic speeches, that one would have thought the North exhausted, and that the South was merely on a little frolic that would end in the course of a day or two.

All this I had to listen to; and by keeping sober I obtained much valuable information; so much, in fact, that when I saw Mr. Welles, the secretary of the navy, and laid my whole history before him, he smiled in a benign manner, at the same time remarking that I had done enough for the Union cause, but could not excuse the course I had deemed it best to pursue.

The fun and drinking waxed fast and furious. Bowls of punch were brought in and emptied, champagne was opened, whiskey was mixed with the rest of the liquors, and just as General Rampage declared that he would sing a song for the entertainment of the company, the steward whispered to me that two sailors were on the dock, and wished to see me for a moment.

I slipped from the cabin, no notice being taken of my disappearance, and saw, as I expected, Mr. Reefpoint and his companion, Barnes, the petty officer, on the dock, in charge of a squad of confederate soldiers.

"Hollo! what are you doing with my men?" I asked the sergeant who commanded the squad.

"Are they your men?" demanded the non-commissioned officer. "They say that they are, and I have come to find out about it. I reckon we want the blue-jackets on our iron-clads in case they don't belong to you. We are short of sailors, and I have orders to pick up all that I can find in the streets, so that they can serve the Confederacy on the water while we fight on the land."

Harry and his companion made a motion as though to leave the dock for the deck of the vessel; but the non-commissioned officer, who was a sharp fellow, and had served a few years in an attorney's office, restrained them, saying, as he did so, —

"Gently, my friends. We need them so much that we must have positive proof that all stragglers belong to the vessel which claims them. Let me see your crew-list, and then all doubts are settled."

"How much do you get for delivering sailors to the captains of iron-clads?" I asked.

"Well, sir, I reckon I may as well be frank with you as not. We are paid twenty dollars per man."

"A small sum, considering the scarcity of the material. But I'll tell you what I am prepared to do. The men are mine; yet I shall not pay for them, neither shall I show you the crew-list."

"Then we must keep them," replied the sergeant.

"Just as you please. Unless the men are returned to me by to-morrow, I shall seek them, and with authority. to take them."

"All right, sir. I do my duty, and you do yours. Right about face. March."

The squad and the sailors trotted up the dock; and when I saw them under way, I had more than half resolved to recall them, and fee the soldiers for the sake of saving the two Union officers, and would have done so had I not been prevented by Harry's positive assurance, as far as signs were concerned, that he wanted to see the interior of one of the iron-clads which had just been completed, and with which the rebels threatened to clean out the Federal ships at some period not very remote.

I had not thought of the subject, and should not have dared mention such an expedition to the midshipman, fearful of the results. But, while standing on the dock, the project had suddenly entered Harry's head, and he had signalized me that he would see one of the iron-clads, and that I must permit him to do so, as he was resolved to undertake the expedition at all hazards.

In the mean time the drinking in the cabin went on fast and furious. I could hear Bowmount's voice, loud above the rest, while attempting an argument on some military point; but as yet he had kept his temper, although he had been opposed on several occasions, and some of his assertions flatly contradicted. Expecting an outbreak every moment, I thought that I would remain on deck, and let the parties wrangle to their hearts' content; and just as I had arrived at this conclusion, and lighted a cigar, General Rampage came out of the cabin, his face flushed and heated, and his whole appearance indicating an intense devotion to the bottle.

His coat was off, his neck-handkerchief removed, and the vest unbuttoned from bottom to top. In fact, the general's appearance did not indicate the great disciplinarian, the man who would punish a soldier for a trifling fault.

He attempted to light his cigar by the aid of mine, but did not accomplish the difficult feat on account of the unsteadiness of his nerves.

"You needn't think I'm drunk," he said, in a severe tone, looking up with a scowl.

"I have no such thoughts," I replied, in a tone of great conciliation.

"Do you think I'm drunk, sir?"

"I'll prove to you that I don't think so, by asking a favor," I replied.

"It's granted, sir. Name it, and you'll see that General Rampage can be generous as well as just. Do you want half my fortune? Take it and be happy."

"I don't want half your fortune; but I do want a favor."

"Good. It is granted without delay. Just mention what it is, and you have it."

"Some of your soldiers," I said, "have picked up two of my sailors, and carried them to one of your iron-clads, just because I would not pay a certain sum for their release. I want you to exert your great influence, and have them restored to me."

"I'll do it. Give me a paper and ink, and I'll write an order to Captain Maulhead of the Palmetto. That will bring them, I reckon. I can write, although you may think that I can't."

"I know you can," I remarked.

And then I called the steward to bring me writing materials; and as soon as they were brought, the general stared at them as though he did not comprehend what they were intended for.

"Eh! what do you want?" he asked.

"The order for the release of the two sailors."

"Yes; but perhaps you think me drunk; so drunk that I can't write."

"No; because you can prove to me that such is not the case. Just write the order, and that will set all suspicions to rest, even if I had any."

"So it will."

And down sat the general, spread the paper on a chicken-coop, frowned savagely, nodded his head several times in a sage and sagacious manner, then closed his eyes, and attempted to go to sleep.

"The order, general," I said, and touched him on the elbow.

He looked up in a gloomy manner, and then muttered, —

"You appreciate me, but the government don't. What can I do for you?"

"Write the order."

"Do you think I can't write it?"

"I shall believe it when you do write it; but not before."

He looked furious for a moment, and then commenced writing, much more carefully than I had anticipated. It took him some time; but at last I had the satisfaction of seeing the work completed, and receiving the note in my own hands.

"There," said the general, with a sigh of relief, "I've done it. I'm not as drunk as I have been; but I'm drunk enough. Old Maulhead is a friend of mine, and I don't think he'll refuse my request. If he does, I'll blow him and his useless iron-clads to the devil; and you may tell him so if you have a mind."

The general attempted to rise; but his legs refused to do their duty. When he found that he could not stand up, he frowned, folded his arms, and informed me that he had no idea of getting drunk; that he was not drunk, and would shoot any man that said he was; after which, he laid down his head, and went to sleep.

In the course of an hour or more, the fun in the cabin began to decrease. I heard Bowmount's voice grow less and less boisterous, the shouts of his companions less wild; the toasts were no longer audible, and only by the occasional smash of a drinking-glass did the carousers indicate that they were trying to keep awake.

At length all was silent. I entered the cabin, and a wonderful sight met my eyes. The Kentuckian was stripped to his shirt and trousers, lying on the transom, his head pillowed by two champagne bottles; his companions, the military gentlemen, were spread all over the cabin floor; some of them with half-emptied bottles by their sides, and others still grasping wine-glasses, showing that drinking was their last conscious act.

I called the steward and some of the men, and had the unconscious inebriates stripped of their gray coats, and then stowed the fellows in state-room berths, where they could sleep off their intoxication without the fear of being seen or disturbed.

General Rampage was next removed from the deck, where he was sleeping, the object of considerable remark from a large number of idle negroes.

The next day we commenced discharging cargo, and in the afternoon I recollected that I had promised Harry Bluff, *alias* Midshipman Reefpoint, to obtain his release from the iron-clads commanded by Captain Maulhead.

Leaving the mate to look after the goods as they came from the ship's hold, I dressed, and started in search of the man who was always promising to blow the Yankee fleet out of the water, and yet did not dare venture beyond the protecting guns of Fort Sumter, for the simple reason that he feared his own vessel would follow the course which he promised his enemies should take.

It was not difficult to find Captain Maulhead and his fleet. Most of the iron-clads were alongside of the dock, undergoing repairs. In fact, they were always being repaired. If they steamed out of the harbor a mile or two, some part of their machinery was sure to break or give out, and a river steamer had to be sent to tow the unwieldy monsters back to a secure resting-place.

Then the Charleston ladies, who had built one of the most destructive looking of the fleet, giving their jewels and money most readily for the purpose, would hold an indignation meeting, and call on Captain Maulhead to explain why he did not carry out his intentions of sinking the Yankee scum, agreeably to promise.

Then Captain Maulhead would drink about a gallon, more or less, of commissary whiskey, and appear before the meeting to explain matters. He was a good-looking man, and when under the influence of liquor, quite eloquent, and appeared as brave as a lion. He said that an apology was due to the young and handsome ladies of Charleston, a city that could boast of more beauty, more patriotism, more real American revolution courage, than any other city in the world. He had intended to sink the whole Yankee fleet, Yankees and all, and he would yet do it, or sink himself to the bottom of the ocean. Had not the iron-clads' shafts broken just as they did, a battle would have been fought, and a victory won, that would have electrified the world.

Then the beautiful ladies would applaud, and the gallant captain was told to try his luck once more, which he did with his usual success, except once, when he sunk one of our steamers, and compelled a second one to run away, while a third surrendered at sight, but still managed to escape.

Such was Captain Maulhead, whom I expected to see, and whose favor I was to secure.

On gaining the deck of the iron-clad Spitfire, which I was only enabled to do by representing that I had urgent business with Captain Maulhead, I sent my name in the cabin by the sentry, and then awaited the result.

In the mean time I made good use of my eyes. I saw that the Spitfire was formidable in appearance only. She had been thrown together in the most unworkmanlike manner. Her bolts were not clinched, as they should have been, her machinery seemed to be patched up, covered with rust, and out of gear, while the guns which I saw were mounted in such a manner that they were liable to pitch overboard, or else kick clean across the deck, knocking down all who were in the course of the ponderous weapons. In a heavy sea it would have been impossible to operate them at any angle except at about sixty-five degrees, sending the charge towards the heavens, instead of in the direction of an enemy.

I had just time to note these things, and in such a manner as to appear perfectly indifferent, — for sharp eyes were on me all the time I was on board, — when the sentry passed the word for me to enter the august presence of Captain Maulhead.

I found the naval gentleman seated at a table, with a chart before him. In his hand he held a rule and a pair of compasses, and he seemed to be measuring distances, and pondering on the results, for he did not look up when I entered the cabin, but muttered in an audible tone, —

" Five miles due west is Fort Wagner, two miles east is Castle Pinckney, and — "

He looked up, as though his calculations had been suddenly interrupted by my presence.

" Well, sir," — and he made a note on a sheet of paper, — " what can I do for you ? "

" My name is Barnwell," I said. " I am captain of the blockade-runner Belle."

"The devil you are! Damn me if I didn't take you for an official from Richmond — some spy from the navy department. Here, steward; clean off these maps and papers, and set on the whiskey again. It's a false alarm, after all. Captain Barnwell, take a seat. You are welcome, sir, to my hospitalities. It's little I have to offer you. Not such fare and pay as you blockade-runners enjoy."

"But the glory," I remarked. "You reap all that."

"Glory be damned! What glory can there be in exchanging shots with the Yankee fleet, and then running for shelter under a sand battery?"

"But you might fight them successfully with an equal force," I suggested.

"Fight the devil!" cried the captain with scorn, pushing the bottle towards me. "Look at my men, and then look at the Yanks. Damn it, what can I do with such cattle as I have under my orders? Half of them are seasick if I run out to Fort Sumter."

"I'm sorry for you, captain, and could wish you better luck. I drink to you."

"Thank you. Now let me know what I can do for you."

"Simply to discharge two of my men, who were picked up in the streets yesterday."

Captain Maulhead struck his fist on the table with a blow that made everything shake.

"Damn me if I didn't suspect what you were after; I did indeed. I told Green that some one would be after those two men, and Green bet me a bottle of whiskey that I couldn't keep them."

"O, I'll discharge the bet if you'll discharge the men," I answered, with a pleasant smile, in hopes of keeping the man in good humor. "I've got a barrel of Scotch whiskey, of the true smoky flavor, on board. Send a demijohn, and I'll fill it."

"That's liberal on your part, and I'll send for the liquor; but, at the same time, I can't give up the men."

"Then I'll be hanged if you can have the liquor," I answered in a blunt tone; for I suspected it was the only method of meeting him on equal ground. "One good turn deserves another, you know."

"The interests of the Confederacy won't permit me to go outside of the line of my duty."

"I supposed that you would view the matter in that light," I remarked, lighting a cigar, and handing half a dozen to the captain, — a prize which he seized upon with avidity, — "so came armed on all points. The men were picked up in the streets while on liberty. I could have had them back by paying a small sum, but it seemed such an imposition that I concluded to test the matter by appearing before you, and pleading their cause and my own."

"If you only knew what damned hard work I have to get hold of the right kind of men, you would not blame me for keeping those two fellows — seamen every inch of them, and smart at that."

"That is the reason I want them. Only smart men can run the blockade, you know."

"But you see you have the pick of all the men in port. So much money is made by cheating the Yankee fleet, that the best sailors go to you."

"You can't blame them for it. It is natural. Human nature is the same with sailors that it is with landsmen."

"I know; but we must draw the line somewhere, or the confederate navy will go to the devil in short order."

"Then you won't give them up?" I asked, none too well pleased at the captain's firmness.

"I don't say that; but I do say that I need a little more time to think the matter over. Suppose you should come and see me in the course of a few days? There is no hurry in such matters, you know."

"Ay, but there is hurry," I answered in a firm tone. "In a few days I shall be ready to sail, and can't leave my men behind."

The captain thought of the matter before he again spoke. Then he leaned forward, and whispered confidentially, —

"To tell you the truth, Captain Barnwell, I am getting ready to make a raid on the enemy. I mean to strike them some night this week, and it will go hard with me if I don't send half a dozen of the Yankee ships to the bottom. My plans are all laid, and can't fail if I muster the right men."

This was the most important information I had received since I had been detailed for secret service. Now the question arose, How could I get the news to the Federal commanders? They must know it, and be prepared to act with promptness when the rebel rams and gunboats stole past Fort Sumter. Unless forewarned, there was danger to the fleet; for we all know that fancied security leads to want of proper vigilance.

There was but one way in which I could send the desired information. That was by the Yankee middy and his friend and shipmate. If I could secure their release, I thought there would be but little trouble in getting them off, by the aid of a boat and a dark night. They could give the alarm, and then Captain Maulhead would get more than he bargained for.

All these thoughts flashed through my mind, while I sat listening to the captain's plans, and assisting him to empty his whiskey bottle. If he could have read my thoughts, I should never have left the cabin alive. But, luckily for me, he did not have the least suspicion that I was not what I assumed.

I was just about to produce the order that General Rampage had written for me, when the steward once more entered the cabin.

"Two gen'men, sar, wants to see you, sar. From Richmond, sar."

"Damnation!" muttered the captain, in an agony of alarm for fear the visitors were agents of the navy department. "Here; sweep off the bottle and glasses. Be lively. On with the charts and tools. — Don't go yet."

I had risen for the purpose of taking my leave, with the request to be allowed to call again in the course of an hour or two.

"Don't go yet. Enter my state-room, and wait till I am free from the fellows, whoever they are. I'll get rid of them unless they want to overhaul everything; and if they do, I'll try and put them off till to-morrow."

I could but obey the captain; and as I retreated the Richmond gentlemen entered the cabin.

"Captain," said one of the visitors, in a tone that sounded quite familiar, "we have ventured to call on you for some information, which the navy department at Richmond assured us you would be willing to give."

"Then you are not agents from the department?" asked the captain.

"No, sir; we are simple Southern gentlemen."

"I'm glad to hear it. Steward, take away these charts and tools, and bring on the whiskey and cigars. Gentlemen, I'm glad to see you. Sit down, and let me hear how I can serve you; for, although I am the busiest man in Charleston, Heaven forbid that I should not be willing to give some of my time to my countrymen when they honor me with a call. Steward, a fresh bottle of whiskey."

"Habn't got a fresh bottle, nor a salt bottle either. I told you dat once afore, sir."

"Ah! so you did. Well, gentlemen, we shall have to make the best of what we have on the table. Don't be afraid of it. Whiskey never hurts any one."

"We hope to be able to present you with a barrel of the best brand to be found in the market before many days," said the gentleman whose voice seemed familiar.

"Thank you, sir. And what must I do to deserve such generous treatment? for I am too much of a man of the world not to know that favors are returned with favors."

There was a momentary hesitation on the part of the visitors, as if they did not exactly know how to commence on the subject nearest their hearts.

"I'm all attention, gentlemen," cried Captain Maulhead. "Help yourself to whiskey. There's some left, I think. No? then I'm devilish sorry, on your account as well as my own."

"The fact of it is, captain," said the visitor who conducted the conversation, "we want your advice as to the proper method of entering the port in the night time. We are about to engage in blockade-running, and desire to know what points will be best on which to display signals of welcome or warning."

While the visitor was speaking, I thought that it was desirable to see his face. I had a suspicion that I should know it; and if such was the case, it was one of the most remarkable circumstances that ever came under my knowledge.

I moved the door of the state-room a little, and was enabled to peer through into the cabin, and obtain a glimpse of those seated at the table. I looked long and eagerly, for I could scarce believe my eyes.

No; there was no mistake in the premises. Unless I was laboring under some hallucination, at that table sat my old employer, Mr. Blank, the Boston merchant, the patriot, the man of wealth, the father of Miss Hatty

Blank, whose curls and bright eyes had captivated my heart the first time I ever saw her in her father's counting-room; and that impression was but strengthened when we met at Washington, where I was the means of rendering her some assistance, which she was gracious enough to acknowledge in terms that set my heart palpitating like a river steamboat under a heavy head of steam.

Nearly opposite Mr. Blank, but so that I could see his face quite distinctly, sat old Crosstrees, the retired sea captain, with money enough to last him all his days, even if he was extravagant in his family and out of it.

That same old fellow had tempted me, one day, on State Street, with the idea that blockade-running would pay; but I had refused to listen to the proposition even for a moment, and on that supposition imagined that Crosstrees had given up the idea. I little thought that I should so soon be engaged in the disreputable business. But such was the case; and now it only remained for me to hear what Mr. Blank and the old captain had to offer, and after they had spoken, to keep out of their way until I could so disguise myself that they would not know me should we chance to meet.

"As far as the signals are concerned," Captain Maulhead said, after a refreshing pull at the whiskey, "you had better arrange that with your consignees. You see, each steamer that enters or leaves the port has different signals, known only to those who arrange them. This is an advantage, because it rather puzzles the Yankees. Of course I'm all ready to help you as far as I can; but as for interfering with signals, it ain't in my line. My duty is to hunt out Yankees, and fight them wherever found. That's what I am here for."

"You wouldn't s'arch long, I guess, if you were very eager," snarled old Crosstrees, who now spoke for the first time, and with considerable twang to his tone. "The

Yankees ain't far off, and they is keen in a fight if they can find some one to battle."

Captain Maulhead smote the table with his fist; but instead of manifesting anger, he laughed.

"Damn me," he said, "if you ain't a Yankee."

"Well," said Crosstrees, shaking himself like a Newfoundland dog after a visit to the water, "I ain't anythin' else, now you may jist believe."

"I have engaged Captain Cross" (he left off part of the name), Mr. Blank said, in his calm, dignified tone, "for the purpose of taking charge of one of the steamers I have purchased in England, and expect in Bermuda next month. His familiarity with the Southern ports and coast qualifies him for the position."

"Of course you can do as you please, but I shouldn't trust all to one of our enemies. A Yankee is a Yankee, all the world over; although I don't mean any offence to you, Captain Cross."

"No; I s'pose you don't; but it's a damn cool way of tellin' me that I ain't on the square, and all sich. However, I'm a old salt, and don't expect nothin' else from a man what was edicated at the expense of the government, and then turned agin her."

I expected to see Captain Maulhead, who had received his education at the Naval Academy, fly into a terrible passion, and order the immediate arrest of Crosstrees; but he did no such thing. He swallowed the whiskey that remained in his tumbler, and then roared with laughter, as he said, —

"Well done, my son of Neptune. Southern air can't break you of quarter-deck habits. The old sea-dog will show his head and let his tongue be heard once in a while. Well, well, I like you all the better for it; that's a fact; but at the same time, let me caution you that all Southern officers are not as good-natured as I am; so take warning."

"I'm sure you will excuse Captain Cross," Mr. Blank said, in that persuasive tone he so well knew how to adopt. "He is a genuine Yankee, and—"

"If he were not, he wouldn't be here," interrupted Captain Maulhead, in a tone so sarcastic, that I thought, if the two visitors had any sense of their own meanness and position, they would wish themselves back at the North, doing what they could for their country, instead of attempting to injure it.

But the men were too intent on the course which they intended to pursue to care for such slight checks as the one they had just received. Money was to be made running the blockade; consequently they forgot all moral considerations in hopes of grasping some of the gold which was showered upon the adventurous. They had entered upon their detested course resolved to perform all the duties that came before them; to swallow all the insults that were thrown at their heads, except on special occasions, such as I have alluded to, when blunt old Crosstrees, unable to restrain his quarter-deck spirit, burst out, and disclosed the fact that he was a Yankee, and possessed some of the real New England independence, that could not be quelled at all times.

But I have wandered from the cabin scene, where three men were seated at a table, with an empty black bottle and two empty tumblers before them. I say two empty tumblers, because the aristocratic Mr. Blank was not the man to burn his throat with new whiskey, or any such liquor. Consequently he made a show of drinking, yet did not allow any of the vile stuff to enter his mouth; while old Crosstrees had no such scruples. He would have swallowed a gallon of the fiery liquor, and then called for more, totally unaware that it was not as mild as milk-punch.

Silence reigned supreme for a moment in the cabin; but

at last Mr. Blank began to talk Southern patriotism, and so interested Captain Maulhead in his conversation, while Crosstrees chewed tobacco and wished for more grog at the same time.

Thus they kept me concealed for nearly an hour; but at last they arose, and left the cabin; and once more I found myself face to face with Captain Maulhead, eager to carry my point, and full as eager to follow my old friends, and find out what they intended to do.

"By the way," said Captain Maulhead, as I took a seat at his table, "you heard all those fellows said — didn't you?"

"Pretty near all. I was not much interested in what they had to say."

"They wanted me to help them; but I'll see them damned first, and then I won't. I go in for my friends."

"I hope that you count me as one."

"Of course. Haven't you promised me a few gallons of whiskey?"

"Yes; but you have not promised me the discharge of my men, captain. It is important that I should have them."

"O, the devil! don't bother me on that point. I want the men more than you do. Come; say no more about them."

"I supposed that you would desire to keep them." I said, with a laugh. "General Rampage told me so."

"Ah! he is a sensible man. He knows how important it is that I should have the men."

"Yes; he is so sensible that he gave me this note, requesting you to discharge the two men I claim."

I handed him the paper. The captain looked mad for a moment, but laughed, as he said, —

"I reckon I'll have to comply with Rampage's request, although I know he was half drunk when he wrote the note."

"How can you tell?"

"O, I know his writing well enough to tell when he is drunk or sober."

"Then you will comply with the request?"

"Of course. Rampage is such a wilful man, that, if I should refuse him, he would hate me forever. Best to conciliate such people, for there is no knowing who will turn up a trump in this war."

The captain struck the bell that stood on the table before him. The steward appeared.

"Tell Lieutenant Drinkhard to discharge those two men who belong to the Belle. And, after you have did that, take the largest demijohn on board, and go to the Belle, and get it filled with whiskey. If I lose the men, I won't the liquor."

In a few minutes the lieutenant entered the cabin with Mr. Reefpoint and his companion, the petty officer. They gave a regular sailor bow, and a twitch at their forelocks, as they stood before the confederate commander.

"Well, boys, hadn't you rather stop with me, and fight the Yankees, than lead a blockade-running life? Think of the glory to be acquired by whipping the enemy."

"Yes, sir; but s'pose we don't whip, but get whipped! then whar is the glory?" demanded the Yankee midshipman, in a tone that was not insolent, although it sounded a little pert.

"Humph," muttered Captain Maulhead; "you are too smart for my ship. If you hadn't said you were a son of John Bull, I should have put you down as Yankees. But go your way. You are discharged; but, if I should get hold of you a second time, I shan't let go in a hurry."

The men left the cabin after a duck of their heads; and in a few minutes I followed them, promising Captain Maulhead to see him again in a few days. On the dock I found Mr. Reefpoint and companion waiting for me. I gave them a sign, and they followed me up the wharf until we reached a point where we could speak without observation.

"Well, Harry, what luck?" I asked.

"Splendid, sir. The iron-clad fleet is as weak as the confederate cause. The ships are all botched in building. If we were ready for them, they couldn't hurt us, although they might do us some damage in the ramming line."

"Your conclusions are right; and now how can you convey the information to the fleet?"

"I don't know, sir, how that can be done; but I'll think of the matter."

"And I have already thought of it. Don't you think, that, if a boat was left in such a manner that you could slip into it unobserved, you could reach the fleet before morning?"

"We might try, sir. If the boat is small and light, we could work past the guards. At any rate it is our only hope for escape."

"You must not fail," I remarked, as I thought of the great amount at stake. "Failure would be disgrace in this case."

"We will do all that Yankees can do under the most trying circumstances," Harry said, in a tone so confident, that I could not help admiring the lad, he was so bold and generous, so handsome and free.

Just at this moment I looked across the street, and saw Mr. Blank and Captain Crosstrees. They were walking along the sidewalk, with heads down, talking in earnest but low tones.

"Harry, do you know the tall gentleman who is opposite?"

The midshipman looked attentively, and then rubbed his eyes as though he could hardly believe them.

"Good Heavens!" he said, "that looks like my uncle Blank of Boston."

The midshipman glanced at my face, and saw that he was correct in his supposition.

"It is him!" he cried, and started to run across the street.

I laid my hand on the lad's arm, and held him fast.

"You must keep away from him," I whispered. "It won't do to speak with him here in Charleston."

"Not speak to my uncle!" the lad cried, in tones of surprise. "Why, what's up?"

"I don't think he would care to have you see him in Charleston," I remarked.

"Why not? He's a good kind uncle, and was always glad to see me."

"I have no doubt of it."

"And, if he is here in Charleston, it is because he is a prisoner, and on parole."

"He is not a prisoner, Harry; and he is not on parole."

"Then what is he, sir?"

"He is here to get ready to engage in blockade-running."

"I can't believe it, sir. My uncle is a great Union man, a patriot, and wouldn't engage in such business. Why, he has given money to aid the cause, and help our sick and wounded soldiers. O, no! don't tell me that he has engaged in blockade-running, or thinks of it. I can't believe it."

"Then I am sorry that I must undeceive you."

"But who are you?" cried the lad in a passionate tone. "What are you? A rebel or patriot? Are you for the Union, or against it? Tell me something concerning yourself. You are full of mystery. At one time I meet you on board a United States ship, and then I find you cutting out blockade-runners, commanding them, hand in in hand with prominent rebels, friends with all, and yet true to none. Forgive me for speaking so plainly,"— for the boy saw an expression of pain on my face,— "but recollect you have just accused a dear uncle of treasonable practices."

"I can make no explanations," I answered. "Some day you may know the truth, but now my mouth is sealed. I can't open it even to enlighten so brave a little fellow as yourself."

"Thank you, sir, I am sure, for the compliment. I hope that it is deserved. But still it must not make me forget the main subject of our conversation — my uncle. See; he has stopped, and is looking up and down the street. Do let me go to him."

"And have him disown you?"

"O, there is no fear of that, sir. You shall see how warmly he will receive me. He is not the uncle to turn a cold shoulder to a nephew."

I thought of the subject for a moment, and concluded that the midshipman could do no harm unless he made a scene in the streets, and thus attracted attention from those who were in the vicinity.

"You can go to him, Harry," I whispered; "but mind and have no words with him. Your safety and the safety of your uncle demands it."

"All right, sir. You just keep quiet for a moment, and see how uncle Blank will welcome me."

"Don't mention my name," I said. "Be careful of that."

"All right, sir. I will recollect."

With these words the lad started across the street, and confronted Mr. Blank. I could hear all that passed between the parties, while concealed behind a fence that had been built as a pen for some small animals.

"Why, uncle Blank, who would have thought of seeing you in Charleston!" cried the lad, advancing with extended hands.

The Boston merchant was so astonished, that he staggered back, blushed red, and then turned white, and trembled violently; and, had not old Crosstrees come to the rescue, he might have acknowledged the nephew's salutation. But the gruff old captain, with a quarter-deck air, roared out, —

"Who's you talkin' to, youngster? What in the devil do you mean by speakin' to us in that style? Go about yer business, or I'll try a rope's end over yer shoulders."

"No, you won't, sir," replied the midshipman, who was a lad of some spirit, and was not in the habit of being addressed in that style by a sea-dog whom he could teach, as far as science was concerned, all that goes to make a naval officer, who has been educated in the United States Naval Academy, perfect.

"No, sir," continued Harry, firmly, but with courtesy. "Because I see fit to speak with my uncle, you must not think I would suffer you to insult me."

"Your uncle, boy! what do you mean?" demanded Mr. Blank, who had now recovered his State Street assurance, and assumed an air that would have told had he been face to face with a rival merchant.

Harry looked at his uncle in astonishment.

"Do you mean to tell me that you ain't my uncle Blank?" he demanded.

"I don't know anything about him, sir," was the gruff answer.

"And haven't you a daughter named Hatty Blank, my cousin?"

"No, sir."

"Are you sure?"

"Do you mean to insult me, boy?"

"No, sir, I do not; but still I hardly know what to say, I am so surprised."

"Then say nothin', boy, but be off to your work, if you

have any," muttered old Crosstrees, in a quarter-deck tone.

"Nay, don't speak so cross to the boy," Mr. Blank said, in a gentle manner. "He has made some queer mistake; but still we must not be angry with him. He is honest in his belief, no doubt."

"That sounds like the voice and sentiments of my own dear uncle," cried the midshipman, who recollected the many acts of kindness which Mr. Blank had performed.

The Boston merchant's face assumed a hard aspect, stern and determined — a regular State Street front; such a face as he would have put on had a poor, unknown man asked him to loan a thousand dollars for ninety days without interest or security.

"Boy," he said, "I may look like your uncle, but that is no reason why I should be a relative. Be off with you, and let's end this nonsense."

"My uncle would not have spoken to me in that manner," the midshipman said, in a sorrowful tone. "No; you are no uncle of mine."

"Then what in the devil's name are you hanging round us for?" roared Crosstrees. "Top your boom, and be off. Steer a straight course, and don't anchor till you have found the harbor of Good Sense. And, arter you has found it, don't you lift your mudhook till you has taken on board a cargo of wit and wisdom."

"Captain," asked Harry, "did you ever visit that harbor?"

"Well, yes, I s'pose I has," was the response.

"Then it seems to me that you didn't take on board much of a cargo, to judge how short of ballast you are at the present time," retorted Reefpoint, with a look that he had learned on the quarter-deck of a national vessel, while associating with men who were apt to think that they were the head and centre of the country, and that the people who paid them for their services should be treated like some of their sailors.

"By St. George, but the boy has you there," laughed Mr. Blank, who was too pleased with the lad's retort to keep silent any longer. Pride of relationship would show itself in all of Mr. Blank's actions.

Old Crosstrees uttered an angry roar, like a hungry sea-lion, and then seized the Boston merchant's arm, and dragged him up the street, leaving Reefpoint standing on the sidewalk, looking after them, apparently undecided as to what course he should take to solve the mystery. For a moment the lad remained watching the forms of the blockade-runners. Then he sighed, and crossed over to where I was concealed.

"Are you satisfied?" I asked.

"Yes, sir; quite so."

"You are sure that the man is your uncle Blank?"

In an instant the boy's suspicions were aroused, and his natural wit appeared.

"Before I am sure on such a point, I want to know how the information is to be applied."

"You fear that I might injure Mr. Blank?"

"I trust not."

"You may be sure of it. He is my friend. I was in his employ for many years. He always treated me well, but kept me at a distance."

"And you would compel him to lessen that distance?" asked the lad in a thoughtful tone.

"Yes; in one respect I would."

"Can you enlighten me a little more, so that I can find my true position?"

"Yes. Some weeks since, you promised to aid me in securing the hand of your cousin Hatty."

"I remember the circumstance, and I still hold to the opinion which I then expressed."

"Thank you. Now you can see the tie which I wish to form between your uncle's family and myself."

"Yes; but still you will allow that your presence in Charleston is as suspicious as—"

"Never mind me, or my presence here. Stick to the subject. Do you still think that the person with whom you have conversed is your uncle?"

"Well," answered the midshipman, with a smile, "I'll tell you when the proper time arrives. At the present moment I am not prepared to answer. If I did, I might endanger the lives and fortunes of those who are innocent of evil intent."

"It is just as well, Harry. I shall never call upon you to bear witness against those whom you love. I know your thoughts, and respect them."

The lad bowed, and then we walked towards the Belle. We went on board, and were met by the mate at the gangway.

"Here are two men I have shipped for the return voyage," I said. "See that they are quartered with the rest of the crew."

"Ay, ay, sir. Go for'ard, lads; and I'll see you in a little while. Two gents come on board this mornin', sir, and wanted to see you about blockade-runnin', I reckon. They look as if they was honest. By George! if they ain't comin' down the dock now!"

I glanced in the direction indicated, and saw that Mr. Blank and Captain Crosstrees were indeed heading towards the steamer; and I debated whether I should meet them or shun them. I resolved to do the latter, and then thought of the disguise which I had in my state-room. This disguise I resolved to assume for the time, and thus hold a free conference with Mr. Blank, and learn his plans.

"Keep those gentlemen on deck till you hear me strike the cabin bell; then send them in to me."

"Yes, sir."

"Where is Mr. Bowmount?"

"Gone up-town, sir. Said he should not come back till near night."

This was just what I desired, so into the cabin I went, and in a few moments assumed my disguise, then struck the bell.

The door opened, and in walked the mate, but he stopped suddenly when he saw such a strange-looking being in the cabin. He did not know me until I had made a sign for him to express no surprise, but even then he could not help muttering,—

"Dowse my toplights! but this is a go, and no mistake," and then the red-faced, broad-shouldered Englishman pointed to the two visitors, and said,—

"These gents wants to see yer, cap'n. Can yer hail 'em now, or shall they wait?"

"O, I am happy to see the gentlemen," I answered, in as gruff a tone as I could assume. "Come to anchor, and I'll order the steward to bring on cigars and wine."

"Our names," said Mr. Blank, with a graceful wave of his right hand towards Captain Crosstrees, "are —"

"No matter about the names," I cried, in a hearty tone, and with a bang of my fist on the table. "As long as you are loyal men, I don't want to know them. You are welcome to the Belle."

The two men colored a little, and for a moment appeared slightly confused, but they rallied, and then Mr. Blank, with charming frankness, remarked,—

"O, you can put trust in us, Captain Barnwell. No more loyal men in the South can be found than ourselves, although my friend here, Captain Cross, is a Yankee."

"And you, sir, I suppose, were born in the South," I asked.

"Yes, sir — in Virginia."

"It is singular," I remarked, in a musing tone, "but your face seems quite familiar to me. I could have sworn that I had met you in Boston."

"It is quite probable, sir," was Mr. Blank's reply, with the old State Street look. "I have purchased many articles in Boston, and visited the city several times."

"Ah! then I must have seen you on one of those visits. A pleasant place is Boston."

"You can bet high on that," Crosstrees cried, a little too enthusiastic for a man who was about to enter the blockade business as a zealous friend of the South.

By this time the wine and cigars were placed on the table; and after a drink, and a puff of smoke, Mr. Blank unfolded his business.

"We are about to engage in the same line as yourself," he said, "and we want a little light on various matters that we can't get except from those who have had experience."

I bowed, and listened.

"We expect to meet two or three steamers in a certain port, and we want to learn the best method of running them into some Southern place of refuge."

"The best plan that I know of is to put on steam, and get past the blockade as soon as possible."

"Yes, that is the principal way; but suppose you meet with blockaders, — run on to them, in fact?"

"O, then haul off, and make the best of it. Get out of the way as soon as possible, and try again."

They did not appear to be satisfied with my explanation; and yet I really had no other to give, even had I desired to serve the two men.

"There is another thing that you must avoid," I continued, after a moment's silence. "You will find at every turn secret agents of the United States. They will watch your movements, and, unless you are sharp, will get the best of you."

I spoke in my natural tone just then, forgetting that I was assuming a character. Old Crosstrees glanced at me as though trying to recollect where he had heard my voice, and, as I ceased speaking, he dashed his fist down on the table, making the glassware dance a merry jig, as he said, —

"I've heard yer voice afore, dang me if I hain't."

"Well," I replied, "if you have, it is no reason, sir, you should break my tumblers and decanters — is it?"

"I'll pay for all I break," the captain said, in rather a sulky tone.

"That is not the question. I don't want you to break my glass, and I don't want your money."

"Well, yer needn't be so afeared of yer property," snarled old Crosstrees, who would not take a hint from Mr. Blank to keep quiet, and have no idle discussion.

"His voice seems familiar to me at any rate," growled the captain.

"I must confess that in this respect Captain Cross is right," remarked Mr. Blank, in his quiet, gentlemanly tone. "Captain Barnwell's voice at times does seem familiar; but I can form no idea where I have heard one like it."

"I know," growled Crosstrees.

"Ah! I should be happy to hear the name of the individual whom I resemble, even in voice," I remarked; for I had an interest in continuing the conversation.

"It was that young chap, Frank Constant, what used to command a ship called the Laughing Mermaid."

Perhaps the reader may have forgotten that Frank Constant is my real name, and that Barnwell was one assumed for Southern purposes. At any rate to hear it pronounced in the cabin of the Belle just at that time was enough to startle me, so I filled a glass, and asked, —

"Was this Constant as old as I am?"

"I should think not," replied Crosstrees, in a tone that savored of contempt at the absurdity of the question.

"He was a young man, and a smart man, and a devilish good-lookin' feller, now I tell yer. He was as promisin' a cap'n as sailed out of Boston at the time this rebellion beginned, wasn't he?" appealing to Mr. Blank, who smiled, and said that he would take Crosstrees' word for it; and then drew back from the table, and announced his intention of leaving, having obtained all the information he could make available.

Crosstrees took another drink, and followed his example; and then both of them went on deck, looked over the steamer, praised her build, and commented on her speed, and at last shook hands with me, and left, incidentally remarking that they should leave immediately for Wilmington, where a blockade-runner was about to sail for Bermuda, and a market.

As the two men walked up the dock, I saw the midshipman looking after them, with a very melancholy expression upon his face, as though he comprehended the infamy of his uncle, and felt grieved at it. I returned to the cabin, and was about to ring for the steward to clear off the table, when I saw a package of papers lying on the deck. I picked it up, and saw that it belonged to Mr. Blank, for his name was on the back of several notes that I looked over.

After a moment's hesitation, I went to my state-room, and examined the papers at my leisure. To me they were more valuable than gold, for I saw they were contracts and correspondence between Mr. Blank and two members of the rebel cabinet, stating upon what terms they would assist him in his blockade-running scheme, and at what price he could have cotton to export.

By these papers I learned all of Mr. Blank's plans, and the plans of those who were connected with him. His own house was involved, and so were two New York firms. Their plans were so well laid, that only the utmost vigilance on the part of the Federal fleet and Federal officials could defeat them.

"These papers," I thought, "are worth thousands of dollars, but money could not tempt me to part with them. The time may come when I can give them up with honor to myself, but not to those who own them."

Just at this moment I heard some one enter the cabin with considerable haste. I suspected who it was, so concealed the papers in a safe that stood in my state-room. A knock at the door caused me to open it. I saw Mr. Blank, with a face that expressed some apprehension, standing before me.

"Excuse me for interrupting you," he said, "but I have returned for some papers which I have dropped from my pocket. I did not know but what I might have lost them in the cabin."

"You had better look round and see," I returned, in as careless a tone as I could assume. "Perhaps you can discover them."

Mr. Blank commenced his search, but didn't find what he was after. He looked at me with a grave and troubled face, as he said, —

"You don't suppose that the stewards could have found the papers — do you?"

"If they had, they would have handed them to me," was my answer; while at the same time I pitied the man, and was at once half tempted to restore the papers to him.

"If you should hear of them, I wish you would seal them up, and send them to me at Bermuda."

"Certainly; or perhaps bring them to you."

"Thank you. I may yet find them before I leave town. I hope I shall, for they are worth to me more than to any one else." With these words the merchant took his departure, and I supposed that I should have a moment to myself; but a noise on deck once more aroused me.

I went on deck, and found that Bowmount had returned, accompanied by a stout negro, whom I had no difficulty in recognizing as Sam, the coachman, who had helped entrap me the night I was kidnapped by John.

"Do you recognize this imp?" asked the Kentuckian; and as he spoke he cut the negro's legs with a cowhide, which produced a rapid movement on the part of Sam.

"O, golly, massa! don't do dat," yelled the coachman. "Don't you know dat it hurts? O, my legs! Please don't do so no more, massa."

And then followed several blows and several capers.

"Do you see this black cuss?" asked the Kentuckian, suspending work for a moment, to talk to me.

"Yes, I see him. I have met the scamp before."

"And so has I," and here came in another cut on the darkey's legs, that made him jump and howl with renewed energy.

"How did you get hold of him?" I asked, as soon as the noise had subsided.

"Mrs. Gowen sent him to you," was the careless answer. Mrs. Gowen has been on the watch for the black scamp ever since he served you such a trick. This afternoon he was took while I was at the house, and she sent him to you, and says you may do what you like with him. If you takes my advice, you will give him two or three dozen, and then send him to the city jail, whar they'll give him as much more."

"For de Lord's sake, don't do dat," cried Sam. "Dis nig is almost cut to pieces now. Him legs is one mess of rings."

I began to have mercy on the fellow, although he did

not deserve it at my hands. He had betrayed and robbed me, insulted me, and committed such crimes that a jury of white men would have condemned him to death on a ten-minutes' hearing. But Bowmount had used a cowhide on the negro's person with such effect that I thought he had been sufficiently punished for the present, at least.

"Sam," I said, "you have treated me vilely."

"Yes, massa."

"You robbed me of my watch and revolver."

"Yes, massa."

"I want them."

"Yes, massa. I has 'em for yer. I intended that you should hab 'em. Do you dink dat dis nigger would steal? I took 'em so dat de udder niggers couldn't get hold of 'em. Bad niggers round Charleston. Take most anything dat dey can carry off, sar. I nebber seed sich ones, in all my experience."

"You is as bad as the rest of them," growled the Kentuckian, and then crack went his instrument of torture to the flesh, and once more the negro danced and howled, although I suspected that he was not hurt as much as he pretended.

"If you will only stop dat, massa," yelled Sam, "I'll gib up de t'ings at once. On my word I will."

Bowmount suspended his barbarous work, and then Sam managed to produce, in some mysterious manner, my gold watch and silver-mounted revolver. The latter was empty, and the former run down, all the darkey's ingenuity not being sufficient to wind up the time-keeper.

"Um don't tick, massa," he said, as he gave up the watch. "I shake 'em eber so much, but it ain't no use. I reckon somethin' de matter wid it, or p'aps it worn out."

"Now go," I said, as I received my property; and, as

the fellow left the vessel, Bowmount said that I was too soft-hearted, and it was no wonder the niggers got sassy.

"What induced you to go to Mrs. Gowen's?" I asked.

"O, merely the desire of talkin' with her on matters connected with her passage. Light a cigar, and come with me," continued Bowmount.

"Where to?"

"The city prison; to see that old scamp of a Rhett, and that nigger, John. They has sent for us."

Without a word, I took his arm, and up the dock we went, towards the prison.

CHAPTER XI.

A VISIT TO THE CITY PRISON. — OFFICER'S OPINION OF THE WAR. — COLONEL RHETT AND JOHN THE MULATTO. — THEIR RELEASE. — ESCAPE OF HARRY AND COMPANION. — SAILING OF THE BELLE. — A DARK NIGHT, AND AN ANXIOUS ONE. — RUNNING THE BLOCKADE. — A MOMENT OF PERIL. — A SHARP PURSUIT. — MORE TREACHERY. — ARRIVAL AT BERMUDA. — DESPATCH-BAG AND ITS CONTENTS. — OLD ACQUAINTANCES.

WALKING to the prison, I learned from the Kentuckian, that while he was on his way to Mrs. Gowen's residence, some one had informed him that Colonel Rhett and John the mulatto desired to see him on business of importance, and that they would be much obliged if he would bring me along, as they wished to consult me on their future welfare; a piece of information that surprised me very much, for after their treatment, they could not suppose that I had much love for them or their plans.

"We'll go and see 'em," the Kentuckian said, as we strolled along, "and hear what they has to say for themselves. I wouldn't refuse to listen to a nigger unless he was sassy; and then I wouldn't listen to him long, now do you think I would?"

I thought not.

"No; dog on me if I would. And yet I have seen some nigs whose word I'd sooner take than some white men's."

As became a true son of South Carolina, I curled a lip in disdain at such sentiments. The Kentuckian saw the sneer, and it roused him to express an opinion that could not be extorted except under great excitement.

"Look 'e here, Barnwell," Bowmount said, "your state allers made a damned fool of itself on the nigger question. It allers went mad when a black skin was mentioned. It never will larn sense, I believe. Why, I've seen men go ravin' mad at the idea of giving a few slaves their freedom, jist as though it would hurt a state to do an act of justice of that kind. Of course, I ain't meanin' you, Barnwell. You is a feller of some sense, and I think, would listen to reason; but some folks don't know any better than to poke their heads agin' a stone wall when they might jist as well butt a feather bed."

"Bah!" I replied, "you are more than half an abolitionist. You had ought to live North, up among the Yankees."

"And a dog-on smart one I should have been, now I tell you," was the reply. "There's wusser people than the Yankees."

To this I made no reply, for, of course, I did not wish to lessen my people in the estimation of so radical a man as Mr. Bowmount, who formed opinions, and then stuck to them just through obstinacy, and the more you talked to him the worse he became.

The Kentuckian, finding that I did not attempt to combat his opinion, after waiting a moment or two to give me a chance, uttered a significant sniff, and said, —

"You don't think like me, dog on it."

"Well," I answered, with a laugh, "you don't always think like me, do you?"

"No; I don't want to. I hate the poor cuss what allers agrees with me, I does. I likes a man what has a opinion of his own."

By this time we had arrived near the jail, where political and other prisoners were confined. A guard of soldiers were lounging near the door, and as we ran towards them, they dropped the butts of their muskets to the ground, and hailed us in a ship-shape manner, after the style of marines, who understand their business.

"You can't pass," said the corporal, "without an order."

"Order be damned," replied the Kentuckian. "Send for the officer of the guard. If he knows me, in we go."

The officer of the guard was sent for. He proved to have been one of the party when the haunted house was visited, consequently we passed in at once, and found ourselves in an office where some dozen officers were smoking, and reading newspapers; and one of them, I noticed with some surprise and considerable wonder, was deeply interested in a copy of THE AMERICAN UNION, which had run the blockade, and was now affording amusement to a good-looking and intelligent member of the Confederacy.

Most of those who were smoking, were talking over the latest news, the various rumors, and matters connected with the war. All looked up when we entered, stared at us for a moment in wonderment, and then resumed conversation just as though we had not been present.

"I tell you what it is," said one of the officers, who

had been reading the Charleston Mercury, " the editor of this sheet may say what he pleases, but I tell you there are Yankee spies in our midst. I know it."

" Well, how do you know it?" asked a captain, whose eyes had not been removed from us since we entered the apartment.

" Why, here is an extract from a Boston paper, and it tells just where our batteries are located, and how many guns each one contains. We have spies in our midst, and it is time they were looked after."

I don't think that the young fellow suspected me, although he did look hard at me while speaking. At any rate, I met his gaze without flinching, or even changing color, for I had learned to control my feelings like a stoic.

"I tell you what I'd do," continued the suspicious officer. " I'd keep a watch on that nigger and white man, I would ; and I'd watch all persons who called to see them. That is what I would do ; and I tell you, if there were spies in Charleston, I would soon find them, and deal with them in a manner they would not like."

" My name," said the Kentuckian, " is Bowmount."

Every one looked up, astonished at the announcement. Those who were reading newspapers, paused in the work.

" Well, sir, what is that to us?" asked the suspicious officer.

" Well, I don't know as it is much, but I want to prevent mistakes in this way. I ain't no spy, and I don't want any man to call me one."

" Well, my man, I haven't called you one, have I ? "

" No ; you have not. But as me and my friend here called to see that white man and that nigger John, I didn't know but you would jump on us, and call us spies and sich like."

" Ah! and who are you, if I am allowed to ask?" demanded the officer, with a wink to his companions.

"I ain't no spy, dog on me if I am, now," was the reply.

"Well, who are you, then? No man should come here on a suspicious errand without giving an account of himself."

"My name is Bowmount, and at one time I commanded the Ninety-ninth Kentucky Cavalry; but arter the Fort Donelson affair, I was paroled, and ain't gone into the service since."

"It is easy to say that you once held a commission. Even the poor cuss in the cell says that he's a colonel, but no one believes him."

"I shouldn't advise you, young man, to doubt my word unless you is prepared to stick to it," remarked the Kentuckian, in a peculiar tone that preceded an outbreak of the most violent kind.

"Look 'e here," said the officer, who had visited the haunted house, "there's no use quarrelling about this matter, for I can set it right in two minutes. General Rampage is an intimate friend of Colonel Bowmount's, and some of our fellows served in the same regiment with him."

"O! if that is the case, of course I am satisfied, and I recall all offensive expressions," and the young fellow touched his cap, and lighted a fresh cigar.

As soon as good feeling was restored, we found no difficulty in obtaining permission to speak with Rhett and John the mulatto.

The two were confined in a cell on the ground floor, where there was none too much light. There was no furniture in the cell; but in one corner was a pile of straw, on which the men slept.

"Well, you miserable cusses," said the Kentuckian, "how does you feel now? Shucks! but you is in a pretty fix, and no mistake. I wouldn't give a picayune for yer chances of life, I wouldn't. If yer necks ain't stretched, it won't be 'cos there ain't enough hemp raised in Old Kaintuck."

"O, Mr. Bowmount," said the soft-voiced Rhett, purring like a contented cat, "you do talk so funny that it is a treat to hear you."

"Shucks! but it won't be a treat to hear you when the rope is goin' round yer neck, now I tell yer."

"You don't mean it, Mr. Bowmount," cried the Virginian. "If I thought so I should telegraph to Richmond without delay, and let the authorities hear of my situation. I should, indeed."

"Then you had better do it, for I tell yer that there ain't much chance for yer lives unless a miracle is to happen; and I'll be darned if I believe the Lord will put himself out for the sake of obliging a vagabond like you, what had rather lie than tell the truth most any time."

"You don't mean it?"

"But I does mean it."

"And does Captain Barnwell think as you do?"

The Virginian caught sight of me, standing in the rear of Bowmount, somewhat in the dark, so made motions for me to come forward.

"You don't s'pose that Barnwell cares, does you? He ain't like to care for a man what tried to hang him. Shucks! I shouldn't think he would."

"It was only in the way of a joke," purred Rhett. "We didn't mean anything serious, you know. Of course we should have let him go."

"You know better," John the mulatto remarked, speaking for the first time. "We intended to hang him, and I'm only sorry that we did not."

"Will you hush, you damned fool!" roared the colonel in a rage, all of his purring gone in a moment. "Curse you! if you don't want to live, I do."

"The nigger is some on truth," cried Bowmount. "He knows that there ain't no hope, and that he might as well come out flat-footed as to sneak behind soft words, what no one believes and no one cares for. An honest confession is good for the soul, as my old mother used to say."

John here stated that he had been led into a bad mess by the colonel, and that such being the case, he was determined not to suffer alone if he could help it.

The Kentuckian laughed, and was about to turn away, when it suddenly occurred to him that he had not asked why he was sent for. He put the question in his usual rough style, and with one or two oaths.

"Because," answered Rhett, in an eager tone, "I know your generosity; and know that if proper efforts are made, you'll do something for us. We must all help each other in this world, and with such a cause before us. A glorious cause! We will fight for it until these aged bones fall to pieces, and this proud flesh drops."

"O, shucks! what damned gammon that is!" cried the Kentuckian; and as he spoke, he left the door of the cell, and went back to the room where the officers of the prison and the soldiers were lounging, leaving me alone to talk with the two men.

"Captain Barnwell," whispered Rhett in an eager tone, "we do not expect much of that man. He is too rough, you know, to feel the finer sensibilities of such natures as yours. You can appreciate our condition. You can forgive and forget. I can read it in your eyes."

"Then you must have a vision like an owl's," I said; "for it is so dark here I can hardly see your face."

"Ha! ha! you are always full of your fun," laughed the colonel. "My daughter said that you was the pleasantest man she ever met. You always had a kind word and sweet smile for every one. I never noticed it before to-day. It is very singular."

"It is. Didn't you notice it when I was about to be hanged through your means?"

"O, don't allude to that little bit of fun, for I can call it nothing else."

"But why don't you appeal to the Richmond government, and get released?" I asked, after a moment's pause, seeing that I could make no impression on the fellow.

"Because, sir, I have particular reasons for the course I have adopted. They are secret and honorable."

"If the latter, confide them to me, and let me judge if such is the case."

Colonel Rhett groaned, and thought for a moment before he replied; and when he did speak, it was in low and feeling tones.

"When this struggle commenced," he said, "I was a rich man, but at the same time, the most imprudent one that you ever saw. I had no thought of to-morrow. It was all to-day. I feasted my friends, lent my money to all who wanted a loan, and at last found myself really embarrassed. A few importuning creditors have since bored me on every occasion, and it is to get rid of them that I now keep secret all my movements. You see how I trust you."

"I can tell how much you trust me after you have answered a few of my questions," I remarked.

"Ask me a hundred, and I'll answer them with that truthfulness which is so characteristic of the Rhetts."

"Bah!" I said, in scornful tones, "you can tell lies as well as other people. Don't disgust me with more exhibitions of your hypocrisy."

"O, that I should hear such words applied to me, and unable to call you to account for them!" moaned the colonel, just as though he was in earnest.

"Stop all such nonsense, or I'll leave you."

He left off his moaning, and immediately became attentive.

"Tell me," I continued, "why you should fear creditors when you are in the military service of the Confederacy. You know very well that military law is superior to civil at the present time."

"Yes, sir; to those who desire to shirk their responsibilities. I am not one of that kind. As long as I had money, I paid as I went along. When the war commenced, and I found that there was no sale for my tobacco, I paid as far as I was able, and trusted to luck for the balance."

"But you have not answered my question," I said. "Who would dare to prosecute a confederate colonel at the present time?"

"Any one who saw that the colonel was not disposed to stand on the order of his rank. My creditors knew that I had some money, so they pressed me. I was sick, and determined to leave the country until my health was restored. By so doing, I knew that I should benefit myself and daughter. Poor child! it makes my heart bleed when I think of her and her desolation."

He pretended to wipe away a tear, but I don't believe it was a real one, for I think that he was well aware that his daughter could take care of herself in most any part of the world, and in most any kind of society.

"Look here, Rhett," I said, "I don't know what to make of you; and for the life of me, I don't understand whether I can class you as a Yankee spy, or a true friend of the South."

The colonel uttered a sound that was intended as a laugh, but it seemed almost a failure.

"Don't think hard of me, captain," he said, in a tone of supplication, "just because I allowed myself to be in the company of those negroes. It was all accident, I assure you."

"Is that the truth, John?" I asked the sullen mulatto, who had not spoken since I had commenced conversing with the colonel.

"I don't want you to ask me a word about that man," John replied. "He don't amount to much. I am sick of him and his yarns. I'll answer no more questions."

"That's right, John. You don't understand these great matters like white men. We'll learn you in time."

The mulatto uttered a roar like a wild beast that has been wounded by an unseen hunter; but after that he remained silent and sullen.

"You will do something to get me out of this?" whispered the colonel. "I'm devilish uncomfortable here. My back is nearly raw, and smarts as though it was pickled."

"I can promise nothing at the present time," I remarked; "but in the course of the day I'll see you once more, and let you know what action I'll take."

"For God's sake, don't desert us. Our only hope is in you," cried the colonel, as I left him."

From the prison, I went direct to the telegraph office, leaving Bowmount to drink whiskey with the officers in the guard-room; an occupation which he liked so well it seemed a pity to disturb him.

I telegraphed to Richmond, to the secretary of war, for information respecting Rhett. In the course of the day a reply came to me that Colonel Rhett was absent from his regiment on sick-leave, and had left the country in company with his daughter.

So far, the story which Rhett had told was a correct one. I was a little staggered as I read the despatch, and could only account for the man's peculiarities on the ground that he hated me, because I had kissed his daughter, and rather snubbed him at times, while we were at Nassau.

But the man had been punished in the most severe manner, so that I felt avenged, and determined to do something for his liberation. I took the despatch, and went to General Rampage, and laid it before him.

"Damnation!" he muttered. "Is it possible that we have whipped a colonel in the confederate service? If such is the case, we can't do better than to set him at liberty, and get him to hush up the matter, for it would cause a stir if it was known. What shall I do?"

"Write a discharge for the colonel and the mulatto John. I'll undertake that they keep quiet about the affair, for their own sakes as well as yours."

"I'll do it," answered the general, and immediately wrote the order discharging Rhett and John from prison.

With the order, I hastened to the place of confinement, confident that for once I had done a generous deed.

When I reached the prison I found no difficulty in gaining an admission, or in obtaining an interview with Rhett and John. Bowmount, I noticed, was still in the guard-room, drinking whiskey as though for a wager, and spinning yarns of his adventures in Tennessee just before the Fort Donelson affair. I did not disturb him, but passed on to the cell where the men were confined. They were astonished to see me, not expecting that I would return so soon, if at all; for the rascals knew that they deserved but little gratitude at my hands.

"This is kind of you," said the colonel, as he came to the grating of the cell, rubbing his hands, and looking as amiable as possible. "I didn't expect to see you so soon, — indeed I did not.

"One word of advice," I said, earnestly. "In a few minutes you will be free. I don't care what becomes of you. You are able to take care of yourself; but that slave, John, had better make tracks for some other section of the country. He has admitted too much to remain here, and live in safety."

I returned to the ship, and the next morning said nothing to Bowmount about what I had done, knowing he would blame me for so doing. It was not necessary for me to allude to the subject, and I suppose Bowmount had too much to think of to remember it.

As I lighted a cigar, and went on deck, the mate came aft, his face showing that he had something on his mind.

"Them men what come on board yesterday has cut for it," he said.

"Are you sure that they are gone?"

"Yes, sir; and, blast 'em, they have taken a boat that was fastened to the dock. It's my opinion they have cut for the Yankee fleet."

"Well, say nothing about it at present. We may hear something in the course of the day. They couldn't run the gantlet of guard-boats and batteries."

"I rather think they could, sir. It was devilish dark, last night, and those chaps in the guard-boats are only a lot of sojers anyhow. If the boat drifted out with the tide, and the chaps didn't use any oars, they wouldn't have been noticed, I reckon."

I hoped that such was the case; for Mr. Reefpoint carried such weighty information to the Federal admiral, that the safety of the Union fleet depended on its reaching him without delay. If Harry and his companion were safe, then I could feel that I had done some good. If they were prisoners, I should have to find other messengers to convey the important intelligence, and I wondered who I could hit upon. John, the mulatto slave, had declared that he was an enemy of the rebels, and that he hated all who were engaged in the rebellion; but dared I to put my trust in him? He had acknowledged that he was in communication with the Yankees, but he had said so only when he thought I was in his power, and that I should never live to tell of it.

I walked the quarter deck, smoking my cigar, and thinking the matter all over, and at last came to the conclusion that I could not confide in John. He had proved himself too hostile to me to trust him. He had shown his vindictive spirit in more ways than one; and as long as he suspected that Mrs. Gowen cared for me, just so long should I incur his hatred, and just so long would he seek revenge.

I was interrupted in my reverie by the sound of heavy guns, far down the harbor. I looked towards Sumter through a glass, and saw that about a dozen of our blockading-fleet were hammering away at the fort with great vigor and determination, just as though a serious attempt at reduction was being made.

"More niggers reached the Yankees last night," a young confederate officer said, as he crossed the gangway-plank, and stepped lightly to the deck.

"Ah! how do you know that?" I asked, for I recognized the young fellow as belonging to General Rampage's staff.

"For the simple reason that every time a deserter or a nigger reaches the Yankee fleet, the Yanks feel bound to wake up, and show that they are alive. There they go; but it's all a waste of ball and powder. Sumter can stand a hundred days' bombardment, and still feel like fighting. It is the strongest fort in the world; for the garrison does not depend upon thick brick walls, but bags of sand, high and thick. Well, I suppose the Yankees like to amuse themselves, but it's devilish expensive fun."

I was delighted to hear the young fellow talk as he did, for it was a half assurance that Harry had reached the fleet in safety. I was so much pleased with his conversation and revelations, that I asked him to take a drink, and smoke a cigar, two offers which were not refused.

He had come on board to invite Bowmount and myself to a dinner, given by General Rampage; and after we had accepted the invitation, the young fellow took a second drink with the Kentuckian, lighted a fresh cigar, and went off, humming Dixie.

That afternoon, I dressed, and paid a visit to Mrs. Gowen, who had sent word that she expected me I found the lady looking more charming than ever, and she welcomed me with such genuine expressions of pleasure, that I could not doubt that she was in earnest. . . .

I was on board again before dark. Bowmount had missed me, but he did not ask where I had been.

"There's a man what wants to ship with us, sir," the mate said, in the course of the evening. "He looks kinder smart like, as though he would do good service. Better see him, sir."

The mate seemed more eager than I ever knew him to be when talking of one of the crew; but at the time I paid no attention to the fact, and merely said that I would look at the man, and that he might be shown into the cabin, so that I could examine him by candle-light. In a few minutes in came the candidate for the position of sailor. I looked the fellow all over, and it struck me that I had seen him before; but where, I could not tell. He seemed about thirty years of age, dark features, dark eyes and hair, stout and active, with a mouth that indicated great determination, and some considerable courage.

"Well, my man, do you want to ship on board the Belle?" I asked.

"Yes, sir," was the prompt answer, with a touch of his cap, in regular man-of-war style.

His voice sounded familiar, although I could not tell where or when. I gave the fellow a scrutinizing look, but he did not flinch.

"Are you an able seaman?" I asked.

"Yes, sir. I can hand, reef, and steer, and, if needed, shovel coals into the furnace. I'm willing to make myself useful."

"Why don't you join the iron-clads, and serve the Confederacy?"

"Because the iron-clads won't fight, and I want to make money."

"Haven't we met before?"

"Not that I knows of, sir."

In spite of the denial, I could not help thinking that I had seen the man on board of some vessel I had commanded; but as there was nothing remarkable in such a suspicion, I concluded to ship the man, so told him to bring his chest on board in the morning, and to swing his hammock in the house.

"Thank you, sir," was the reply. "You don't know what a favor you have conferred on me." And with a touch of his cap the man left the cabin: but as he turned from me I thought I saw a dangerous glitter in his dark eyes, as if he would like to express his triumph in words and gestures, yet dared not.

"Humph!" grunted Bowmount, who had been smoking a cigar during the interview, yet had not uttered a word; "do yer know I think that feller is a sneak?"

"What makes you think so?"

"I don't know; but I has that impression. That man's face don't look right; I don't like the glance of his eye. I ain't got much of what you'd call college larnin', but I tell yer I can read humans like a book. If that fellow ain't a sneak, then I'm no Kentuckian, that's all."

"If you think so, I will not take him on board. It is not too late to change our resolution."

"No," said the owner of the steamer, after a moment's thought; "let him come. I have a curiosity to see what he will turn out. I ain't afeared of him. Let him come, and welcome. I'm a match for him if he turns out vicious."

So the next day the new hand came on board, and commenced his labors. The mate said that he took hold with much readiness, and that he was a smart fellow, and knew his duty; which was high praise for the first officer to utter; for he seldom praised any one, being more pleased to swear at the men than to laud them, and more given to knocking them down than to setting them up.

We completed our cotton loading, stowing on board some sixteen hundred bales of soft, silk-like Sea-Island, which we had concluded to purchase instead of common cotton, thinking that the profit on the same would more than recompense us for the trouble of waiting a few days and collecting our cargo.

The evening before we sailed, Mrs. Gowen came on board, attended by a black girl, who had been freed some year or two before the war, so that in case she desired to run, on reaching the soil which does not tolerate slavery, the lady would not be a sufferer in purse or in feeling. Bowmount uttered a growl when the lady came on board, and took up her quarters in one of the best state-rooms in the ship; but he said not a word in remonstrance, for he knew that it would be useless, as far as I was concerned. She had made up her mind that she would go with us, and I had resolved that she should; consequently neither of us was to be changed in our fixed resolves.

The night that we sailed was a busy one to all on board. We had kept quiet the hour of our departure, for fear the news would be carried to the blockading-fleet, and an extra lookout stationed to discover us. Only Bowmount and myself were in the secret, and it is certain that we did not divulge it. Late in the afternoon about a dozen passengers were notified that it was desirable they should be on board at sundown, at the latest, for no one could tell what would happen. All were prompt, and among them was a despatch-bearer from Richmond, on his way to England, loaded down with communications from Davis and cabinet. The night was dark and squally, with showers of rain, which fell heavily, and at times shut out all the lights that were intended to guide blockade-runners in and out of the port. Even the pilot, whom I had engaged to take the ship as far as Sumter, seemed a little inclined to shirk the job, and intimated that the night was not such a one as he should have chosen for the work before him.

"Ye see," he said, after a long and anxious glance over the harbor, "the tide will begin to ebb at ten o'clock, and it will run like a sluice. Since the damned Yankees sunk their old ships on the sands, the channel has changed, and I reckon it's mighty onsartin in a dark night, taking out a ship that draws more'n fifteen feet of water aft."

"Then you are unwilling to run the risk?" I demanded.

"I didn't say that. I reckon I'm as willin' and as bold as most of 'em, but you see there's risk in it. I'll do the best I can, but if I touches, don't blame me, 'cos ye see how dark the night is, and the lights ain't much for showin' a feller where the deep water is."

I laid the matter before the Kentuckian, and he decided to make the attempt at all hazards; for he was impatient to move. The night was favorable for avoiding the fleet, and he thought we could do it if we only exercised caution. A little after ten o'clock the engineer reported that a full head of steam was on, and that the engines were in perfect running order. There were some anxious faces around me when this was made known, for on our success depended freedom or imprisonment, Fort Layfayette or Bermuda and Nassau.

"Gentlemen," I said, as the passengers gathered around me, "the risk is great, and the danger considerable. Are you willing to encounter it?"

"Yes," was the answer.

"Remember, then, to keep cool and calm, and remain in the cabin without lights, or else on deck without talking."

As I turned to go on deck, I saw standing at the cabin door, where he could have overheard all that was uttered, the strange sailor, whom I had shipped a few days before.

"What are you doing here?" I demanded, a little sternly.

He pointed to a carpet-bag which he held in his hand.

"The mate told me to carry this into the cabin, sir."

"And how long have you been standing here listening to what was said?"

"Don't know what you mean, sir; 'cos I has no object in listenin', sir."

The fellow appeared so honest, that I could but believe him.

"Drop the bag," I said, presently, "and go to your duty."

"Yes, sir."

He handed the carpet-bag to the steward, and left the cabin, touching his hat respectfully as he did so.

"It is singular," I muttered; "but I can't help thinking that I've seen that fellow's face before. Where, I can't for the life of me tell. His voice, too, seems familiar."

But in the hurry and confusion of leaving the dock, I forgot all about the sailor and my suspicions; for I had other matters demanding my attention. We dropped into the stream, slowly turned the steamer's head, and commenced moving towards Fort Sumter, a light on the battlements of Fort Moultrie being our only guide; a slight warning against the numerous bars and other dangers of the harbor. The pilot took his station on the wheelhouse, and I stood beside him.

"It's a devilish dark night," muttered the official; "and I wish that you had chosen some other time for starting. How the deuce I'm to get ashore on Sumter, in my boat, is more than I can tell."

I did not inform the man that I had no idea of stopping the engines for any such purpose in case there was a clear field before us. It struck me that Mr. Pilot would go farther than he anticipated; a common occurrence with blockade-runners, and sometimes a very profitable one for the pilot.

We crawled along with but little steam on, for the tide was ebbing fast, and carried us as rapidly as we desired, with men in the fore-chains taking soundings, and calling off the fathoms of water by feeling of the knots, instead of using a light, and being governed by the color of the rags. For two miles we met with no reverse of any kind, managing to keep in the channel, and clear of the shoals; but after the light at Fort Pinckney was off our beam, the difficulties of navigation began to increase in a very perplexing manner. The first warning came from the man in the starboard chains.

"By the mark three!" he cried, in a low tone, yet sufficiently loud to reach our ears.

There was just water enough to show that we were grazing the bottom, with not an inch to spare.

"Port," said the pilot; and then he muttered, "damn such a dark night, and not a light-house to steer by."

We edged away from the sand-bank, and once more got into water three and a half fathoms deep. Then we run along half a mile or so, when the man in the larboard chains shouted out a warning.

"Quarter less three!" he said.

"Stop her!" cried the pilot.

The engineer's bell conveyed the order. But it was too late; we were on a sand-bank, and still moving slowly along with the full force of the tide.

Then for the first time Mr. Bowmount spoke. He had been on the wheel-house from the time we left the dock, but had not uttered one word until the ship's keel touched the bottom.

"Is she hard and fast?" he asked.

"No; for we are still moving a little, as far as I can judge."

"How far are we from Sumter?" the Kentuckian next demanded.

"A mile or more," replied the pilot. "We must be under its guns."

"Then we are safe from the Yankees."

"Yes; they don't dare to come up as far as this."

"Barnwell, what does you recommend?" demanded the owner.

"Putting on the whole of the steam, and attempting to work over the shoal."

"And you, pilot — what does you say?"

"I say that we should only get stuck deeper. As it is, we must remain here till the next tide. I feared it all along."

"And have the Yankees discover us, and pitch into us at long range. No, sir; I don't stand that. Barnwell, put on all the steam, and see if you can't jump her over the shoal."

"I wash my hands of the whole matter!" cried the pilot.

"Wash, and be damned!" was the blunt reply. "Crowd on the steam, and let's see what we can do."

But just at that moment the engineer opened a valve, and commenced blowing off steam, making a noise that could be heard for miles.

"Hell and furies! what is the man about?" roared the Kentuckian and the pilot with one voice.

I went to the skylight that ventilated the engineer's room, and shouted to him to save the steam, and asked him what he meant by opening the valve.

"Tell him to come on deck," roared the Kentuckian. "Up here with him, and let's understand what all this means. By the Lord Harry, I'll see if we have traitors on board. Shucks! but the man what tries to sell me to the Yankees dies, or I'm a nigger."

The engineer came on deck, surprised and indignant, leaving one of his assistants in charge, who had orders to reverse his engines, and put on all the steam that he could raise, and see if we could not back the steamer from her uncomfortable position, and once more float in water deep enough to keep her keel from the ground.

"Well, sir," roared the irate Kentuckian, "what in the devil do you mean, sir, by such conduct?" and here he uttered a string of oaths that sounded most emphatic as well as profane.

"Look a-here, Mr. Bowmount," said the engineer, in a mild but firm tone, "if you talk to me, talk as one man should talk to another, for I'll be damned if I will be swore at as though I was a brute. Now understand that at once."

With all the Kentuckian's faults, with all of his hasty temper and liberal expenditure of oaths, he was a man who respected true courage wherever he found it, in enemy or friend; so I was not surprised to note that Bowmount lowered his tone considerably when he again spoke to the engineer.

"Mr. Crankpin," he said, "what in the devil's name did you blow off steam for? That's what I want to know. And I puts the question, like good whiskey, right square afore you; and dog on me, if I don't want an answer as quick as I can get it, and no mistake."

"I let off steam, sir, because I was ordered to do so by the captain; that's why I did it," was the confident answer.

The Kentuckian fairly yelled his astonishment, as he dashed his old wide-awake hat on the deck, and stamped on it, and then deliberately kicked it overboard.

"Do you hear him?" gasped the Kentuckian, turning to me. "Well, dog on me, if this ain't a leetle the greatest thing that I ever heard in all my born days. Why, damn it, man, Captain Barnwell was standin' right alongside of me jist at the time the steam began to blow off. Now, there."

"But he sent a message by one of the men," urged the engineer.

"He didn't send no message. He ain't spoke to no man except me and the pilot there; I has been here all the time, and seed all that has taken place. You didn't send no word like that, did you, Barnwell?"

"No," I replied, watching the effect of the struggle that was going on between our powerful engines and the soft sand on which the steamer had touched.

"Do you hear that? He didn't send no sich message," roared Bowmount. "I knowed he didn't."

"Then some one has played me false," said the engineer, in a tone so frank, that even Bowmount could not help believing him.

"Go find the man what brought you the word. If we has traitors on board, we will find 'em to make examples of. I don't stand no damned nonsense when a fortune is at stake, now I tell yer. I'd hang my own grandfather if he should but wink in a suspicious manner."

I saw that all efforts to back off the sand were useless. We were wasting time, for the tide was still ebbing quite rapidly, and every moment but added to our perplexities; consequently I said, —

"Let the engineer return to his post, for we need his services more than ever just at this time. I am satisfied that he is no traitor, but an honest man."

"Thank you, Captain Barnwell, you' but do me justice. I am as true as steel," replied the engineer, in a gratified tone.

"All right. So back to your post, as Barnwell says. P'int out the feller what told yer arter we is out of this scrape. if we ever does get out of it."

As the engineer turned away, I said to him, —

"Put on all steam, and go ahead; I will see if we can't lift her over the bar. It is our only hope."

"I'll do my part," was the reply; and the instant he entered the engine-room he kept his word, and had the elements to help him. and the rest of us, just as he had started the engines, and was letting on steam to send the vessel ahead.

The wind, which had blown off shore, suddenly chopped round, and struck us on the bow, dead ahead.

At first this might seem a misfortune, but we did not so regard it, for with the wind came quite a heavy swell, long at times, and then sharp and choppy, showing that the elements were at war outside. The waves raised the steamer, and dropped her on the sand, but so softly that no injury was done; not a seam was opened, not a bolt displaced.

Little at a time steam was let on, and then the pressure began to tell. The huge wheels revolved so rapidly that they beat the water as if punishing it for its misdeeds; the hull groaned, and creaked, and rolled, and pitched, while at the same time heavy squalls of rain were dashed on the deck, and in our faces, almost blinding us for the moment, but still not driving us from our posts.

The men who were in the chains, taking soundings, reported every few seconds. With their heavy leads resting on the sand, they could tell if the ship moved ahead or astern.

"Does she forge ahead?" I asked every second, and still the answer came back that she did not move an inch in the right direction.

But still the wheels continued to revolve, and the ship to groan and roll; and just as I had given up all hope of once more getting afloat, a huge swell came tumbling in from the sea, striking on our bow, and instead of going over us, and sweeping the deck, passed under us, lifting the steamer from its bed of quicksand, and for a moment allowed the paddles to be of some service in moving ahead.

But that moment saved us, for the vessel seemed to have gathered strength for a spring, like a well-trained hunter, and when the waves passed, and the keel once more touched the bottom, we moved over the shoal, slowly but surely, as the men in the chains informed us.

It was hard work, for the quicksands were as tenacious as pitch, and stuck to us like it; but the power of our engines and the aid of the heavy swell did wonders, so that we soon had ten inches of water under our keel, and were moving along past Fort Sumter at the rate of eight knots per hour, all hands on the lookout for a stray but vigilant member of the Federal fleet.

"You did that well. Dog on me, ef I ever seed anything like it, old feller," said Bowmount, speaking for the first time since we had been afloat. "Here; take some whiskey, old Bourbon, and drink to our future good luck."

I really needed the stimulant, for I was wet and cold, in spite of my rubber boots and coat. The liquor was therefore acceptable. I took a drink, and passed the bottle to the pilot. That worthy gentleman threw back his head, and the fluid gurgled down his throat, and continued to do so until I thought he would strangle.

But no such misfortune happened to him. He removed the bottle from his mouth, and after a long-drawn sigh, asked, —

"Is there much of that 'ere kind of stuff round here?"

"Two or three barrels full," returned the Kentuckian. "You wouldn't have a man go to sea short of provisions, would you?"

"No; but two or three barrels ain't much for a crowd what is on their drink, now is it?" asked the pilot, in an argumentative tone.

"No; but the passage will be short."

"There's somethin' in that, sir," and then, after a moment's consideration, the pilot continued, "It's too rough to land at Sumter, and I should capsize if I attempted to beach my boat under the walls of Fort Moultrie. I don't know what to do."

"Go with us," I said. "You are safer here than in your boat."

"And you shall have an allowance of a quart of whiskey per day," suggested the owner; thus touching the man's heart.

"Count me in," he said; and just as he had announced his readiness to accompany us, almost directly in our course a blue light was revealed, exposing the frowning broadside of a blockading steamer.

For fifteen seconds it threw its ghastly pale and weird light over the water, then died out, the darkness seeming ten times more dense than ever.

"Damn 'em, they is on the watch," muttered the Kentuckian, who stood at my elbow.

"The fleet heard the noise of escaping steam," I remarked, "and the ships have moved to prevent our escape. Ha! there goes a second light, and on board of another vessel. The Yankees are wide awake, and no mistake."

As the light died out, three or four red-white-and-blue rockets flew into the air, from various directions, and I knew that they meant, as plain as words could tell, " Our ships are in position, and the enemy is in sight."

"Shall we 'bout ship?" asked the pilot. "There is time enough for us to run under the lee of Sumter, and so escape."

I turned to Bowmount for an answer, for he was the man most interested, and while waiting for a reply, touched the engineer's bell to signalize slower speed of the engines.

The owner did not reply immediately to the question. He seemed to be turning it over in his mind, and calculating the chances for escape; for he was not one to turn back unless there was cause. At length he spoke.

"What does you think of it, Barnwell? Is there any hope for us? Can we break through the lines, and show 'em our heels?"

"If we were once through the line, we could out-steam the best boat on the coast," I answered, in a non-committal style.

"I know that, but it ain't the question. Can we get through, and not carry off shots between wind and water?"

"If you say go on, I'll do the best I can. The night is dark, and that is favorable for us. We may have the luck to slip by."

An exclamation of surprise from the pilot attracted my attention. I turned, and saw, soaring heavenward, direct from the bow of the Belle, a red rocket, which burst, and sent down upon the dark waters a thousand bright stars.

"We have damned traitors on board," yelled the Kentuckian, and leaving the bridge, jumped to the spar-deck, and started forward, bowie-knife in hand, determined to kill or maim the person who had sent up the signal, and thus gave the Federal fleet our exact position.

"Shall we go on?" asked the pilot, as soon as he found that we were alone.

I was just about to order the engineer to reverse his engines, and back towards Fort Sumter, when a black mass suddenly appeared alongside, and then I knew that it was too late. We were under the guns of a Federal gunboat, and would be blown out of the water if we but made a motion to escape. Nothing but coolness and impudence could save us now.

The pilot saw the apparition, and commenced drinking all the whiskey he had in his flask. In a few minutes he was in a state of blind drunkenness, and didn't know the points of the compass, or Fort Sumter from a brick-bat.

In a moment, fore and aft, there was such stillness came over the vessel, that any one could have told that great danger was at hand. Even Bowmount, whose loud swearing I had heard but a moment before, suspended his hard words, and seemed to have sheathed his knife, and awaited the development of events, with a patience that most all rash men can assume under certain circumstances.

"Is that you, Hubbard," asked the commanding officer of the dark frowning mass that was ranging alongside.

The officer had made a mistake, owing to the darkness. A thought entered my head that there was yet hope for us. Mr. Midshipman Reefpoint had mentioned the name of Commander Hubbard of the Highflyer, a steamer that carried ten guns, and two hundred men; and it struck me I had met some one who supposed that he was alongside of Hubbard's ship, the dark hull of the Belle favoring the deception.

I did not for a moment hesitate as I replied, —

"Yes, this is what is left of me, but I'm almost washed away by the rain and sea," and then, thinking that I would first cry "thief," added, —

"I wish that blockade-runners were to the devil, rousing a man out on such a night as this on a wild-goose hunt. If one started, he turned back as soon as he saw our blue light."

"I guess that's so; but what the deuse did you throw up that rocket for just now? You know that it is not the right signal, don't you?" asked Commander Hubbard, in all honesty.

"Of course I do, but the gunner made a mistake, and let it pass, supposing that every one would understand it. It was intended to let the admiral know that I could see nothing as far as I had gone."

"How far did you run in, sir?"

"Close to Sumter; but I did not dare to show a glim, for fear the active gentlemen who man the fort would salute me with a few of their heavy shells. They are capable of it, at any time."

"I believe you; for I notice that they have grown spiteful lately. I should like to have a hack at them, although it would be of no use. Wooden walls won't stand against stone and sand, and the rebels know it."

"It is true, but at the same time I should like to stir —"

I had proceeded so far, when some one, who, I could not tell, put his head through a port hole, or looked over the rail, and yelled out in a loud tone, —

"Treason! Treachery! A blockade-runner. Fire on us."

My heart jumped into my mouth, and I thought I was done for; but still did not lose my presence of mind. I knew the cries would startle Commander Hubbard, and that he would hasten to ask some awkward questions, but

I determined to forestall him, as the only method of banishing his suspicions.

"Take that man back to the sick-bay," I said, in a tone that would reach the quarter deck of the other steamer, "and tell the surgeon to put a guard over him as long as he is out of his head."

I dreaded that the traitor whom we had on board would once more proclaim our character, but he did not, for the reason that all our crew and passengers, armed with heavers, handspikes, knives, and revolvers, were rushing around the decks, poking blades into dark corners, and looking sharp for the scoundrel who had attempted to betray us. If he had been caught in the act of giving an alarm, certain and speedy death would have been his portion. The crew and passengers would not have waited for the formalities of a trial. They would have taken the law into their own hands, and despatched their victim without a pang of remorse.

"What is the matter?" asked the commander of the Federal steamer, in a tone a little sterner than the one he had before used; for it was a grave breach of discipline for one of the crew to utter even a whisper when two captains were carrying on a conversation.

"One of my poor fellows was sun-struck a few days since, and owing to carelessness, escaped from the sick-bay. I hope that he will get over it in a short time; but it is a tough case. All owing to this confounded climate."

"Too true. Hope he will recover. But where is the blockade-runner?"

"Gone back to Charleston, I guess. He'd be a fool to attempt to run out such a night as this."

"So I think. Good by. Come and dine with me to-morrow."

"I will; and now I must run down and report to the

admiral." And with these parting words I touched the bell that notified the engineer a little more steam was wanted.

We edged away, and soon lost sight of the gunboat, the captain of which did not receive his expected guest the next day; and when he charged Commander Hubbard with neglect, the latter repudiated the charge in emphatic terms, and by comparing notes, they came to the joint conclusion that some rebel blockade-runner had performed a most prodigious game of humbugging which would not be best to try on the second time.

Mr. Reefpoint afterwards told me that the whole matter was talked over in the fleet for a week; and that the admiral swore like a seventeenth-century pirate at the carelessness in not trying the Belle with secret signals, the only sure method to bring out the truth when meeting a strange vessel on a dark night.

To some of the gallant sailors who served on the Southern station at the time of which I write, these few facts will prove interesting, and explain some points which were rather clouded with darkness. At any rate, if they read this, let us hope they will not bear any malice for the little trick which circumstances over which I had no control compelled me to perform.

As soon as we had lost sight of the gunboat, and had passed the outer circle of the blockading fleet, the Kentuckian came to me, wet as I was, and took me in his arms, and wanted to kiss me; but that I objected to in decided terms, for I remembered that in the cabin were a softer and sweeter pair of lips, which I preferred to those of the owner.

"Barnwell," cried the enthusiastic Kentuckian, "you are a trump, and no mistake. To you I owe my ship and cargo. No other man but you, dog on me, could have took us through that scrape, now I know. Shucks! how

I loves a noble-hearted man, what comes up to my expectations! Here, drink; and let me swear to you universal friendship, that shall last forever and ever. Amen.

"Barnwell," continued the owner, "is there more dangers? Can a feller yell just as much as he pleases, and not run no risk of waking up the Yankee fleet?"

"Shout as much as you please," I answered. "No one can hear you in this breeze, or if you are heard, it won't make much difference. It will not be noticed."

The Kentuckian commenced a mad dance, and then made a second rush for the purpose of embracing me; but this encounter I declined, to the intense amusement of the passengers, who had recovered from their fright, and renewed their good-nature, although I did not feel like rejoicing with them at the cheat which had been imposed upon the Yankees.

"Blast it, old feller, let me show my gratitude in some way! Let me do somethin' to prove that I'm grateful for savin' ship and cargo. Egad! how the Yankees would have chuckled over the long and silky Sea Island what we has on board, and is worth most a dollar and a half of any man's money! Whoop! let's begin. Whiskey for all of us, you stewards. Set it out on the table, in the cabin, and give us a cold bite. Pipe all hands to liquor, and let 'em splice the after downhaul, or whatever you call it. Hoop! wake snakes, and let's liquor."

The owner and passengers rushed to the cabin, and once more left me in possession of the quarter-deck. I wanted to be alone, to think over what had passed, and to wonder who had managed to get on board with the firm determination of betraying the vessel into the hands of the Federals; something that I should have rejoiced at, under other circumstances, although I had too much at stake to care about meeting my Union friends just at that time. While I was looking astern, to see if there was any evidence of commotion in the fleet, I saw a flash, and then the report of a heavy gun, while at the same time a flight of rockets darted into the air, and burst, showering down green and red stars in profusion.

"They have waked up to the fact that you have escaped," some one said, close to my elbow; and, turning, I saw the man who had come on board with despatches from the Richmond government, and with which he was to make the best of his way to Europe, while I had resolved that if the fellow did visit the continent he should go empty-handed; for the despatches I was determined to have, even if I had to resort to a little violence for the sake of obtaining them.

"Yes," continued the despatch-bearer, "the Yankees have discovered that their prize has slipped through their hands. There will be a devil of a commotion to-morrow morning, and some of the commanders will get a wiging."

"I shouldn't be surprised if such was the case," I answered.

"We slipped through much better than I anticipated," continued the despatch-bearer. "Do you know that at one time I had weights attached to my despatch-box, so that I could throw the papers overboard, and sink them, in case we were captured? This contains too much valuable information for the Yankees to get hold of. It would be a godsend to them."

He touched a carpet-bag, that seemed to contain the box and papers which he alluded to. It was hanging to a belaying-pin in the fife-rail, around the mizzen-mast, and consequently swung back and forth with the motion of the vessel; and although we rolled and pitched considerably, yet not enough to displace the bag, and even if it had slipped from the pin, it could not have rolled overboard, for the rail was too high to admit of such a thing, and we were not shipping enough water to wash it into the sea.

I have been somewhat particular in stating this fact for reasons which will soon appear.

While the despatch-bearer was chuckling at having avoided the Yankees, one of the crew came on the quarter-deck, and began to coil down some of the ropes which had worked loose. I supposed that the mate had sent him, so did not look at the man, or notice what he was about. In a few minutes he had concluded his labors, and went forward, while my passenger and myself remained on the quarter-deck, smoking, and talking of various topics, all relating to the Southern Confederacy.

All at once Bowmount, who was in the cabin, brewing punch, missed me, and yelled to me to come to him, and submit to have my health drank; a proposition that was hailed with cheers of enthusiasm by the passengers.

"We must go and see them," said the despatch-bearer. "They are mixing punch, and I think I smell its perfume even here. I long for a drink. Shall we join the jolly dogs."

"I have no objection. I think that we are now safe."

The despatch-bearer went towards the mizzen-mast for the purpose of recovering his carpet-bag which contained important papers from the Richmond government. Suddenly he uttered an exclamation of horror, fell on his knees, and commenced searching the deck, all the time uttering the most passionate exclamations.

"What in the devil's name is the matter?" I asked; for I thought the fellow had been attacked by a fit.

"It's gone!" the man howled; "it's gone!"

"What's gone?"

"My carpet-bag, containing all my despatches. O, my God! what will become of me? A moment ago it was here, on the rail, and now it is gone. Some one has stolen it. I am betrayed. There's traitors on board this vessel. They have got possession of my despatches, and I shall be shot if I ever return to the Confederacy."

At this moment Bowmount came on deck to hurry me to the cabin. He overheard the wailing, and said, —

"Then it's my advice to you to keep away. Don't be a damned fool, and go and put yer head in the wolf's mouth. That's my advice, I reckon, and, shucks! you may take it for what it is worth, or let it alone."

"I've lost my despatches. I'm a ruined man," moaned the agent, still searching on the deck for his carpet-bag.

"Well, then, don't you go for to tell every one that you is ruined, 'cos if you does they is sure to believe yer. Keep cool, and matters to yerself, and then ye can hold up yer head, and no one will be the wiser for what ye has lost."

"O, my despatches!" moaned the man.

"Damn yer despatches! they wan't of any use, no how," pettishly exclaimed the Kentuckian. "Let 'em go to thunder; and come in the cabin, and have a drink. I wouldn't give a bottle of whiskey for all the despatches in creation." And with a growl like that of an angry bear, Bowmount returned to the cabin to drink success to the voyage with the enthusiastic passengers.

"What shall I do?" asked the despatch-bearer, turning to me for consolation.

I did not know what to answer. The loss surprised me as much as it did the confederate agent. It was improbable that the bag could have disappeared without the aid of hands; for the motion of the ship would not have loosened it from the pin in the rail. At first I thought that the man at the wheel might have stolen the property, but he could not have left his post without being detected. Then I thought of the fellow who had come aft, and coiled up the ropes. He must have committed the robbery, and if such was the case, detection was probable. I approached the sailor at the wheel, an Englishman, and one who had made the run with me to Charleston, and asked, —

"Jack, who was the man who coiled up the ropes a few minutes since, on the quarter-deck?"

"I don't know, sir; I didn't look at him. I was too busy watching the compass, and keeping the ship on her course."

"Humph!" I thought. "I wonder if you are always so particular."

"You saw a man come aft?" I said.

"Yes, sir; but I didn't look up to see who it was."

The mate was forward, stowing the chain and anchor. I sent for him, and he was prompt in coming aft.

"Mr. Cringle," I said, "do you recollect whom you sent to the quarter-deck to coil up ropes?"

The mate canted his head over one side, and thought of the matter for a moment.

"No, sir," he answered. "I didn't send any one aft, 'cos I has been so busy that I didn't think of it."

The despatch-bearer uttered a howl of anguish.

"I 'opes no one has been sassy on the quarter-deck, sir," said the mate. "If any one has, jist pint 'em out, and I'll warrant he don't do it agin."

"No one has been impudent as far as words are concerned, but some one has come aft, and stolen a valuable package of papers, which were in a carpet-bag."

The mate scratched his head, not knowing what else to do; and then he turned his quid, and said, —

"There is some one on board what hadn't ought to be here. He is a rum customer, and if I could lay hands on him he'd go overboard afore he had time to say his prayers, now I tell ye. I has been huntin' for him from the time that he sent up that bloody rocket to the time when he hailed the Yankee gunboat. He is a sly one, but I think we can nab him yet; and if we does, why, we will settle his coffee jist as sure as fate."

"The man who gave the signals might have been the

one who stole the carpet-bag. To you I intrust the duty of finding it. Search every part of the ship if it is necessary. Find it," and then I sunk my voice to a whisper, " and if you do find it, don't fail to give it to me, and say not a word about it to any one."

" Yes, sir ; " and the mate was turning away, when I stopped him, by asking, —

" Do you think that Dick Smith, the new hand, is concerned in the matter ? "

" Lord bless ye, no, sir. Dick is as stanch as oak, sir, and has been close to me all night. He's a trump, sir, and a smart sailor. That's what he is."

" Was he alongside of you when the gunboat was hailed ? "

" No, sir ; 'cos I'd jist sent him to see that the men didn't make a bit of noise. O, I'll go bail that he's a slap-up true man."

" Well, perhaps he is ; but keep an eye on him, and see if you can notice anything suspicious."

" Yes, sir," and the mate went forward, while the confederate agent retired to the cabin, and endeavored to forget his misery by drinking whiskey punch, a task that all seemed to enjoy ; for after I had given the course of the ship, and performed some other duties, I left the deck in charge of the mate, and joined the happy company that mustered around the cabin-table, some of them so jolly that they did not know whether they were on shore or the sea.

" Three cheers for the cap'n of the Belle ! " yelled one fellow, as I entered the cabin, and I must confess that the cheers were given with a will, and that a glass of whiskey punch was thrust into my hand, which I drank with infinite relish ; and then all eyes were directed towards Bowmount, who was telling of the trouble he had experienced in searching for the traitor who was on board, and who had managed thus far to elude all attempts at discovery. While this was going on, I heard a commotion on deck; such a one as indicated that my presence was required.

"Light off the starboard-bow," cried the lookout.

"A steamer in sight off the starboard-bow," cried half a dozen voices; and then the revellers in the upper cabin started from their seats, and dashed on deck.

"Silence, fore and aft," was the first order I gave. "Let the men go to their stations. Gentlemen, you must retire to the cabin, or keep quiet. Don't let me hear a loud word."

"Blast me, if I don't keep 'em quiet," said the Kentuckian, who had drank so much that he did not know what was going on for some minutes. Our sudden danger had almost sobered him, so he was just the man to keep the others still.

The mate pointed out the suspicious steamer, about a mile off our starboard-bow, and apparently edging towards us; for she was heading in the same direction that we were, but without that regard to secrecy which was so essential to ourselves, for we could see the light of her furnaces as she rolled and pitched with the heavy sea, and no attempts seemed to have been made to screen them from observation.

I looked at the stranger, long and earnestly, through a powerful spy-glass, but the night was so dark that I could not tell whether we had fallen in with one of Uncle Sam's cruisers or not. The fellow might be a blockade-runner, waiting for a chance to get in; or he might have escaped from some port, and was now running along, under easy steam, for Havana, Nassau, or Bermuda.

"What is he?" chorused half a dozen of the most sober of the passengers.

"Silence!" roared Bowmount; "we won't have no noise here on the quarter-deck."

"Gentlemen," I said, "I don't know what to make of the stranger, but, if you will keep quiet, I'll let you know in the course of time."

With this all seemed satisfied, even if they were not, while I ordered the steamer to be kept away a couple of points, wishing no company under our circumstances. I was soon satisfied that the stranger desired a closer acquaintance, for the fellow edged away to meet our movements, and after we had run along for a mile or more without much change in our relative distances, a light was flashed from the rigging of the steamer, and then three lanterns formed a triangle, changing from the latter to a square, and from a square to a diamond, all of which meant, as plainly as words could express, that our number and name were desired, if it was not too much trouble on our part. I could read the signals as plain as a book, but I could not answer them while surrounded by a dozen or more rebel gentlemen, who would have relished such information, and used it on other occasions. No; if I was chased even into the harbor of Bermuda, I would not allow those on board to penetrate the mysteries of the United States signals.

"Better drop the cuss," said the owner, who had thrust his head into a pail of water, and now was as sober as man could be. "We don't want no such sneaks as that round us — do we?"

"No; and I'll try and throw him off. At any rate, we will see if he has speed; for I tell you candidly that it's one of Uncle Sam's ships on the outer station, ready to pick up all that crosses its course."

I touched the bell to notify the engineer that more steam was wanted. A prompt answer was returned in the shape of smoke and a rush of the paddle-wheels. The steamer started ahead with increased speed, plunging into the waves, throwing the spray high in the air, and sometimes landing huge masses of water on the deck, which swept aft, to the intense disgust of the passengers, who would jump on chicken-coops and chairs for the purpose of saving their feet from being wet. Fifteen minutes' such running settled one point, and that was that the gunboat could travel as fast as the Belle. Such at least appeared to be the case; for we did not increase our distance from the stranger. He held his own in spite of us, which fact caused me some uneasiness. The passengers, those who were sailors, and could stand head seas and bad weather without sickness, also saw that we had caught a tartar, and were disposed to grumble, as men will sometimes when they are in distress or danger. Their alarm, and the cold spray, mixed with rain, began to sober them, so that we no longer had snatches of wild songs and enthusiastic bursts of self-glorification.

"Mr. Cringle," I said to the mate, in a quiet tone, "send the chief engineer to me."

"Yes, sir;" and off he went on his errand.

In the course of a minute or more Mr. Crankpin stood before me, black with smoke, and smelling strongly of oil.

"Mr. Crankpin," I said, in a low tone, so that no one should hear me, "are your boilers making steam as fast as desirable?"

"Yes, sir; they are doing all that I could wish."

"And the machinery is in perfect order?"

"Every part is perfect."

"And the coal. Does it burn well?"

"Yes, sir. Sends out as much heat as any that I ever used."

"Then why is our speed slower than usual?"

"Don't know, sir, unless it is the head sea, and the wind."

"No; the Belle can make ten knots an hour, even with a head sea and strong wind."

"Certainly, she has done better, sir; but at the present time I am doing all that can be done, and if you have any doubts on the subject, just send for my assistant, and see what he thinks on the subject; or you can give him full charge of the engines, and I'll retire."

"You will do nothing of the kind. I have confidence in you, and believe that you perform your duties as well as any man. Ah! that shows the gunboat is waking up, and disposed to try the effect of shot and powder."

The latter part of my remark was caused by the report of a heavy gun on board the Federal vessel, the captain of which seemed disposed to see what could be done in the way of bringing us under his lee without the benefit of a long chase. I don't know where the shot struck. The night was too dark to see. But I noticed that some of the passengers left the deck suddenly; while others, who had been under fire more than once, laughed at the shot, and the man who thought that he could hit a vessel that was bobbing about on a heavy sea, on a dark and stormy night, with only the glowing smoke-stack to aim at.

"Let him waste his powder," growled Bowmount. "He won't hurt us by it."

I was not so sure of that; for unless my eyes deceived me, the gunboat was gaining on us at such a rate, that in the course of two or three hours we should be under his guns and sunk, unless we surrendered.

"If we are pressed too closely, do you want me to throw overboard some of the cotton that is stowed in the cabin and on deck?"

"Not a damned bale," was the profane remark. "I'll carry it all into port, or I'll sink it in the ocean, ship and all. No half ways for me. A big haul or none. Dog on me if that ain't my course, now I tell yer."

"All right," I answered; and then turned to exchange

a few words with Mrs. Gowen, who would persist in remaining on deck in preference to retiring.

"Is there danger of being taken?" she asked.

"I hope not," I answered.

"You are not confident of escape;" and as she spoke she laid one of her hands on my arm.

"To tell you the truth, the Belle is not doing as well as we could hope."

"Then there must be some reason for it," the lady replied.

And those words, thoughtlessly spoken, set me to thinking; and after a moment's thought I determined to act. I called the mate to me, and told him to make a thorough examination of the steamer fore and aft, and see if all was right; and while he took the larboard side I took the starboard. We were both rewarded for our trouble before we reached the wheels; for, while I found a huge fender towing in the water, Mr. Cringle discovered that some sixty fathoms of a small hawser, which we had used while in dock, was towing overboard, although I could have sworn that it was nicely coiled up near the house.

"How in —— came this overboard?" roared the mate, whose rage was not confined to narrow limits when he saw the trick that had been played us.

No one answered the direct question, although I could hear the men mutter how they would serve the rascal who had played us such scurvy tricks from the time we had left the wharf until the present.

"Lay hold of it, and rouse it in, some of you," roared the mate.

The men did so, and then secured the fender, while I continued my walk forward, and was rewarded with another important discovery. I saw a rope hanging over the bow, and on attempting to haul it in, found that I could not do so. A few moments' investigation showed that a sail was attached to the rope, which the evil genius whom we had on board had managed to slip under our stem, and so impeded our progress all of half a knot per hour. I called to the men, and they came rushing forward. The strength of a dozen of them was required to haul the sail on board, and then we found that it was the forecastle awning, which had missed being stowed away, for some reason which the mate could not account for. Among those who were especially active in hauling in the sail and fender was the new hand, Dick Smith. He swore vengeance on the mean cuss who would do such a dirty trick, and thought a search should be made fore and aft for the traitor.

"Some one is determined," he said, " to have us fall into the hands of the Yankees, and so share the prize-money; but I reckon he will miss it this time."

The man seemed so interested that I thought he was quite an addition to our crew, and so noticed him more than the others, and had half a mind to station him near the machinery, the part on deck, so as to be sure no one played pranks with it; but some trifling thing prevented me, and I set a raw-boned Scotchman on the watch, with orders to cut down any one who dared to meddle with the works unless authorized to do so.

As soon as the drags were on board, the Belle appeared to recover her usual swiftness; and this the Federal cruiser discovered in a short time, for he began to hammer away at us in the most lively manner, first with his bow-chasers, and then with his midship gun, a heavy Parrott, that sent shell after shell through the air, on each side of us, astern of us, and sometimes ahead of us. But none of his shots touched us, and the more he fired the more ground he lost; and this was soon discovered by the captain of the gunboat, for he shut his ports, secured his guns, and crowded on all the steam that he could stand; but still we dropped him, and even saved some of our power while doing so.

At daylight the gunboat was hull down. We could see nothing of her but her masts and smoke, and, as the wind and sea fell, even those were soon lost to view, and we were alone upon that part of the ocean. At sunrise the passengers once more assembled upon the deck, those who were not too sick, and drank gin-cocktails and coffee, and wished all manner of luck to the confederates, and all sorts of confusion to the Yankees. The despatch-bearer, however, was rather glum, and did not participate in the festivities; and once he said to me, with a sullen frown on his brow, that he almost wished the Belle had been taken; because, if such had been the case, no one would have blamed him for the loss of his papers.

"Cheer up, old feller," I said; "perhaps we shall yet find them before we reach Bermuda."

But the comfort I afforded was not of a substantial kind, and the agent mourned, and refused to be consoled. No accident occurred to us, and we saw no vessels except peaceable merchantmen, which gave us a wide berth, fearing, from our snake-like appearance, that we were on the privateer order, and so bound not to respect neutrals, or those who hoisted the English flag for the purpose of covering American bottoms.

At length we sighted the reef-bound Island of Bermuda, and steered for St. George's Harbor, where we took on board a pilot, who asked for two things as soon as he touched the deck — first, for a drink of ale or brandy, he did not care which; secondly, the news. Had the confeds succeeded in establishing their independence? God bless 'em! They were a noble-hearted people, and deserved to be free. Luff a little, so that we can clear the coral reef that runs out at this point. The taking of Fort Sumter was the greatest thing that ever happened in the world. Were there any Yankee men-of-war in the harbor? O, yes! there was one — the Stingeree, Captain Switchell. She had arrived the day before, and would remain a week or more; although there was no telling what would happen, as the officers were close-mouthed fellows, and did not mix much on shore with the citizens or the officers of the garrison.

Thus the pilot run on, till we dropped anchor not far from the Stingeree, whose officers were on the quarter-deck, and pretended to take no notice of us, although I have no doubt that it galled them in the most cutting manner to see a blockade-runner enter the port. In a few minutes we were surrounded by shore-boats, and into them our passengers tumbled, bag and baggage, and so took leave of us without ceremony, as is customary at the end of all voyages, long or short. While the men were deserting us, I entered the cabin, and spoke to Mrs. Gowen. I saw that she had made no attempts to pack up her effects, and, in fact, appeared as calm as if she were at home.

"Shall you leave us this afternoon, Mrs. Gowen?" I asked.

"Are you anxious for me to go?" she demanded, with a troubled face.

"No."

"Then let me remain with you as long as possible."

"And your future plans. What of them? Can you trust me with them?"

"I have no future," she sighed; and I saw tears in her eyes.

"But you expect to join your husband here, do you not?"

"Perhaps I shall. I am not certain."

Further conversation was interrupted by Bowmount, who called me on deck on business; but as I was leaving the cabin, and in passing the mate's state-room, I saw that the door was open. Glancing in, I saw, lying behind a chest, a bag that looked like the one the despatch-bearer had lost.

It was the work of a moment to step into the room, and pull the bag from behind the chest, and examine it. I was convinced that it contained the lost despatches; but how did it happen to be in the mate's room? This was a question that I could not answer, and I did not work at a solution of the mystery very long, for I seized on the bag, carried it to my own state-room, shut the door and locked it, and then out with a knife, and soon ripped the bag open. In it I found a tin box, but the lock yielded to a strong pressure, and then I was rewarded by the appearance of a dozen or more documents, addressed to various rebel agents in Europe. I did not have time to glance over the papers, even if I had desired to break the seals of the letters; so thrusting them into a safe, where I knew they would be secure, as I alone had the key, returned the carpet-bag and tin box to the place where I found them, and then went on deck, quite well satisfied with my five minutes' work, yet still wondering who had stolen the despatches in the first place.

I argued that some one would soon go for the bag, so as to get it on shore, and avail themselves of its contents; and it struck me that the presence of a Federal gunboat in the harbor had something to do with the despatches. Word might have been sent from Charleston to the commander of the fleet that the Belle was intending to touch at Bermuda, and that an important bundle of documents would go on board of her in charge of a special messenger, fresh from Richmond. To be sure, I had tried to keep secret our destination, but the Kentuckian had more than once blurted out that Bermuda was the point we should aim at, and that he could obtain cash for all of his cotton if he once landed it there. It was an easy matter to send word to the admiral, and more easy for him to despatch the Stingeree to the port we were expected to touch at, in hope that important documents would be placed in the hands of Captain Switchell. Even while I was turning these matters in my mind, I happened to glance at the quarter-deck of the Stingeree, and read, as plain as in print, a signal in the mizzen-rigging, which said, —

"If you have the papers, bring them on board as quick as possible."

The signals were not formed to express those very words, for only a little piece of red-and-blue bunting was hanging in the rigging; but still it was intended to convey just what I have written, yet no one, unless acquainted with the Union secret service could have made out of the little flag anything more than an innocent piece of bunting.

"Now," I thought, "here is a chance to discover the person who has done all he could to deliver us into the hands of the Union fleet."

But I looked in vain for an answer to the signal. As far as I could tell, no reply was returned; although I noticed that Dick Smith, the new hand, jumped on the rail, and waved his hat several times; yet, when I ordered him down, he said that he was bidding farewell to some of the passengers who were bound for the shore, full of fun and impudence. In less than an hour's time I saw Dick Smith, with a jacket in his hand, walking towards the cabin.

"Now I have you, my man," I thought, and watched the fellow like a cat watching a mouse.

As Smith walked towards the cabin, the mate's jacket hanging on his arm, I pretended not to notice him, for I saw him glance at me several times, as if wondering whether I would object to his coming aft. I did not even look at the fellow, yet not one of his movements escaped me. He entered the cabin, and I followed him, but not quick enough to notice if he looked behind the chest where the despatch-bag was concealed. He was placing the coat on a hook when I came upon him suddenly.

"Hollo, Smith!" I said, "what are you doing here?"

The man did not exhibit the least signs of disappointment or surprise as he turned and faced me.

"Mr. Cringle told me to hang the jacket in his stateroom, sir, and that is the reason I am here."

"You are sure that another motive did not induce you to come?" I asked.

"I don't know what you mean, sir, unless it is that I wanted a glass of grog, and hoped you would give it to me if you saw me aft."

The man touched his cap in true man-of-war style, and smiled in so good-natured a manner that all of my suspicions vanished in an instant, and once more I looked upon the fellow in the light of a true-hearted, careless sailor.

"You shall have your grog, if only for your impudence," I said, and ordered one of the stewards to give the man a tot of whiskey.

"Your health, cap'n," he said. "You are one of the lucky men; may it continue!"

I did not like the tone in which the fellow spoke, yet there was nothing I could seize upon so that I could take him to task. It seemed to me as though a sneer was intended.

Smith swallowed the liquor, and then said, —

"I suppose, cap'n, that I'm free now. I can go on shore when I please, can't I?"

"Yes, you know you shipped for the run. You can leave me this afternoon, if you like."

"Thank you, cap'n. I think that I'll go on shore without delay, and the next time we meet I hope that we shall be even."

"What do you mean by that?" I asked a little sternly.

"Why, that I may be the skipper of a craft as large and as swift as the Belle."

"O, yes! I see."

"That would make us equal, wouldn't it, sir?"

And the fellow grinned, and left the cabin, leaving me wondering where I had heard his voice and seen his peculiar smile before.

But all thoughts of Smith were banished from my mind by the duties which I was called upon to perform; for the ship was crowded with shore people, eager, hungry Bermudians, who sympathized with the South because they could make money by the operation, not on account of the justness of the conflict. How the descendants of pirates and convicts did fawn upon us, praise us, and coax us for a chance to sell some of the tempting cotton that lumbered our decks! They offered all manner of inducements, boasted of their harbor, their enterprise, and ended by drinking whiskey with Bowmount until one half of them were piled up under the dinner table, and the other half were in a state of kissing and crying drunkenness; and in this condition they were sent on shore, where it is to be hoped they met with a warm reception at the hands of their indignant wives.

But the result was that the cotton was sold at a most fabulous sum, all payable in gold, and the day that we commenced discharging, which was soon after we had entered port, I was on shore, in company with Mrs. Gowen, when whom should I meet, face to face, but my old acquaintance, Colonel Rhett, whom I had assisted in obtaining a discharge from prison in Charleston. I could scarcely believe my eyes. I rubbed them, and then, sailor-like, was inclined to damn them for deceiving me. But there was no deception in the matter. Before me stood Colonel Rhett, with his white beard and white eyebrows, long gray hair and keen black eyes. Even the gold-headed cane, that looked so substantial and respectable, was in his right hand; and when the Virginian saw me, he brought the cane down upon the ground with a ring, and an oath from his mouth.

"Well, I reckon we have met once more," the colonel said, in a tone that was far from pleasant.

In fact, I thought it was rather threatening than otherwise.

"Yes, colonel, we have met again, and I am very sorry for it, for I hoped never more see your ugly, treacherous face."

"You are complimentary, sir. Damn me if you ain't."

"I don't intend to be."

"No; I see you don't. A man like you don't stand on trifles, that is a fact."

"Speaking of standing, will you be kind enough to stand out of my path, for I want to move on?" and as I spoke, I endeavored to pass on; but the fellow was not in the humor to give way.

"Look a-here, Captain Barnwell," Rhett said. "You have crossed me at all points."

"Well, how do you intend to help yourself?"

The colonel banged down his stick, and seemed inclined to take offence; but concluded that he wouldn't just then, so continued: —

"You have had wonderful luck, sir; or else you bear a charmed life. All plots against you have failed; the best-laid schemes have been defeated. When we reckoned that we had you sure, you would wriggle out of the net. How did you do it?"

"Do you want to know very bad?"

"Yes, sir; I reckon I do."

"Well, then, listen and learn. Honesty has ever been my guide, my counsellor, my friend."

"O, what damned bosh! what nonsense! what trash!"

Down went his stick to the ground, and once more I attempted to pass him; but the colonel was so urgent that I should remain and listen to him, I concluded to do so; for I had foiled the old fellow so many times I could afford to joke a little with him, and bother him on matters of a purely personal nature.

"Even when I was taken from the deck of the Growler to that of the Belle you got the best of me."

"Yes; I recollect that you were not transported with joy when you found you were in the presence of a man whom you had attempted to injure."

"True; I didn't know but you might give me a push overboard, to pay me for what I had done."

"I suppose that you deserved such treatment; but I am a gentleman, and not an assassin."

"You came very near it, at any rate, when you took me by the throat, the night we entered Charleston."

And the colonel rubbed his neck as though it were still sore from the tremendous squeeze which I gave it.

"Do you know," I said, "that I am quite sorry I did not finish you on that occasion? You deserved it, if ever a man did."

"You think so?" and the colonel smiled in a provoking manner.

"I know so; for I heard you plotting with that mulatto, John, one day in your state-room. I did not hear enough to convince me that you meant treachery, but I was on the watch for you, nevertheless."

"But you did not watch me sharp enough to prevent me from swinging a lantern, and making other signs to the Federal fleet," and the old wretch smiled in the most insulting manner.

"No, I did not; but you had only a moment to wave your lantern; then I think you went to the deck in a sudden manner, and only by my interference did you escape with life. In a moment more, had I not stayed him, the Kentuckian would have given you a taste of his bowie-knife."

"That man is the devil," the colonel said. "He is worse than all other men. He is like a grizzly-bear, all teeth and claws; and, curse him, he comes at you head first, tail first, sideways, and every other way, so that you don't know how to receive him. I had rather meet the devil than that same crazy, drunken Kentuckian."

"I don't blame you; for some time he will break your neck, unless you keep clear of his course. He will never forgive you for your tricks on the night we run the blockade."

"Ha, ha!" and the colonel laughed heartily. "If he knew all, he would have more of a grudge against me. I reckon he would cut me up into inch pieces, and feed me out to the dogs."

"What do you mean?"

"Just this," answered the colonel. "I had the honor to take passage with you from Charleston to this port."

"It is a lie," I said. "I did not see you on board during the passage."

"O, yes you did; and talked with me several times. In fact, Captain Barnwell, I made the signals to the Federal fleet, and hailed it; I sent up the rocket, and threw fenders over so that the Belle could not out-steam the gunboat; and when I found that she was likely to do so, I pitched the awning over the bow, and would have smashed some part of the machinery if you had not set a watch so that I could not approach it without detection."

The scamp stood before me, and grinned in triumph at

the recital of his treachery. I was so angry at what he said, that I put my hand in my bosom for the purpose of drawing a revolver, and shooting him dead on the spot; but the scamp saw the motion, and divined the object.

"Don't do that," he said, in a cool tone; "if you do, you will repent it. Recollect that you are not now in the Confederacy; you don't stand on Southern ground, and ain't backed by rebel bayonets. Here I am as good as you: you are in Bermuda, and under the British flag. If I am shot, you will be hanged. Put up your revolver, and listen to me, for I have some disagreeable truths to tell you."

"Curses on you," I replied, "I have no desire to talk with you. Let me pass, or I fear I shall do you mischief."

"I have no fear of it. Don't keep your passions quiet, if you have the least inclination to curse. You can't hate me more than I do you."

"And on account of that hatred you tried to make me lose my ship."

"Yes; to pay you for the stripes which still grace my back, and smart with every movement of my body. Do you think that I have forgotten your agency in the matter?"

"I hope not."

"Every time the stripes smart I remember you."

"I am glad of it, because every time I see a rope I think of your exertions to hang me, and how near you succeeded. You remember, I suppose?"

"Yes; and I am sorry that I did not succeed. Curses on my luck for the failure A few minutes more, and I should have seen the last of you."

"You forget that I saved your life after it was forfeited. That I took you from prison, even when you had not a friend to speak a good word for you. At least such kindness deserves a word of gratitude."

"But I have none to give you. You are too successful to find favor in my eyes. From the first time I saw you I hated you."

"And your hatred increased from the moment you saw your daughter's friendship for me," I said, with a smile.

"Curses on you," returned the venerable colonel, with an angry stamp of one of his feet, and a rap of his cane, "did you never suspect that she was my wife, and not my daughter?"

"The devil! No, I never thought of such a thing. What possessed an old fool like you to marry such a young woman?"

To my surprise, the colonel nearly exploded with laughter, and only after he could command his face did he venture to reply to my sarcasm.

"You are smart, Captain Barnwell, but you ain't so smart and so wise as you think for. You are pretty good looking, but you can't come in."

"Heaven forbid that I should disturb that serenity of mind which is so much needed in your venerable head. But I can't stand here all day talking with you. Go and join your young and handsome wife, and may your days be long in the land. Give my regards to her when next you meet."

I once more attempted to pass on, but the colonel stopped me by the motion of his hands.

"Don't leave me so soon," he entreated, with a mocking smile. "I want to tell you that I am as smart as you are, although you don't seem to think so."

"Prove it, sir; and I'll be convinced that your words are true. I make no pretensions to smartness, while you do. Go on. Let me hear what you have done."

"I will; because concealment is of no use any longer. I am ordered home, but before I leave you I will let you into a secret."

"Good. Go on. I am listening."

"You know when I attempted to signalize the Union fleet, on entering Charleston Harbor?"

"Yes."

"Well, that was the result of a conspiracy between John and myself. You know that John hated you a little worse than I did."

"Yes; I suspect that such was the case. But I care nothing for the matter."

"But we annoyed you, nevertheless. We leagued together to imprison you in the haunted house. There we should have finished you, or given you up to the Yankees, if it had not been for that damned Kentuckian."

"I suppose that you were in favor of finishing," I said.

"No; I did not want to kill you, although John did. I reckon he would have knocked you on the head in short order if I had not persuaded him to keep still, and let the Yankees deal with you."

"It was very kind on your part, and I am fearful that I shall never repay you," I cried, still maintaining a contemptuous coldness, that I saw annoyed the fellow more than downright rage.

"Perhaps not; but still, let me tell you that you have precious little to be thankful for as far as I am concerned. I have done my best to annoy you, and failed. I own it."

"Go on, and repeat some more of your rascalities. I should like to hear the rest of them."

"You shall. When you released John and I from the Charleston prison, we laid our heads together."

"I hope with no disagreeable result to either of you. With your heads together, I do not know which would fare the worse."

"There spoke the South Carolinian," said the old vagabond, with more than usual energy. "I never saw one from your State who did not hate a negro."

I could not refrain from laughing; for the remark showed that my secret was not even suspected by the Virginian.

"I'm not an abolitionist," the colonel continued; "but I have got some little feeling for the negro."

"Look here, old fellow," I cried, out of patience, "are you a colonel in the confederate service, or what the devil are you?"

"Didn't you telegraph to Richmond, and find out who I was? I reckon I'm Colonel Rhett, of Virginia. If I ain't, who the deuse am I?"

"That I should like to know. The telegraph said that you were all right; but I don't believe it at the same time."

The old scamp chuckled, and then rapped the ground quite smartly with his gold-headed cane, and said, —

"I'm on British ground, my friend."

"Don't call me your friend," most indignantly.

"Just as you please. I don't suppose that I have acted a friendly part as far as you are concerned. But that ain't here nor there. We are now talking of business."

"Yes; go on, and confine yourself to business."

"I will; for I want to take the conceit out of you, and show that you don't know so much, and are not so smart as you think for."

"Bah! you can't surprise me."

"Can't I?"

As the fellow spoke, he tore off the gray beard and hair from his head and face, and stood before me as Dick Smith, late foremast-hand on board the Belle.

CHAPTER XII.

A COMPLETE SURPRISE. — A UNION SPY. — AN INTERVIEW WITH CAPTAIN SWITCHELL. – MRS. GOWEN AND HER HUSBAND. — A PAINFUL SCENE. — THE KENTUCKIAN IN A NEW CHARACTER. — A TERRIBLE REVELATION. — THE KENTUCKIAN'S STORY. — MAGNOLIA'S HISTORY. — A SHARE OF THE PROFITS. — SALE OF THE BELLE. — MEETING OF OLD FRIENDS IN NEW YORK. — OFF FOR WASHINGTON. — PROMOTION TO THE RANK OF COMMANDER. —- SMITH IS ASTONISHED. — A LITTLE LOVE-MAKING. — AN INTERRUPTION. — A STERN PARENT. — TERMS. — AN AGREEMENT. — A WEDDING.

I MUST confess that I was more than surprised, I was most intensely astonished, to see the transformation of the gallant Colonel Rhett into the common sailor, Dick Smith, whom I had shipped in Charleston, owing to his urgent solicitations. I could hardly believe my eyes; and I rubbed them to make sure I saw aright, and that it was no optical illusion.

Still I did not speak, but looked at the grinning fellow; and he looked at me with an impudent leer on his face, that spoke of triumph and success.

"You're a little astonished, my sweet captain," remarked Colonel Rhett, *alias* Dick Smith. "Why, even the Yankees at Bull Run were not so surprised and astonished as you are at this moment."

"What are you," I demanded; "a Confederate or a Federal? a spy or a devil?"

"What should you think, my gallant captain?" asked the fellow, with a laugh. "Don't I look as though I could be most anything?"

"Yes."

"Well, then, I will tell you what I have been for the past six months; and hard work I found it, I assure you."

"Tell on."

"A Union spy."

"The devil you are!"

And once more I was astonished; for I saw at a glance how we had crossed each other, and fought each other, under the impression that each was rendering great service to the Federal cause. But the time had not yet arrived for me to betray my connection with the Unionists; for I commanded the Belle, and still associated with prominent rebels. So, when the colonel, *alias* Smith, told me he was a professional Union spy, I managed to assume a look intended for virtuous indignation, and thundered out, —

"You scoundrel! I have a great mind to shoot you!"

Of course I had not the least intention of so doing; but I put my hand in my breast pocket, as if feeling for a revolver.

"Don't do it, my gallant captain," cried Smith, who saw the movement, and knew from experience what it meant. "You are not in South Carolina now, — you are on John Bull's territory; and if you shoot me you'll be hung. Don't doubt it; for a Yankee man-of-war is in port, and would insist on justice."

"Don't be alarmed," I said. "I won't hurt you."

"O, I ain't alarmed, my gallant captain. I have run too many risks to be alarmed at an angry threat. I have carried my life in my hand for many months, and have had some wonderful escapes from the cord and bullet. To be sure," the fellow continued, in a tone that showed he was sincere, "if we were alone, and in some place where the law would let us up, I wouldn't mind taking a crack at you, with revolvers, at ten paces, provided you felt a little aggravated at me for what I have done."

"You have played a bold game," I remarked, "and have lost. You tried to secure the capture of my ship;

but failed through my vigilance. I am safe in port, and in future will take care that no such sailor as you ships in my craft."

"You may be as cautious as you please; but Uncle Sam is powerful, and has many arms and many eyes. In spite of your efforts, he will know what you are doing."

While the man was speaking, I made one of my secret service signs; but there was no response. Three times I tried him, and failed to elicit a reply; so I came to the just conclusion, that Smith was a volunteer spy, and not attached to the higher order of secret service, such as I had undertaken at the request of President Lincoln and Secretary Welles.

Then we separated, the spy going in one direction, and I in another; but I had not walked along forty fathoms before who should I stumble on but a young friend, Midshipman Reefpoint, looking as fresh and handsome as when I first met him. The boy saw me, and would have run towards me and offered his hand, if I had not made a sign which he understood. It informed him that I did not wish to speak to him on the street, in sight of so many eager, jealous Bermudians.

"All right," he replied, with an almost imperceptible nod of his head; but as he passed me he whispered, —

"Let me see you for a moment — can't you?"

"Yes," I replied. "Follow me."

I led the way towards a second-class house, where mates and petty officers of men-of-war congregated when on shore, off duty. I knew that I could there find a room and a glass of ale, and that we could talk without being disturbed, if we were lucky. Harry followed me into the house, up one flight of stairs, into a room that was small and uncomfortable; but it overlooked the harbor, and answered our purpose. Just as we sat down, I saw Captain Switchell, of the Growler, land, and walk up the street;

a proceeding that called forth some few groans from the fun-loving Bermudians, who, like John Bull and the rest of his tribe, were extremely neutral during the war.

"Now, Reefpoint," I said, as I shook hands with the young man, " tell me how you managed to reach the fleet."

" We had a tough time of it, but made our escape, after some risk and danger. Your welcome information was well received by the admiral, and saved the fleet, I have no doubt. But — "

Just at this moment a noise was heard on the stairs. Then the door of our room was burst open ; and into the apartment tumbled Captain Switchell, and Smith, the Union spy, with the first lieutenant of the Growler.

As Captain Switchell, and Smith, the spy, entered the room, Reefpoint and I started to our feet, surprised at the interruption ; for no warning had been given that we were to receive callers, and we could not comprehend what was meant by the intrusion.

Smith was the first to speak ; and when he did open his mouth he revealed his purpose in so decided a manner there was no misunderstanding him.

"Captain Switchell," said the spy, "I have brought you here to let you see that one of your officers is holding a close and confidential conversation with one of the most dangerous rebels of the South. I know him, sir, as a rebel, and as commander of the blockade-runner Belle, now lying close under the guns of your ship."

Captain Switchell, his fat, red face steaming with perspiration, the effect of unusual exertions and the warm sun combined, had been staring at me from the moment he entered the apartment, his eyes expressing astonishment, and his huge mouth open to its widest extent, as though he was thinking by its aid and tasting treason. For a moment he did not speak, for his gaze wandered from Reefpoint to me, and then from Smith to the lieutenant, and from their faces to the table, to see if there was anything on it of a liquid nature.

Smith noticed that Captain Switchell did not speak; so made another remark, calculated to draw him out.

"I tell you, captain, this man is a dangerous one," — he pointed to me while he spoke, — " and he is attempting to corrupt one of your young and inexperienced officers."

Then Captain Switchell, who had recovered his presence of mind, it seemed, no longer kept silent, for he roared out a hoarse sort of chuckle, that was intended for a laugh; but it was such a laugh as a sea-lion would have uttered when in a jovial mood.

" Inexperienced ! " cried the captain, with another chuckle. " Why, damn it, man ! an old head is on those young shoulders; and I defy all the rebels in ——, or out of it, to corrupt him."

And then the captain gave me a wink, and made a sign to keep quiet, and that he would make matters all right.

" You don't know Captain Barnwell as well as I do," said the spy, in an appealing tone. " I have had so much to do with him that I understand him most thoroughly."

" O, belay that," returned the captain. " The master of the blockade-runner don't look so bad, after all; and I'll lay a wager he was not talking treason with Mr. Reefpoint. Come, I'll bet the wine that he was not; and I'll leave it to Captain Barnwell to decide."

" On my word of honor I was not," I replied.

" And on my word of honor he did not mention politics," cried Master Reefpoint, with so much earnestness, that I could not avoid laughing; which circumstance so surprised Smith, *alias* Rhett, who had expected to see me

27

humbled by the presence of Captain Switchell, that he remarked, in a surprised tone, —

"It appears to me that I have made a mistake in conveying my information. Had I known that Captain Switchell did not care for the reputation or temptation of one of his officers, I should have held my peace."

"Bah!" retorted the captain, with an internal chuckle that sounded as though a number of men were at work rousing up a chain-cable in his interior arrangements. "Bah! Don't be suspicious of every one. We are now in a neutral port; and it won't do to board every craft that we fall in with. Put aside all hard feeling, and let us see if this crib can furnish us with a bottle of claret; for I'm almost roasted, and dry as a marine."

Smith looked disappointed, and a little hurt, when he saw the turn matters had taken.

"If you don't want to foil rebels, after they are pointed out, I must carry my news to another market."

And with these words Smith left the room, although he did return, poking his head in at the door, and firing a parting shot.

"I don't have much hard feeling against Captain Barnwell because he's a rebel, bound to make things tell, and put money in his pocket, and it's all in his line; but when there is a chance to squelch such a man, it should be done at once."

He closed the door, and was off; and then Captain Switchell opened a bottle of claret that the landlord had brought, filled the glasses, emptied his own, and remarked, —

"How in the devil's name did you manage to escape the blockading fleet? Ships were all around you, I am told; and yet you went through them like a race-horse. How was it done? That's what I should like to know."

"It was through luck."

"Thunder! Don't you think that it would have been a little better for some of our brave tars to have clapped their paws on you, and shared the prize money?"

"I can't say that I see matters in that light."

"If I only knew how far your instructions lead you," mused the captain, "I might tell whether I thought you had done wrong or right."

The captain wanted to discover if I had authority for doing what I had done; just the information I did not wish him to possess.

"The end more than justified the means," I answered; "so we will not discuss the subject. Mr. Reefpoint tells me," I continued, changing the conversation, "that the information he was enabled to bring did good service to the Federal fleet."

"I believe you, my boy. Without it we should have had to raise the blockade; for we should have been taken by surprise."

"I hope you will impress upon the navy department the distinguished services of Mr. Reefpoint. I tell you, in his presence, he displayed a gallantry and courage, while in Charleston, that should entitle him to promotion. He put his head into a noose, and deserves thanks and gratitude for getting it out safe."

"And what do you deserve for the risk you have run?" demanded Captain Switchell.

"O, I have no doubt but that I shall be rewarded in the course of time," was my indifferent answer.

"Well, I hope so; although promotion ain't rapid in the United States navy. But, to come home, and talk of other matters, do you know what I was sent here for?"

"I imagine that it is for the purpose of receiving some despatches which my ship was to bring from Charleston."

"Yes: damned important things I was told, they were."

"And have you got them?"

"No; and what is more, Smith, who shipped with you for the purpose of stealing them, did manage to secure them, but lost all in some unaccountable manner. So I made the trip to this den of sympathizers for nothing."

"I am sorry for it."

"So am I; for it would have been a feather in my cap, I assure you. Certain promotion would have been the result of placing those despatches in the hands of Mr. Welles."

"Then I don't think that I would despair. If you will promise that you will do all in your power to get Mr. Reefpoint a lieutenant's commission — "

"O, kind and generous-hearted friend!" murmured the midshipman, with a voice choked with emotion.

"I will place those coveted despatches in your hands between now and sundown," I said, finishing the remark which I had commenced, and which Mr. Reefpoint had prevented me from completing.

"Damn me if I don't do it!" cried the hearty sailor, in a burst of enthusiasm. "Give me the documents; and I'll stir heaven and earth but the lad shall have his swab. And now tell me how it is to be done."

"Ask no questions, but meet me here this afternoon, and you shall have the papers."

"I'll do it; and an hour after they are in my hands, I shall steam out of the harbor."

And, with this assurance, Captain Switchell and I shook hands, and parted; and then I had a chance to exchange a few more words with Reefpoint.

"You will soon be home," I said, "and perhaps will have a chance to run on to Boston. If you do, see Miss Blank, and tell her that she is not entirely forgotten. Speak as well of me as you can, but do not hint to her that I have been blockade-running."

"I understand. Everything shall be made lovely as far as you are concerned."

"And do not distress the young lady with the knowledge that her father is running any risks for the sake of adding to his fortune."

"You can be assured of that. I like my cousin too well to say one word to her that would cause her the least uneasiness. She is one of the best girls I ever saw; and I hope will look with favoring eyes upon a certain gentleman whose kindness I shan't forget in a hurry."

And with a smile the lad turned away, and I hastened on board the Belle. The first person I met was Bowmount, who was, to my surprise, perfectly sober.

"Look a-here, old fellow," he said, "I've sold all the cotton at a big figure, cash down, on the nail, and all in gold. We shall make a big vige, — the best one that ever entered the port, by all odds; and I tell you, Barnwell, dog on me, if I don't feel as though I had almost got enough. Shucks! you may think that I'm jokin'; but it's the case."

I did not reply to the remark, but thought that I would let the Kentuckian take his own course until I got ready to lay out mine, which was already defined in my own mind. However, just as Bowmount was about to explain, a shore boat ran alongside; and up the accommodation-ladder came a gentleman, who, after he reached the deck, I recognized as Mr. Gowen, the husband of my handsome cabin passenger.

"Your sarvant, sir," said Bowmount. "This is an unexpected pleasure, sir. What can we do for you, sir?"

"I hear that Mrs. Gowen is on board; and I have come to see if such is the case. Business called me most unexpectedly from Nassau to Bermuda; but I did not think of meeting my wife here."

"Yes, sir; the lady is on board. And delighted enough

she will be to see you. Shucks! she'll be so pleased she'll shed tears of joy."

And the Kentuckian, with a sneer on his lips, and a smile on his face, lighted a cigar, and walked aft, leaving Mr. Gowen a little unsatisfied with the position of affairs; for he turned to me, and said, —

"Will you let the steward announce that I am on board?"

"Certainly."

One of the stewards happened to come aft just at that moment; so I told him to tell Mrs. Gowen that her husband desired to see her.

Five, ten minutes elapsed, and still the lady did not appear on deck. Mr. Gowen manifested some impatience. He could not keep still, but wandered about in a listless manner. At length, seeing that he was growing angry, I entered the lower cabin to speak to the lady, and found her on her knees, her head on a table, weeping most bitterly, while her servant was addressing the mistress in words of comfort and encouragement.

"Missus feels powerful bad, sar," said the negro servant, who had accompanied Mrs. Gowen from Charleston, and really loved the lady.

"For what reason?"

"Can you ask?" demanded the lady; and she raised her tear-stained eyes to my face. "Mr. Gowen is here to claim me. He will insist that I shall accompany him, and live with him."

"He is your husband," I said. "You must see him. He is impatient for an interview."

"I suppose that I must meet him," she sighed.

"Then wipe your eyes, and go on deck, and greet Mr. Gowen; or would you prefer to see him in the cabin?"

"In the cabin," she replied; and then, by the aid of a

damp towel, she removed the traces of tears, and motioned to me that she was ready for the interview.

"You will remain near me, and protect me if violence is offered," Mrs. Gowen said, as we entered the outer cabin.

"If you wish it, yes."

"I do wish it. Mr. Gowen has a most ungovernable temper. He is accustomed to have his own way; and the least opposition makes him furious. Remain near me and save me from violence."

"I will. And woe be to him if he offers the least rudeness."

I left her in the cabin, and went on deck.

"Mrs. Gowen is ready to see you," I said.

"Well, she was a long time about it," was his reply.

And into the cabin he went, I following close to his heels.

"Magnolia!" he cried, and opened his arms; but she did not rise from her chair to receive him.

He suddenly stopped, and looked at her in a surly manner.

"What kind of a reception is this?" he asked. "What does it mean?"

"It means that I can no longer live with you as your wife," was the answer, delivered in a firm tone, but without the least display of passion.

"Magnolia," he said, after a moment's silence, "are you aware of what you are saying? Have you considered the whole matter?"

"Yes: I have considered all things. I have done but little more than think of my past life during the last two weeks."

"You are mad," Mr. Gowen said, in a tone that was deep and stern; "utterly mad and foolish."

"No, I am in my senses, if I ever was," she answered, in a low tone.

I did not like to remain, and listen to their conversation; yet I had promised to be present during the interview, so that I could assist her, in case her husband gave way to his usual sudden bursts of passion, which only a resolute man could encounter. Neither party seemed to take the least notice of me. I retreated, and entered my stateroom, leaving the door open, and ready to go to the lady's assistance, in case she required it. From the position which I occupied I could hear all that passed, and see the parties at the same time.

"No," answered the lady, with a grave smile, and a sad shake of her head; "I am not mad now: but I have been nearly mad for three long years."

"Well, then, what is to be the final result of all this nonsense? Do you expect me to support you, and yet not enjoy your society?" demanded the man impatiently."

"No; I expect nothing at your hands. If we separate, it will be in peace, and without promises on either side."

"And how do you expect to live without my aid?"

"I can work. I am a good musician, can embroider, teach French, school, or even play the nursery maid."

"All very fine; but you can't return to the South. You know that if you did, I could detain you at any time we chanced to meet."

"And would you do so?" she demanded.

"I would."

"Then I will go North, where protection is afforded all such unhappy creatures as I am."

"But you can't go without revealing your secret."

"Would you reveal it?" demanded the lady, with more excitement than she had yet manifested.

"I would, so help me Heaven!"

"Have you no mercy?" pleaded the lady.

And I thought her voice was tremulous, as though her eyes were filled with tears.

"None in this respect. You have resolved to leave me; and I am resolved to keep you if possible, even if I have to make a clean breast of it."

"O, my God!" the lady cried, and wrung her hands, as if with the most bitter anguish.

"Besides, you must remember that I have the law to aid me; and even in these islands the law is powerful, and has a powerful arm."

"But the law is powerless in your case," said a deep bass voice.

And into the cabin walked the Kentuckian, with such a look upon his face that even I was surprised at its expression.

For a moment the lady and gentleman were too astonished to speak; but at last Mr. Gowen, who still remembered the treatment which he had experienced at the hands of Bowmount at Nassau, and, therefore, feared his evil temper, spoke: —

"I am talking to my wife, sir, and requesting her to go with me. In a few minutes we will have left your vessel."

"That is, if the woman is willing," said the Kentuckian. "If she ain't willin', shucks! you know she can't go."

"Then Mrs. Gowen will speedily tell you that she is anxious to go on with me. Speak, my dear, and let him hear such words from your own lips."

"Yes; I'd like to hear 'em."

And the Kentuckian canted his head one side, as if to listen.

"I do not wish to go with Mr. Gowen," the lady said, in a tone so distinct and firm that no one could misunderstand her.

"Then you shall go with me," said the husband, in a rage. "I'll let you know that I'm master, and that I will be obeyed. You belong to me; and I will have you, if I have to spend ten thousand dollars in the effort."

"Softly," cried the Kentuckian. "Let's see how you is going to get her from this ship unless she is a mind to go. Barnwell," he continued, calling me from the stateroom, "come here, and see about this."

"He must hear all, know all," said the Kentuckian, in a low, firm tone. "I have kept your secret most faithfully, even from a man what I likes as well as if he was my own brother, father, wife, or children, all crowded into one. Now it must come out; 'cos why, it's the only way to save you."

And then he turned to Mr. Gowen, and continued:—

"You say that this woman is yer wife?"

"Yes, sir; I claim her as such."

"Very good. Jist fork over yer sartificate, so that I can tell if yer was married in form."

"I have no certificate with me."

"Whar was yer married?" demanded the Kentuckian.

"Is that any of your business?" Mr. Gowen asked.

"Never you mind. You jist answer all the questions what I puts to you. Now, whar was you married?"

"O, save me! spare me!" moaned the lady.

"I shall not answer the question," was the sullen rejoinder.

"Very well. Then you needn't. We comes, now, to the next p'int. What was the name of the parson what married you? Come, I knows most all the parsons in Georgia; and if you tell me, I may recollect his name."

Another sob from Mrs. Gowen, and a sullen look from the husband.

"You won't tell?" demanded the Kentuckian. "O, very well. How does you s'pose that you can get your wife unless you prove that she is your wife?"

"By the law."

"The law be damned! You jist try it on, and see how you makes it. I've had some experience in law, during my long and eventful life; and I know that the law won't affect you much."

"A writ of *habeas corpus* will not be disregarded on board this vessel, I take it," Mr. Gowen intimated.

"Jist try it on, and see," was the reply. "You bring your *habeas corpus* on board this ship, and you'll find more than one corpse round here, now I tell you. I don't want to be violent, 'cos I'm in a friendly and neutral port; but damn me if you wouldn't see sights arter you shake a law paper in my face. But few men would dare do it, even in old Kentuck; and that is a State what can show some tough cases."

"I don't wish to provoke your ire," said Mr. Gowen, in a tone that was intended to be conciliatory; "but you must acknowledge that I want my wife."

"We admit that," the Kentuckian said; "but prove to us that the woman is your wife."

"Spare me! O, spare me!" murmured the lady.

And she cast upon me such a look of anguish that I pitied her, and would have saved her feelings if it had been possible.

"We has opened the sore," cried the Kentuckian; "and now we must cleanse it, even if we does cause pain. It is the best thing that we can do. Don't you think so, mum?" addressing Mrs. Gowen.

"God only knows! I don't," was the subdued answer.

"Mr. Gowen," said Bowmount, "you had better go on shore, and let the woman take what course she sees proper to take. She don't seem to have much love for you, so it is better that you should part."

"You have a cool way of separating man and wife," retorted the visitor.

"O, shucks!" cried the Kentuckian, in a tone of contempt. "This thing has been goin' on long enough. I can't hold in no longer, no how. I didn't want to speak it; but you know that you ain't married to this woman at all; now don't you?"

A wild shriek on the part of the lady, and her hands went up to her face; and then both hands and face were buried in her lap; but the sobs which she uttered were like stabs in my heart; and I would have gone forward, and assisted her, in spite of my surprise, if Bowmount had not motioned me to remain where I was.

"I don't like to see a woman cry, or hear one cry," the Kentuckian continued; "but in this instance I must speak, 'cos it is for the good of all of yer."

While the Kentuckian was speaking, I stole a look at Gowen's face, and saw that it did not manifest that indignation which would have appeared had the words uttered a moment before been false. He seemed a little surprised, but nothing more.

"You have made a grave statement," Mr. Gowen said. "Perhaps you can't prove it."

"By your own lips will I prove it. I didn't want to let on about it, dog on me if I did! but when you talk of takin' the woman out of the ship by a *corpus*, then it's time for me to talk, and to talk to the p'int, now I tell yer."

"The woman is mine, — my wife," said Mr. Gowen.

"O, what a lie! Come, your game is up. The rig is run out. The woman is free to go or stay, just as she pleases."

"She is not free to do as she pleases," responded Mr. Gowen.

"Don't you provoke me, old feller; 'cos I can't stand it. I'm as playful as a kitten; but damn me if I stand everything!"

Suddenly Mrs. Gowen arose, and looked as though she had made up her mind on an important subject.

"SHE IS MY SLAVE." — Page 429.

"There is no need of quarrelling about me," she said. "I'm not worth the hot words which you would utter. Don't let my presence be the means of involving you in trouble. I will go on shore, and end the strife."

"Well said!" cried Mr. Gowen. "I knew you wouldn't desert me, Magnolia."

"It is not well said," the Kentuckian remarked. "She don't utter them words 'cos she wants to go; and, by the living jingo! she shan't go. I say that, and I mean it."

"You must have a greater claim on the lady than myself," Mr. Gowen remarked, "if such is the case."

"I haven't any claim on her; but I see that she don't want to go with you, and that's enough. She ain't your wife; you will admit that."

"Well, suppose I do admit it?"

"And she ain't *your slave*," persisted the Kentuckian.

Mrs. Gowen uttered sob after sob, and once more covered her face with her hands.

Mr. Gowen looked at the Kentuckian, and then, to my intense astonishment, deliberately said, —

"*She is my slave;* and in my pocket I hold a bill of sale, signed by the heirs of old Colonel Grantly, of Georgia. You may have heard of the man."

"Yes, I have heard of him," responded the Kentuckian, in a tone that sounded to me more mournful than anything I ever heard from his lips.

As soon as Mr. Gowen had uttered the word "slave," the lady dropped her head, and fell back, perfectly insensible. I was taken so much by surprise, so shocked, that a minute or two must have elapsed before I regained my presence of mind and went to her assistance. When I did start forward, and raised the poor thing's head, the Kentuckian, with more feeling than I ever gave him credit for, remarked, —

"That's right, Barnwell. Handle her as gently as you

would a two-year-old colt that promises to make a racer. Give her a little water, and then swab her mouth and nostrils with some weak wine."

His advice showed that the rough genius was more familiar with stables than a lady's boudoir.

I did give the lady some weak wine, and was enabled to restore her; but she seemed to suffer so much that I doubted whether I had performed an act of kindness.

As soon as she could speak, or even whisper, she looked at me with such a mournful glance that it cut me to the heart.

"O God! what will you think of me?" she moaned.

"Is that man's statement true?" I asked.

"It is true," was the reply. "I am his slave. He bought me just as he would a dog; and for two years I have lived with him under the assumed title of wife. O, how you must despise me!"

"No; far from it. Do not think so meanly of me as all that. If you have been a slave, you are one no longer. From this moment you are free."

"Yes; that's so, Barnwell," the Kentuckian replied. "If she was never free afore, she is now."

"Let him relate my whole history, or what he knows of it; then you will see that I have been wicked, but not voluntarily," Magnolia said.

"I'll do it; 'cos I know it will interest Barnwell and the man what claims her. Hey, Gowen? Well, don't get mad, and tear yer shirt; 'cos it's no use. You jist listen to me, and be edicated and enlightened."

Mr. Gowen made a motion of impatience; but it did not affect the Kentuckian, who lighted a cigar, in the most deliberate manner, as though through its aid his thoughts would flow more freely, and he could tell his story with less embarrassment.

"Now," said Bowmount, after taking one or two puffs

at the cigar, and finding it was well lighted, "I am all ready to begin my yarn. Six years ago, I think, while I was in South Carolina on business, selling mules and other truck, and pickin' up money here and there, I saw there was to be an auction sale at a plantation some ten miles from Charleston. So I thought I'd go and see if I could make a thousand dollars, buying stock or land. When I got to the plantation, there warn't many people there, for some reason or other; and I thought I should have some nice bargains; but, shucks! there warn't anything worth pickin' up, except a few slaves, and them I didn't want. In fact, the old plantation was all run out, 'cos the owner and his sons had paid more attention to whiskey drinkin' and hoss-racin' than to cultivatin' cotton and rice."

The Kentuckian puffed away at his cigar for a moment, while the rest of us remained silent, anxious listeners to his story.

"Wall, you see," the Kentuckian continued, "I didn't want to buy the niggers, 'cos none of 'em was promisin'; and I was jist about to mount my hoss, and go back to the city, when the auctioneer said that he had a prize to offer, and we had better stay and see it. I did remain; but most of the fellers cut off, and raced their horses back to town."

Another puff of the cigar, and a sob from Magnolia.

"Arter I had waited a bit, the auctioneer led for'ard a little girl, not more'n fourteen years of age, and as white as I am."

I looked at the Kentuckian, and did not think that indorsement amounted to much; for Bowmount was dark and bilious. Another sob, still more violent from Magnolia.

"I liked the looks of the little thing," continued Bowmount; "for she appeared so innocent like, so timid, and she cried like a little baby. I saw at a glance that she was the darter of the old feller what owned the place, and I s'posed that he wouldn't let her be bid on; but the cuss hadn't any heart; for the auctioneer said she must be sold, and axed for an offer."

Another long pause, and a more vigorous puffing of the cigar. Magnolia still bowed her head, and listened to the Kentuckian's yarn.

"An old chap, what didn't look none too good," continued the Kentuckian, "bid one thousand dollars for the child; and then I called fifteen hundred, and the other chap two thousand, and that made me mad. The old Kentuck blood began to tell. I looked at the pretty little gal, and thought that I would go it blind but I would have her; so I jist called out three thousand dollars, and that brought her. The old cuss couldn't rake down the pile. She was mine."

Another long puff, and a sob from Magnolia.

"The gal what I bought that day now sets there. She's a woman, now, and can tell if I warn't a kind master. Speak, Magnolia, and let 'em hear the words from yer own lips."

"You were always kind to me," she managed to say.

"Thank you for that, Magnolia. If I warn't kind to you, I'm sure I tried to be, in my own rough way; although when we first met, at the dinner table at Nassau, when you riled me, by sneering at the Yankees, I did cut up kinder strong; 'cos I didn't know you then, and I reckon you didn't know me. You had kinder outgrown me. Wasn't that so?"

"Yes," the lady murmured. "I did not once think of you until you had smashed the glass in Mr. Gowen's face."

"Well, we'll let them things go; and I'll finish my yarn. You know, Magnolia, that arter I had bought you, and paid for you, I didn't know what to do with you. I didn't have no wife, and so couldn't let you tend her; and you was too young to act the part of a wife, even if I had wanted yer for sich, which I didn't, 'cos you know, Barnwell, I'm rough and tough, but I ain't quite so bad as some men, now is I?"

"No, I don't think you are," was the response.

"Thank you for that. It kinder does a man good, sometimes, to have a compliment. It tickles him almost as much as a young gal what has jist got her fust real live lover. But let us haul up on the track, and trot back to the subject. And I suppose most of it is new to Mr. Gowen."

"Yes, it is," responded that gentleman, who had listened with much patience to the narrative.

"So I thought; and I'll amble on. Wall, I took the gal with me to Charleston; and I said to a woman what cut out clothes, and sich fixens for gals, to dress her up in all that was needed to make her comfortable and nice. And that woman did it; and when she was dressed, she looked nice enough to be the darter of the best white man in the land, and I had many a chap ax me if she was my own child, and if she had, I'd been proud of her, now I tell yer. You remember, don't you, Magnolia?"

"Yes," in a faint whisper.

"Well, arter she was dressed, I took her to old Kentuck; and then I sent her to school, where she had music, and all manner of sich like advantages. She studied for a year; and she jumped ahead, in all manner of larnin', like a young colt what has just been trained. O! she was a wonder, now I tell yer."

The Kentuckian lighted a fresh cigar, smoked for a few minutes in silence, and then resumed:—

"Now comes the worst part of my yarn, and the only portion I'm ashamed of. One day, a Mr. Dabney, of

Georgia, an old man, and I believe a good one, was visiting me; and he seed Magnolia. He said that he took a fatherly likin' to the gal, and wanted her. He would give me twice what I had paid for her; 'cos he wanted her for his daughter, only as a companion. I refused; but the old gentleman kept urging, and, at last, agreed to give me five thousand dollars for the gal; and then he swore a solemn oath that when she was eighteen years of age he would let her free, and give her a start in the world, or, if he died before that, he would leave her free papers where she would find 'em. And, on these terms, I let her go; but it almost broke my heart to do it; and I believe that the gal shed some tears at partin' — didn't you, Magnolia?"

"Yes; I can remember the time, and the tears that I shed," was the answer.

"I has no doubt of it. Let me tell you that you is the last one, woman, or child, that I ever sold, or ever wanted to, now I tell yer. But you went with Mr. Dabney, and he done well by yer — now didn't he?"

"He was kind and fatherly, and sent me to school, even to a Northern school with his daughter, where I passed as her sister, and his child; but he died suddenly, and did not leave me free, as he intended."

"Just so," the Kentuckian cried. "It was imprudent on the part of Dabney; 'cos he was a good man, and meant what he said. He thought that he was long-lived, but whiskey and high living takes off the strongest of us, and don't stop to ax questions. Well, Magnolia, s'pose you tell what remains. You can do it much better than I can."

"When the estate was settled, by Mr. Dabney's eldest son," the lady said, "I was offered one of two choices; either to be sold with the rest of the slaves, or to live with the heir as his mistress. I preferred to be sold, and sold I was."

Another passionate burst of grief, and not a heart in that cabin but felt for the sufferings of the poor girl.

It was a long time before Magnolia could command her voice sufficiently to continue her narrative; and it was only after I had forced a glass of wine upon her that she could compose herself to proceed, and relate the remaining facts connected with her life. Twice she attempted to speak, and twice she failed to accomplish the task that she had entered upon. Mr. Gowen, who appeared to feel for one whom he had called wife for some years, noticed her distress, and came to her aid.

"Let me relate how we became acquainted," he said. "As long as so much is known, it is best that the rest should also be told. Have I your permission, Magnolia?"

She made a gesture of assent, and Mr. Gowen continued:—

"On the day that Mr. Dabney's slaves were sold, I attended the sale; for I had heard that a girl of marvellous beauty was to be disposed of by young Mr. Dabney, who, in a moment of jealous rage and ugliness, had disregarded his father's well-known wishes, and his sister's tears and entreaties. He was determined that the girl should be sold; and, for fear that his sister would interfere at the last moment, he sent her off to a distant part of Georgia, on some pretext or other."

"He was a likely pup," muttered the blunt Kentuckian. "I'd like to have cracked his head for him, I would."

"He was punished. He fell at Bull Run," Mr. Gowen said.

"God bless the Yankee that fired the bullet that killed the mean cuss that would sell a gal agin his dead father's wishes!" reverently responded Bowmount.

Mr. Gowen resumed his story, which we were all interested in.

"There was a large attendance at the sale, for it was noised abroad that Magnolia was to be disposed of; and many young men, and some old ones, desired the prize if it did'not go too high. I won't weary you by telling you how impatient we were until the chief attraction was put up, and her good qualities paraded to an appreciating audience. You remember, Magnolia?"

"O God! shall I ever forget that moment?" the lady ejaculated. "Shall I ever forget the horror of standing up on a block, before an eager, gaping crowd, and told to exhibit my good points?"

"Your blushes of shame showed that you felt the position," Mr. Gowen said; "but all appearance of modesty only caused your audience to inwardly vow that they would bid higher than they intended to for the purpose of receiving the prize."

"I wish I'd been thar. I'd have had a cut at 'em, if it cost me my life," muttered Bowmount.

"After all the good points which Magnolia possessed had been pointed out, the sale commenced; and the first bid was for two thousand dollars, then three, then four, then four thousand five hundred, and so on, until she was knocked down to me at six thousand dollars. But she did not hear the final bid, for the girl fainted before it was offered; and, when she revived, the crowd had dispersed, not until I had received the congratulations of my friends, and an advance offered on the price that I had given, from a negro trader, who could have made a pile on the transaction, at New Orleans, or some other large city at the South. But I was resolved not to sell you, Magnolia. You know I told you that I would not, as soon as you were able to comprehend me, and listen to my protestations."

"Yes, I know," murmured the lady.

"Well, I kept my word, did I not? When the war

commenced, I told you the part that I desired you to play. I gave you my name; and, when we sailed for Nassau, where I was to receive the cotton that was shipped to that port, I called you my wife, and you were looked up to, and respected, as such, and no one ever knew that you had been a slave, even the most rabid of Southern women not suspecting such a thing. I believe that your every want was gratified at Nassau, Magnolia."

"Yes," she answered; "I was almost contented. You were kind to me."

"And I trusted you — did I not?"

"Yes."

"And you know that I loved you, Magnolia."

I could see, by the lady's eyes and face, that Mr. Gowen's influence was returning; that he had touched her heart by his kindness and consideration, even in spite of herself.

"You always said that you did," returned the lady, in a low tone.

"Come with me," said Bowmount. "We ain't wanted here."

And we left them.

An hour later Mr. Gowen and Magnolia emerged from the cabin. Both looked as though they had shed tears, yet on each face was a look of confidence. Gowen came towards me, and said, —

"Captain, we are much obliged to you for your kindness. Will you please to order a boat, so that we can be set on shore?"

"Is the lady to go with you?"

"Yes, sir."

"Of her own free will and accord?"

"Yes; of course."

He looked a little surprised, as though wondering what I meant.

"Will you allow me to speak with the lady for one moment? I wish to be assured on that point."

"Certainly, sir."

I went to Magnolia, who was standing near the cabin doors, her back towards me.

"Mrs. Gowen," I said, "do you wish to leave the steamer?"

"No."

"Then why do you go?"

"Because he has promised to make me his wife in reality. He has, indeed he has."

We then went to the quarter-deck, where Gowen and Bowmount had remained.

"Well, Barnwell, are you satisfied?" asked the Kentuckian.

"Perfectly."

"They mean arnest — don't they?"

"Yes."

"A regular hitchin' affair — hey?"

"I should think so."

"Wall," drawled the Kentuckian, "I ain't seed a weddin' for a long time. I think it would do me good to look at one. S'pose we have one to-night?"

Mr. Gowen looked a little astonished.

"We have no clergyman," he said, at last.

"O, I'll find one. All ships of war have 'em. Barnwell, jist take one of the boats, and ax the cap'n of the Stingeree if he will lend us his parson to splice a couple. He may look black at you, but he can't look black at the cause of yer visit unless he has a uproarer for a wife. In that case he wouldn't favor matrimony."

"This is so sudden that I am not prepared," Mr. Gowen said.

"O, fudge! shucks! what does a man want to prepare himself for, jist to be married? Go and get the parson,

Barnwell. The woman is a kind of ward of ours; and we must look arter her interests, you know."

I should have been loath to propose such a plan, but readily agreed to it; for I thought it the best one that could be adopted, on account of the lady's interests, for I was bound to protect them as long as she remained on board the ship, and was man enough to know that promises are not always kept when made to a woman.

"I think," said Mr. Gowen, after a moment's silence, "that, as this is a private matter, we had better settle it to suit the parties most interested. The shore is the place for such negotiations; and a certain degree of time is allowable for the completion of them."

"Shucks!" cried the blunt Kentuckian. "If we should let you off, to-morrow mornin' you'd have a different mind. I know what men is, dog on me if I don't!"

"I won't be forced into a marriage," pettishly exclaimed the candidate for matrimony.

"We don't want to force you, man alive. It is your own proposal. We didn't ax yer to marry the woman. We didn't say one word about it. And, shucks! now yer come to me, and say that we is forcin' yer to take a bold step. Now I'm a plain man, and speak my mind; and I want yer to understand that the woman don't leave the steamer till she is a wife. Dog on me if I stand it!"

I no longer hesitated. I saw that the Kentuckian had made up his mind, and all creation could not move him. I wanted to visit the Stingeree, and leave the important papers I had taken from the despatch-bearer, and which I had promised to hand over on shore in the course of the afternoon or evening. Now, here was a chance, and I determined to improve it.

"I will return with the parson, in fifteen minutes," I said.

And, after diving into the cabin, and securing the papers,

I was pulled alongside the Stingeree, where my appearance caused some sensation. I went on deck, and was received with cold courtesy by the officers; but still, at the same time, they treated me politely, and sent my name in to Captain Switchell, without delay; but they did look as though they wondered what I wanted. The captain granted me an interview immediately, and, as soon as he could speak without being overheard, held out his hand for the papers.

"You've brought 'em," he said. "Don't tell me that you haven't. Don't crush me, by sayin' that some one has stolen 'em from you."

I placed the documents in his hands; and the old salt would have thrown up his cap, and given three cheers, if he had not been fearful of exciting suspicion by such a demonstration.

"I'll leave port this very night," he said. "I'll not lose a moment. Damn me if this ain't the greatest hit that I ever saw. You don't know how much government owes you."

As soon as his enthusiasm had subsided a little, I asked for the loan of the chaplain, and explained why I wanted him.

"Take him, and welcome. I'd like to keep him at work, for ten hours a day, at just such business. Orderly, pass the word for the chaplain."

Mr. Bangum came into the cabin, with a sedate smile on his face. He thought that he was wanted to take a hand at whist, and, perhaps, drink a glass of wine; and he was prepared to do either.

"Mr. Bangum," said the captain, " this is Mr. Barnwell, the master of the blockade-runner that lies near us. He's a rebel, but still claims to have the consideration of a Christian. He wants you to splice a couple on board his ship; and you have my permission to do so. Be as lively as you can, for I intend to get up steam, and sail as soon as possible."

Mr. Bangum said that he was ready to do all required; and then I took a cold and guarded leave of the captain, bowed to the officers on deck, and was soon alongside of the Belle.

"They are already in the cabin," whispered Bowmount. "Clinch 'em, and then we'll have a rousing feast. I've got one under way now; the best the cook can get up."

We all entered the cabin, and found that Mr. Gowen and Magnolia were awaiting us; the latter in tears, and the former looking rather sober for a bridegroom.

Mr. Bangum looked at the candidates for matrimony, and then glanced at the table, on which stood, in loving proximity, several bottles of wine and whiskey. He rubbed his hands, and smiled in an encouraging manner, as though to assure the parties contemplating marriage that there was nothing so very dreadful in the act, even if they thought there was. Then he put his hand to his mouth, and coughed a delicate little cough, as if he was affected with a bronchial trouble, yet did not desire to pain his friends by giving them notice of the fact.

"Mr. Bangum," cried Bowmount, "you have a cold. Let me recommend a glass of whiskey. It will relieve you at once, clear your throat, and enable you to do your duty with the utmost despatch."

The chaplain did not refuse, and neither did he say that he would accept; but he gave another little cough, and smiled; and, before the smile had died away, the Kentuckian had thrust a glass into his hand, and poured out a stiff dose of whiskey, which Mr. Bangum stowed away in a very short time, and appeared to like it. Then he smacked his lips, and turned to the matrimonial candidates, a smile on his face, and a bright light on the tip-end of his nose.

"My dear young friends," he said, " I am informed that

you contemplate marriage. It is a sacred and divine institution; although there are men who scout the latter consideration of the question. Such people are to be looked upon with suspicion, and their domestic lives are to be taken into account as one reason why they entertain such notions. You, my friends, I hope, love each other with all sincerity, and will continue to do so until death. Captain Barnwell informs me that it is a long attachment. I hope that you will find that perfect bliss which you so fondly anticipate. Join hands if you please."

Trembling, and with downcast eyes, the parties joined hands, and were pronounced husband and wife; and I think I was never more rejoiced than when I heard the words uttered.

"Give 'em each a sartificate," cried the Kentuckian; "and, while you is writin' 'em out, we'll all have a drink. Here's long life and happiness to the newly wedded couple. May they find that their trials is over, and that they is anchored in the haven of rest at last, never more to be disturbed by the billows of commotion! Amen."

Mrs. Gowen, as soon as she had received our congratulations, retired to her state-room, and gave vent to her feelings by a passionate burst of tears. I could understand her emotions, and appreciate them. The change which she had undergone was so sudden, so unexpected, that I did not wonder she was nearly prostrated by emotions of a conflicting nature. . . . .

The next day a ship hauled alongside, and we commenced discharging our cotton into her, Bowmount having sold the whole cargo to a company of speculators, who were neutrals, and, consequently, bound to make money out of both parties. In two days the cargo of the Belle was discharged into the ship, and we had received pay for the same in good bills of exchange on Baring Brothers, London. Bowmount handed to me a draft that represented fifty thousand dollars in gold. It was my share of the speculation, and pretty good pay it seemed for some four months' labor at Nassau and Charleston.

"Now," said the Kentuckian, "let's take a drink, and have a talk, a real serious one. Light a cigar. So; that's all right. Now, then, look at me, and answer on your honor."

"What is coming now?" I thought; but I gave no sign that I was anxious.

"Crowd on," I said.

"I will. What do you think of blockade-runnin'?"

"It seems to me to pay pretty well. I should judge so by looking at the piece of paper you just gave me."

"Yes; it does pay. We've been lucky. The next trip might cost us dear."

"True."

"I've got money enough to give me a start in the world," the Kentuckian resumed. "If I should sell the Belle for eighty thousand dollars, I'd have near three hundred thousand salted down; and that had ought to support a moderate man like me, what ain't got no vices, except love for a glass of whiskey once in a while."

"Do you ask my advice, Bowmount, what to do?"

"No, not exactly. You know I has a mind of my own — don't you?"

"Yes; I am aware of that."

"Well, what I mean is, don't you think that blockade-runnin' is damned mean business for two men like me and you, what really don't care about this quarrel?"

"I don't know but it is."

"Well, Barnwell, since I've made my pile, my feelin's has undergone a change. Besides, there's more risk every day; 'cos the Yankees will keep putting on ships till they won't permit a rat to escape from out the Southern ports."

I saw what the man was driving at, and determined to

encourage him to the best of my ability. I wanted to quit the vessel, and return home; and I had been puzzled how to manage it. Now here was a chance, without an effort on my part. I could leave the business without exciting the suspicions of the Kentuckian. We could part good friends, and go our several ways without a word of discord. The very thing that I had wished for had come to pass; for I had done with blockade-running.

"Bowmount," I said, "don't beat about the bay any longer. Say, at once, that you are tired of the business, and want to get out of it."

"Well, I do."

"That's right. Own up like a man, and then I'm with you. I don't want to risk what I've got in another attempt at blockade-running. You feel the same. The matter is a simple one, since we both agree on the most important point. Sell the vessel; then we can go on shore, and wait until we can take passage North, or leave for Europe."

"And you won't feel as though I'd left you out in the cold?" asked the Kentuckian, in an anxious tone.

"By no means."

"I didn't know; you are sich a desperate Southerner. A rigular fire-eatin' South-Car'linian, and no mistake."

"O, gammon!" I replied, with a conscious blush.

"Yes, you is. But I'm glad to see that you is sensible. We'll sell the Belle for what the Englishmen offered, and then have a run to Europe. Hey?"

I acquiesced in the agreement; and, the next day, the arrangement was carried out. The vessel was sold, and the new owners took possession. Our crew were paid off; but most of them remained in the steamer, preferring to take their chances at a second attempt to enter the Southern ports to going on shore, and waiting for another fast-sailing ship.

On shore the Kentuckian and I took up our quarters at the St. George Hotel, where we were treated with the utmost distinction on account of our Southern connections. We found ourselves quite comfortable, with good society to pat us on the back, and call us smart fellows for our success; while the same men who thus encouraged us would have cast us off had we been unfortunate. The Kentuckian knew this as well as myself; so, as a matter of course, he framed some of his speeches to a blunt tune. But all that he said was glossed over; and he was called eccentric instead of impudent, witty instead of rude, a noble specimen of the South, such as any nation might be proud of.

For four days we were destitute of excitement. The Belle had loaded with powder, rifles, cannon, clothing, and provisions, and sailed for Wilmington, under the charge of a new captain, who was inexperienced in the art of blockade-running. And he met a fate that delighted the captains and crews of three of Uncle Sam's gunboats; for the Belle, in spite of her speed, got in a tight place, and was compelled to surrender, even without the firing of a shot. Our English friends did not make much out of that trip, even if they did out of others.

But, at last, all Bermuda was electrified by the arrival of a large steamer with three thousand bales of cotton on board. She was from Wilmington; and the rumor was that she had met with no opposition in leaving port. The names of the owners and captain did not transpire; and I was ignorant of them, until, one day, who should enter the hotel but my old friend, Mr. Blank, the polite and successful Boston merchant, whom I had met in disguise in Charleston, in company with old Crosstrees. I think that Mr. Blank was a little astonished when he saw me. He hesitated, colored, and did not know whether he should acknowledge my acquaintance or not; but, before he had decided, I accosted him.

"Why, Mr. Blank!" I cried, "who would have thought of meeting you in this part of the world?"

"Perhaps I can say that the surprise is mutual," the merchant returned; but, as he spoke, he held out his hand, which I took.

"Of course you have come here for your health," I remarked. "Nothing else could induce a man like you to visit such a barren spot as this."

"O, yes! Yes. Of course. My lungs. A little out of order, you know."

"I am sorry for that; because Bermuda is a bad place in the summer time, and I fear that you won't do well here. It is cooler at the North in July."

"Yes; I suppose so. But it was necessary that I should come. I am surprised, however, to see you here. What good wind sent you in this direction?"

"O, I'm here waiting for orders; and I hope that I shall see a good deal of you."

"Yes; perhaps you may."

And the merchant was about to turn away, when I asked, —

"Was your daughter well when you left Boston, Mr. Blank?"

"Yes, sir; quite well."

"I wish that you had brought her with you."

"Why so, sir?"

And the proud merchant frowned a little; for he recollected that I was once in his employ, and, consequently, his inferior.

"Simply because I like her society," was my blunt answer; for I saw that I might as well commence a movement that would make an impression, as to hold off, and pretend to be awe-stricken in his presence.

"Mr. Constant," said the stately Boston merchant, "you rendered my daughter valuable service in Washington. You have been thanked for it. If you need more, say so; and you shall be rewarded to the extent of any reasonable amount of money."

"I am much obliged to you for your kindness," I remarked, without manifesting the least sign of temper; " but you know that I would not accept money for such services as I have rendered, and it is but an insult to talk of it in this connection."

The merchant bit his lips, and was silent for a moment.

"You spoke so pointed," he said, "that I thought you wanted some reward for the services you rendered my child at Washington."

"So I do."

"Name it, sir."

"Not at present. The time may come when I shall be enabled to do so."

"I do not understand your meaning, sir."

"No; I suppose not. It would surprise you very much if you knew my aim and purpose."

I don't know what Mr. Blank would have said, if, at that moment, old Crosstrees had not come rolling to the piazza where we stood, apparently to speak to the merchant. As soon as the old salt caught sight of me, he stopped his roll, gave his trousers a hitch, and said, —

"Blast me if this ain't you, and no mistake! What are you doin' here? By the sixteen of spades! but this is a good one. I don't understand it."

"I suppose not; and, what is more, you ain't likely to, unless you stop that bellowing. You ain't on the quarter-deck of a ship, and in a gale of wind; so take in sail, and come to anchor."

I saw the old salt look at Mr. Blank, as though asking advice on the subject. The latter motioned to him, and then walked off a few fathoms, so that they could consult without being overheard. They whispered together for a minute or two, and then Mr. Blank strolled off, and left old Crosstrees to deal with me as best he could. I guessed his object. It was to pump me, and find out how much I knew, and what I was doing at Bermuda.

I lighted a cigar, and sat down to wait for the contest. Old Crosstrees took a seat near me, and opened the campaign in his usual blunt manner.

"I say, Constant," Captain Crosstrees remarked, "we allers was friends — now wan't we?"

"O, yes."

"And you know that me and Mr. Blank would do most anything to oblige you."

"I suppose so."

"We would, on honor."

"I don't doubt your word."

"Now as we feel so towards yer, jist tell us what you is doin' here."

"With pleasure. I'll exchange confidences with you. Tell me what you are doing here, and I'll do the same."

Old Crosstrees colored and hesitated, while he rolled his quid in his capacious mouth.

"Well, the fact of it is, Constant, the government sent us down to look arter its affairs in this region. Mum, you know. Don't say a word."

"Not for the world. But how does it happen that you arrived on board a blockade-runner?"

For a moment old Crosstrees was taken completely aback; but, when he rallied, he blurted out, —

"That's the joke of the thing. We have wormed out important secrets; and no one knows that we are from the North."

"I suppose that was the reason you were in Charleston."

"Hey?"

"You know you were in Charleston one or two days."

"How did you know that?"

"I saw you there."

"It ain't so. Damn me, if it is so! I ain't been in Charleston for years."

"You've been there within four weeks," I answered, in a short, dry tone.

"No, I ain't, either."

"Yes, you have."

"How do you know?"

"Because I saw you there."

"You?"

"Yes."

"What in the devil are you talking about, Constant?"

"Just what you hear."

"Are you in earnest?"

"Never more so, I assure you."

Crosstrees looked at me, in solemn silence, for a moment; and then he growled out, —

"Cuss me, if I know what you is drivin' at!"

"No; I suppose not. Yet let me assure you that I saw you and Mr. Blank in Charleston less than four weeks since."

"I don't believe it."

"Very well; disbelieve it. Some time I may be called upon to prove my assertions."

"Look a-here, Constant. Damn it, man! be fair and square, and let an old shipmate know what you mean — won't you?"

"No; the time has not arrived. Mr. Blank and you have nothing to fear from me. Only certain remarkable circumstances can induce me to utter one word regarding the nature of your late transactions."

"Name 'em, Constant. Do you want any money?"

"No; none of yours."

"Then what do you want? Come, be frank with me. Treat an old shipmate and sailor like a friend."

"Just as you have treated me, hey?"

"Hem."

"No, Crosstrees, I shall not confide my secret to you at present. It is better in my keeping. You are safe; and so is Mr. Blank. Go on, and sell your cotton. Make all the money that you can; but let me warn you to no longer tempt fortune by running the blockade. It is playing with fire. Keep on, and you will get burned. I assure you that such is the case. You see that I know all, so be advised in time."

"I don't know how you know all these things; but you has hit the nail on the head in some manner; and, damn me, if you couldn't ruin us with a turn of your paw! But you won't do it — will yer?"

"I have said that you and Mr. Blank are safe at present; but do not repeat the experiment if you wish me to remain your friend. Be warned in time."

"Yes, I will. A heap of thanks for what you have said. Count on me, in any latitude or longitude, you know. You has some secret understanding under yer jacket, and when it is time to come out jist h'ist a signal, and I'll square away, and run down to yer. I will, so help me sixty!"

The old sea-dog made me take his hand, and then he left me, and sought Mr. Blank; but I don't think the information he imparted to that dignified gentleman was consoling; for the Boston merchant managed to find me in the course of half an hour after Crosstrees left me, and, with a short, genial smile, took my hand, and remarked, —

"Constant, you and Crosstrees have been having some conversation together. May I ask you to keep matters secret for my sake?"

"Certainly, you may ask me; and I tell you that it will depend entirely upon your own conduct as to my course. You know better than to violate the laws of your country. You have wealth and position, and need not embark in such business."

"I know it; and I promise you that I will not repeat the experiment. As soon as I sell ship and cargo, or send them to Liverpool, I'll return to Boston without delay."

"Where I shall have the pleasure of seeing you; as I sail for home as soon as possible."

Mr. Blank did not look so delighted at this information as one might have expected. He merely said, —

"Ah, indeed!"

"Have you any message that you wish me to take to your daughter?" I continued.

"O, no! She does not know that I'm here. It is not necessary that she should hear from me oftener than once a month."

"She still remains in Boston?" I suggested.

"Yes, sir; I presume so. It is not probable that she would leave the city for any length of time without consulting me."

He did not ask me to call on Miss Hatty, but I determined to do so in spite of him; and, if I could get the start of him for a week or two, so that I could talk to the young lady without much restraint, I had great hope of winning her for a wife, for that was the extent of my ambition.

We parted, with formal bows; for, somehow, each of us felt as though there was a difference between us, a gulf that needed bridging over, — yet neither of us was willing to make the least advances towards a mutual understanding. I don't think he even dreamed that I loved his daughter; but he knew that something made me a little cold and distant.

I saw no more of Crosstrees and Mr. Blank during my stay on the island. They retired to their ship, and kept out of sight, — a wise proceeding on their part, which I commended most heartily; for I feared that they and Bowmount might meet, and then an explanation ensue that would damage me somewhat in my projects.

But a steamer was advertised to sail for New York, and in her the Kentuckian and I took passage. Before she weighed anchor, however, I saw Mrs. Gowen, and had a long and tender interview. She was much happier in her new relation than she had anticipated. Mr. Gowen was kind and considerate, tender and judicious; and his wife thought that she should live happy with him. At least she would try to do so, which resolution I highly commended; and, after a few words of good advice, I kissed her, shook hands, and we parted the best of friends.

Let me, in a few words, describe her career; for she was no ordinary woman. Her husband turned all his property into gold, and removed to Paris, where he is still residing. He has a fortune equal to a million or more, dispenses the most generous hospitality to all, from the North or South, is free from all bitterness on the subject of the war, and loves his wife most devotedly; and one reason for this is, that she is the most lovely lady, one who creates the most excitement and admiration of any American in France. The emperor was partial to her company, while the empress was really fond of her, and made a pet of her at all times.

No one has discovered her secret. It is guarded by friends, who would on no account reveal it; while it is useless to attempt to identify the parties by the names which I have given them. Of course they are fictitious; but the characters are realities, faithfully drawn, and not in the least exaggerated. They have but one child, born soon after their arrival in Paris. It is a boy; and the mother, in her letters to me, speaks of it in the most glowing terms. It is a sturdy little fellow, and as handsome as an angel. Mr. Gowen is much attached to it, and, consequently, is in a fair way to spoil it. I hope, some day, to see it. May the family live long and happily together! Their trials were severe, and their courage well tested. Their reward is great.

We left Bermuda, and steamed for New York, arriving in the latter city after a five days' passage. As soon as we landed we sold our bills of exchange at a great advance, — for gold was at a premium, — and then found ourselves in possession of quite a fortune, in greenbacks and government stocks; for I noticed that Bowmount showed his confidence in the stability of the United States by investing most of his spare funds in seven-three tenths bonds; and when I rallied him on that point, he wanted to know if I thought he was a fool.

"Don't I know which side is comin' up, and which side is goin' to win? I have watched this thing for some months, and know what I'm about; and while I'm on the subject, let me explain to you that it's best to keep shady while you is here. Don't let any disloyal notions drop out; 'cos, if you do, there'll be men ready to hear 'em, and report 'em. Be as strong for the North as you can, at least in all your yarnin'. Don't let on that you was born in South Carolina. There ain't no occasion for it, you know; and you might get into trouble if you should blart too much."

I gravely promised to mind what he said, and after a few days spent in New York, we started for Washington, where I was anxious to report myself, and get assigned to more agreeable duty than that which I had performed. I was tired of secret service, and its anxieties and dangers. I longed for more noble strife; where I could distinguish myself, and prove that I was worthy of Hatty Blank.

I feared that the Kentuckian would remain with me in Washington, and thus prevent me from communicating with the proper authorities; but, to my great joy, he met a party of gentlemen from his own State, acquaintances, and they carried him off home. We parted the best of friends, and months elapsed before Bowmount knew that I was in the service of the United States. When he first heard of it, he swore that he wouldn't believe it; and when forced to do so, smiled a grim smile, and said, —

"Shucks! Dog on me! but he was smart, now I tell yer. So, he is a Yankee, is he? Well, damn me! but I was half a Yankee at the time, and knowed the North was right all along. I'd like to see that Barnwell, or Constant, or whatever his name is; 'cos I shall never forget that he saved me and my vessel, and put money in my pocket. He's a trump, and no mistake."

And so well did the Kentuckian think of me, that he came North when he heard that I was wounded, for the express purpose of seeing if I was likely to get well. A few words more, and his history will be brought to a close. After his return to Kentucky, he threw the whole of his influence on the side of the Union, raised a regiment, was colonel of it, then made a general, and did as much as any other man to capture and disperse Morgan's band of raiders, and save Kentucky and Ohio from pillage. He was in the army till the close of the war, and now owns an immense plantation in his native State, where he raises tobacco and animals, and makes money as fast as his generous nature permits. This spring I received a present from him, in the shape of a span of black horses, some of his own raising, and now I'm debating what I shall do with the animals. I don't want to sell them, for it wouldn't be proper; and I don't know how I can keep them, and make them useful. Still I feel grateful to Bowmount for the gift, and think that I will acknowledge it by sending him a splendid specimen of a royal Bengal tiger. We will see how he likes it.

But I must return to my narrative, for it is drawing to

a close. Soon after Bowmount left Washington, I waited upon Mr. Secretary Welles, and reported myself. The venerable gentleman refused to see me, until I sent in my card, with certain mysterious signs on the same, which were expressive, even if they were not beautiful.

With the secretary, I found Mr. Fox, his assistant. The latter recollected my face at once, and explained to Mr. Welles who I was, and what duty I had been engaged in. The venerable secretary thereupon gave me his hand and his photograph at the same time, — the latter gift being designed as a special mark of honor, to be prized above all things; and as I knew a few of the good man's peculiarities, I told him that I should always cherish it, and hang it up in my state-room the next time I went to sea.

"We have work for you, sir, plenty of work," cried the secretary, who watched me most attentively while I was placing the photograph carefully in my note-book. "I see that you are one we can rely on. You have performed most valuable service to your country, sir. I hear you praised by all hands, from the quarter-deck to the — to the — "

He looked to Captain Fox for relief from his dilemma. Captain Fox was examining a chart, and did not notice the appeal.

"Ahem!" said Mr. Welles, after a moment's silence. "I have heard you praised by all the captains on the station; for you was prompt with your information as a marine at — at — "

Another look at Captain Fox for assistance, and more disappointment.

"Ahem! Yes, sir; you were reliable with your news. The sailor in the main-foretop and the officer in the cabin are now living, to bless you for saving their lives by your promptness."

I expressed myself pleased to learn that such was the

case, and wondered where the secretary picked up his immense stock of sea terms.

"That blockade-running was rather tough sort of work. I don't know but I should condemn it, if I went according to a taut bowline backstay, as sailors say; but as you did the cause so much good, why, we must overlook all little errors, I suppose. Those despatches from the Richmond cabinet were invaluable. Worth to us millions of dollars. I don't know how we should have got along without them."

"They were precious as jewels," Captain Fox remarked. "They enabled us to block a nice little game."

"Yes; we blockaded their game, and now we have another mission for you; a little less dangerous than the last, perhaps, but still just the thing for a sensible, adventurous fellow like yourself."

"Perhaps Mr. Constant would like a furlough of a few weeks, after his arduous duties," remarked Captain Fox.

"I really don't see how we can spare him. We were never so pressed for good men, reliable men, regular sheet anchors, you know. You won't object to being ordered away at short notice, — will you?"

"I fear that I must object," I replied; "for I have a great desire to visit some friends in Boston."

"Yes, I know; but still you will be gone but a few days. Now I want you to undertake a mission to Georgia. Away down in Savannah, and let us know how that city is fortified. Find out all about the iron-clads, the feeling of the people, and report to this department as soon as possible."

"You have laid out considerable work for me," I remarked.

"No more than you are capable of performing, judging from past performances," the secretary remarked, with a grave smile, combing his whiskers with his fingers.

Now I thought this rather tough. I had run more risks, while at the South, than I cared to again undertake. I had escaped with a whole skin, but only through good luck, not by any wit of my own; and, just as I supposed that my work was done, another job was put before me, more repugnant to my feelings than the last. I determined to refuse the mission, let what would happen; for I was ambitious to shine in a new sphere, on the quarter-deck of a first-class gun-boat or frigate.

Captain Fox must have read my thoughts, for he said,—

"You think of refusing the mission?"

"Yes."

"I thought so; and, to tell you the honest, sailor truth, I don't blame you."

"Avast, there!" nautically cried Mr. Welles. "Take a round turn there, and belay all that."

"Mr. Constant is right in refusing the mission," Captain Fox repeated. "He is known at the South, at the present time; and it would be a miracle if he escaped from there with his life. Under such circumstances, I don't blame him for hesitating over the job. Why not make a commander of him, and give him charge of a gunboat? He has earned his promotion."

"It is just the position I would have asked, above all others," I cried.

"But who is to go South?" asked the secretary, in a tone that showed he was hesitating over the project."

"O, I'll find a man," was the answer.

"Well, if Lieutenant Constant refuses the mission, why, I must do the best that I can. But we did depend on him."

"O, I'll find a man who will answer every purpose; and I'll send him off in a day or two."

And this assurance seemed to satisfy the good-natured secretary; for he once more opened his desk, and handed me his photograph, forgetting that he had already given me one.

"You can keep it," the secretary said, "to remember me, and to recollect that I'm not the most arbitary of men, although some people say so."

"I shall consider you the kindest of men, if you will write on the photograph, 'Commander Constant, from Secretary Welles.'"

"Well, so I will," cried the secretary.

And down went the words; and that is the manner I obtained my promotion.

"The new gunboat Firefly, fitting at the Charlestown Navy Yard, needs a commander," suggested Captain Fox.

"Then see that Commander Constant is appointed to her."

And with a nod of his venerable head, the secretary intimated that the interview was terminated; and once more thanking both gentlemen, I retired from the department; and just as I was leaving the building, who should I meet, face to face, but the Union spy, Colonel Rhett, *alias* Smith, *alias* half a dozen other names.

"Well," cried Smith, in the most profound astonishment, "if I ain't damned!"

"If you ain't, you ought to be," I remarked, and was about to pass on, when Smith laid one hand on my shoulder, and beckoned to a police officer.

"Well, captain," the man said, in a tone of triumph, "now I have you on my own ground. Now I can settle old scores, and in a manner satisfactory to myself, if not to you."

"Indeed!" I remarked, in so cool a tone that the man looked a little more astonished than ever, if such a thing were possible.

"Yes; you will find it so. Here, officer, take charge

of this man. He is a Southern spy, a captain in the rebel navy."

"You are my prisoner," said the detective, and laid a hand on my shoulder.

"He's slippery, officer," cried Smith, who appeared to feel that I was not safe, but would escape. "Put the bracelets on to him. Make sure of him. He's the devil for getting out of a small hole."

Just as the officer was about to produce his irons, who should come towards us but Captain Fox, as he left the department building.

"Ah! you are just the person I want," the assistant-secretary said, as his eyes fell upon Smith, and, for the moment, did not notice me. "I want to see you on business; it is important."

"I have some now," replied the Union spy. "Here's business that will last me for a few days. I've made a capture that will astonish you. Damn me, if it won't startle you! Just look at the most unblushing rebel in the Southern States, and one that is capable of doing much harm."

Captain Fox did look at me, and after his first glance of astonishment, began to laugh.

"Why, man alive!" the secretary said, "do you know whom you are talking about?"

"Yes, sir; the worst rebel in the South."

Again the secretary laughed, as he replied, —

"This is some strange mistake, sir. You have arrested Commander Constant, of the United States Navy. Officer, release him immediately."

The detective removed his hand from my shoulder, while Smith's face was a puzzle. It showed mingled astonishment and rage at the prospect of being deprived of his prey.

"Look here, Captain Fox," Smith cried, "you don't

know this man. He's dangerous, — damned dangerous, I tell you. I've met him in South Carolina, and heard him plot against the government. Once he had me flogged, and once I had a rope around his neck. You never know where to find him, and how to put your finger on him. He's like an eel."

"O, what nonsense you talk!" replied the secretary. "You have been making too free with whiskey this morning. It's apt to affect the brain, unless care is exercised. Come, Constant, walk with me. I want to speak with you."

He put his arm through mine; and we were about to move off, when Smith made one more appeal.

"I tell you, Captain Fox," he said, "you are mistaken in this man."

"No, I am not. You are the one mistaken."

"Good God!" cried Smith, trotting along by our side. "It can't be possible that the captain is in the Union service."

There was no response to this."

"O, damn it! I see it all now," muttered the spy. "What a fool I've been. No wonder he didn't want me hanged. He knew me, and I didn't know him. We've been fighting at cross purposes all this time. Well, I'm dead beat this time, and no mistake. But I'll give you the credit of being a little smarter than I am. I don't bear any malice; so here's my hand. Hereafter I shall keep my mouth shut."

We shook hands, and parted; and the next day Smith assumed the character of a paroled confederate soldier, and started on his tour through the South. He returned in safety, and is now an officer on a gunboat, having fought well at Fort Fisher and Mobile, and received his promotion through sheer merit and hard work. I meet him once in a while, and we talk over the adventures of the past; but when he speaks of the flogging which he received at the time he and John were so anxious to hang me, his shoulders are shrugged, as though some of the pain still remains in them, and is darting through the scars which the cruel whip left. I hope that his career will be successful and honorable in the future as in the past, as I have no doubt that it will be.

The next day I left Washington, and started for Boston, which city I was anxious to reach as soon as possible, for the purpose of having an interview with Miss Hatty Blank. Much of my future happiness depended upon the manner in which she met me; so no wonder I felt a little nervous, and desired to look my best while in her presence.

The first day I arrived in Boston I had a commander's uniform made; and when it was finished, donned it, and then took a good look at myself in the glass. I felt so well satisfied with my appearance, that I determined to call upon Miss Hatty in my new dress; for I knew that women like the appearance of a neat uniform, and do not disdain casting glances at a good-looking man inside of one.

Miss Hatty resided on the new lands on the Back Bay, in a large freestone house, one of the best in a block of four. Mr. Blank's name was on the door, so I had no trouble in finding the building; but I must confess that my heart beat rather wildly as I touched the bell, and awaited the arrival of a servant.

I thought of a dozen things while standing on the stoop. Perhaps she was not in, or was sick, or would not see me. Or, it might be her father was at home, and would interfere with the interview which I so much desired. But all speculations ceased as the door opened, and a colored servant appeared.

"Is Miss Blank at home?" I asked.

"I will see, sar, if you will walk in," was the answer.

I was shown into an elegantly furnished reception-room, handed my card to the servant, who received it on a silver salver, and then disappeared. He was gone five minutes before he returned. Then he said, —

"Miss Blank is in, sar. Will you be kind enough to walk into the drawing-room, sar?"

I complied with the request, and found it even more brilliant than the reception-room. French-plate looking-glasses were over the mantles and at each end of the room. The walls were covered with pictures, and the furniture was rosewood; while the carpet was so thick and soft that a footstep could not be heard on it. By all odds, I think that it was the richest room I had ever entered at the time; and all things considered, I do not wonder that I felt a little taken aback at such evidences of wealth and refinement.

I sat down, and waited ten minutes. All that time I felt my courage sinking lower and lower; and had it not been for shame's sake, I should have run away, and waited till some other day before seeking an interview.

"Courage," I said, with a thump on my heart. "She is but a girl, and can't hurt a man like me. Why should I be afraid? I won't be intimidated. I'll see her, if I have to remain here all day."

"Why, Captain Constant! how glad I am to see you!" a soft, sweet voice said; and turning, and starting up, I saw Miss Blank more lovely than ever, standing near me, with outstretched hands. She had entered the room so quietly that I had not heard her.

"Miss Blank!" I cried, and caught her hands in both of mine, and looked at her, too full of emotion to say another word.

"I am glad to see you," the young lady said, and made an effort to free her hands from my strong grasp; but I resisted, so she gave up the attempt, with a smile and a blush. "Haven't you a word to say to me, Captain Constant?" asked the lady, seeing that I remained silent.

"I am so happy at seeing you once more," I replied, "that I find words fail me just when they are needed most."

"I am sure I hope that you did not leave your tongue with the rebels. You used to talk fast enough when we met in Washington. Do you remember the fellow who insulted me, and how kind you were in defending me? Come, sit down, and tell me all about your wanderings. You don't know how glad I am that you have returned home. I have thought of you quite often. It was only yesterday, I wondered what had become of you. You may laugh, but it is true."

I led her to a seat; and not till then did I release her hands, and ask,—

"And how often do you think I have thought of you, while absent?"

"O, I don't know. Perhaps once or twice. You gentlemen are rather fickle-minded, I believe. I have heard so, at any rate."

"I can only answer for myself," I returned; "for I have thought of but you since absent."

I forgot, for the moment, that I had ever looked upon Mrs. Gowen's face. Even if I had recollected it, I was not such a fool as to acknowledge the fact. Men generally know better than that.

We talked for a long time quite confidentially; and I felt myself more in love than ever. At last I rose to take my departure; but Miss Hatty insisted that I should not go just yet; so I was forced to resume my seat.

"I am so sorry that my father is absent from home," the lady said, as we resumed conversation. "He has often spoken of you, and in such high terms that you would be pleased if you knew what he said."

"May I ask where he is?"

"O, he went to New Orleans, to see about some land he owned there. I expect him home in the course of a week or two."

So the daughter knew nothing about the father's engaging in blockade-running. If such was the case, I was not the one to enlighten her. As far as I was concerned, his disgrace should never reach her ears.

"I met a cousin of yours while I was South," I said, after I had thought over the matter of the father's absence, and how cunningly he had kept the reason from his family.

"O, yes, — Charley Reefpoint. He has spoken of you ever so many times. I suppose you know that he is in the city."

"No; I did not."

"He has been here more than a week. And don't you think, he once admitted that he had seen papa in Charleston; and when I expressed surprise, he seemed quite confused, and denied that he had said so. I must have misunderstood him, he argued; but I am certain that I did not. What did he mean?"

I comforted the dear girl as well as I was able, and told her that her cousin might have been playing a practical joke, and then repented of his rashness. At any rate, there was nothing to fear. If Master Reefpoint met her father at all, it was in New Orleans, where he was looking after his property, and trying to prevent its being confiscated by the Federals.

While we were conversing, who should enter the house but the person of whom we were speaking, — Master Midshipman Reefpoint, — looking as bold, as handsome, and as intelligent as ever. He was glad enough to see me; and I was pleased to see him, and more than pleased to tell him that his commission as lieutenant was already made out, and that further promotion awaited him, in good time, if he was prudent and considerate.

The delight of Charley was so great that he would have kissed his cousin if she had been willing to receive the embrace. She probably thought that it was not just the thing to be kissed by a lieutenant of the navy, however pleasant it might be to the young gentleman; so she refused to allow Reefpoint to touch her lips, which did not, in the least, disconcert her cousin, for he had the impudence to turn to me, and remark, —

"Never mind, Constant. I have kissed her; and you may if you are smart enough."

"You are a saucy boy," replied the indignant Hatty, her face flushing scarlet. But Master Reefpoint did not stop to hear a lecture. He saw that he was not wanted; so after making an appointment to meet me on board the Firefly the next morning, he took his departure, and once more left us together, thus enjoying several hours of complete happiness. When I left the house, I promised to call the next day, and did so, and continued to call quite frequently, until one day I resolved that I would disclose my passion.

"Hatty," I said, one afternoon, "do you recollect the first time I ever saw you?"

"O, yes; it was in my father's counting-room."

"And do you know from that time to the present I have loved you most dearly?"

She turned deadly pale, then flushed scarlet, while tears came into her eyes, and she covered her face with her white hands.

"Dear Hatty!" I whispered, and stole an arm around her waist, and pressed her to my heart; while her fair head fell on my shoulder, and I felt her sweet breath on my cheek.

She did not answer me, but continued to shed tears. I was pretty well assured that they were not tears of anger.

"Dear Hatty," I continued, and managed to touch her lips, " please speak to me, and tell me that you do not hate me."

" No, I don't hate you," was the answer.

" And you will love me a little ? " I asked.

" Yes, just a little," was the whispered response ; and then a smile stole over her handsome face, and mischief beamed from her dark eyes.

" O! but I want to be loved a good deal," I said.

" But you only asked for a little."

" I know ; but now that you have assured me of a little, do give me as much as you can."

Then she came out serious. She raised her head, and looked me full in the face.

" Frank," she said, and placed both little hands on my shoulders, " do you love me with your whole heart ? "

" As God is my judge, I do love you with my whole heart and soul."

" And you will always love me as dearly as at present ? "

" Such shall be my prayer, Hatty. Every day since we parted at Washington I have thought of you, and the more I thought of you, the more I learned to love you."

" Now hear me," said the young girl, still in a serious tone. " From the time we separated at Washington, until the present, I have loved you."

" And do you mean to intimate that you do not still love me ? "

" No, far from it ; " and down went her lovely face on my shoulder. " I mean," she whispered, " that I love you more than ever ; but not more than you deserve, I am sure."

Did I feel a pang of reproach at these words, as I thought of Mrs. Gowen, and my kindness towards her? No; man-like, I only congratulated myself that Hatty did not know that there was such a person as Mrs. Gowen in the world, and was not likely to unless young Reefpoint was disposed to open his mouth, and tell what he knew, which I did not think at all likely. He had loved the lady most dearly; and, although it was but a boy's passion, short and sweet, still I judged that he would not care to inform the world of the fact, much less speak of my private affairs.

"Ten thousand thanks, darling," I said, after she had made her confession. Now there is but one more promise that I require on your part, to make me supremely happy."

"Name it;" and she looked up as she spoke, a smile on her face, as though she anticipated the request which I had to make.

"The promise of this dear hand at an early day."

"It is yours," she answered; "but you must first obtain my father's consent."

"And that he will not obtain in a hurry," said a stern voice at the door.

Hatty uttered a little scream, started up, and then ran towards her father, who stood looking at us in a sullen manner, as though angry at what he had witnessed.

"O, papa!" the lady cried, "how pleased I am, that you have returned home!"

She would have thrown her arms around his neck; but he refused the embrace, putting her away from him haughtily and sternly.

"So!" he said, "while I am away on business, you occupy your time in love-making, do you? Go to your room this instant; I am ashamed of you."

"Dear papa," the young lady cried, "I have done

nothing to be ashamed of. I will tell you all that has passed between Mr. Constant and myself. I am sure that you will not disapprove of it."

"I will hear nothing. Go to your room, I tell you. I have other designs for you besides one of my shipmasters."

Hatty gave me one tearful look, and then left the room, her father closing the door after her.

During the whole of this scene I had sat on the sofa, and listened in silence to what had passed, knowing that the time would soon come when all of my courage and calmness would be required to meet a crisis.

"Now, sir," said Mr. Blank, facing me, after having closed the door, "I am ready to attend to you."

"I am glad to hear it, for I am prepared," I replied.

"Don't you think, sir," Mr. Blank continued, "that you have done a mean action, to thus take advantage of my absence, and sneak into my house for the purpose of making love to my only child?"

"To tell you the truth, I don't see the mean point," I replied, with unruffled temper. "As for sneaking into your house, you are mistaken. I entered it as other gentlemen do, — by the front door, and in an upright manner. Your daughter received me as a friend, and I trust that I am one."

"She will have no further occasion for your friendship, sir, She will leave town to-day, and you will see her no more."

"I am sorry for that," was my reply, "for a moment ago I asked her to be my wife."

"And what answer did she return?" demanded Mr. Blank, his face expressing the rage he felt.

"An answer that gave me much pleasure. If you were willing, she was."

"Well, sir, understand me at once. I am not willing. So let that settle the matter, if you please."

"Pardon me, Mr. Blank, if I am persistent; but I must say that I cannot consent to such an arrangement. I love your daughter, and she loves me. I mean to marry her."

"The devil! Are you mad, man?"

"No; I am quite sane. I shall marry her, and with your consent."

"Do you recollect who you are?" thundered the hot-blooded merchant.

"Yes, sir," I replied, loftily; "I have the honor to be a commander in the United States naval service."

"And do you know who I am?"

"Yes, sir. You are a merchant, and reported worth a million dollars."

"Precisely, sir. Well, now answer me this question. Is it the girl or my money that you want?"

"The question is an insult; but still I will answer it. I do not want your money. I have enough of my own. I can command a hundred and fifty thousand dollars; and that is a comfortable sum for a man like me."

"And pray how did you make so much money in so short a time?" asked Mr. Blank, with a sneer, which showed he did not believe my statement.

"By running the blockade, and capturing blockade-runners. We cut one out at Nassau which gave me about forty thousand dollars in prize-money."

When I mentioned blockade-running, Mr. Blank manifested some little uneasiness. He showed guilt at once; but still he was determined to brave me, and drive me from the house; and I was equally determined in my resolution not to be driven.

"I am glad that you have been successful, Constant," the merchant said, his tone a little modified; "but still you will see that I can't change my views. My daughter is no wife for you."

"And may I ask the reason?"

"The reason, sir!" he exclaimed, growing angry again. "Why, look at my position, and then at yours, and let that answer you."

"Well, I have looked the matter over, and I still see nothing discouraging."

"You don't?"

"No, sir; and to tell the truth, I think that the proposed alliance would confer great honor on you."

"The devil you do! Well, you are a cool one, I must say. Pray explain what you mean by it."

"Simply this. I rank as a captain in the United States service."

"Yes. You have once before mentioned that point."

"Just so. Well, the position is an honorable one, is it not?"

"Certainly. No one disputes that. Still, it is not high enough to justify you in aspiring to my daughter's hand."

Mr. Blank, as he uttered these words, looked the rich merchant in every feature of his proud face.

"I am coming to that point," I continued, still as cool as man could be under the circumstances. "Now, who do you think is deserving of reward, — a man who is willing to serve his country by fighting for it, or one who forgets himself so far as to plot against it?"

Mr. Blank sprang to his feet, and his face glowing with anger, as he asked, —

"Do you mean to insinuate anything? Do you dare to insult me?"

"I ask a question, and you become enraged. I insinuate nothing, but want an answer."

"No answer can you receive until you explain yourself. It is the basis of an understanding between us."

"Very well, sir; then I will explain. You must remember that I met you at Bermuda, in company with Captain Crosstrees."

"Yes; but what of it?"

"Much, as you will see. A few weeks before, we had the pleasure of meeting in Charleston, South Carolina."

"It is false!" thundered the angry merchant. "Leave my house this instant."

"It is not false; and I shall not leave your premises until you have heard the whole of my story. Then I will start quick enough to please even you."

He made no further remark, so I continued:

"I met you at Charleston, aboard the enemy's iron-clad, where you had a long conference with Captain Maulhead on the prospect of blockade-running."

"It is false!"

"After you left the Palmetto, you were accosted in the street by your nephew, Mr. Reefpoint; but you pretended that you did not know him. I saw the interview, and heard all that passed."

"Curses on you!" muttered the merchant, grinding his teeth.

"Then you went on board the blockade-runner Belle, and had a long interview with the captain."

"How do you know that?"

"I was present."

"Impossible. Only three persons were in the cabin."

"Yet I was there."

"I don't believe it."

"I can prove it by producing a package of papers which you dropped on the cabin floor. You remember that you came back for them."

A look of dismay passed over the man's face. He trembled for the first time. He saw that he stood over a mine, and that an explosion was likely to occur at any moment.

"Are those papers safe?" he presently asked, in a faltering tone.

"Yes; so safe that I know where to place my hand on them at any time."

"Name your price for them."

"Your daughter's hand."

"I mean in gold."

"Your daughter is more precious to me than gold."

"Are those the only terms?"

"Yes; although I tell you, candidly, I have no intention of using the papers to your injury. I have too much respect for you to see an honored name disgraced."

"Thank you." And the merchant smiled somewhat bitterly. "If you are so noble, be man enough to place the papers in my hand, and trust to my generosity."

"No; I am too well acquainted with human nature for that."

"Has any one excepting yourself seen the papers?"

"No one but myself."

"And will you tell me how you obtained possession of them?"

"Yes. I found them on the cabin floor of the Belle."

"And why did you not give them up when I returned for them?"

"Because I thought them safer with me than with you."

Mr. Blank drew a long breath. Then, after a pause, he asked, —

"Where were you when I was talking with the captain of the Belle?"

"Right before you. Captain Barnwell and I are one."

Mr. Blank was astonished.

"I never should have suspected such a thing," he muttered.

Then he walked to the window, and looked out upon the Common and Public Garden.

I arose, and moved towards the door, intending to take my leave. Mr. Blank heard me, and turned from the window.

"Where are you going, Constant?" he inquired.

"To my ship."

"Can't you remain to dinner?"

"Yes, if you will treat me as an equal and a friend."

"Wait," he said, and touched a bell.

A colored servant appeared.

"Inform Miss Blank that I wish to see her without delay," the merchant said.

Five minutes elapsed before the young lady appeared. In the mean time Mr. Blank did not utter a word, nor did I speak.

When Hatty entered the apartment, I saw that she had been weeping; for her eyes were red and swollen.

"Hatty," said her father, taking her hand, "this gentleman wants you for a wife; are you willing to take him for a husband?"

"Yes, papa, if you consent."

"And are you sure that you love him, my child?"

"Quite sure, papa."

And the young lady left her father, and came to me, placing both her hands in mine, in token of her confidence and love.

"I am glad, my child," said the merchant, "that you have placed your affections on so worthy a man. You have my approval and blessing. May you both be as happy as you deserve."

Then he left us alone.

"What has changed papa in so short a time?" asked Hatty, wonderingly, as she nestled down by my side.

"A frank statement of my affairs," was the reply.

And that satisfied her; for she was too happy to investigate, or else did not care to. She never knew the means that were employed to bring her father to terms, and she never learned the reason of his absence from home while in the South.

From that day Mr. Blank treated me like a son. His house was my home. All my projects he was ready to second as heartily as I could wish; and instead of opposing an early marriage, he readily acquiesced when I suggested that the wedding should take place before I sailed in the Firefly.

It was a quiet wedding. Only our intimate friends were present. Hatty had insisted on this, and she had her own way. I was enabled to remain with her two months before my vessel was ready. Then we parted; and when next we met, I was suffering from a wound received at Fort Fisher. She tended me like an angel through my illness, but declared that I should give up the sea, and love her on the land. And she is as precious to me now as on the day we were married.

And so I close my log, by wishing my readers as much happiness as I really enjoy in the possession of a young and lovely wife. Mr. Blank is loyal to the core. All of his money is in government bonds, and so free of taxation; consequently he is happy. His grandchildren expect to fare well in his will. Let us hope they won't be disappointed.

www.ingramcontent.com/pod-product-compliance
Lightning Source LLC
Chambersburg PA
CBHW051231300426
44114CB00011B/695